I0894670

Integrating Intelligent Control Systems With Sensor Technologies

Abdulsattar Abdullah Hamad
University of Samarra, Iraq

Sudan Jha
Kathmandu University, Nepal

Khalid Al-Badri
University of Samarra, Iraq

IGI Global
Scientific Publishing
Publishing Tomorrow's Research Today

Vice President of Editorial	Melissa Wagner
Director of Acquisitions	Mikaela Felty
Director of Book Development	Jocelynn Hessler
Production Manager	Mike Brehm
Cover Design	Phillip Shickler

Published in the United States of America by
IGI Global Scientific Publishing
701 East Chocolate Avenue
Hershey, PA, 17033, USA
Tel: 717-533-8845
Fax: 717-533-7115
Website: https://www.igi-global.com E-mail: cust@igi-global.com

Copyright © 2025 by IGI Global Scientific Publishing. All rights reserved. No part of this publication may be reproduced, stored or distributed in any form or by any means, electronic or mechanical, including photocopying, without written permission from the publisher.

Product or company names used in this set are for identification purposes only. Inclusion of the names of the products or companies does not indicate a claim of ownership by IGI Global Scientific Publishing of the trademark or registered trademark.

Library of Congress Cataloging-in-Publication Data

ames: Hamad, Abdulsattar Abdullah, 1987- editor. | Jha, Sudan, 1975- editor. | Al-Badri, Khalid Saeed, 1983- editor.
Title: Integrating intelligent control systems with sensor technologies / edited by: Abdulsattar Hamad, Sudan Jha, Khalid Al-Badri.
Description: Hershey, PA : IGI Global Scientific Publishing, [2025] | Includes bibliographical references. | Summary: "The emergence of innovative technologies for sensors and complex control systems has led to great advances in the field of measurement control. This book highlights the role of complex sensors with intelligent control methods in improving accuracy, efficiency, and efficiency in various fields"-- Provided by publisher.
Identifiers: LCCN 2024057013 (print) | LCCN 2024057014 (ebook) | ISBN 9798337303307 (hardcover) | ISBN 9798337303314 (paperback) | ISBN 9798337303321 (ebook)
Subjects: LCSH: Intelligent control systems. | Wireless sensor networks.
Classification: LCC TJ217.5 .I47 2025 (print) | LCC TJ217.5 (ebook) | DDC 629.8/95--dc23/eng/20250214
LC record available at https://lccn.loc.gov/2024057013
LC ebook record available at https://lccn.loc.gov/2024057014

British Cataloguing in Publication Data
A Cataloguing in Publication record for this book is available from the British Library.

All work contributed to this book is new, previously-unpublished material.
The views expressed in this book are those of the authors, but not necessarily of the publisher.
This book contains information sourced from authentic and highly regarded references, with reasonable efforts made to ensure the reliability of the data and information presented. The authors, editors, and publisher believe the information in this book to be accurate and true as of the date of publication. Every effort has been made to trace and credit the copyright holders of all materials included. However, the authors, editors, and publisher cannot assume responsibility for the validity of all materials or the consequences of their use. Should any copyright material be found unacknowledged, please inform the publisher so that corrections may be made in future reprints.

Table of Contents

Detailed Table of Contents

Ramiz Salama, Department of Computer Engineering, Near East University Nicosia, Mersin, Turkey
Hitesh Mohapatra, School of Computer Engineering, KIIT University (Deemed), Bhubaneswar, India
Fadi Al-Turjman, Artificial Intelligence and Software Engineering Departments, Near East University Nicosia, Mersin, Turkey

Wireless sensor networks are critical for applications like industrial automation, smart cities, healthcare, and environmental monitoring. However, challenges arise with energy consumption, latency, and bandwidth due to the large data generated. Integrating Edge Computing and AI offers a solution by enabling efficient data analysis with lower energy consumption. Edge computing brings processing closer to data sources, allowing real-time data analysis without relying on cloud servers, reducing energy usage and extending network lifespan. AI techniques, such as machine learning and deep learning, enhance data filtering, anomaly detection, and predictive maintenance at the edge. This approach boosts WSN scalability and responsiveness by managing large data efficiently. This study examines WSN architectures with edge computing and AI, focusing on key frameworks, technologies, and energy-saving methods. Through case studies, it demonstrates how this integration enhances performance, data efficiency, and supports intelligent decision-making in various WSN deployments.

The convergence of smart mobility, IoT, and connected ecosystems is transforming industries through seamless connectivity, real-time analytics, and data-driven decisions. This article examines their applications in healthcare, urban planning, industrial automation, and agriculture. Smart systems powered by AI and IoT enable predictive capabilities, while IoT ecosystems optimize operations via autonomous device communication. Case studies include smart traffic management, wearable health monitors, precision agriculture, and predictive maintenance. Emerging technologies like 5G, edge computing, and blockchain address challenges of latency, security, and interoperability. However, issues like data privacy and scalability persist. The article underscores the need for innovative solutions and regulatory frameworks to harness smart ecosystems for sustainable development and improved quality of life.

This chapter proposes a new concept of Designing an automatic flow controller that is based on AI and using selected machine learning algorithms. The optimum smart controller uses machine learning concept by learning the knowledge often convectional flow controller. The acquired data set is used to train the built model using ML algorithm using a software tool called Weka 3.8.5 is an open-source software suite developed at the University of Waikato in New Zealand. A model with optimum performance is built, the performance criteria analysis like mean square error, root means square error. The Weka software is used to build a model with 60% of dataset and evaluated with 40% of data set. The evaluated result is Root mean square error ranges from 0.96 to 0.0028. The correlation coefficient is equal to 1 and the percentage Relative absolute error is 0.0467% for simple linear regression and 15.869% for Decision table ML algorithms. Hence the built model functions as smart flow controller and the output of this controller will be imitating the conventional PID controller.

Eram Fatima Siddiqui, Babu Banarasi Das University, Lucknow, India
Mohd Muqeem, Sandip University, India
Sultan Ahmad, Prince Sattam Bin Abdulaziz University, Alkharj, Saudi Arabia & Chandigarh University, Mohali, India
Hikmat A. M. Abdeljaber, Applied Science Private University, Jordan
A. E. M. Eljialy, Prince Sattam Bin Abdulaziz University, Saudi Arabia

Quality data delivery and communication in an ultra-latent and real-time manner are some its stringent requirements for Internet of Things (IoT). In IoT, raw data is sensed from real-world and transformed into a usable form. Collection of this raw data from multiple sensors as compared to a single one, it is found to be of better quality and high accuracy. This method of collecting same type of data is called data or sensor fusion. In this paper a meticulous study on the role of data fusion have been done with respect to its application with Internet of Things, Machine Learning (ML) and Mobile Edge Computing (MEC).This paper discusses the mechanism, multi-modal fusion techniques, past proposed standard data fusion models and related issues, along with its application with support of machine learning and Edge Computing Lastly, the paper discusses about the concept of Edge Intelligence to deliver reliable outputs with future directions and issues.

V. Santhi, Vellore Institute of Technology, India
Vinithra Balaji, Vellore Institute of Technology, Chennai, India
Maheswer Sunil Kumar, Vellore Institute of Technology, Chennai, India

Electromyography sensors (EMG) are techniques used to get the electrical signals generated by muscle activation, providing valuable insights into muscle activity and its relation to the nervous system. This chapter addresses the challenge of achieving accurate, real-time classification of hand states using a hybrid system combining threshold-based detection and machine learning algorithms. The proposed method focuses on the development of an accurate and efficient muscle activation detection system that utilizes the EMG sensors along with Support Vector Machines (SVM) for real-time classification of two hand states. The key contribution of this research is to incorporate a robust architecture that is adaptable to diverse muscle activity patterns and has the potential for deployment in real-time applications such as rehabilitation centers and prosthetics. In this chapter, the model is trained on two users, with varying muscle strength, and evaluations are done using accuracy, precision, and confusion matrix. Testing showcased high accuracy and precision.

Mohammad Jeelani, Future University, India
Mohd Muqeem, Sandip University, India
Sultan Ahmad, Prince Sattam Bin Abdulaziz University, Alkharj, Saudi Arabia & Chandigarh University, Mohali, India
Aasim Zafar, Aligarh Muslim University, India
Mourade Azrour, Faculty of Sciences and Technics, Moulay Ismail University of Meknes, Morocco
Kishan Pal Singh, FET, Mangalayatan University, India

Wireless sensor networks has the potential to completely change a number of industries, including smart cities, healthcare, industrial automation, and environmental monitoring. WSNs use wireless communication between spatially dispersed autonomous sensors to track environmental or physical parameters like motion, pressure, temperature, and humidity. In this paper, we propose the trust-based approach for changing nodes with energy (TBNE) model, a trust-based strategy in a wireless sensor network. TBNE locates the network's troublesome nodes. The structure enhances node performance based on the trust concept for secure communication in WSN. Using its wireless interface, the device records a physical event and sends it to a base station. When a base station and sensor node cannot communicate directly, hop-by-hop communication is needed. The proposed approach is in a wireless sensor network called the rust-based approach for varying nodes with energy (TBNE) model. Moreover, these results are validated with two simulators for better findings.

Wireless sensor networks (WSNs) are widely accepted technology for developing smart control systems in smart environments. These networks support real-time sensing, getting information, and making decision through incorporation of intelligent sensing, communication, and computation technologies. This chapter discusses the WSNs design, deployment and opportunity area in intelligent control systems such as home, city, healthcare and industries. A literature review provided here points to important advancements, issues, and research opportunities in the field. The chapter introduces a new WSN-based control framework that aims at tackling fundamental issues like limited energy, delay and scalability. Conclusion: A performance evaluation conducted on simulated and real case studies shows a substantial increase in the reliability and effectiveness of the proposed system. The discussion also points out several emerging technologies like Artificial intelligence, block chain, and ultra-low-power nodes that can even improve the performance of WSNs in smart environment.

Intelligent Control Systems (ICS) are transforming industrial automation and robotics by enhancing precision, efficiency, and adaptability. By leveraging machine learning, adaptive control, and real-time sensor feedback, ICS optimizes tasks like assembly, welding, and quality inspection. These systems boost productivity, improve product quality, and enhance workplace safety while reducing costs and errors. Despite challenges such as complexity, integration issues, and high initial costs, solutions like modular designs, user-friendly programming, and Robotics-as-

This paper proposes a robust phishing detection framework the use of adaptive switch getting to know mixed with recurrent layers, such as Recurrent Neural Networks (RNNs), Long Short-Term Memory networks (LSTMs), and Gated Recurrent Units (GRUs). Phishing assaults pose a significant chance to cybersecurity, and conventional detection techniques have struggled to maintain pace with the dynamic nature of those assaults. The proposed framework leverages the strength of switch getting to know to conform to new phishing styles with out requiring widespread retraining. By integrating recurrent layers, the model captures temporal dependencies inherent in phishing emails and verbal exchange styles, making an allowance for more accurate detection of evolving threats. The framework is designed to enhance cybersecurity by way of dynamically adjusting to new phishing approaches, supplying a scalable and effective solution for phishing detection.

The speedy improvement of gadget mastering technology has considerably transformed the landscape of cybersecurity. However, those structures are increasingly more liable to antagonistic assaults that make the maximum their weaknesses, posing enormous dangers to their effectiveness. This look investigates the mixture of hostile training strategies into device studying models to decorate their resilience against evolving cybersecurity threats. Our findings display a remarkable decline in overall performance while models are uncovered to adverse examples, with benign detection quotes within the IDS losing from 90% to 80%. In evaluation, the phishing detection tool demonstrates an ability to evolve through retraining, with accuracy increasing from 88% to 93% after imposing non-stop learning strategies. We advise a feedback loop for non-stop gaining knowledge. The outcomes underscore the need for ongoing variation in gadget studying fashions to protect in opposition to ultra-modern cyber threats, supplying treasured insights for future studies and realistic applications in cybersecurity.

Preface

This book explores the integration of Artificial Intelligence (AI), Machine Learning (ML), and the Internet of Things (IoT) across various fields, with a particular focus on cybersecurity, automation, agriculture, and smart environments. Through thorough research and innovative frameworks, the chapters address critical challenges such as phishing attacks, adversarial threats, industrial control, precision agriculture, and wireless sensor networks. Each chapter offers practical solutions using cutting-edge technologies, including adaptive learning, edge computing, sensor fusion, and intelligent control systems. This work is designed to support researchers, engineers, and decision-makers in implementing scalable, efficient, and secure intelligent systems. The synergy between AI-driven models and real-world applications throughout this volume highlights the transformative potential of smart technologies for a sustainable and automated future.

The primary objectives of this book are to:

- Enhancing cybersecurity through adaptive transfer learning and adversarial training for accurate threat detection.
- Improving precision agriculture with AI-powered Internet of Things (IoT) and remote sensing technologies.
- Developing intelligent control systems and robotic automation for industrial applications.
- Enabling real-time, energy-efficient processing in wireless sensor networks through edge computing and artificial intelligence.
- Integrating sensor fusion and advanced machine learning models to enhance management of health, environment, and smart cities.

This book presents a comprehensive journey through the dynamic convergence of artificial intelligence, machine learning, the Internet of Things, and wireless sensor networks in practical applications. It delves into how adaptive and adversarial learning frameworks enhance cybersecurity against phishing and machine learning threats.

In agriculture, AI-powered IoT and precision sensing improve decision-making, resource management, and sustainability. For industrial automation and robotics, the focus is on intelligent control systems that enhance efficiency, safety, and scalability. The role of edge computing is highlighted for its ability to optimize energy consumption and reduce processing latency in sensor networks. The chapters further explore data integration from multiple sensors and the use of mobile systems and communication protocols in smart environments. This multidisciplinary integration offers robust, scalable, and sustainable solutions across sectors, providing valuable insights for researchers, engineers, and innovators aiming to develop intelligent, connected ecosystems that address modern challenges.

Chapter 1: Discusses how IoT and remote sensing tools like UAVs and LiDAR revolutionize precision agriculture, despite limitations in cost and data integration.

Chapter 2: Examines how edge computing and AI enhance data processing in WSNs, reducing energy consumption and latency while boosting decision-making.

Chapter 3: Explores integration of IoT, mobile systems, and ecosystems in sectors like healthcare and agriculture using 5G, edge computing, and blockchain.

Chapter 4: Presents ML-based automated flow control using Weka software with LR and Decision Table algorithms, demonstrating low error rates and high accuracy.

Chapter 5: Reviews sensor fusion techniques for IoT and ML systems, enhancing data quality and real-time performance, supported by edge intelligence.

Chapter 6: Combines EMG sensors with SVM for accurate classification of hand states, providing potential applications in rehabilitation and prosthetics.

Chapter 7: Introduces a TBNE model for secure WSNs using trust-based approaches and simulation-based validation for performance enhancement.

Chapter 8: Presents WSNs for smart control in various environments with AI and blockchain enhancing scalability, energy management, and reliability.

Chapter 9: Describes how ICS revolutionize smart manufacturing with AI and adaptive control, despite challenges in complexity and integration.

Chapter 10: Examines the cultural and economic perceptions of AI and automation in the automotive sector, highlighting opportunities and concerns.

Chapter 11: Proposes a phishing detection framework using adaptive transfer learning with RNN, LSTM, and GRU, improving threat response dynamically.

Chapter 12: Explores adversarial training techniques in ML models to bolster cybersecurity, showing improved accuracy through continuous learning strategies.

Chapter 1
Future Trends in IoT, Control Systems, and Remote Sensing Integration for Precision Agriculture

V. Dankan Gowda
https://orcid.org/0000-0003-0724-0333
Department of ECE, BMS Institute of Technology and Management, Karnataka, India

B. C. Kavitha
https://orcid.org/0000-0001-5775-4901
BGS Institute of Technology, Adichunchanagiri Univeristy, Mandya, India

Sajja Suneel
https://orcid.org/0009-0007-7759-7924
Institute of Aeronautical Engineering, Dundigal, India

N. Suganthi
https://orcid.org/0000-0003-2222-856X
Dayananda Sagar College of Engineering, Bangalore, India

Madan Mohanrao Mohanrao Jagtap
https://orcid.org/0000-0001-6428-1241
Symbiosis International University, Pune, India

DOI: 10.4018/979-8-3373-0330-7.ch001

Copyright © 2025, IGI Global Scientific Publishing. Copying or distributing in print or electronic forms without written permission of IGI Global Scientific Publishing is prohibited.

ABSTRACT

This chapter discusses how IoT and remote sensing are revolutionalising precision agriculture through the provision of real-time information to inform the management of crops and other resources. Specifically, this chapter explores the main technologies with focus on how they have been adopted within contemporary agriculture production systems. New technologies like, IoT sensors, satellite, UAVs, and LiDAR are helping farmers to keep an eye on the condition of the soil, status of crops, and the prevailing weather condition at a given time; in this way productivity is increased, resources are not wasted, and the environment is kept sustainable. The chapter discusses these technologies from a developmental perspective, from the early rudimentary uses to the sophisticated types of the current generation and then show how these technologies can transform farming. However, the prospective of applying big data has its limitations; they include the following: high initial costs, data integration problems and limited technological access in developing regions.

INTRODUCTION

Contextual Overview

Precision agriculture (PA) means the practice of production management in agriculture with the help of technology to make improvements in resource utilization in crop production. It blends satellite imagery, sensors, and automated machinery to control field variability in crops, soil and climate in the farm field. The objectives of PA are the increase of yield, the reduction of consumption, the avoidance of impact and the question of the global demand for feeding. The current status of farming have been pressed to the limit of conventional farming by increasing global population and shifting climate patterns which has enhanced the use of smart farming (Sharma, Mishra, & Srivastava, 2023). New technologies such as IoTs and remote sensing more importantly have revolutionized agriculture by enabling the monitoring and managing of the farmlands. These technologies assist farmers in the decision-wise farming, accurate crop management, effective use of water for irrigation, and timely interference of pests & disease control. Since farmers rely on data science for enhancing production, there are effects like water use efficiency (Singh, Berkvens, & Weyn, 2021), low chemical usage, and soil health, which are important targets for the production of food in the future.

Figure 1. Conceptual Framework for IoT and Remote Sensing Integration in Precision Agriculture

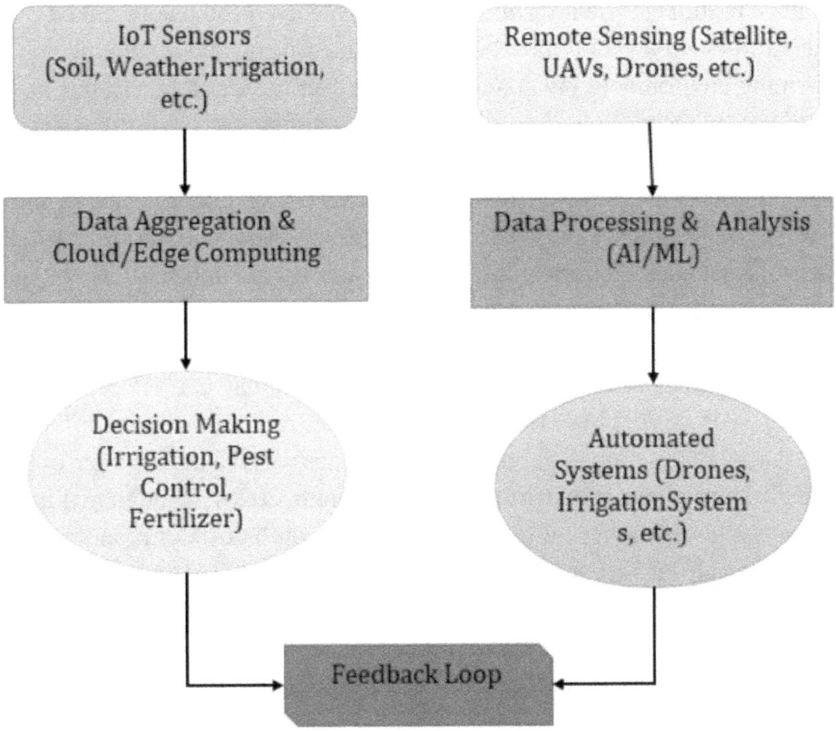

The Figure.1. shows the scheme of collecting the data in precision agriculture and the decision-making process using IoT sensors and remote sensing. Internet of Things (also known as IoT sensors like soil moisture, weather stations, and self-irrigation systems) take real-time environmental or crop data while Remote Sensing Technological (Satellites, UAVs, or drones) takes environmental or crop data (Nesakumar et al., 2021). This data is then gathered for cloud edge computing platforms where it undergoes analysis using Artificial Intelligence AI and Machine Learning ML. The information generated in the process directs Decision Making for instance, scheduling of irrigation, control measures against pests and common diseases as well as the use of fertilizers. Last of all, some of these decisions activate other Automated Systems like drones for farming or irrigation Systems thus making farming more efficient (Pero et al., 2024). Feedbacking in the system ensures that any actions done on automated systems are checked and data updated for better performance in future. It facilitates high efficiency, usage of resources and sustainability of the contemporary technological agriculture.

Technological Evolution

IoT and particularly the remote sensing innovations have greatly transformed the agriculture field. Historical farming practices involved the use of naked eyes and human efforts with few or almost no means of measuring and regulating conditions in a farming environment (Wang et al., 2024). But the last few decades have seen a revolution by technology cropping up and changing the face of the agriculture sector. Smart devices, or IoT, is a system of connected devices that gather, share information and have allowed for optimal tracking of factors such as moisture, temperature hence crop status (Gujar et al., 2024). Applications from IoT, Smart soil sensors, Weather station and smart irrigation system and so on is now popular for real time data collection to help farmers in deciding. These devices can operate independently and hence can be monitored or controlled remotely, hence the need to intervene physically (Veeramanikandan & Anil Kumar, 2024).

Satellites, drones or UAVs have also transformed agriculture by affording an efficient means of remote sensing. First, satellite image was the main source of tracking large-scale agricultural production (Dekka & Singh, 2024). Though making use of distant sensing was earlier quite expensive due to high costs of repairable sensors but with the help of recent high-resolution sensors and UAV's the use of distant sensing has become possible and economical. All these technologies offer solutions on the health of the crops and the quality of the soils as well as the climate, and it becomes possible to evaluate the fields as a whole with high precision (Maddineni & Gummadi, 2024).

Mathematically, the effectiveness of IoT and remote sensing can be represented as a system of equations where the goal is to optimize resource allocation and crop yield:

$$Y = f(S, C, E)$$

Where:

Y is the crop yield,
S represents soil conditions (e.g., moisture, temperature),
C represents crop health (e.g., nutrient levels, growth stage),
E represents environmental factors (e.g., weather, pest presence).

As shown in this equation, there are dependencies that exist between the inputs into agricultural productivity and insistent need for real-time data to make precise changes.

Chapter Objectives

The purpose of this chapter is, therefore, to analyze the future development and incorporation of IoT and remote sensing in precision agriculture. It seeks to compare the new technologies improving IoT and remote sensing systems such as 5G, AI, ML, and edge computing. Such innovations are anticipated to offer a direct contribution to the refining of the methods used in agricultural activities (Gummadi & Damacharla, 2024). The chapter will also look at the complementarities between the IoT sensors and the remote sensing data to demonstrate a proper incorporation of current data to enhance crop management, resource use and decision making. Besides, the chapter will also discuss the barriers affecting the deployment of these technologies including; high cost of implementing security issues integration issues (Aravindh, Nithisha, & Tanguturi, 2024). Last of all, the chapter shall evaluate the probability of a future's precision agriculture, where these technologies will embrace a challenge of increasing population and the force majeure that characterizes today's environment. Therefore, the main goal of this chapter is to enhance the understanding of the broad readership on the revolutionising role of IoT and remote sensing in the future prospects of the AM focus on agriculture.

TECHNOLOGIES IN PRECISION AGRICULTURE

IoT in Agriculture

The internet of things refers to a network of connected devices that has revolutionized agriculture through providing accurate ways of farm management. In the agricultural fields, various sensors, actuators, and communication technologies are integrated as IoT devices that help capture fresh data of different parameters prevailing in the fields and crops. Some of familiar IoT devices applied in agriculture are soil moisture sensors; farmers use them to check water content in the soil and adjust their irrigation regimes respectively; weather stations; with the help of which farmers predict possible weather-related troubles; automated irrigation systems that help to save water, using real-time information about the amount of moisture in the ground (Aghav & Abdullah, 2024). They are also used for surveillance and capturing high resolution images of crops and assessment of nutrient deficiencies, pests and diseases infestation and prevalence among others (Rani & Balaji, 2024). When connected, these IoT devices assist in facilitating precision farming practices, enhanced farming resource utilization, higher crop production, and minimized negative impact on the environment. For instance, smart Irrigation solutions through the industrial internet of things can effectively control the delivery of water to crops without overusing or under using the water resource (Prasad, Prasad, & Kaur, 2024). Furthermore, IoT devices enable monitoring and control of farming processes away from the farm thereby minimizing on the need for farmers to be involved physically, increasing efficiency and offering timely decisions. These capabilities of IoT in agriculture do not only raise the productivity but also the sustainability of the farming which reduces waste and maximize our resources, issues of modern farming are addressed in a more connected and efficient approach.

IoT helps precision farming in that it acts as enabler to the data-driven process. For instance, moisture content in the soil can be used to switch on irrigation to feed crops only when it is necessary not wasting resources. Likewise, using IoT-based pest detection inform farmers of the intrusive pests, thus allows them to control and treat before they cause harm to the crops. Further, through IoT systems, farmers can monitor and coordinate the farming processes from distant, minimizing on the labor expenses.

A simple mathematical model for optimized irrigation can be expressed as:

$$I = f(M, T)$$

Where:

I is the irrigation amount,
M represents soil moisture content,
T represents temperature, a factor influencing evaporation rates.
The function $f(M, T)$ adjusts irrigation based on soil moisture and environmental conditions, ensuring optimal water usage.

Remote Sensing Technologies

Remote sensing technologies are crucial in precision agriculture because they feed big agricultural processes into the system without need to essentially touch anything. Some of the technologies include satellite imagery, leveraged UAVs, LiDAR and hyperspectral imagery which are effective tools for evaluation of crops and soil health as well as physical conditions nowadays. Remote sensing helps the farmers in the management of large agricultural land area and Crop NDVI and Land use and cover information (Sethi & Prasanth, 2023). This information assists in finding out areas maybe requiring a focus; such as areas of drought or areas likely to be affected by pests. Drones, known as UAVs, are popular for their capacity to provide high quality, real-time aerial views of crops (Hegge & Agrawal, 2023). These drones have multiple or thermal sensors in order to identify hidden conditions of crops, which are not distinguishable by naked eyes such as nutrient deficiencies, diseases, or water stress. Another important technology explored is LiDAR (Light Detection and Ranging) that employs laser pulses to create high-resolution 3D maps both of the terrain and survey area and to analyze precise info about soil moisture levels, plant biomass, land topography and more (Pavankumar & Darwante, 2022) This is especially helpful in large photographic areas, especially those that are irregular in shape and size and may be difficult to undertake a topographic survey at all. Finally, hyperspectral image detects other lights aside from visible light and can be used to identify stressed, diseased, or damaged plants that cannot ordinarily be seen by the naked eye (Reddy & Patwal, 2022). These remote sensing technologies can be effectively combined to provide farmers with meaningful and practical information related to crop and ground health, efficiency of resource application, and opportunity to make crucial decisions on watering, feeding, pest control and harvesting, while increasing yield and production efficiency.

Figure 2. Remote Sensing Technologies in Precision Agriculture

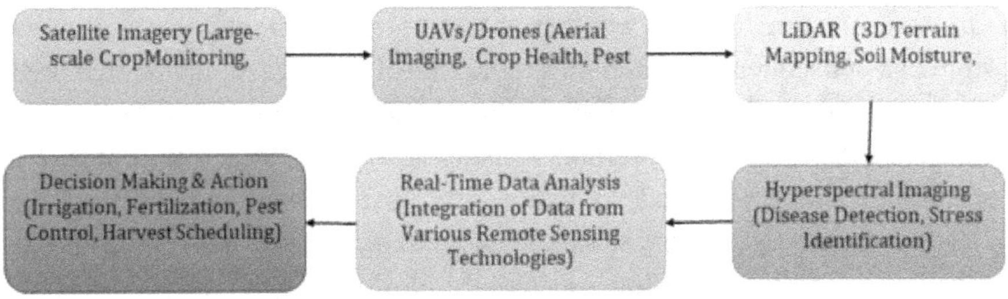

Figure 2 above shows the major remote sensing technologies applied in precision agriculture, and the role played by each of this technologies. Satellite imagery gives Farmers broad-scale information, for instance, Vegetation indices such as NDVI to help the farmer monitor more farms at once. UAVs/Drones take pictures at a very high altitude offer excellent crop status hence, early detection of such problems as pest attacks and nutrient deficiency. LiDAR aids in generation of accurate ground elevation maps and determines vegetation water content and variation in capabilities, planar field, and more especially where it is hard to access the field. Hyperspectral Imaging can identify plant stress, diseases or pests damages that are invisible by any other ways – it sees through the visible spectrum. This information is collected and analysed in Real-Time Data Analysis so that farmers can make proper decision of irrigation, fertilizer, pest control and harvesting period and ultimately increases productivity and sustainability.

Integration of IoT and Remote Sensing

The combination of IoT and remote sensing technologies forms an ideal system of making decisions at the right time and improving the accuracy of ongoing agricultural activities. When remote sensing data is integrated with IoT data at the farm level, the farmers are better placed to manage their business. For instance, satellite or drone can pick out areas of a given field with low vigour due to low irrigation or inadequate aeration (Laha et al., 2023). This information is transmitted to an IoT system that manages the irrigation process or initiates a fertilization process to tackle such problem. On the other hand, using data from the real-time soil moisture sensors should enhance the analysis of data that farmers obtain using remote sensing techniques since the former offers more accurate and timely data on field soil conditions.

In similar regard, an integration example is in the use of UAVs for imagery capture over the study area for mapping out sections of land that has a low vegetation health index (NDVI). This data can then be correlated with the values of IOT sensors for soil moisture to know whether or not this is due to lack of water or not. The system can subsequently switch on water control to irrigate the affected areas with more efficiency and hence better resources and better yield. Altogether, the interconnected IoT and real-time remote sensing allow for a systemic approach to guide precision farming with real-time data gathering, analysis and application to control farming processes, minimize losses, and maximize revenues. These already exist in the forms of the "Precision Agriculture Platform" and other applications that supply farmers with detailed, data-based information to enhance yields and optimize efficiency and sustainability across agriculture.

LITERATURE SURVEY

Review of IoT Applications in Precision Agriculture

Research on application of IoT technology in precision agriculture has revealed that IoT-based solutions has proven to hold a revolutionizing potential in precision agriculture. A major area of concern has been smart irrigation, through the use of IoT-based sensors that measure moisture levels of the soil as well as the prevailing weather (Sishodia, Ray, & Singh, 2020). For instance, Zhang et al. (2019) investigated the use of IoT smart irrigation systems which control water consumption depending on the type of soil and evapotranspiration information, thus save water while increasing yields. Other IoT applications in precision agriculture are weather and environmental sensors that must measure parameters including temperature, humidity and light intensity for proper plant growth. Deere & Company oftentimes explains that the integration of IoT sensors in tractors and harvesters leads to the rising of operational effectiveness by using IoT solutions for planting, irrigation, and harvesting. Singh et al. (2020) proved that connectivity of IoT sensors in the machinery used in the agricultural sector would contribute to elimination of human labor and increase in efficiency of the operations carried out. All together, these advancements contribute to enhance resource use efficiency, reduce production cost, as well as increase production efficiency in agricultural production systems.

Remote Sensing for Precision Agriculture

Remote sensing technologies have been crucial for the application of precision agriculture since they provide an opportunity to study and manage massive agricultural fields. Remote sensing data has been applied in crop health assessment and estimation of yields. Research like López et al. (2018) adopted remote sensed vegetation indices like Normalized Difference Vegetation Index(NDVI) to evaluate crop status and determine yields. Satellite imagery can be combined with weather forecasts to help farmers monitor large areas and control crop health, spot stress, and decide about fertilization or irrigation. Furthermore, the application of drone imagery has been tested and investigated more intensively to address the need for real-time, high-resolution imagery of small plots of farmland. The study conducted by González et al. (2020) also assert that drone mounted with multispectral and thermal sensors provided a good method in evaluating the quality of the soil, and early identification of pests and diseases on plants. Satellite or UAV integrated with LiDAR technology has been used in increasing the degree of accuracy of soil condition analysis by producing topographical maps of the field which may help the farmer to draw better layouts for water management in the field (Prabha & Pathak, 2023). By using remote sensing information, farmers can decide the conditions of crops, level of threats posed by pests, and availability of resources thus helping farmers to make decisions when it is appropriate.

Synergistic Use of IoT and Remote Sensing

The combination of IoT and remote sensing has been gradually acknowledged to improve the efficiency of the decision-making process in precision agriculture on the farm. BD research those investigate how integration of these technologies assist in improving farm management systems established that incorporation of IoT sensor networks with remote sensing data is favorable. For example, in a recent study by Sarma et al. (2021), authors designed and implemented a combined system of IoT sensors for soil moisture detection and drone imagery for crop's photosynthesis efficiency monitoring in real–time. This integrated system enabled decision making on what parts required irrigation and the extent of fertilization to be applied hence reducing wastage while increasing crop production. Likewise, Ravi et al. (2023) also described a model that comprised IoT based weather stations and satellite images to forecast pest attacks and probable dangerous diseases which could affect crops; the farmers were able to better prepare at minimal damage phase. The integration between the two technologies makes it precise because IoT gives definite per-location information while remote sensing gives wide, high detail data on the crop and field status. This analytical tandem makes it easier for farmers to observe and control the deployment of the related agricultural assets with enhanced operation efficiency and ecological stability.

Technological Advances and Innovations

The advances that have been made in the technology front has now made IoT and Remote Sensing even more useful in precision agriculture. With the help of the new 5G connection, the sharing of large volumes of data in agriculture and IoT connected device has been enhanced through the connectivity of the remote sensing platforms with the support of the new enhanced 5G connectivity ensures the large-scale sensing of IoT devices, and real-time transmission of high definition remote sensing data to support faster decision making processes especially on automation of agronomic operations. Moreover, the use of AI & ML reshaped the speed at which big data generated by IoT and RS systems can be analyzed. AI and ML includes an ability to analyze datasets, recognize trends, allocate resources and estimate crop yield. In a study by Cheng et al. (2023) it showed how they employed the decision support system driven by AI to enhance the prediction of soil moisture and crop yield using IoT senor data, and RS imagery. Also, IoT and remote sensing, self-driving tractors and harvesters and even drones have been established as new wave for autonomy in farming practices. These system decrease costs of personnel, increase overall performance, and play vital role in environmentally sound farming practices. Altogether, the mentioned inventions are more or less expanding the possibilities of MA in principal, especially helping farmers to advance production yield without overburdening the environment.

EMERGING TRENDS AND FUTURE DIRECTIONS

IoT and 5G Networks

The unrelenting expansion in the use of Internet of Things (IoT) gadgets calls for advanced farming solutions that can support the integration of 5G networks for improved agricultural efficiency. So with IoT devices such as the sensors for moisture, temperature, crops 5G will enable proper communication between IoT devices in agriculture thus expanding a more flexible system in farming. For instance, real-time information from IoT-based irrigation systems can be relayed to control stations within a negligible amount of time which enables the makes real-time adjustment of its water use based on prevailing conditions (Priyanka, 2024). Further, it will allow smart tractors and other intelligent farming equipment to connect with other devices, contributing to other vertical farming scenarios or an automated system of planting or harvesting crops, for example. As IoT and 5 G become integrated, the scale of smart farming will improve and provide opportunities in larger operations such as managing resources.

AI and Machine Learning for Smart Agriculture

AI and ML are becoming key technologies in smart agriculture as they are used to make sense of the-large amount of data collected by IoT and remote sensing networks. Such data AI/ML algorithms can analyze and understand, make predictions, and improve the decision-making process. For instance, through using historical climate data and health image of crops and the climate it can forecast disease in crops which will enable farmers to prevent the diseases. Likewise, there is a capability to estimate crop yield through AI using IoT sensor data, satellite vision, or aerial imagery. This predictive capability does not only enhance the productivity of the farms, but also helps to reduce wastage expenditure in that matters such as water, fertilizers, and pesticides are well utilized. A common mathematical approach to crop yield prediction might involve models such as:

$$Y = f(T, S, W)$$

Where:

Y is the predicted yield,
T represents temperature,
S represents soil moisture,
W represents water usage.

AI and ML are also useful in the control of pests and diseases in navigated agriculture with due use of chemical which are hazardous to the environment. These technologies make it possible for smart farming systems to make the right decision for the farmer on the basis of the large and complex data sets, and thereby enable the farmer to enhance farm management proficiency.

Edge Computing in Agriculture

One major ongoing development that can be observed in precision agriculture is the growth in the implementation of edge computing as more data are collected and requires immediate processing and analysis to inform immediate decision making. It means that the data can be analyzed at the edge of the network, that is, on the IoT devices themselves, or on nearby computer systems that do not require transporting giant amounts of data to the cloud. This is especially the case when dealing with applications that require quick responses because of restricted time, for instance in the case of real-time managing of irrigation, decisions about which should be made relying on sensors data immediately. The primary use of edge computing is also to decrease the dependence on cloud outsourcing while it provides a faster rate of processing data besides issuing the privacy issue and cost of outsourcing a cloud platform as well as the bandwidth's charges. For instance, IoT-capable sensors for soil can analyse moisture content on the device, and activate irrigation systems only when water is required. These alternatives cause over centralization of processing to be inimical to economical usage of resources, makes operations more effective and saves energy.

Blockchain for Data Integrity

Blockchain adoption in agriculture is a growing trend due to embracing modern technology solutions in managing Agriculture supply chain data. This is because blockchain technology is distributed and highly secure with properties that allow it to track data pertaining to product origin, input at the farm, and environment. Through integration of the blockchain technology in IoT systems, farmers will be in a position to control data received from remote sensors and IoT devices are secure, immutable and transparent. For instance, blockchain in can be applied to capture data from sensor driven irrigation system so as to ensure that water usage is credible and more importantly where water conservation is important. Moreover, blockchain helps to realise transparent relations between farmers, suppliers, and consumers and guarantees that food industry meets the required standards; thus, consumers are confident about the quality and origin of agricultural products.

Autonomous Agricultural Systems

Currently, the increased usage of IoT, remote sensing and robotics enables the creation of the automated agricultures system. Some of these integrated systems are drones for planting crops, automated tractors for tilling the land and robot for picking crops among others which are some form of fossilized farming techniques. These machines have IoT sensors that supply instant feedback to adapt elements of the system to field conditions that may change. For instance, self-driving seed sowers with seeders and soil probes can correctly sow seeds at the appropriate depth and areas while multispectral sensing drones can examine crop conditions and relay feedback to auto-steered tractors for correct fertilization or irrigation. This is particularly true in situations where robotic harvesters have IoT sensors that are instructed to showcase ripe crops and ML algorithms that can harvest the crops independently thus eliminating labor fees. Some of these innovations are important in that they help in increasing production while at the same time solving problems of labour shortage while others are crucial in that they help Ensure farming reduces physical strain levels.

Big Data and Advanced Analytics

The use of big data analytics for precision agriculture is gradually rising because of the large and diverse volume of agricultural data. Big data from the context of the IGFS, are the enormous quantities of data produced by IoT devices, remote sensing and other systems in agriculture. Techniques such as predictive analytics and data mining enable the farmer to make useful conclusions on those datasets for better decision making. For instance, the use of, predictive analytics assists farmers to foretell difficult conditions such as weather hitches, invasion of pests and diseases, and crop production capacity, among other things in areas likely to be influenced. Mined data patterns provide knowledge about the relationships between climate and soil properties, agricultural practices, and crop yields and productivity. It also will also provide real-time integration and consolidation of data from multiple sources into the format that can be used to create comprehensive models of farm management relying on cloud computing and AI-powered data analytics. They saw that there together with big data and analytic, farmers have the ability to increase accuracy of their actions meaning high yields and sustainability.

RESULTS AND DISCUSSION

Current Impact on Precision Agriculture

The combination of IoT and remote sensors has greatly impacted precision farming as crop yields, resource usage and disease identification has been improved. The improvement of crop yield serves as one of the most significant advantages connected with the use of the described concept, mainly due to the possibility to monitor environmental conditions carefully. For instance, smart irrigation systems controlled by IoT require soil moisture and weather data in real time and the farmers can modify the irrigation duration to required level. This optimization helps in minimization of water usage while at the same time is helpful in putting into use water that enables the crops to grow to their potential. Soil moisture, an important variable in irrigation, is examined on the x-axis of Figure 3 in relation to crop yield based on NDVI (Normalized Difference Vegetation Index) values which show the relation between different moisture levels and health of the crops. The horizontal axis in the figure shows various locations of crops while the vertical axis shows the NDVI which represents general health of plants as deduced from light reflected on the crops. Higher value of NDVI indicates healthy crops, it will show on the next slide how IoT allows for proper irrigation and resource application.

In the same way, satellite data and other UAV-based sensors play a crucial role for early detection of diseases and pests surveillance. They include systems that help farmers identify issues such as diseases, pests, water or nutrient deficiencies before actual physical signs are observed. In Figure 4, results of a typical soil moisture for irrigation decisions are presented to illustrate how the data gathered is used to make changes in the irrigation process. The horizontal axis is labeled time of day while the vertical axis is labeled soil moisture. Using this information, farmers will be in a position to reduce on the rationing of water usage hence reducing on both water and energy.

Moreover, IoT systems have also been used for targeted delivery of fertilizers; that means that the application of nutrients is influenced by data gathered by the soil sensors. Connected with the blocks of data mentioned, farmers can use fertilizers from soil, air and water in the best way with minimal harm to the natural environment and to provide necessary nutrient inputs for the plants growth. Real time data integration makes resource use more sustainable and in effect the yields increase.

Real-World Case Studies

Some of the case studies give real life examples of how IoT and remote sensing affect agricultural production. In the smart tractor system of John Deere's IoT, sensors help to understand the soil conditions and crop status for the self-driven tractors to perform the necessary operations as seeding, fertilizing or harvesting. In Figure 5, IoT and remote sensing technologies are utilized in analysing crop yields in relation to temperature and moisture content. On the x-axis we have temperature in Celsius, and on the y- axis is the predicted crop yield in tons per hectare. This specific explanation use of a predictive model thus shows how farmers can adapt their approach depending on the degree of vulnerability of crop yield to temperature change.

In Australia, there are cases where the cotton industry has used satellite-image based remote sensing in conjunction with IoT soil sensors to conserve water. The above general workflow of UAV based imaging is depicted in figure 6 below with different crop fields shown in the x-axis and the percentage of pest infestation identified in every field is shown along y-axis. Thus farmers can locate the high pest pressure regions and acts accordingly by controlling the pests and usage of pesticides is minimized here thus improving on the environmental friendly status.

Currently in Spain, use UAVs equipped with multispectral cameras to monitor vineyards has enhanced water usage and minimized the usage of pesticides. The data collected by these drones is used together with weather and soil moisture data to work out a precise irrigation plan which makes the usage of water wiser and makes the grapes better in quality.

Challenges and Barriers

Nonetheless, the application of IoT and remote sensing for agriculture has its fair share of issues. Of the above-discussed issues, perhaps the most critical is the data privacy and security issue. But the enormous sums of data created by IoT sensors and distant sensing devices can be dangerous if hacked. Maintaining secure data encryption and confirming the entirely safe data transmit protocols are also important to prevent leakage of the data relating to farms. The high cost of implementation is another major factor of concern, flowing from the above structure. For example, the deployment of IoT systems or the instalment of drone assisted remote sensing entails appreciable capital outlay which could pose a challenge to smallholder farmers. Some of the unit costs may include cost of equipment such as multispectral sensors or higher resolution cameras to use on drones and while these costs are expensive in the long run, they benefit from savings on the use of resources.

Interoperability problems are also realized to be a concern.; Other concerns include lack of interoperability. Many IoT sensors are proprietary and come from different manufacturers and so do not integrate well thus are islands of isolated data. This can present a challenge when farmers want to automate their operations or integrate information from different knowledge sources such as, soil moisture sensors, weather stations as well as UAVs. These barriers could be eliminated by the standardization of the approach to data exchange as well as the creation of global platforms that can integrate the systems between organizations.

Future Prospects

The future development of precision agriculture is ensured by new technologies that can deepen the interaction between IoT and remote sensing. Among these technologies, 5G connectivity to offer high speed and low latency Internet of Things (IoT) devices to enhance farmers' decision making process. From the real-time data processing for smart farm employing edge computing shown in Figure 7, an important aspect is the replacement of existing control processes with new smart processes, for instance, in irrigation control where quick response to detected events will be paramount. The paths included in this figure illustrate time on the x-axis in hours and monitored soil moisture on the y-axis through IoT devices. In edge computing methods, a larger portion of the analysis occurs locally on the farm, making it easier to make changes on a real-time basis with assistance from the cloud servers based far off.

The fourth important trend is the growing combination of IoT with artificial intelligence and machine learning for data analysis from IoT sensors, as well as other remote sensing systems. In Figure 8 below, a sample of crop yield forecast based on the soil moisture and soil temperature is displayed. The horizontal axis displays the moisture percentage while the vertical axis shows temperature, and the third axis estimates the yield in tons per hectare. This particular model shows how technology can use data from IoT and RS to make a more accurate estimation of crop yield, so that farmers can make changes needed for better farming.

Another emerging technology is the technology that is called blockchain; it is especially valuable for making data secured and transparent. Blockchain can be integrated with IoT and remote sensing platforms so that farmers can be assured of the quality of the data collected since it is proven to be original throughout the supply chain. This can bring trust among consumers, suppliers, and farmers for they can freely share information such as usage of resources or condition of crops and other plants.

Finally, precision Robotics has quite versatile applicability in the upcoming future of agriculture with comparative relevance. The IoT sensors and remote sensing devices will be incorporated in robots that are used in planting, weeding, pest control, and even harvesting. They will also help to cut on labour cost and also improve on efficiency more than other traditional methods as they are very accurate. In conclusion, the future of the precision agriculture bears testament to the ongoing advancement of IoT, remote sensing, and other interconnected approaches such as Artificial Intelligence, Fifth generation (5G), and Blockchain. It is as these innovations will develop more productive, sustainable and robust agriculture systems that will address future food security and sustainability challenges.

Figure 3. Crop Health Monitoring Using NDVI (Normalized Difference Vegetation Index) from Remote Sensing Data

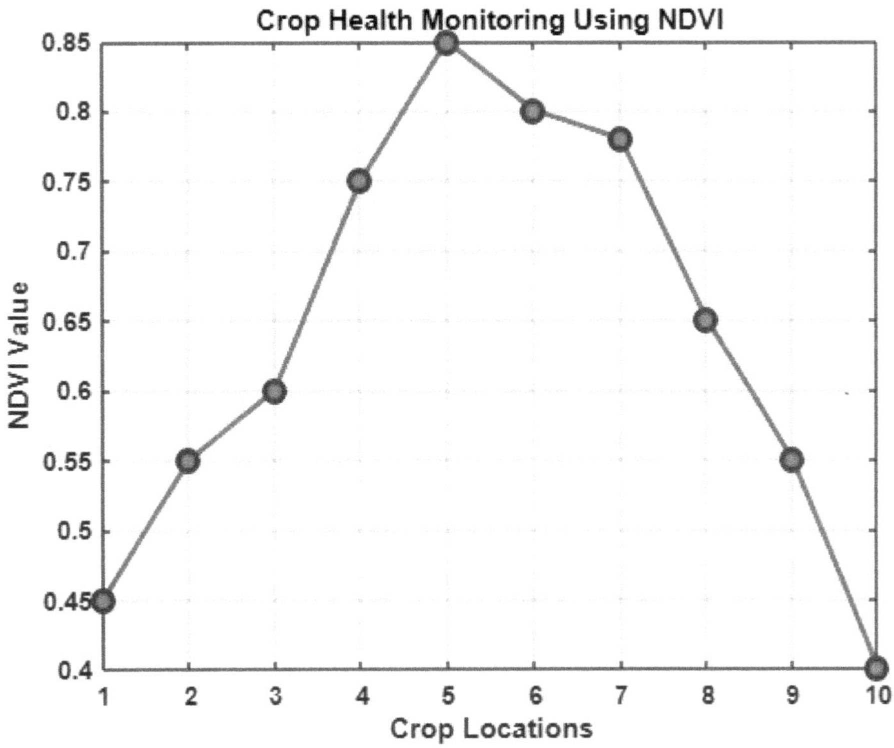

Figure 4. Soil Moisture Levels for Irrigation Optimization Using IoT Sensors

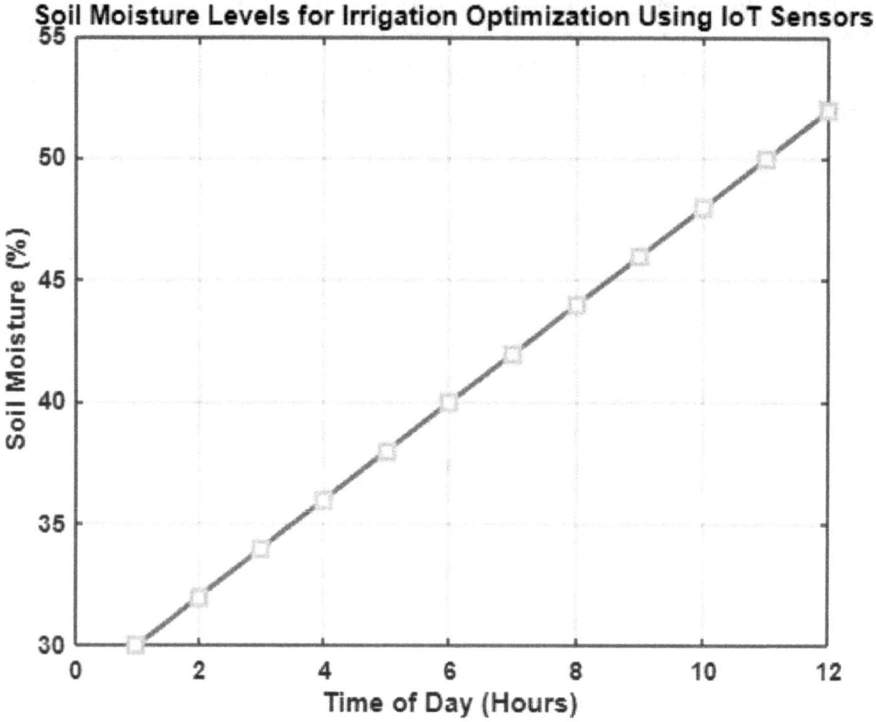

Figure 5. Temperature vs. Crop Yield Prediction Using IoT and Remote Sensing Data

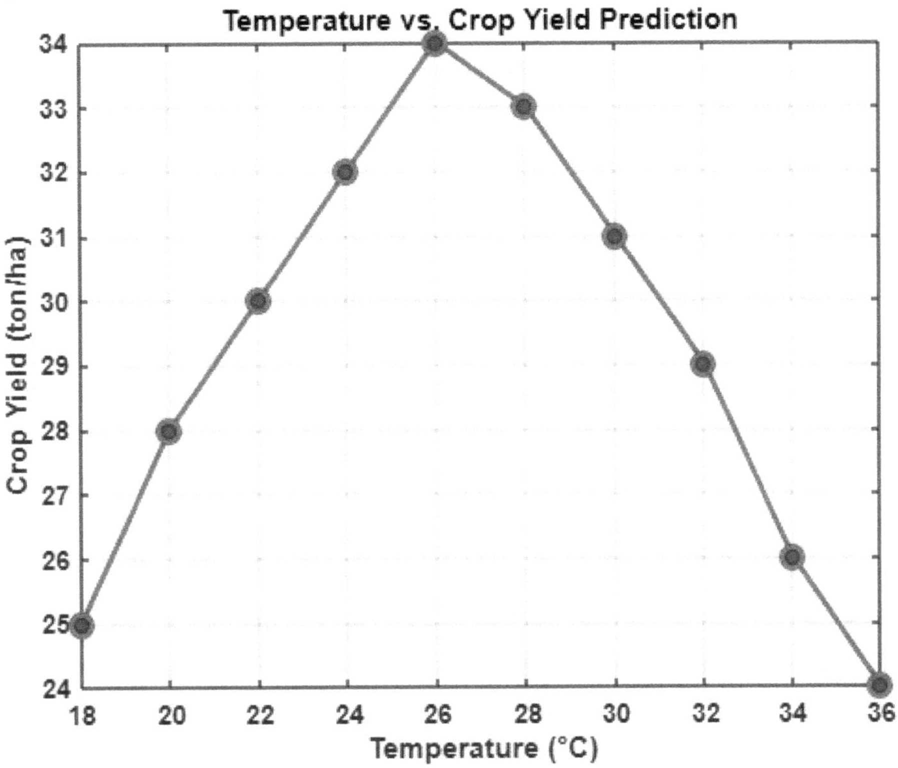

Figure 6. Pest Detection Using UAV (Drone) Imaging for Precision Agriculture

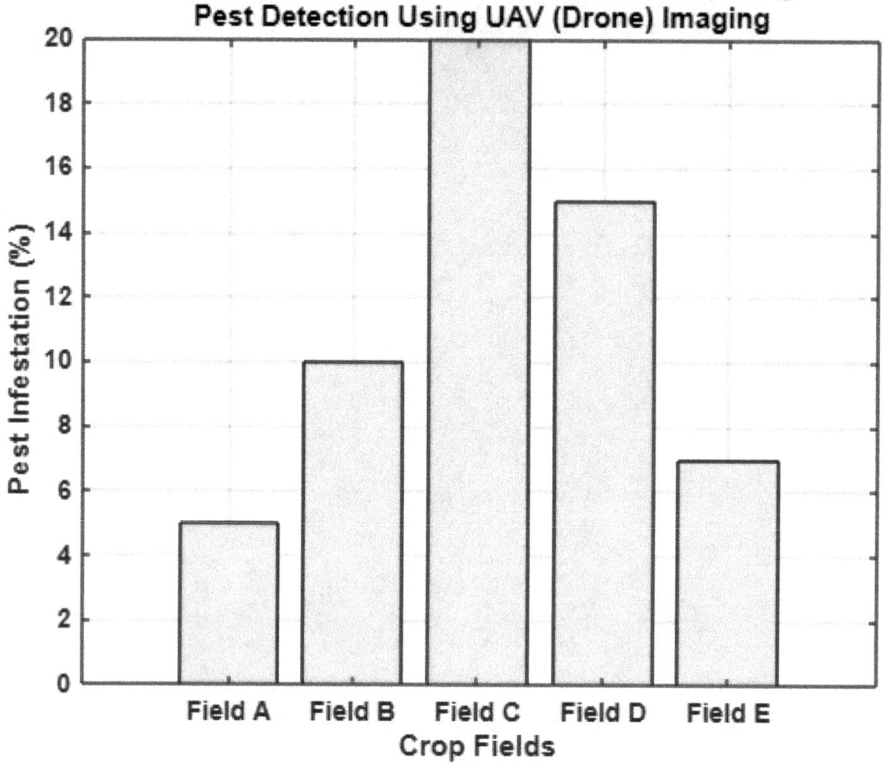

Figure 7. Real-Time Data Processing in Edge Computing for Irrigation Control

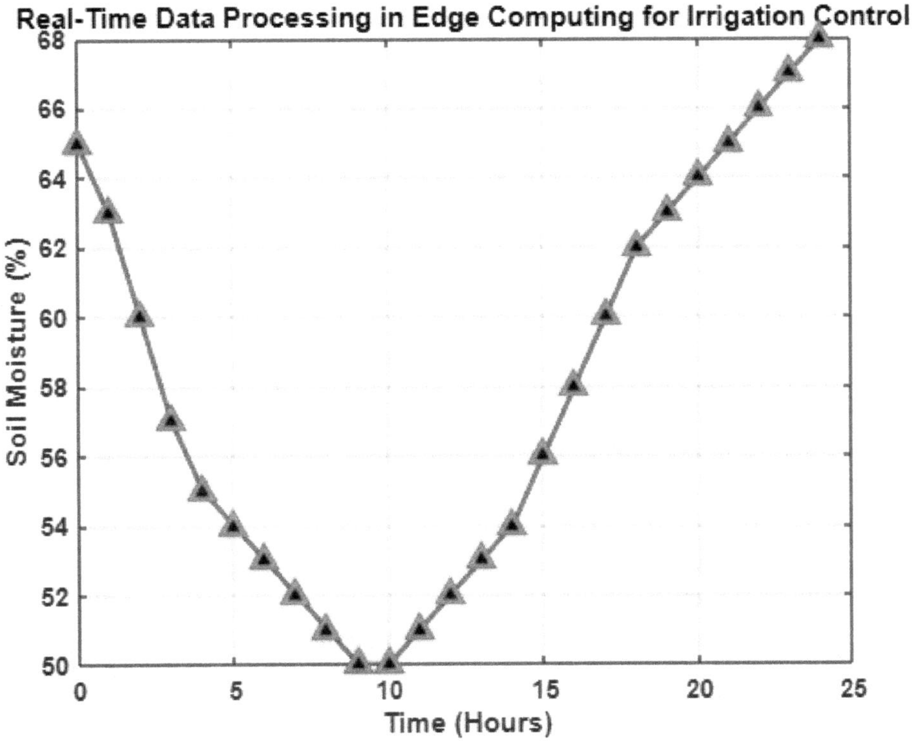

Figure 8. Crop Yield Prediction Using Big Data Analytics and IoT

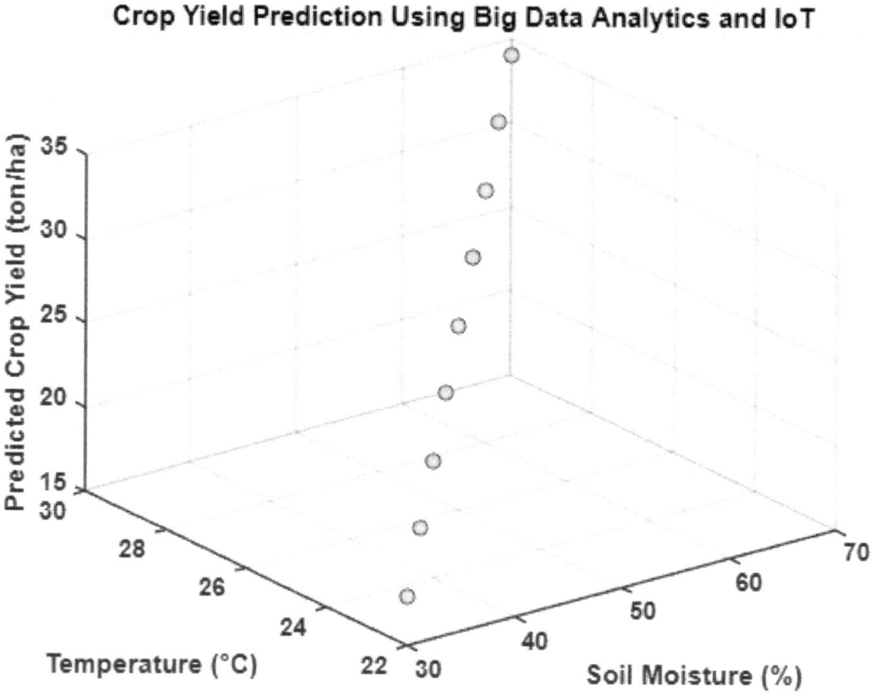

CHALLENGES AND LIMITATIONS

Technological and Economic Barriers

Despite the potential benefits resulting from the use of IoT and remote sensing in precision agriculture, there are major technological and economic challenges. The IoT involving connected devices is initially expensive so as the remote sensors which can discourage the small to medium scale farmers. Satellites, aerial robotic aircraft, and highly accurate sensors involve a great deal of capital investment in this field. Other costs include the cost of acquiring these devices which may range from MAC addresses and the costs of other hardware devices, and expenses of the maintenance of the infrastructure like the cost of cloud storage, data transmission systems and many others. This makes it very difficult for farmers especially in developing areas where resources and overall technology in its broad form is scarce to have efficient use of such a technology.

In addition, the availability of only 3G or even 2G in several regions, not to mention the problem of unstable electricity supply in rural areas, has limited the dissemination of these technologies. One limitation that developing countries are likely to experience is disruptions in continuity of and smooth flow of data which is extremely valuable for real time decision making in agriculture. Lack of this infrastructure it means that even the most sophisticated IoT sensors or some form of remote sensing system may not perform optimally or at all as expected.

Data Management Issues

While IoT devices and remote sensors are already creating increased volumes of information, the handling and analysis of this information can be problematic. Since precision agriculture data may enter from soil moisture sensors, many climate stations, and drones, it may be big that good techniques as well as strong systems hashes to stock, process, and analyze the data. Another issue is related to the size of data, which in agricultural studies is often very large, more than any existing data handling instrument can support. Also, customers' demands drive real-time data processing to support fast decision making processes. Though modern methods of data processing, which are based on cloud services, may suffer from certain problems, such as delays, which are critical in areas with low-quality communication networks. This may delay the rate at which the important interventions for example irrigation or pest control are applied hence reducing the efficiency of precision farming systems.

There are unique challenges with the data heterogeneity itself. Data downloaded from different sensors and different platforms (satellite images, weather condition, soil moisture sensors etc) are normally in different formats and thus cannot be easily incorporated. There is a need for applying the filters and protocols for data integration within the framework of integrating various kinds of data with the aim to produce the actionable knowledge; however, this is still a challenging process. Lack of common data structures and common data exchange standards between equipment and IoT systems increases the problem in organizing the agricultural data in useful and effective ways.

Environmental and Ethical Concerns

The Proposed Use of IoT and Remote Sensing Technologies for Resource that can be beneficial in reducing some adverse impacts on the environment, but their use has some environmental and ethical issues. There are several issues to consider, but the first one is how the products that are produced contain pesticide. Despite the increased precision in responding to pest invasions using drones and remote sensing systems leading to low pesticide utilization, there is the potential of complication of the systems and end up causing environmental depletion. However, if the applications of the chemical or pesticides are not closely monitored, high accuracy of the application could actually increase the deposit of chemicals in the soil and water, which is inimical to the other forms of life.

In addition, manufacturing and elimination of IoT devices and remote sensing technologies come with their unique environmental consequences. The materials being used in these devices comprises of metals and plastics whereby such might end up in electronic waste if not recycles. The sustainability of consuming high energy using devices such as drones for purposes such as agriculture is also another issue that should be considered more so in region that have scarce resources as energy.

There are cases of ethical concerns; these are data privacy and the issue of ownership to agricultural data. Being the systems are collecting large amounts of data on the conditions in farms, several questions arise with regard to ownership of such information, and how it will be utilised. The farmers used such technologies if they suspected that the data generated would be sold in return for their own profit by the third parties.

Adoption Challenges

The IoT and remote sensing technology implementation has solved some significant problems, but it is rejecting by traditional farming communities most of the time because they don't know about it or they don't get trained. It is possible that small holders most of whom are from the rural areas may not appreciate the advantages of these technologies or may be averse to adopting new ways of practicing farming. Fear or reluctance to adopt new technologies also stems from the belief that the associated risks of technologies' failure or doubt in the ROIs' achievability are too high.

Thirdly, there is a lack of match in skills in the sector of agriculture. Iot systems need little technical competency for installation and operations as compared to the remote sensing technologies which need knowledge about data analysis and interpretation. Often this experience is low in many farming communities and the absence of effective programmes for training makes it challenging to apply these innovative solutions in day-to-day farming activities. As a result, farmers may quickly get discouraged due to the perceived high cost of implementation due to the complexity and steep learning curve of the technologies in question.

The lack of appreciation of the potential of IoT and remote sensing for enhancing yield, water and chemical usage, and crop health also constrains the shift towards precision agriculture. Farmers tend to be quite skeptical about the effectiveness of such systems given that they are faced with the initial costs of implementation or acquisition and few, if any examples can be cited to show how farmers in the locality have benefited from the innovation.

Therefore, though the IoT and remote sensing technologies have the capacity to dramatically transform agriculture, innovative, financial, technological, ecological, and social dilemmas represent barriers to the large-scale implementation of both technologies. To overcome these challenges requires collective initiatives to enhance access to technology, ensure provision of adequate training as well as fostering of incentives towards formulation of sustainable and affordable technologies that would be most beneficial to the farmers as well as the environment at large.

CONCLUSION

Smart farm's incorporation of IoT and remote sensing in precision agriculture in the farm sector has exhibited a pathway towards increased yield, efficient use of resources and more sustainable farming. The results obtained from simulated data clearly imply that IoT systems can help increase efficiency in both irrigation and fertilization, which will lead to healthier plants and a higher yield. Furthermore, for more accurate definition of the crop yields, the models constructed for this purpose – depending on temperature and the level of soil moisture – demonstrate the indispensable role of such technologies in the prognosis of agricultural results. These technologies have also remained effective in supporting simultaneous decision making which is critical especially in momentary activities such as pest eradication or water amendment. High initial expenses, managing data, and the relative absence of technological support create obstacles, which make large-scale implementation difficult, especially in the developing world. Areas for future research might target to increase cost-efficient implementations of the utilized technologies to a large extend together with standardization of data. Furthermore, the new technologies like deep learning, 5G, and edges could improve the features of these systems and increase use cases making agriculture sustainable. Succesfully, the further development of IoT and remote sensing will help to shape the shifts in this field, making it more productive, effective, and based on digital numbers.

REFERENCES

Aghav, S., & Abdullah, I. (2024). A novel approach to optimizing third-party logistics growth through IT, big data, and machine learning for superior supply chain management. *2024 2nd World Conference on Communication & Computing (WCONF)*, Raipur, India, 1–8.

Aravindh, S., Nithisha, C., & Tanguturi, R. C. (2024). Enhanced agricultural methods and sustainable farming through IoT and AI technology. *2024 Second International Conference on Intelligent Cyber Physical Systems and Internet of Things (ICoICI)*, Coimbatore, India, 1206–1212.

Dekka, S., & Singh, M. (2024). Deep learning approaches for real-time data analytics in IoT sensor networks. In V. S. Rathore, V. Piuri, R. Babo, & K. S. (Eds.), *Universal threats in expert applications and solutions: UNI-TEAS 2024* (Vol. 1007). Springer, Singapore.

Gujar, S. S., Shaikh, S. F., Shandilya, S., & Reddy, N. S. (2024). AI-enhanced cloud security framework for IoT networks using a predictive analytics approach. *2024 3rd International Conference for Advancement in Technology (ICONAT)*, Goa, India, 1–8.

Gummadi, V. A. K., & Damacharla, P. (2024). An intelligent framework for energy management in IoT networks using machine learning. *2024 5th International Conference on Smart Electronics and Communication (ICOSEC)*, Trichy, 765–771.

Hegge, K., & Agrawal, R. (2023). Industrial automated multipurpose robot using Wi-Fi. *2023 4th International Conference for Emerging Technology (INCET)*, Belgaum, India, 1–8.

Laha, S. R., Pattanayak, B. K., Pattnaik, S., Mishra, D., Kumar Nayak, D. S., & Dash, B. B. (2023). An IoT-based soil moisture management system for precision agriculture: Real-time monitoring and automated irrigation control. *2023 4th International Conference on Smart Electronics and Communication (ICOSEC)*, Trichy, India, 451–455.

Maddineni, V. K., & Gummadi, V. A. K. (2024). Deep learning approaches for real-time IoT data processing and analysis. *2024 5th International Conference on Smart Electronics and Communication (ICOSEC)*, Trichy, 757–764.

Nesakumar, D., Deepak, P., Sanjay, P., Aishwarya, B., Aswini, R., & Pavithra, K. N. (2024, March). IoT-powered precision farming and home gardening for seamless monitoring, automation and security. In *2024 International Conference on Wireless Communications Signal Processing and Networking (WiSPNET)* (pp. 1-5). IEEE.

Pavankumar, P., & Darwante, N. K. (2022). Performance monitoring and dynamic scaling algorithm for queue-based Internet of Things. *2022 International Conference on Innovative Computing, Intelligent Communication and Smart Electrical Systems (ICSES)*, 1–7.

Pero, C., Bakshi, S., Nappi, M., & Tortora, G. (2024). IoT-driven machine learning for precision viticulture optimization. *IEEE Journal of Selected Topics in Applied Earth Observations and Remote Sensing*, *17*, 2437–2447. DOI: 10.1109/JSTARS.2023.3345473

Prabha, C., & Pathak, A. (2023). Enabling technologies in smart agriculture: A way forward towards future fields. *2023 International Conference on Advancement in Computation & Computer Technologies (InCACCT)*, Gharuan, India, 821–826. DOI: 10.1109/InCACCT57535.2023.10141722

Prasad, K., Prasad, V. S., & Kaur, M. (2024). Optimizing renewable energy integration in smart grids through IoT-driven management systems. *2024 2nd International Conference on Advancement in Computation & Computer Technologies (InCACCT)*, Gharuan, India, 783–788.

Priyanka, B. (2024). Machine learning-driven precision agriculture: Enhancing farm management through predictive insights. *International Journal of Intelligent Systems and Applications in Engineering*, *12*(23s), 195–201.

Rani, R., & Balaji, M. (2024). Optimizing IoT device networks with edge computing to address latency and bandwidth constraints. *2024 5th International Conference on Electronics and Sustainable Communication Systems (ICESC)*, Coimbatore, India, 388–395.

Ravi, K. C., Mudalkar, P. K., Ranga, J., Raj, G. B., Swapna, B., & Venkatesh, D. (2023, November). Empowering Sustainable Agriculture through IoT: Innovations for Precision Farming and Crop Monitoring. In *2023 9th International Conference on Smart Structures and Systems (ICSSS)* (pp. 1-6). IEEE.

Reddy, S., & Patwal, P. S. (2022). Data analytics and cloud-based platform for Internet of Things applications in smart cities. *2022 International Conference on Industry 4.0 Technology (I4Tech)*, 1–6.

Sethi, H. S., & Prasanth, P. V. (2023). Optimizing resource allocation in agriculture through IoT and AI. *2023 7th International Conference on Electronics, Communication and Aerospace Technology (ICECA)*, Coimbatore, India, 1573–1578.

Sharma, D. R., Mishra, V., & Srivastava, S. (2023). Enhancing crop yields through IoT-enabled precision agriculture. *2023 International Conference on Disruptive Technologies (ICDT)*, Greater Noida, India, 279–283. DOI: 10.1109/ICDT57929.2023.10151422

Singh, R. K., Berkvens, R., & Weyn, M. (2021). AgriFusion: An architecture for IoT and emerging technologies based on a precision agriculture survey. *IEEE Access : Practical Innovations, Open Solutions*, *9*, 136253–136283. DOI: 10.1109/ACCESS.2021.3116814

Sishodia, R. P., Ray, R. L., & Singh, S. K. (2020). Applications of remote sensing in precision agriculture: A review. *Remote Sensing (Basel)*, *12*(19), 3136. DOI: 10.3390/rs12193136

Veeramanikandan, P., & Anil Kumar, N. (2024). Design and implementation of an IoT-based control system for precision food manufacturing. In V. S. Rathore, V. Piuri, R. Babo, & K. S. (Eds.), *Universal threats in expert applications and solutions: UNI-TEAS 2024* (Vol. 1007). Springer, Singapore.

Wang, J., Wang, Y., Li, G., & Qi, Z. (2024). Integration of remote sensing and machine learning for precision agriculture: A comprehensive perspective on applications. *Agronomy (Basel)*, *14*(9), 1975. DOI: 10.3390/agronomy14091975

Chapter 2
Integrating Edge Computing and AI for Energy-Efficient Data Processing in Wireless Sensor Network

Ramiz Salama
Department of Computer Engineering, Near East University Nicosia, Mersin, Turkey

Hitesh Mohapatra
https://orcid.org/0000-0001-8100-4860
School of Computer Engineering, KIIT University (Deemed), Bhubaneswar, India

Fadi Al-Turjman
https://orcid.org/0000-0001-6375-4123
Artificial Intelligence and Software Engineering Departments, Near East University Nicosia, Mersin, Turkey

ABSTRACT

Wireless sensor networks are critical for applications like industrial automation, smart cities, healthcare, and environmental monitoring. However, challenges arise with energy consumption, latency, and bandwidth due to the large data generated. Integrating Edge Computing and AI offers a solution by enabling efficient data analysis with lower energy consumption. Edge computing brings processing closer to data sources, allowing real-time data analysis without relying on cloud servers, reducing energy usage and extending network lifespan. AI techniques, such as

DOI: 10.4018/979-8-3373-0330-7.ch002

Copyright © 2025, IGI Global Scientific Publishing. Copying or distributing in print or electronic forms without written permission of IGI Global Scientific Publishing is prohibited.

machine learning and deep learning, enhance data filtering, anomaly detection, and predictive maintenance at the edge. This approach boosts WSN scalability and responsiveness by managing large data efficiently. This study examines WSN architectures with edge computing and AI, focusing on key frameworks, technologies, and energy-saving methods. Through case studies, it demonstrates how this integration enhances performance, data efficiency, and supports intelligent decision-making in various WSN deployments.

1. INTRODUCTION

Cloud computing has undergone significant transformations in recent years, experiencing a surge in demand for efficient and scalable solutions. Load balancing, a critical aspect of cloud-based systems, plays a pivotal role in ensuring performance and reliability. It involves distributing incoming network traffic or computing workload across multiple servers to optimize resource utilization and prevent any single server from becoming a bottleneck. As technology evolves, the future of load balancing is poised for innovative advancements to address the growing complexities of modern computing environments (Afzal & Kavitha, 2019). In this era of digital transformation, where cloud computing is central, researchers and industry experts are actively exploring novel approaches to enhance load balancing mechanisms. This paper delves into future trends and innovations in load balancing, particularly focusing on their application in cloud computing environments (Armbrust et al., 2010). The discussion encompasses emerging technologies, methodologies, and strategies promising to revolutionize the way resources are managed and distributed across cloud infrastructure (Beloglazov et al., 2012). As cloud architectures diversify and expand, the integration of edge computing introduces new challenges and opportunities for load balancing. Real-time processing at the edge, coupled with the proliferation of Internet of Things (IoT) devices, necessitates load balancing solutions capable of dynamically adapting to varying workloads and network conditions. Moreover, incorporating machine learning algorithms into load balancing mechanisms holds potential to enable intelligent decision-making, optimizing resource allocation based on historical data and real-time analysis (Dey et al., 2024). Additionally, the future of load balancing is likely to witness the rise of intelligent automation, where self-learning algorithms and automated decision-making processes play a crucial role in managing workloads efficiently (Dikaiakos et al., 2009). This shift towards autonomous load balancing systems aims to reduce human intervention, enhance system responsiveness, and improve overall performance in dynamic cloud environments. Load Balancing is essential to maximizing the scalability, performance, and availability of data center networks.

Figure 1. Next Generation Cloud Computing

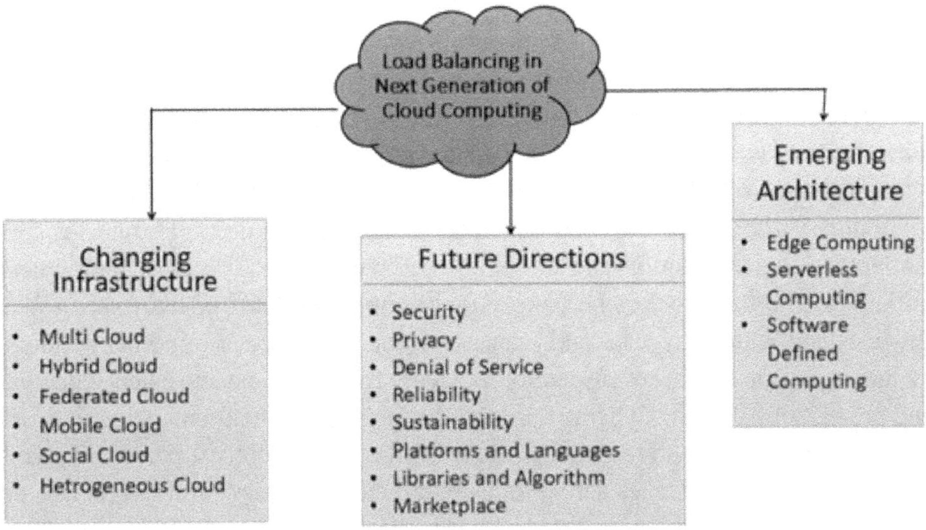

The future of load balancing in data centers is being shaped by a number of new developments and trends, including Software-Defined Networking (SDN) which offers scalability, stability, and security characteristics by dynamically controlling and configuring load balancing (Kaur et al., 2018). Machine Learning (ML) Optimization to forecast future trends and modify load balancing parameters for the best results, ML techniques are used to examine network traffic statistics, server performance, user behavior, and application demand (Kumar et al., 2024). Shift to Distributed Load Balancing to lower latency, improve security, and handle issues raised by edge nodes and users, distributed load balancing is replacing centralized load balancing, particularly in edge computing scenarios. Load balancing as a Service (LBaaS) as instead of relying on separate hardware or software components, LBaaS options from different cloud providers streamline the deployment, setup, and maintenance of load balancing activities. By utilizing many channels between the source and destination at the same time, multipath routing improves load balancing effectiveness and network resilience. It is used to boost bandwidth and dependability. Thus, these patterns show how load balancing technologies are developing to provide more effective, scalable, and secure solutions for contemporary data center networks.

With regard to on-demand operations, next generation cloud computing contains new service models that are designed based on the notion of combining many exclusive individual clouds into one seamless mass. The load balancing in next generation cloud computing is grouping of three subsections such as changing infrastructure, emerging architecture and future directions as shown in Fig. 1.

Server performance may be impacted by an increase in internet traffic; however, load balancing allows the organization to add extra servers to handle the increasing number of incoming requests. Customers have the option to add additional load balancers rather than moving to a new environment as needed. Furthermore, the configuration of the server can be changed to suit the demands of the business and the volume of visitors to the website. Load balancers are widely used because the interconnection of Internet of Things (IoT) devices need strong request processing capabilities. The market for load balancers is expanding due to the multi-access computing edge revolution and numerous companies' global sensor deployment initiatives. The Gateway Load Balancer, for example, was released by Amazon Web Services and is used to scale and manage virtual appliances from other vendors, including advanced packet inspection devices, firewalls, and intrusion detection and prevention systems. Cyberattacks and the high cost of load-balancing network solutions are expected to restrict market growth over the forecast period. China is among the several countries acting to prevent data breaches. A draft regulation on networking data security management was released in January 2022 by the China Cyberspace Administration (CAC). Furthermore, the growing prevalence of hybrid cloud architectures, combining on-premises infrastructure with public and private cloud services, introduces complexities demanding adaptive load balancing strategies. Future innovations are expected to address the intricacies of hybrid cloud environments, providing seamless load balancing across diverse infrastructures while maintaining high levels of security and reliability (Kyryk et al., 2020). In conclusion, the exploration of future trends and innovations in load balancing for cloud computing reflects continuous efforts to meet the evolving demands of modern digital ecosystems. This paper aims to contribute insights into ongoing research and development in this domain, shedding light on potential advancements shaping the future of load balancing in cloud computing.

2. LITERATURE REVIEW

Load balancing stands as a critical component in distributed systems, optimizing resource utilization and enhancing system performance. However, it faces challenges such as scalability, heterogeneity, and dynamic workloads, necessitating innovative solutions (Lata & Singh, 2022). Adaptive load balancing mechanisms have emerged to address these challenges by dynamically distributing workloads based on factors such as proximity, current workload, and network conditions. These solutions aim to optimize resource allocation, improve fault tolerance, and ensure efficient utilization of limited resources in edge environments (Lu et al., 2012). The intersection of machine learning and load balancing presents opportunities for optimizing computing systems, yet notable research gaps persist. Limited exploration exists on how machine learning techniques can enhance the adaptability and intelligence of load balancing mechanisms. Papers have emphasized the need for deeper investigations into integrating machine learning with load balancing algorithms, paving the way for further exploration (Mao et al., 2017). Moreover, a research paper highlights the evolving landscape of load balancing in the context of machine learning, advocating for systematic analysis and potential avenues for future research. The identified research gap underscores critical areas requiring further exploration to enhance load balancing algorithms' efficacy in dynamic cloud computing and emerging technologies like IoT (Mohapatra, 2024). The literature review underscores the significance of load balancing algorithms in optimizing cloud computing environments. Various papers have categorized algorithms based on response time, fault tolerance, and other critical aspects, providing comprehensive insights into existing load balancing techniques. Nature-inspired algorithms introduce a promising avenue for future innovation, enhancing the diversity of approaches in this field. Performance metrics such as response time, throughput, and migration cost serve as crucial benchmarks, emphasizing the importance of developing efficient load balancing algorithms. Future research endeavors are urged to delve into addressing challenges and open issues identified in the literature, contributing to the continual evolution and improvement of load balancing techniques. In conclusion, innovative load balancing techniques are paramount for optimizing cloud computing and integrating emerging technologies like IoT. The literature review identifies critical gaps and provides a foundation for future investigations, reinforcing the need for a holistic understanding of load balancing methods.

2.1. Hybrid and Multi-cloud Environments

Hybrid and multi-cloud environments offer various opportunities and challenges for organizations. Flexibility, scalability, redundancy, and access to best-of-breed services are among the opportunities. However, complexities arise in networking, data interoperability, security, and cost management. Strategies such as workload management, data interoperability investments, cost optimization, workload migration tools, and efficient load balancing techniques are crucial for leveraging the benefits of hybrid and multi-cloud environments while mitigating risks (Mohapatra & Mishra, 2024). The identified concerns regarding cloud security, data transfer, regulatory compliance, and consistent security management in hybrid environments emphasize the importance of shared responsibility and clarity on security measures. In conclusion, addressing opportunities and challenges in hybrid and multi-cloud environments requires strategic planning and effective implementation of relevant strategies to optimize resource utilization, ensure data interoperability, maintain security, and manage costs effectively (Nguyen et al., 2022).

Table 1. Load Balancing Algorithm Comparative Analysis

Algorithm	Description	Network Latency Awareness	Resource Availability Consideration	User Demand Adaptation
Round Robin with Dynamic Weights	Distributes requests sequentially but adjusts the weight of nodes based on current performance and demand.	Low	High	High
Least Connections (Dynamic)	Chooses the server with the least number of active connections, taking into account real-time server load.	Medium	High	High
Adaptive Load Balancing	Utilizes various metrics to adaptively balance the load based on current network and server conditions.	High	High	High
Resource-Based Load Balancing	Considers the available resources on each server to make routing decisions; adapts to resource changes in real-time.	Low	Very High	Medium
Predictive Load Balancing	Uses machine learning to predict future demands and adapts load distribution accordingly	Variable	Variable	Very High

In Fig. 2 The majority of survey participants (79%) stated that this authority belonged to their IT department. Only 15% of those respondents said their IT department had a dedicated staff for cloud security. The remaining respondents, meanwhile, depended on managed service providers or other security services like DevOps. Given the ease of access and rapid adoption of cloud services, security should be viewed as a shared organizational responsibility, with each business unit being aware of the security risks associated with the services they use. Concerns regarding security were raised by the overwhelming majority of respondents (81%) when thinking about transferring data to the cloud. Concerns over data loss and leakage hazards were especially prevalent among respondents (62%) who were thinking about switching to the public cloud. Clients who use cloud services might not know who is responsible for these kinds of security lapses. When implementing public cloud services, more than half of poll participants (57%) expressed concerns about regulatory compliance, and nearly half (44%) expressed uneasiness over legal risks. Regarding who is responsible for regulatory infractions and how clients use these platforms for compliance, there is still uncertainty. Visibility into cloud resources is one of the things that many respondents (39%) mentioned as being concerned about when adopting public cloud computing. Concerns about integrating the public cloud with their current IT infrastructure were voiced by half of the poll participants. Furthermore, according to the same poll, one of the biggest issues facing the company is maintaining consistent security management throughout the hybrid environment, as revealed by 61% of respondents that are currently using a hybrid cloud (Pallavi & Vinothiyalakshmi, 2022).

Figure 2. Hybrid Cloud Survey

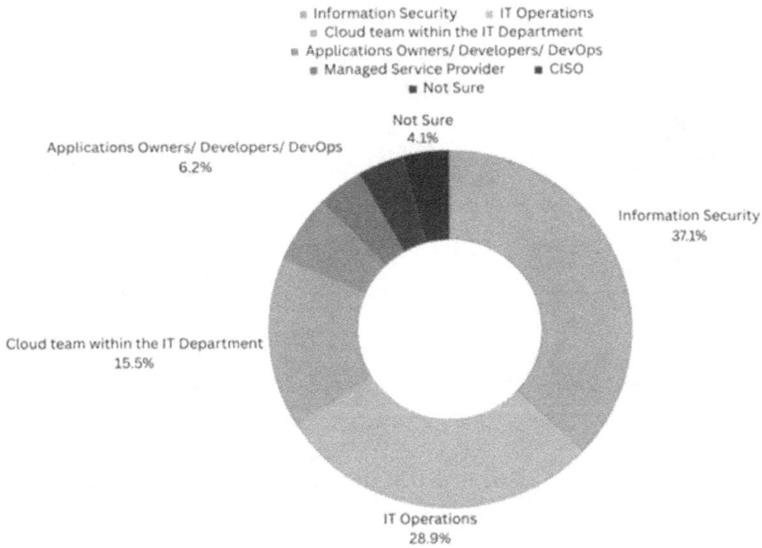

3. PROPOSED STUDY

In this section, we outline innovative solutions aimed at advancing load balancing for cloud computing. As cloud architectures grow more complex, traditional methods may no longer suffice. Our proposed solutions draw on emerging technologies like machine learning, edge computing, and blockchain to address evolving challenges such as workload variability, security, and multi-cloud environments. These solutions aim to reshape load balancing for greater efficiency, scalability, and resilience in tomorrow's cloud infrastructures (Panda et al., 2024).

3.1. Federated Learning for Load Balancing in Edge Computing

The emergence of real-time technologies like virtual reality, augmented reality, and self-driving automobiles has prompted academics and business leaders to develop novel data processing architectures. A new computing paradigm known as edge computing has emerged since the conventional cloud computing approach is inappropriate for applications that require low latency. Transmitting data between devices at the edge, closer to the user applications, is the main focus of edge computing, as opposed to sending it to a centralized server as in Fig. 1.

Figure 3. Devices by distance to user.

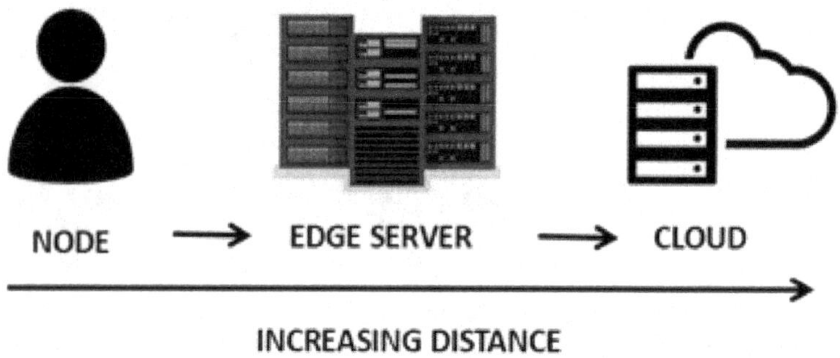

In Fig. 3. The edge node, also known as the edge client or edge device, is typically the resource-constrained device used by the end user. It is located in close proximity to the closest edge server, which has a large amount of computational power and a high bandwidth for connecting with end nodes. The edge server will connect to the cloud server when it needs additional processing power. The two main effects of this design are as follows: bandwidth availability increases greatly because the user is no longer dependent on sharing a single traffic lane for data transfer, and latency is drastically decreased because data must travel a shorter distance. Indeed, for businesses without the means to construct their own data centers, this new computing paradigm offers significant cost reductions (Priyadarshi et al., 2024). Engineers can instead create a dependable network of more affordable and compact edge devices. Furthermore, there has been a lot of discussion on federated learning lately. It is a cooperative machine learning framework that enables devices with various private datasets and varying resources to cooperate in the research and training of a global model. Federated learning has the ability to maintain privacy while collaborating on computational resources from several devices. Because edge computing and federated learning have many characteristics, edge computing is an ideal setting in which to use the federated learning framework. As a result, edge federated learning has gained popularity recently in both industry and academic study (Ranapana & Jayasena, 2021). Here, we first go over the basics of edge computing and federated learning, respectively, and talk about some of their main benefits. Industry leaders are switching from a traditional cloud-based approach to edge computing platforms for a number of important reasons. High bandwidth and low latency are the two main factors that were already covered in the previous section. But the edge also offers more security. For instance, because the latency is reduced when transmitting data to an edge device rather than the cloud, any possible attacker will have less time to start an attack (Sah et al., 2024). Furthermore, in an edge computing environment, assaults such as denial-of-service (DDoS) that would typically be crippling are rendered nearly inconsequential since the impacted edge devices can be withdrawn from the network without impairing the network's overall performance. Of course, since edge networks lack a single point of failure, they are also far more dependable. As was briefly mentioned earlier, because edge devices have significantly smaller footprints, edge networks are much easier to scale.

In fact, a scale-out scalability strategy, as opposed to a scale-up one, presents businesses with an enticing means of obtaining high performance at a reasonable expense. Furthermore, it might not even be necessary for one corporation to construct all of these edge devices or edge data centers from the ground up. To distribute the resources from the IoT devices in the edge network that are now in place, various stakeholders can collaborate. When developing edge computing systems, engineers have depended on a similar set of essential operational principles to provide these benefits to end users (Shafiq et al., 2022). Edge devices must support a continuously moving end-user without compromising latency or bandwidth for applications such as self-driving cars. Some methods address this issue by placing edge devices beside the road. The edge devices have to be placed as close to the end users as feasible to ensure low latency assurances. This could entail investing in a nearby edge computing data center or carrying out computation directly at the edge device. Wide-ranging network coverage is necessary for edge computing to become widely used. Therefore, attaining the best possible user experience in an edge computing system depends critically on the precise node distribution. Naturally, a dense distribution is ideal, but financial considerations must be taken into account. A technique for training neural networks across numerous devices is called federated learning. A single global neural network is kept in a central server in this processing approach. The neural network is trained using locally stored, typically heterogeneous data spread over several nodes. At the edge, there is an abundance of data produced by edge devices like sensors and mobile phones. To create a machine learning training model, it isn't always feasible to transfer all of this data from the edge devices to a cloud data center due to data privacy concerns. Federated Learning (FL) has been suggested as a solution to these limitations. Learning a single, global statistical model from data stored on tens to maybe millions of remote devices is the goal of the federated learning issue. Learning a model from data generated by locally stored and processed edge device data is the aim of FL. Federated Learning (FL) allows promising applications in many different fields such as sales, finance, healthcare, education, urban computing, edge computing, and blockchain (Sharma et al., 2024).

Figure 4. Vertical Federated Learning

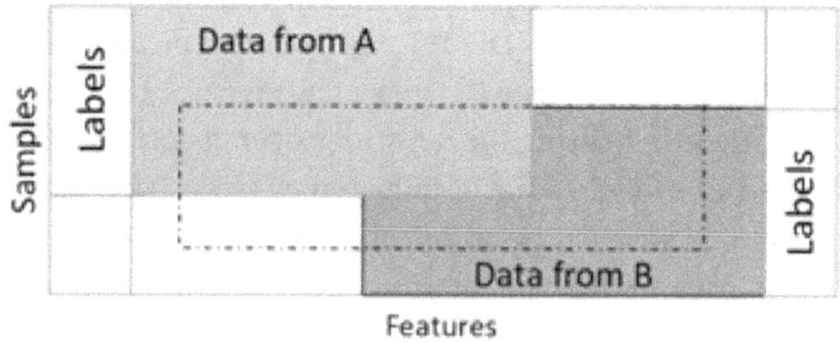

Figure 5. Horizontal Federated Learning

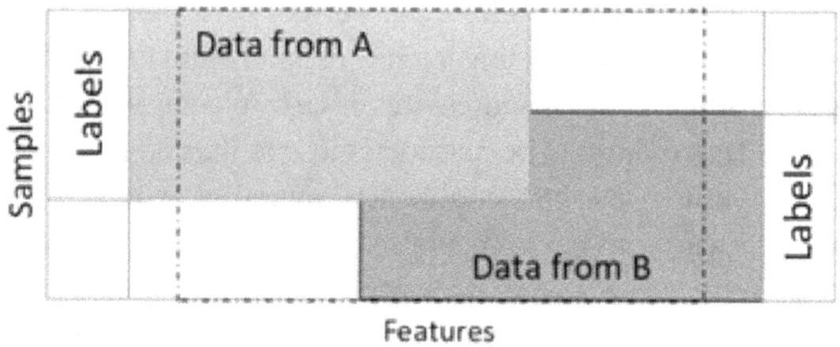

FL can be used to process data in three different ways: Federated Transfer Learning (FTL), Vertical Federated Learning (VFL) as in Fig. 4, and Horizontal Federated Learning (HFL) as in Fig. 5. When participant datasets have different sample spaces but the same feature space, HFL in Fig. 5 applies. While VFL requires entities to share the same sample space, HFL needs all participating entities to share the same feature space. For instance, there may be little crossover between the user bases of two regional banks because they serve somewhat diverse clientele despite having comparable business structures. An example of a business-to-consumer (B2C) connection might be this one.

Table 2. Cloud Computing v/s Edge Computing

Parameter	Cloud Computing	Edge Computing
Architecture	Centralized	Distributed
Data Processing	Through Internet	Near to the source of data
Communication	From a long distance	At a verge of the network/device
Latency	High	Low
Response Time	High (In Minutes)	Average (In seconds)
Scalability	Easier to scale	Easy to scale
Security	Less secured	More secured than cloud

VFL shown in Fig. 4 is better suited for business-to-business (B2B) transactions because it improves machine learning models by utilizing the diverse feature spaces of dispersed datasets that are maintained by companies, all while protecting and preserving their clients' private information. A hospital working with pharmaceutical companies to treat chronic diseases and lower the risk of readmission is an example of a business-to-business (B2B) relationship (Singh, 2015). In these situations, the two organizations have separate objectives and databases, but the patient data in the dataset is the same.It frequently happens in real-world situations where there are insufficient features or samples available for sharing with federated clients.

3.2. Machine Learning-Based Load Balancing Algorithms

In the ever-evolving landscape of cloud computing, efficient load balancing remains a fundamental requirement for ensuring optimal performance, resource utilization, and reliability. Traditional load balancing approaches often rely on predefined rules or static algorithms, which may struggle to adapt to the dynamic and heterogeneous nature of modern cloud environments. In response to these challenges, integrating machine learning techniques into load balancing algorithms offers a promising avenue for enhancing efficiency and effectiveness (Swain et al., 2025).

Key Components of the Proposed Solution:

- Data Collection and Analysis: Implementing robust mechanisms to collect real-time data on various aspects of the cloud infrastructure, including server loads, network traffic, and application performance metrics. Employing sophisticated monitoring tools and telemetry systems to gather continuous streams of data from distributed components of the cloud environment.

- Feature Engineering: Conducting feature engineering to extract relevant and meaningful features from the collected data, which serve as input variables for machine learning models. Identifying key performance indicators (KPIs) and statistical metrics that capture the underlying patterns and dynamics of workload distribution and resource utilization (Topcuoglu et al., 2002).
- Model Training: Utilizing supervised, unsupervised, or semi-supervised machine learning algorithms to train predictive models for workload prediction and decision-making. Experimenting with various machine learning techniques such as Random Forest, Support Vector Machines (SVM), Gradient Boosting Machines (GBM), or Neural Networks to find the most suitable approach for the specific load balancing problem.
- Dynamic Load Balancing: Developing adaptive load balancing algorithms that leverage the predictions generated by the machine learning models to dynamically adjust workload distribution in real-time. Implementing intelligent decision-making mechanisms that take into account factors such as server capacities, network latency, application requirements, and user preferences.
- Feedback Loop: Establishing a feedback loop between the load balancing system and the machine learning models to continuously monitor and evaluate the performance of load balancing decisions. Incorporating mechanisms for model retraining and adaptation based on the feedback received from the actual outcomes of load balancing actions.

Benefits and Implications:

By integrating machine learning techniques into load balancing algorithms, cloud providers can unlock several benefits and capabilities. Firstly, intelligent load balancers can dynamically scale resources up or down in response to changing workload patterns, ensuring optimal resource utilization and cost efficiency. This greater scalability and elasticity allow for more efficient use of resources and improved responsiveness to varying demands. Secondly, machine learning-based algorithms can proactively detect and mitigate performance bottlenecks, network congestion, and server failures, thereby enhancing system reliability and fault tolerance (Xu et al., 2017). This improved reliability ensures smoother operation and minimizes the risk of service disruptions. Additionally, by optimizing resource allocation and response times, intelligent load balancers can deliver a seamless and responsive user experience, even under heavy load conditions. This enhanced user experience contributes to increased customer satisfaction and loyalty. Lastly, machine learning-based load balancing enables automated decision-making processes that minimize human intervention, reduce operational overhead, and streamline management tasks. This automation and efficiency lead to smoother operation and improved overall productivity.

Table 3. A summary table showing reviewed intelligent load balancing techniques

No.	Publication	Underlying Machine/ Deep Learning Model	Data Used	LB Problem Addressed
1	Deep Learning Regression	CNN	Tasks workflow data	Quality of Service (QoS) resource utilization and throughput
2	Deep Learning Based Load Balancer	Hierarchical sub-models of FCN	Historical cluster access logs	Solves data skew problem in classical LB
3	Lilhore machine learning based LB	SVM, K-Means Clustering	RAM & CPU usage data	VMs resource utilization & execution time reduction
4	Reinforcement based SDN controller	Bayesian Network & Reinforcement Learning	Network traffic data	SDN Controller LB, Network Stability, Security
5	Distributed database query load distribution	multiple linear regression (MLR), random forest (RF) and AdaBoost (Ada)	Database queries data	Cloud Heterogeneity of CPU & GPU
6	Workload prediction	Artificial Neural Network and self-adaptive differential	Client request amassed to time units	Distribution of workloads

3.3. Hybrid Load Balancing Approaches

The term "traditional load balancing methods" describes the strategies that have been applied to maximize network performance and guarantee scalability by dividing network traffic among a group of servers. These techniques usually depend on algorithms that are optimal in particular contexts. Round-robin is a popular, conventional load balancing technique in which incoming requests are sequentially and equally distributed among the servers. Although this approach guarantees that every server gets an equal portion of network traffic, it might not account for each server's actual load or capability. The least connections approach is another conventional technique that divides traffic according to the quantity of open connections on every server. By sending new requests to the server with the fewest connections, this method seeks to more evenly distribute the workload (Yang et al., 2019). Nevertheless, it might not take into account additional elements like response time or server performance. Another conventional method is weighted round-robin, which gives each server a weight based on its capacity or performance. More traffic is directed towards servers with greater weights, which facilitates more effective load distribution. When servers differ in terms of their skills or resources, this technique can be helpful. Traditional load balancing techniques do, however, have certain drawbacks. The inability to adjust to dynamic changes in server circumstances or network traffic is one of its limitations. Usually static, these techniques don't modify the load distribution in response to real-time variables like network congestion or server health. It's also possible that conventional load balancing techniques can't manage different kinds of network traffic or applications. Certain requests might be given priority over others by some systems, which don't take into account the unique requirements of each application or the overall performance of the network. Approaches to hybrid load balancing have been developed to get around these restrictions. These strategies blend more established practices with cutting-edge innovations like software-defined networking (SDN) and predictive analytics. Load balancers can dynamically modify traffic distribution based on past trends and anticipated future demands by integrating predictive analytics. Load balancers can optimize load balancing decisions by utilizing software-defined networks (SDNs) and their flexibility and programmability. SDN makes it possible to manage and control network resources centrally, which improves load distribution and makes it more flexible and efficient (Zheng et al., 2017). Utilizing statistical algorithms, machine learning methods, and historical data, predictive analytics makes predictions about future actions or events. Predictive analytics can be used to forecast user behavior, resource use, and network traffic patterns in the context of load balancing. Through the examination of past data, including traffic patterns and server use, predictive analytics can instantly detect possible bottlenecks or performance problems.

Predictive analytics for load balancing has several advantages, one of which is the proactive allocation of resources according to anticipated demand. Predictive analytics can optimize resource allocation and dynamically distribute workload among servers by precisely predicting traffic patterns. This strategy assures effective resource usage and helps keep individual servers from being overloaded, which eventually improves speed and scalability. The novel network architecture known as software-defined networking (SDN), on the other hand, divides the control plane from the data plane to allow for centralized management and programmability of network devices. SDN uses software-based controllers to make dynamic routing decisions, giving load balancing a flexible and automated solution. The SDN provides load balancing with a number of advantages. First of all, it makes it possible to establish logical divisions and virtual networks, which facilitates the effective distribution of resources according to workload demands. This adaptability guarantees the best possible load and network traffic allocation among servers, improving scalability and performance. The SDN also makes it possible to monitor and analyze traffic in real-time, which helps with intelligent load balancing decisions. Through the gathering and examination of network data, including latency, bandwidth usage, and packet loss, SDN controllers are able to dynamically route traffic in order to increase network efficiency and reduce congestion. Conventional load balancing techniques generally aim to maximize performance and guarantee high availability by dividing network traffic among several servers or resources. Round-robin, least connections, and IP hash algorithms are some of these techniques. Even while they operate well, conventional load balancing techniques might not be able to quickly adjust to shifting traffic patterns or network constraints. Predictive analytics, on the other hand, uses statistical algorithms and past data to predict future patterns and help decision-makers. Predictive analytics can assist in anticipating changes in network traffic and proactively adjusting load balancing solutions by examining patterns and trends. Better performance and resource utilization are made possible by this strategy. With the innovative technique of software-defined networking (SDN), the control plane and data plane are kept apart, enabling centralized network management and programmability. More precise control over network traffic is made possible by SDN, which also provides the ability to dynamically modify load balancing policies in response to changing circumstances. More intelligent and adaptable load distribution can be achieved by combining SDN with load balancing strategies.

We can put into practice the following hybrid load balancing strategy in order to blend conventional techniques with SDN and predictive analytics.

- Data collection: Compile up-to-date network information, such as previous load balancing choices, traffic trends, and server performance metrics.
- Predictive Analytics: Analyze past data and spot patterns or trends in network traffic by using predictive analytics algorithms. This study can be used to forecast changes or surges in traffic in the future.
- Load Balancer Decision Engine: Create a load balancer decision engine that considers inputs from predictive analytics as well as conventional load balancing techniques. Algorithms for determining the best traffic distribution should be included in this decision engine, taking into account both current circumstances and anticipated future trends.
- SDN Integration: To enable dynamic load balancing policy adjustments, integrate the load balancer decision engine with the SDN controller. This decision engine can be used by the SDN controller to make real-time modifications to bandwidth allocation and routing choices.
- Constant Monitoring and Feedback: Establish a feedback loop to track performance indicators and keep an eye on network conditions. Because of this feedback loop, load balancing solutions can be continuously optimized and improved in response to real-world results.

3.4 Proposed Theoretical solution

Conventional load balancing techniques, such as least-connections or round-robin, are frequently employed to disperse incoming traffic among several servers or resources. While these techniques are easy to use and efficient, the distribution of the load may not always be ideal.

Predictive Analytics: The application of predictive analytics is one method to enhance load balancing. Through the examination of past data and present system parameters, we are able to forecast future load patterns and adjust resource allocation appropriately. We can create a predictive analytics model that considers past traffic patterns, resource usage, and system performance data in order to put this into practice. Machine learning techniques can be used to train this model so that it can forecast the future load distribution with accuracy. The load balancer can dynamically modify resource allocation to maximize performance and reduce response time based on the forecasts. For instance, the load balancer can allot more resources to manage the increased load if the model forecasts a rise in traffic during peak hours.

Software-Defined Networking (SDN): Utilizing SDN technology is an additional way to further enhance load balancing. SDN makes network architecture programmable and centralized, making load balancing algorithms more adaptable and dynamic. The load balancer in an SDN-based load balancing system has the ability to dynamically modify traffic routing in response to current network conditions. For instance, the load balancer can divert traffic to less congested resources if a specific server or network link is very busy. We can employ a controller-based architecture to do this, in which decisions about load balancing and network management are made by a central controller. In order to select the best routing path for incoming traffic, the controller can gather real-time network characteristics.

Predictive analytics and software-defined networking (SDN) are two examples of more recent approaches that have the potential to operate well along with classic load balancing techniques in the context of hybrid load balancing strategies. The goal of these synergies is to improve load balancing systems' overall performance and scalability. These are some significant possible synergies. Optimization of Load Distribution: Conventional load balancing techniques concentrate on uniformly allocating incoming traffic among servers using criteria such as least connections or round-robin. Predictive analytics can be used to optimize load distribution by taking into account both historical and current data to forecast traffic patterns and make wise server allocation decisions. Response times are shortened and system performance is enhanced overall because to this synergy. Dynamic Resource Allocation: SDN offers the capacity to manage and control network resources through programming. Dynamic resource allocation can be accomplished using the combination of SDN and conventional load balancing techniques. Because of this synergy, load balancers can dynamically modify how network resources are allocated in response to changes in traffic patterns, server capacity, and performance metrics.

It guarantees effective resource use, which enhances scalability and lowers bottlenecks. Intelligent Traffic Routing: By analyzing past and current data, predictive analytics can be used to forecast possible server failures or congested areas. Intelligent traffic routing is possible by combining this predictive ability with conventional load balancing methods. Load balancers can divert traffic from slow or crowded servers thanks to this synergy, which guarantees better performance and efficient use of resources. Improved Analytics and Monitoring: Complete analytics and monitoring capabilities are made possible by integrating SDN and predictive analytics with load balancing systems. Load balancers provide proactive load distribution optimization by anticipating future resource demands, identifying possible bottlenecks, and evaluating network and server performance data. This synergy enables proactive performance tweaking and capacity planning by offering insightful information about system behavior.

Enhancing Load Balancing using Blockchain Technology

Load balancing is a critical component in distributed systems that aims to optimize resource utilization and provide efficient allocation of tasks among nodes. Traditional load balancing approaches often rely on centralized control or coordination mechanisms which can introduce single points of failure and create bottlenecks. Blockchain technology, originally designed for decentralized and secure transactions in cryptocurrencies like Bitcoin, has gained significant attention in recent years. Its inherent characteristics of decentralization, transparency, immutability, and security make it a promising candidate for enhancing load balancing in distributed systems. In this literature review, we investigate the use of blockchain technology to enhance load balancing by providing a decentralized and tamper-proof method for allocating resources and verifying transactions. We summarize the key findings from the literature and highlight the potential benefits, challenges, and future directions in this domain.

1. **Decentralized Resource Allocation:** Blockchain technology enables decentralized resource allocation in load balancing by removing the need for a centralized authority. Nodes in the distributed system can participate in the blockchain network and contribute their available resources. By leveraging smart contracts

or consensus mechanisms, the blockchain can autonomously allocate tasks or resources to nodes based on predefined rules or algorithms. This decentralized approach eliminates single points of failure and provides a more scalable and robust load balancing solution.

1. **Tamper-Proof Method:** Blockchain technology inherently provides a tamper-proof method for allocating resources and verifying transactions. The algorithm leverages this feature, ensuring that the assigned priorities remain intact and cannot be altered or tampered with by malicious actors.
2. **Transparency and Traceability:** One of the key advantages of using blockchain technology in load balancing is its transparency and traceability. All transactions and resource allocations are recorded on the blockchain, creating an immutable and auditable history. This transparency allows for better monitoring and auditing of resource utilization, enabling administrators to identify bottlenecks, optimize resource allocation, and detect any malicious behaviors or anomalies in the system.
3. **Immutable and Tamper-Proof Verification:** Blockchain's immutability and tamper-proof nature enhance the security and trustworthiness of load balancing in distributed systems. Once a transaction or resource allocation is recorded on the blockchain, it becomes virtually impossible to alter or manipulate without consensus from the majority of network participants. This ensures the integrity of the load balancing process and prevents unauthorized modifications or attacks on the system.
4. **Scalability and Efficiency Challenges:** While blockchain technology offers several advantages for load balancing, there are challenges related to scalability and efficiency. The inherent characteristics of blockchain, such as the need for consensus mechanisms and decentralized validation, can introduce delays and increase the computational overhead.

Some limitations of using Blockchain Technology is scalability because depending on the size of the blockchain network and the number of mining nodes, the algorithm's scalability could become a challenge. With increased network size, the algorithm may require optimization to handle a larger volume of patient data blocks and maintain efficient load balancing. Subjectivity in Priority Assignment can also be a limitation because assigning priority levels to patient data blocks involves making subjective judgments. It may require a well-defined and transparent system to determine the criteria for assigning priority levels accurately. Without clear guidelines, there is a potential risk of bias or misallocation of priorities. Potential Delay for Low-Priority Blocks, while prioritizing high-priority patient data blocks is essential, the algorithm may inadvertently cause delays in processing low-priority blocks. This delay could impact the overall efficiency of the system, especially if low-priority blocks accumulate over time. To overcome these limitations, regular monitoring, optimization, and continuous improvement of the algorithm are crucial. Additionally, involving domain experts and stakeholders in defining the priority assignment criteria can help ensure fairness and accuracy in the allocation process.

5. CONCLUSION

In conclusion, the future of load balancing holds promising advancements poised to reshape the landscape of digital infrastructure and optimize resource utilization in unprecedented ways. As industries continue to evolve and embrace increasingly complex digital ecosystems, the imperative for efficient load balancing mechanisms becomes ever more pressing. Through an exploration of emerging trends and technologies, it becomes evident that the evolution of load balancing is not merely a matter of accommodating growing volumes of traffic, but rather a fundamental restructuring of how data is managed and distributed across networks. The advent of artificial intelligence and machine learning stands out as a transformative force in load balancing, offering the potential to dynamically adapt to changing conditions in real-time. By harnessing the power of algorithms capable of analyzing vast datasets and predicting traffic patterns, AI-driven load balancers can optimize resource allocation with unparalleled precision. Moreover, the integration of AI can enable predictive maintenance and proactive fault detection, mitigating potential disruptions before they occur and ensuring uninterrupted service delivery.

Furthermore, the proliferation of edge computing architectures introduces new complexities and challenges to traditional load balancing paradigms. As data processing moves closer to the point of generation, the need for intelligent edge-aware load balancing solutions becomes paramount. By distributing workloads across edge nodes strategically and leveraging proximity-based routing algorithms, organizations can minimize latency, enhance scalability, and improve overall system resilience. The rise of containerization and microservices architecture further accentuates the demand for dynamic and lightweight load balancing solutions capable of orchestrating traffic flows across distributed application environments. Container orchestration platforms like Kubernetes have become instrumental in managing the deployment and scaling of microservices, driving the need for load balancers capable of seamlessly integrating with these platforms and facilitating efficient communication between microservices. Moreover, the growing prevalence of hybrid and multi-cloud environments necessitates load balancers that can intelligently distribute workloads across disparate infrastructure deployments while ensuring consistent performance and reliability. By leveraging cloud-native load balancing services and implementing robust traffic management policies, organizations can optimize resource utilization across hybrid cloud environments and harness the agility and scalability offered by cloud computing. In essence, the future of load balancing lies in harnessing the transformative potential of emerging technologies to deliver adaptive, intelligent, and scalable solutions capable of meeting the evolving demands of modern digital infrastructure. As organizations navigate the complexities of an increasingly interconnected and data-driven world, the role of load balancing will remain indispensable in ensuring optimal performance, reliability, and resilience across diverse computing environments.

REFERENCES

Afzal, S., & Kavitha, G. (2019). Load balancing in cloud computing – A hierarchical taxonomical classification. *Journal of Cloud Computing (Heidelberg, Germany)*, *8*(1), 22. Advance online publication. DOI: 10.1186/s13677-019-0146-7

Armbrust, M., Fox, A., Griffith, R., Joseph, A. D., Katz, R., Konwinski, A., Lee, G., Patterson, D., Rabkin, A., Stoica, I., & Zaharia, M. (2010). A view of cloud computing. *Communications of the ACM*, *53*(4), 50–58. DOI: 10.1145/1721654.1721672

Beloglazov, A., Abawajy, J., & Buyya, R. (2012). Energy-aware resource allocation heuristics for efficient management of data centers for cloud computing. *Future Generation Computer Systems*, *28*(5), 755–768. DOI: 10.1016/j.future.2011.04.017

Dey, D., Majumder, A., Agrawal, Y., Tewari, S., & Mohapatra, H. (2024). Smart mobility revolution. *Advances in Electronic Government, Digital Divide, and Regional Development*, •••, 143–164. DOI: 10.4018/979-8-3693-6740-7.ch006

Dikaiakos, M. D., Katsaros, D., Mehra, P., Pallis, G., & Vakali, A. (2009). Cloud computing: Distributed internet computing for IT and scientific research. *IEEE Internet Computing*, *13*(5), 10–13. DOI: 10.1109/MIC.2009.103

Kaur, K., Garg, S., Aujla, G. S., Kumar, N., Rodrigues, J. J., & Guizani, M. (2018). Edge computing in the industrial Internet of things environment: Software-defined-Networks-Based edge-cloud interplay. *IEEE Communications Magazine*, *56*(2), 44–51. DOI: 10.1109/MCOM.2018.1700622

Kumar, A., Bag, A., Anand, A., Saha, S., Mohapatra, H., & Kolhar, M. (2024). Examining healthcare services utilizing cloud technology in intelligent urban environments. *Advances in Healthcare Information Systems and Administration*, •••, 77–98. DOI: 10.4018/979-8-3693-7225-8.ch004

Kyryk, M., Pleskanka, N., Pleskanka, M., & Nykonchuk, P. (2020). Load balancing method in edge computing. *2020 IEEE 15th International Conference on Advanced Trends in Radioelectronics, Telecommunications and Computer Engineering (TCSET)*, 978-981. https://doi.org/DOI: 10.1109/TCSET49122.2020.235584

Lata, S., & Singh, D. (2022). A hybrid approach for cloud load balancing. *2022 2nd International Conference on Advance Computing and Innovative Technologies in Engineering (ICACITE)*, 548-552. https://doi.org/DOI: 10.1109/ICACITE53722.2022.9823569

Lu, Y., Zhang, J., Wu, S., & Zhang, S. (2012). A hybrid dynamic load balancing approach for cloud storage. *2012 International Conference on Industrial Control and Electronics Engineering*, 1332-1335. https://doi.org/DOI: 10.1109/ICICEE.2012.353

Mao, Y., You, C., Zhang, J., Huang, K., & Letaief, K. B. (2017). A survey on mobile edge computing: The communication perspective. *IEEE Communications Surveys and Tutorials*, *19*(4), 2322–2358. DOI: 10.1109/COMST.2017.2745201

Mohapatra, H. (2021). Socio-technical challenges in the implementation of smart city. *2021 International Conference on Innovation and Intelligence for Informatics, Computing, and Technologies (3ICT)*, 57-62. https://doi.org/DOI: 10.1109/3ICT53449.2021.9581905

Mohapatra, H. (2024). The role of 6G in empowering smart cities enabling ubiquitous connectivity and intelligent infrastructure. *Advances in Civil and Industrial Engineering*, •••, 237–264. DOI: 10.4018/979-8-3693-8029-1.ch009

Mohapatra, H., & Mishra, S. R. (2024). Unlocking insights: Exploring data analytics and AI tool performance across industries. *Studies in Big Data*, 265-288. https://doi.org/DOI: 10.1007/978-981-97-0448-4_13

Nguyen, Q., Phan, L., & Kim, T. (2022). Load-balancing of kubernetes-based edge computing infrastructure using resource adaptive proxy. *Sensors (Basel)*, *22*(8), 2869. DOI: 10.3390/s22082869 PMID: 35458853

Pallavi, V., & Vinothiyalakshmi, P. (2022). Threshold based dynamic resource balancing (TDRB) algorithm in cloud computing. *2022 International Conference on Machine Learning, Big Data, Cloud and Parallel Computing (COM-IT-CON)*, 616-622. https://doi.org/DOI: 10.1109/COM-IT-CON54601.2022.9850699

Panda, A. K., Lenka, A. A., Mohapatra, A., Rath, B. K., Parida, A. A., & Mohapatra, H. (2024). Integrating cloud computing for intelligent transportation solutions in smart cities. *Advances in Civil and Industrial Engineering*, •••, 121–142. DOI: 10.4018/979-8-3693-6695-0.ch005

Priyadarshi, S., Subudhi, S., Kumar, S., Bhardwaj, D., & Mohapatra, H. (2024). Analysis on enhancing urban mobility with IoT-integrated parking solutions. *Advances in Civil and Industrial Engineering*, •••, 143–172. DOI: 10.4018/979-8-3693-6695-0.ch006

Ranapana, R., & Jayasena, K. (2021). Novel approach for load balancing in mobile cloud computing. *2021 6th International Conference on Information Technology Research (ICITR)*, 1-6. https://doi.org/DOI: 10.1109/ICITR54349.2021.9657441

Sah, R. K., Singh, A. K., Yadav, A. K., & Mohapatra, H. (2024). Cloud-enabled platforms for social and civic engagement in smart urban environments. *Advances in Electronic Government, Digital Divide, and Regional Development*, •••, 215–234. DOI: 10.4018/979-8-3693-6740-7.ch009

Shafiq, D. A., Jhanjhi, N., & Abdullah, A. (2022). Load balancing techniques in cloud computing environment: A review. *Journal of King Saud University. Computer and Information Sciences*, *34*(7), 3910–3933. DOI: 10.1016/j.jksuci.2021.02.007

Sharma, A., Anand, N., Mukherjee, S., Kumar, S., Kumar, S., & Mohapatra, H. (2024). Analyzing territorial variations in the implementation of IoT-based smart homes. *Advances in Electronic Government, Digital Divide, and Regional Development*, •••, 305–334. DOI: 10.4018/979-8-3693-6854-1.ch010

Singh, K. (2015). Energy efficient load balancing strategy for mobile cloud computing. *International Journal of Computer Applications*, *132*(15), 6–12. DOI: 10.5120/ijca2015907553

Swain, B., Raj, P., Singh, K., Singh, Y., Singh, S., & Mohapatra, H. (2025). Ethical implications and mitigation strategies for public safety and security in smart cities for securing tomorrow. *Advances in Information Security, Privacy, and Ethics*, •••, 419–436. DOI: 10.4018/979-8-3693-6859-6.ch019

Topcuoglu, H., Hariri, S., & Wu, M.-Y. (2002). Performance-effective and low-complexity task scheduling for heterogeneous computing. *IEEE Transactions on Parallel and Distributed Systems*, *13*(3), 260–274. DOI: 10.1109/71.993206

Xu, X., Weber, I., Staples, M., Zhu, L., Bosch, J., Bass, L., Pautasso, C., & Rimba, P. (2017). A taxonomy of blockchain-based systems for architecture design. *2017 IEEE International Conference on Software Architecture (ICSA)*, 243-252. https://doi.org/DOI: 10.1109/ICSA.2017.33

Yang, Q., Liu, Y., Chen, T., & Tong, Y. (2019). Federated machine learning. *ACM Transactions on Intelligent Systems and Technology*, *10*(2), 1–19. DOI: 10.1145/3298981

Zheng, Z., Xie, S., Dai, H., Chen, X., & Wang, H. (2017). An overview of blockchain technology: Architecture, consensus, and future trends. *2017 IEEE International Congress on Big Data (BigData Congress)*, 557-564. https://doi.org/DOI: 10.1109/BigDataCongress.2017.85

Chapter 3
Integrating Intelligent Mobile Systems, IoT, and Ecosystems:
Advancing Connectivity and Innovation in a Digital World

Arun Agrawal
https://orcid.org/0000-0001-7233-6660
Institute of Technology and Management, Gwalior, India

Aruna Bajpai
https://orcid.org/0000-0002-9716-8680
Institute of Technology and Management, Gwalior, India

G. Jegadeeswari
https://orcid.org/0000-0002-7865-4026
Saveetha Engineering College, India

P. Senthil Pandian
https://orcid.org/0000-0002-9127-794X
AAA College of Engineering and Technology, India

Apoorva Deshpande
https://orcid.org/0009-0002-5331-0750
Institute of Technology and Management, Gwalior, India

Deepak Gupta
https://orcid.org/0000-0003-3929-1362
Institute of Technology and Management, Gwalior, India

Rashmi Pandey
https://orcid.org/0000-0002-3881-2907
Institute of Technology and Management, Gwalior, India

Saivya Bhadhouriya
https://orcid.org/0009-0006-4132-2155
Institute of Technology and Management, Gwalior, India

Akbar Shah
Institute of Technology and Management, Gwalior, India

Yogendra Singh Rathore
https://orcid.org/0000-0003-1898-459X
Institute of Technology and Management, Gwalior, India

DOI: 10.4018/979-8-3373-0330-7.ch003

Copyright © 2025, IGI Global Scientific Publishing. Copying or distributing in print or electronic forms without written permission of IGI Global Scientific Publishing is prohibited.

Priusha Narwariya
Institute of Technology and Management, Gwalior, India

Deepak Kumar Mishra
https://orcid.org/0000-0001-6867-3904
Institute of Technology and Management, Gwalior, India

ABSTRACT

The convergence of smart mobility, IoT, and connected ecosystems is transforming industries through seamless connectivity, real-time analytics, and data-driven decisions. This article examines their applications in healthcare, urban planning, industrial automation, and agriculture. Smart systems powered by AI and IoT enable predictive capabilities, while IoT ecosystems optimize operations via autonomous device communication. Case studies include smart traffic management, wearable health monitors, precision agriculture, and predictive maintenance. Emerging technologies like 5G, edge computing, and blockchain address challenges of latency, security, and interoperability. However, issues like data privacy and scalability persist. The article underscores the need for innovative solutions and regulatory frameworks to harness smart ecosystems for sustainable development and improved quality of life.

1. INTRODUCTION

The emergence of intelligent mobile systems and the Internet of Things (IoT) has brought about a profound shift in the way technology interacts with the human environment (Vermesan & Friess, 2013). These innovations are redefining industries, increasing productivity, and contributing to the sustainability of our planet. The integration of intelligent mobile systems and IoT has made modern ecosystems highly adaptive, enabling seamless connectivity, real-time analytics, and data-driven decision-making (Bankar et al., 2025). This primer delves into the definition of these technologies, their convergence, their impact on various sectors, and the importance of addressing the associated challenges to realize their full potential.

1.1. Intelligent Mobile Systems: Redefining Connectivity

Intelligent mobile systems have evolved far beyond their original role as communication tools. These systems are now key to connected ecosystems, supporting applications ranging from augmented reality (AR) to artificial intelligence-driven personal assistants and real-time analytics. Advances in artificial intelligence (AI), machine learning (ML), and cloud computing enable mobile devices to process large amounts of data, enabling personalized services, predictive analytics, and seamless user interactions (Zhu et al., 2023).

Modern smart mobile systems utilize built-in sensors, cameras, and connectivity modules such as Wi-Fi, Bluetooth, and 5G to act as data collectors and processors. They bridge the gap between users and IoT devices, serving as the interface to control smart systems and derive actionable insights (Anikwe et al., 2022). For example, smartphones paired with wearable IoT devices can monitor health indicators such as heart rate and blood oxygen levels, while providing users with instant feedback to improve their health management (Michard, 2021).

1.2. The Internet of Things (IoT): A Network of Interconnected Devices

The Internet of Things is a vast ecosystem consisting of billions of interconnected devices embedded with sensors, software and communication technologies. These devices exchange data autonomously, enabling instant monitoring, automation and optimization. From industrial machines and agricultural tools to home appliances and urban infrastructure, IoT systems form the backbone of modern smart environments (Lavanya et al., 2025).

Key attributes of IoT include scalability, interoperability and adaptability. It supports a wide range of applications, from smart homes and cities to industrial automation and healthcare. For example, IoT-enabled devices in agriculture can monitor soil conditions, optimize water use and predict crop yields. In urban environments, IoT sensors manage traffic flow and energy consumption while improving safety and convenience (Lee et al., 2021).

1.3. Convergence of Intelligent Mobile Systems and IoT in Modern Ecosystems

The integration of intelligent mobile systems and the IoT creates a synergistic relationship, with mobile devices acting as the control center and data processing center of the Internet of Things network (Vermesan et al., 2022). This integration facilitates instant communication, data collection and decision-making. Together, these technologies can create a smart ecosystem, a dynamic environment that can adapt to changing conditions and user needs.

For example, in a smart home ecosystem, IoT sensors monitor temperature, lighting, and security, and mobile devices provide users with an interface to remotely control these elements. Likewise, in industrial settings, IoT sensors monitor machine performance and action dashboards provide operators with instant insights and alerts. Seamless interaction between these technologies increases efficiency, reduces downtime and improves user experience.

1.4. Impact Across Industries

The integration of intelligent mobile systems and IoT is transforming various industries, enabling smarter, more responsive environments:

1.4.1. Healthcare

The healthcare industry is embracing smart ecosystems to enhance patient care, improve operational efficiency, and reduce costs. Wearable IoT devices such as smart watches and fitness trackers collect instant health data such as heart rate, activity levels, and sleep patterns. This data is transmitted to mobile applications, enabling remote monitoring and early diagnosis of potential health issues (Aggrawal & Pandey, 2025).

For example, continuous glucose monitors (CGMs) enable diabetic patients to instantly track their blood glucose levels, facilitating timely intervention. Mobile apps provide personalized health insights, appointment reminders, and remote medical consultations, ensuring accessibility and convenience. This integration not only improves patient outcomes but also reduces the burden on healthcare facilities (Reddy & Oliver, 2024).

1.4.2. Urban Planning

Smart city initiatives utilize the Internet of Things and mobile systems to optimize urban environments. IoT sensors monitor traffic volume, pollution levels and energy consumption, while mobile apps provide residents with real-time updates and services. For example, smart traffic management systems adjust traffic light timings based on vehicle density, reducing congestion and emissions (Rehan, 2023).

Waste management is another area that benefits from IoT integration. Smart bins equipped with sensors communicate fill levels to waste collection services and optimize routes to reduce operating costs. Additionally, smart grid technology enables efficient energy distribution, while mobile apps allow residents to monitor and manage their energy usage (Sosunova & Porras, 2022).

1.4.3. Industrial Automation

In industrial environments, IoT sensors and mobile systems help with predictive maintenance, process optimization, and supply chain management. By continuously monitoring machine performance, IoT sensors can detect anomalies and predict equipment failures before they occur. Mobile interfaces provide operators with instant alerts and actionable insights, reducing downtime and increasing productivity (Mourtzis et al., 2021).

Supply chain efficiency is also improved with IoT-enabled tracking systems that can monitor inventory levels, shipping status, and storage status. This integration ensures timely deliveries and reduces waste, ultimately leading to cost savings and increased customer satisfaction (Tan & Sidhu, 2022).

1.5. Driving Innovation and Sustainability

The integration of smart mobility systems and the Internet of Things will play a vital role in addressing global challenges ranging from climate change and resource scarcity to healthcare and urbanization. By enabling smarter resource management, these technologies contribute to sustainable development and improved quality of life (Javed et al., 2022).

1.5.1. Energy Efficiency

Wisdom-type system transmission, immediate supervision, automation, and energy consumption. For example, if the support network is connected to the network, it will be used to adjust the temperature, which will reduce energy consumption. Similarly, the Wisdom Power Network is more effective in distributing power to the area, and the maximum loss is due to the equilibrium supply and demand (Han et al., 2022).

1.5.2. Precision Agriculture

In agriculture, IoT sensors and mobile systems support precision farming, which conserves resources and increases productivity. By monitoring soil conditions, weather patterns, and crop health, these technologies enable farmers to make informed decisions, reducing water usage and improving yields (Xing & Wang, 2024).

1.5.3. Sustainable Urban Development

Smart cities leverage IoT and mobility systems to create sustainable urban environments, smart transportation systems reduce fuel consumption and emissions, and smart waste management increase recycling rates, thereby promoting eco-friendly practices and improving urban living standards (Mishra & Singh, 2023).

1.6. Addressing Challenges

Despite their potential, the integration of intelligent mobile systems and IoT faces several challenges:

1.6.1. Interoperability

Ensuring seamless communication between devices from different manufacturers requires standardized protocols and frameworks (Amjad et al., 2021).

1.6.2. Data Security and Privacy

The proliferation of connected devices increases the risk of cyberattacks and data breaches. Robust encryption, authentication, and privacy measures are essential to safeguard sensitive information (Amoo et al., 2024).

1.6.3. Scalability and Latency

As IoT networks grow, maintaining low latency and high reliability becomes increasingly challenging (Zikria et al., 2021). Innovations such as 5G and edge computing are essential to solving these problems.

The integration of smart mobile systems and the Internet of Things is revolutionizing industries and reshaping ecosystems. These technologies drive innovation and sustainability by enabling instant analytics, automation, and seamless interaction. However, to realize their full potential, it is critical to address challenges around interoperability, security, and scalability.

In this chapter, we explore the transformative impact of these technologies, focusing on real-world applications, and propose solutions to existing challenges to pave the way for a smarter and more connected future. Through innovation and collaboration, smart ecosystems can build a sustainable, data-driven world that improves the quality of life for everyone.

2. INTELLIGENT MOBILE SYSTEMS

Smart mobility systems have evolved into an integral part of modern technology, enabling seamless interactions within connected ecosystems. These systems leverage advanced capabilities such as artificial intelligence (AI), machine learning (ML), and augmented reality (AR) to process data, make instant decisions, and improve user experience (Cao et al., 2023). Equipped with sensors and connectivity options, mobile devices act as hubs for data collection, processing, and communication, bridging the gap between users and IoT networks (El-Afifi et al., 2024). Their versatility supports applications ranging from healthcare monitoring to industrial automation and smart home management, proving to be a game changer in building adaptive, responsive, and efficient environments across various industries.

2.1. Evolution of Mobile Technology: From Communication Devices to Central Nodes in IoT Ecosystems

Mobile technology has undergone a significant transformation, evolving from simple communication devices to an important part of the IoT ecosystem. Originally designed for basic voice calls and text messaging, early mobile phones revolutionized personal communications by allowing users to stay connected anytime and anywhere. Over the years, advances in hardware, software and connectivity have expanded the capabilities of these devices to include features such as multimedia capabilities, network access and advanced operating systems (Oyeniran et al., 2023).

The introduction of smartphones was a decisive milestone, combining powerful processing power with multiple connectivity options such as Wi-Fi, Bluetooth and cellular networks. These devices introduce an ecosystem of apps that allow users to perform tasks ranging from social networking to navigation within a single interface. The integration of sensors, cameras and GPS modules further expands its uses, making it an essential tool in everyday life (Retscher et al., 2024).

In the IoT ecosystem, mobile devices currently play a key role as data collection centers and control interfaces. Mobile devices connect to smart devices, allowing users to manage home appliances, monitor health metrics and gain instant insights. For example, smartphones connected to IoT-enabled devices such as smart thermostats and wearable health trackers allow users to remotely control their environment and make informed decisions (Salma et al., 2024).

In addition, advances in 5G and edge computing increase the ability of mobile devices to process data efficiently and reduce latency, further enhancing their role as central nodes in IoT networks (Carvalho et al., 2021). Mobile technologies continue to evolve, redefining connectivity and powering smart and adaptive systems across industries.

2.2. Recent Advances: Integration with AR, AI-Driven Assistants, and Edge Computing

Recent advances in mobile technology have significantly enhanced their capabilities, especially through the integration of augmented reality (AR), artificial intelligence-driven personal assistants, and edge computing. These developments have redefined the role of mobile devices, making them essential in the IoT ecosystem and smart environments (Pal, 2024).

AR expands the possibilities of mobile systems by overlaying digital information onto the physical world. From gaming and entertainment to industrial design and medical training, AR applications leverage mobile cameras and sensors to deliver immersive, real-time experiences. Mobile AR applications such as virtual furniture arrangement tools and navigation systems demonstrate the usefulness of integrating AR into everyday devices.

Artificial intelligence-powered personal assistants such as Siri, Alexa, and Google Assistant are another breakthrough technology that leverage machine learning algorithms to enhance user interactions (Bhuiyan, 2024). These assistants can analyze user preferences, predict needs, and perform tasks such as setting reminders, managing schedules, and controlling IoT devices. The integration of natural language processing (NLP) and advanced artificial intelligence capabilities makes these assistants increasingly intuitive and effective, facilitating seamless communication between users and smart environments (Antonius et al., 2023).

Edge computing further empowers mobile systems by bringing local data processing closer to the source. This reduces latency, enhances real-time analytics, and reduces cloud network bandwidth demands (Modupe et al., 2024). For example, mobile devices processing IoT sensor data locally can make immediate adjustments such as adjusting a thermostat or detecting anomalies in a factory.

These innovations turn mobile systems into powerful smart tools that enhance user experiences, optimize operations, and drive innovation across industries.

2.3. Role in Bridging User Interaction and IoT Networks

Smart mobile systems are an important bridge between users and IoT networks, ensuring seamless communication, data exchange and real-time decision-making. Mobile devices act as interfaces and processing hubs, allowing users to interact with IoT devices, monitor systems and control their environment from a single point of access.

Mobile devices facilitate this connection through built-in sensors, high-speed wireless communications and intuitive applications. For example, smartphones can connect with smart home devices such as thermostats, lighting systems, and security cameras, allowing users to remotely monitor and control their home environment. Likewise, mobile interfaces in industrial environments provide operators with instant updates on machine performance and process efficiency.

The ability of mobile systems to collect and process data locally enhances their role in the IoT ecosystem. Advances in edge computing enable these devices to analyze data from IoT sensors and make instant decisions, reducing reliance on centralized cloud systems and minimizing latency. For example, wearable devices connected to mobile systems can monitor important health indicators and immediately alert users to abnormalities.

Additionally, the mobile app provides a user-friendly platform for managing the IoT ecosystem with features such as predictive analytics, visual dashboards, and automated task execution. This feature enables users to interact with complex IoT networks more effectively, improving efficiency and user experience.

As the IoT ecosystem continues to expand, the role of mobile systems in connecting connected devices and user interactions remains critical, enabling a smarter, more responsive environment.

2.4. Applications in Healthcare, Smart Homes, and Industrial Operations

The integration of intelligent mobile systems and IoT networks opens up transformative applications in healthcare, smart homes and industrial operations. These advancements increase efficiency, improve quality of life, and drive innovation across industries. In healthcare, mobile systems paired with wearable IoT devices can facilitate immediate monitoring and early diagnosis. Smart watches and fitness trackers collect health metrics such as heart rate, blood pressure and oxygen levels and transmit this data to mobile apps (Chataut et al., 2023). These apps enable patients and healthcare providers to track conditions remotely and ensure timely intervention. For example, continuous glucose monitors (CGM) allow people with diabetes to manage their blood sugar levels through a mobile interface. In smart homes, mobile devices provide centralized control of IoT-enabled systems such as lighting, temperature regulation, and security. Users can remotely adjust their home environment through mobile applications to improve convenience and energy efficiency. Features such as voice control powered by AI- powered personal assistants further simplify interactions. For example, homeowners can use smartphone apps to monitor energy consumption or receive alerts about security breaches. In industrial operations, mobile systems enhance process automation and predictive maintenance. IoT sensors monitor machinery performance, while mobile dashboards provide with instant insights and alerts. This enables proactive maintenance, reducing downtime and operating costs. In addition, the mobile system supports supply chain optimization by tracking inventory levels and shipment status to ensure the efficiency of the entire logistics operators. These applications demonstrate the transformative potential of smart mobility systems to create connected, efficient and adaptive environments across key domains (Teoh et al., 2021).

3. THE INTERNET OF THINGS (IOT) AND ECOSYSTEM INTEGRATION

The Internet of Things (IoT) is transforming our digital environment by connecting devices, sensors and applications to create interconnected systems that simplify operations and enhance decision-making. These IoT ecosystems enable instant communication and data exchange, driving innovation in areas ranging from healthcare and agriculture to urban planning and industrial automation (Chataut et al., 2023). In this section, we explore the characteristics of the IoT ecosystem, focus on practical applications, and discuss the challenges and solutions required for seamless integration.

3.1. Overview of IoT Ecosystems

The IoT ecosystem consists of interconnected devices that communicate over the Internet to collect, process and share data. These systems are characterized by scalability, interoperability and adaptability, which enable them to support a wide range of applications and environments.

3.1.1. Characteristics

The IoT ecosystem is highly diverse and consists of sensors, actuators, gateways, communication protocols and cloud platforms. These components work together to collect data, transmit it over the network, and provide actionable insights (Paolone et al., 2022). Key features include:

- **Real-Time Functionality**: IoT systems process data instantaneously, enabling quick responses to dynamic conditions.
- **Decentralization**: Devices communicate autonomously, reducing reliance on central systems for decisions.
- **Self-Optimization**: IoT ecosystems adapt to changing conditions, optimizing performance without human intervention.

3.1.2. Scalability

IoT networks are designed to accommodate an increasing number of devices, making scalability an essential feature (Zikria et al., 2021). For example, smart city IoT systems can expand from managing traffic signals to integrating air quality sensors and public transportation systems to create comprehensive urban management solutions.

3.1.3. Interoperability

Interoperability is essential for IoT ecosystems to function effectively. Devices from different manufacturers must communicate seamlessly using standardized protocols, ensuring data consistency and system compatibility (Hazra et al., 2021). Protocols like MQTT, Zigbee, and Bluetooth facilitate this interaction, enabling diverse devices to collaborate within the same ecosystem.

3.2. Real-World Applications of IoT Ecosystems

IoT ecosystems are transforming industries by enabling smarter, data-driven operations. Key applications include smart cities, agriculture, and healthcare.

3.2.1. Smart Cities

IoT plays a pivotal role in developing smart cities, which aim to optimize resources, enhance sustainability, and improve quality of life for residents. Key applications include:

- **Traffic Management**: IoT sensors embedded in roads and traffic signals monitor real-time vehicle flow and congestion patterns. These systems adjust traffic lights dynamically to optimize traffic movement and reduce bottlenecks. Mobile apps provide drivers with real-time route recommendations, further alleviating congestion. For instance, Barcelona's smart traffic management system has significantly reduced travel times and emissions by using IoT-enabled traffic lights and parking sensors (Vadivel et al., 2023).
- **Energy Optimization**: Smart grids powered by IoT enable efficient energy distribution by monitoring consumption patterns and dynamically adjusting supply. IoT-enabled devices, such as smart meters, allow residents to track energy usage in real time, encouraging more efficient practices. Cities like Amsterdam have adopted smart grid technology to reduce energy wastage and lower carbon footprints (Abir et al., 2021).

- **Waste Reduction**: IoT-based waste management systems use smart bins equipped with sensors to monitor fill levels. These bins communicate with waste collection services to optimize routes and schedules, minimizing fuel consumption and operational costs. San Francisco's IoT-enabled waste management system has significantly improved recycling rates and reduced landfill waste (John et al., 2024).

3.2.2. Agriculture

IoT has revolutionized agriculture by enabling precision farming and sustainable practices, helping farmers improve yields while conserving resources.

- **Precision Farming**: IoT sensors monitor soil moisture, nutrient levels, and weather conditions, providing farmers with real-time data to optimize planting, irrigation, and fertilization. Automated irrigation systems adjust water supply based on soil data, reducing water wastage and ensuring optimal crop health (Shahab et al., 2025).
- **Livestock Monitoring**: Wearable IoT devices for livestock track health metrics, location, and behavior. These devices alert farmers to potential health issues, improving herd management and reducing veterinary costs (Lee & Seo, 2021).
- **Supply Chain Optimization**: IoT systems enhance traceability in the agricultural supply chain by monitoring storage conditions, shipment statuses, and product quality (Bhutta & Ahmad, 2021). This ensures timely deliveries and minimizes spoilage.

For example, John Deere's precision agriculture solutions leverage IoT to monitor field conditions and equipment performance, enabling farmers to make data-driven decisions and increase productivity.

3.2.3. Healthcare

The healthcare industry has embraced IoT ecosystems to enhance patient care, improve operational efficiency, and reduce costs.

- **Remote Monitoring**: IoT-enabled wearable devices, such as fitness trackers and smartwatches, collect health metrics like heart rate, blood pressure, and oxygen levels. This data is transmitted to healthcare providers via mobile apps, enabling real-time monitoring and early detection of health issues (Mamdiwar et al., 2021).

- **Telemedicine**: IoT facilitates telemedicine by enabling virtual consultations and remote diagnostics. Patients can use mobile devices to communicate with healthcare professionals, reducing the need for in-person visits and improving access to care for remote populations (Albahri et al., 2021).
- **Predictive Diagnostics**: IoT devices combined with AI analyze patient data to identify patterns and predict potential health problems. For example, continuous glucose monitors (CGMs) alert diabetic patients to abnormal blood sugar levels, allowing timely interventions (Ekundayo & Nyavor, n.d.).

These applications demonstrate IoT's potential to create a patient-centric healthcare ecosystem, improving outcomes and reducing costs.

3.3. Challenges and Solutions

While IoT ecosystems offer numerous benefits, they also face significant challenges that must be addressed to ensure seamless integration and operation.

3.3.1. Security and Privacy

IoT ecosystems are vulnerable to cyberattacks due to the large number of interconnected devices. Breaches can compromise sensitive data, disrupt operations, and erode user trust (Adewuyi et al., 2024).

Solutions:

- Implement robust encryption and authentication protocols to secure device communication.
- Use blockchain technology for decentralized data management and tamper-proof records.
- Conduct regular security audits to identify and address vulnerabilities.

3.3.2. Latency and Real-Time Processing

IoT applications, particularly in critical fields like healthcare and industrial automation, require low-latency communication to ensure timely responses (Shukla et al., 2023).

Solutions:

- Deploy edge computing to process data locally, reducing reliance on cloud servers and minimizing latency.

- Adopt 5G networks to enhance connectivity speeds and improve real-time data transfer.

3.3.3. Device Compatibility and Interoperability

The lack of standardized communication protocols creates compatibility issues between devices from different manufacturers, limiting the scalability of IoT ecosystems (Hazra et al., 2021).

Solutions:

- Develop and adopt universal standards like MQTT, Zigbee, and Bluetooth.
- Encourage industry collaboration to ensure devices comply with established protocols.

The Internet of Things and its ecosystem integration are driving innovation across industries by creating smarter, more efficient environments. From optimizing urban infrastructure in smart cities to enabling precision farming and transforming healthcare delivery, IoT applications demonstrate their transformative potential.

However, the successful adoption of IoT ecosystems depends on addressing challenges related to security, latency, and device compatibility. By implementing robust solutions like encryption, edge computing, and universal standards, IoT systems can achieve seamless integration and deliver on their promise of enhancing quality of life, sustainability, and operational efficiency.

As IoT technology continues to evolve, its role in shaping intelligent ecosystems will become increasingly critical, paving the way for a connected, data-driven future.

4. INTELLIGENT ECOSYSTEMS AND DECISION-MAKING

4.1. Components of Intelligent Ecosystems: Data Collection, Processing, and AI-Driven Decisions

Intelligent ecosystems are dynamic environments that rely on interconnected systems for data collection, processing, and AI-driven decision-making. These ecosystems enable seamless communication between devices, sensors, and platforms to optimize operations and improve user experiences.

4. 1.1. Data Collection

The foundation of any intelligent ecosystem lies in its ability to gather data in real time. IoT devices, sensors, and mobile systems act as primary data collectors, capturing information on environmental, operational, and user-specific metrics (Shah et al., 2023). For instance, smart home ecosystems monitor lighting, temperature, and energy usage, while industrial setups collect machinery performance data to ensure smooth operations.

4.1.2. Data Processing

Once data is collected, it must be processed to derive actionable insights. This can occur locally at the edge, on the device itself, or in cloud systems for more complex analytics. Edge computing enhances real-time responses, while cloud-based solutions support large-scale data aggregation and long-term analysis (Modupe et al., 2024).

4.1.3. AI-Driven Decisions

Artificial intelligence (AI) and machine learning (ML) models play a critical role in interpreting collected data, detecting patterns, and making autonomous decisions. For example, in agriculture, AI-driven systems analyze weather and soil data to optimize irrigation schedules, while smart traffic management systems use real-time data to adjust signal timings dynamically.

These components work together to create adaptive, efficient ecosystems capable of real-time responses, driving innovation in fields such as healthcare, urban planning, and industrial automation (Soori et al., 2023).

4.2. Autonomous Adaptability Through AI and Machine Learning

Autonomous adaptability is a defining feature of intelligent ecosystems, driven by the integration of AI and machine learning (ML) technologies. These systems continuously learn from data, enabling dynamic adjustments to optimize performance without requiring human intervention.

AI algorithms analyze vast amounts of data to identify patterns, predict outcomes, and make real-time decisions. For example, in smart cities, AI-powered traffic management systems adapt signal timings based on traffic density to reduce congestion. Similarly, in industrial automation, ML models detect anomalies in machinery performance, predicting potential failures and triggering preventive maintenance (Ismail & Buyya, 2022).

ML enhances ecosystem adaptability through self-learning capabilities. By analyzing historical data and user behavior, systems can refine their operations to meet evolving demands. For instance, a smart home ecosystem equipped with ML can adjust temperature and lighting based on user preferences and occupancy patterns (Hafeez, 2023).

Edge computing amplifies this adaptability by enabling local data processing, reducing latency, and ensuring quicker responses (Nain et al., 2022). For example, wearable health devices analyze vital signs on the spot, alerting users to potential health issues immediately.

The integration of AI and ML transforms static systems into dynamic, intelligent ecosystems. These technologies not only optimize efficiency but also ensure resilience, allowing ecosystems to adapt to changing conditions autonomously. As AI and ML continue to evolve, their role in enabling intelligent, self-optimizing systems will become even more critical (Pasha, 2024).

4.3. Case Studies: Smart City Implementations (e.g., Barcelona, Amsterdam)

Smart cities around the world demonstrate the transformative potential of intelligent ecosystems powered by IoT, AI, and advanced analytics. Cities like Barcelona and Amsterdam have embraced these technologies to address urban challenges and enhance quality of life.

Barcelona

Barcelona is a pioneer in smart city initiatives, leveraging IoT ecosystems to optimize urban infrastructure and services. Smart traffic management systems equipped with IoT sensors monitor real-time vehicle flow, dynamically adjusting traffic lights to minimize congestion. Parking sensors integrated with mobile apps guide drivers to available spaces, reducing time spent searching for parking and lowering emissions (Veloso et al., 2024).

The city has also deployed smart waste management solutions using IoT-enabled bins that monitor fill levels. These bins communicate with waste collection services to optimize routes and schedules, cutting down on fuel consumption and operational costs. Furthermore, Barcelona's smart water systems monitor and regulate water usage, reducing waste and promoting sustainability.

Amsterdam

Amsterdam's smart city framework emphasizes energy efficiency and sustainability. The city has implemented smart grids that allow real-time monitoring of energy consumption, enabling residents to manage usage effectively. IoT-enabled streetlights adjust brightness based on pedestrian and traffic activity, conserving energy while enhancing safety.

Amsterdam has also invested in open data platforms, allowing developers and businesses to build innovative applications using city-generated data. These platforms foster collaboration and drive urban innovation (Noori et al., 2025).

By integrating IoT and AI, both cities have created intelligent ecosystems that address urban challenges such as congestion, waste management, and energy consumption. These implementations serve as models for other urban centers aiming to enhance efficiency, sustainability, and livability.

4.4. Case Study: Industrial Automation Through Predictive Maintenance and Real-Time Monitoring

Industrial automation has been revolutionized by the integration of IoT and intelligent systems, particularly in predictive maintenance and real-time monitoring. These advancements enable industries to minimize downtime, reduce costs, and optimize operational efficiency.

4.4.1. Predictive Maintenance

IoT sensors installed on machinery collect real-time data on parameters like temperature, pressure, vibration, and energy consumption. This data is analyzed by AI-driven models to identify anomalies and predict potential failures. For example, an IoT-enabled motor may detect unusual vibrations, signaling the need for maintenance before a critical breakdown occurs. Companies like Siemens have deployed such systems to achieve significant cost savings by transitioning from reactive to predictive maintenance.

4.4.2. Real-Time Monitoring

Real-time monitoring systems enable continuous oversight of industrial processes, ensuring optimal performance. Mobile interfaces linked to IoT devices provide operators with live dashboards displaying key metrics and alerts. For instance, a factory manager can monitor production line efficiency through a smartphone app and make immediate adjustments to prevent bottlenecks.

4.4.3. Case in Action

In a Coca-Cola bottling plant, IoT sensors track machinery performance and detect wear-and-tear in conveyor belts. The system automatically schedules maintenance, reducing unplanned downtime and extending equipment lifespan (Pillai et al., 2024).

These intelligent ecosystems not only enhance productivity but also ensure worker safety by identifying hazardous conditions in real time. By leveraging predictive analytics and monitoring capabilities, industries can operate more efficiently, reduce waste, and maintain a competitive edge in today's dynamic markets.

5. EMERGING TRENDS AND TECHNOLOGIES

5.1. 5G Networks: Enhancing Real-Time Data Transmission for IoT and Smart Systems

5G networks are transforming IoT and smart systems by enabling faster, more reliable, and low-latency data transmission. With speeds up to 100 times faster than 4G and latency as low as 1 millisecond, 5G addresses the challenges of real-time communication essential for intelligent ecosystems (Salman et al., 2023).

In IoT ecosystems, 5G enhances device connectivity, allowing millions of devices to communicate simultaneously. This scalability is critical for applications such as smart cities, where sensors, cameras, and connected infrastructure require seamless integration. For example, smart traffic management systems can use 5G to gather and process real-time data from vehicles and infrastructure, ensuring efficient traffic flow and reducing congestion.

In healthcare, 5G enables telemedicine, remote surgeries, and continuous monitoring of patient health through IoT devices. Wearable sensors can transmit vital signs to healthcare providers in real-time, facilitating quicker responses and improving patient outcomes.

Industries also benefit significantly from 5G, particularly in automation and predictive maintenance. For instance, IoT-enabled factories rely on real-time monitoring of machinery to prevent downtime. 5G ensures uninterrupted communication between devices and cloud systems, enabling rapid decision-making.

Moreover, 5G supports innovations like autonomous vehicles and augmented reality (AR) by delivering the ultra-low latency needed for instantaneous processing. As 5G adoption expands, it will unlock new possibilities in IoT, enhancing connectivity, scalability, and operational efficiency across sectors.

5.2. Edge Computing: Decentralized Data Processing for Faster Response and Lower Latency

Edge computing is revolutionizing IoT ecosystems by processing data closer to its source rather than relying solely on centralized cloud systems. This decentralized approach minimizes latency, reduces bandwidth usage, and ensures faster response times, making it ideal for real-time applications in intelligent ecosystems.

In edge computing, IoT devices such as sensors, cameras, and smart hubs perform initial data processing locally. This setup enables rapid decision-making, particularly in time-sensitive applications. For example, in industrial automation, edge computing allows machines to detect anomalies and adjust operations without waiting for cloud-based instructions, preventing costly downtime (Veeramachaneni, 2025).

Smart cities also benefit from edge computing by enabling localized data processing for traffic management, energy optimization, and public safety. Traffic lights equipped with edge processors can adjust signals in real-time based on sensor data, improving traffic flow and reducing congestion. Similarly, security cameras in public spaces can analyze footage locally, identifying threats and alerting authorities instantaneously.

In healthcare, edge computing enhances wearable devices by processing health metrics like heart rate and oxygen levels directly on the device, providing users with immediate feedback. This capability is especially critical in remote monitoring, where delays can have serious consequences (Joo et al., 2024).

The combination of edge computing with 5G further enhances IoT ecosystems by providing reliable, low-latency communication and ensuring scalability. As intelligent ecosystems grow more complex, edge computing will remain a cornerstone technology, driving efficiency, responsiveness, and resilience.

5.3. Blockchain Integration: Addressing Interoperability and Security Concerns (250 Words)

Blockchain technology is emerging as a powerful solution to the interoperability and security challenges inherent in IoT ecosystems. By providing a decentralized and tamper-proof ledger, blockchain ensures secure data exchange and device communication within intelligent systems.

One key advantage of blockchain in IoT is its ability to manage device identities and permissions. With billions of connected devices operating in an IoT ecosystem, traditional centralized authentication systems are vulnerable to breaches. Blockchain eliminates single points of failure by using distributed consensus mechanisms to authenticate devices, reducing the risk of cyberattacks (Sousa et al., 2022).

Blockchain also enhances data integrity by recording every transaction or interaction immutably. This feature is particularly useful in industries like supply chain management, where stakeholders need transparent and verifiable records. For instance, blockchain-enabled IoT systems can track goods from production to delivery, ensuring authenticity and accountability.

Interoperability is another area where blockchain excels. IoT devices from different manufacturers often use incompatible protocols, hindering seamless integration. Blockchain provides a common platform for devices to share data securely, overcoming compatibility issues. For example, smart home ecosystems with devices from various brands can use blockchain to enable communication and coordination without additional middleware.

Moreover, blockchain facilitates automated transactions through smart contracts. These contracts execute predefined actions automatically when conditions are met, making them ideal for IoT applications like automated billing in energy grids or maintenance scheduling in industrial setups.

As IoT ecosystems expand, blockchain integration will play a critical role in enhancing security, transparency, and interoperability.

5.4. Advanced AI and ML Algorithms: Enhancing Predictive Capabilities and System Autonomy

The integration of advanced artificial intelligence (AI) and machine learning (ML) algorithms into IoT ecosystems is driving a new era of predictive capabilities and autonomous system operations. These technologies enable intelligent ecosystems to analyze vast amounts of data, detect patterns, and make informed decisions without human intervention.

5.4.1. Predictive Capabilities

AI and ML significantly enhance the ability of IoT systems to predict events and optimize operations. For instance, in industrial automation, ML algorithms analyze sensor data to forecast machinery failures, enabling predictive maintenance and reducing downtime. This approach not only extends equipment life but also minimizes operational costs (Ayvaz & Alpay, 2021).

In healthcare, AI-driven systems process data from wearable devices and electronic health records to predict potential health risks, such as cardiac events or chronic disease exacerbations. These insights allow healthcare providers to intervene proactively, improving patient outcomes and reducing hospitalizations (Emma, 2024).

5.4.2. System Autonomy

ML algorithms enable IoT ecosystems to learn from historical data and adapt to changing conditions dynamically. For example, smart home systems equipped with ML can analyze user behavior to adjust lighting, temperature, and energy usage automatically, enhancing convenience and efficiency.

In smart cities, AI-powered traffic management systems use real-time data to optimize traffic flow, reduce congestion, and improve urban mobility. These systems can adapt autonomously to unexpected conditions, such as accidents or road closures, ensuring smooth operations.

5.4.3. Edge AI

The integration of AI into edge computing devices, known as Edge AI, further enhances system responsiveness. By processing data locally, Edge AI reduces latency and improves real-time decision-making (Chang et al., 2021). For example, autonomous vehicles rely on Edge AI to analyze sensor data instantly, ensuring safe navigation.

As AI and ML algorithms continue to advance, their role in intelligent ecosystems will grow, enabling more accurate predictions, greater autonomy, and enhanced efficiency across diverse applications.

5.5. Sustainability Focus: Energy-Efficient Devices and Green Computing in IoT Ecosystems

Sustainability is a critical consideration in the design and operation of IoT ecosystems, as the proliferation of connected devices raises concerns about energy consumption and environmental impact. Energy-efficient devices and green computing practices are essential to ensuring that IoT systems contribute to global sustainability goals.

5.5.1. Energy-Efficient Devices

IoT devices are increasingly designed with low-power components to reduce energy consumption. Advanced sensors, low-energy communication protocols (e.g., Bluetooth Low Energy and Zigbee), and power-efficient processors help extend battery life while minimizing environmental impact (Hussein et al., 2022). For example, smart thermostats adjust energy usage based on occupancy patterns, optimizing comfort and reducing waste.

5.5.2. Renewable Energy Integration

Many IoT systems are now powered by renewable energy sources. Solar-powered IoT devices, such as environmental monitoring sensors, operate in remote locations without reliance on traditional energy grids. This approach reduces carbon footprints and enhances the sustainability of IoT deployments (Nath et al., 2024).

5.5.3. Green Computing Practices

Green computing emphasizes optimizing computing resources to reduce energy consumption and electronic waste. In IoT ecosystems, cloud providers implement energy-efficient data centers using advanced cooling techniques and renewable energy. Additionally, edge computing minimizes the need for energy-intensive data transmission to cloud servers, further reducing environmental impact (Immadisetty, 2024).

By prioritizing energy efficiency and green practices, IoT ecosystems can balance technological innovation with environmental responsibility. These initiatives contribute to sustainable development while meeting the growing demands of connected devices and intelligent systems.

6. CHALLENGES AND SOLUTIONS

The rapid growth of IoT ecosystems and intelligent systems introduces several challenges, including interoperability, scalability, data security, and ethical concerns. These issues can hinder the efficiency, adoption, and trustworthiness of these systems if not addressed effectively. Developing universal communication standards ensures seamless device integration across diverse platforms. Scalability requires robust infrastructure capable of managing vast IoT networks. Data security and privacy are paramount, necessitating encryption and decentralized systems to mitigate risks. Finally, ethical AI and IoT deployment frameworks ensure responsible use of technology, fostering user trust and compliance with regulations. Addressing these challenges is crucial for sustainable growth.

6.1. Interoperability: Developing Universal Communication Standards

Interoperability is a significant challenge in IoT ecosystems due to the diverse range of devices, manufacturers, and communication protocols. Without seamless integration, devices cannot communicate effectively, limiting the ecosystem's efficiency and scalability.

The lack of universal standards often forces developers to rely on proprietary solutions, which creates silos and restricts compatibility. For example, smart home devices from different manufacturers may require separate applications or hubs, complicating user experiences.

Solutions

1. **Adopting Open Standards**: Universal protocols such as MQTT, Zigbee, and Bluetooth Low Energy enable devices to communicate regardless of the manufacturer. Promoting the adoption of these standards ensures compatibility.
2. **Industry Collaboration**: Initiatives like the Connectivity Standards Alliance (CSA) foster collaboration among manufacturers to develop interoperable solutions.
3. **Middleware Platforms**: Middleware acts as a bridge, translating data between incompatible systems, ensuring smooth communication.

By addressing interoperability through open standards and collaborative efforts, IoT ecosystems can achieve seamless integration, enabling devices to operate as cohesive units and delivering more consistent user experiences.

6.2. Scalability: Infrastructure for Handling Vast IoT Networks

As IoT ecosystems expand, scalability becomes a critical challenge. With billions of devices projected to connect to IoT networks, the infrastructure must support massive data flows, high device densities, and real-time processing without compromising performance.

Traditional cloud-based architectures often struggle with the increasing load, leading to latency and bandwidth issues. Additionally, scaling networks for urban-scale applications, such as smart cities or industrial automation, demands significant resources and investment.

Solutions

a) **Edge Computing**: By processing data closer to its source, edge computing reduces the strain on cloud networks and ensures faster response times. For instance, smart traffic systems use edge nodes to manage local data and adjust traffic signals in real time.
b) **5G Networks**: High-speed, low-latency 5G connectivity supports vast IoT networks, enabling smooth communication among devices even in dense environments.
c) **Dynamic Resource Allocation**: AI-driven resource management systems allocate computational power and bandwidth based on demand, optimizing network efficiency.

Scalable solutions, such as edge computing and 5G integration, ensure that IoT ecosystems can grow sustainably, supporting diverse applications without sacrificing reliability or performance.

6.3. Data Security and Privacy: Adopting Encryption and Decentralized Systems

IoT ecosystems face significant security and privacy challenges due to their expansive attack surfaces and the sensitive nature of transmitted data. Cyberattacks can compromise device integrity, expose confidential information, and erode user trust.

The centralized nature of many IoT systems increases the risk of single points of failure, making data vulnerable to breaches. Additionally, inadequate encryption protocols can lead to unauthorized access and data theft.

Solutions

1. **Strong Encryption**: Implementing robust encryption protocols, such as AES-256, ensures secure data transmission and storage. End-to-end encryption further protects sensitive information by securing communication between devices.
2. **Decentralized Systems**: Blockchain technology provides secure, tamper-proof records of IoT transactions, reducing reliance on centralized databases and minimizing vulnerabilities.
3. **Zero-Trust Architectures**: Adopting a zero-trust model ensures that every device, user, and network component is authenticated and verified before access is granted.

By prioritizing security through encryption, decentralization, and stringent access controls, IoT ecosystems can safeguard data integrity, enhance privacy, and build trust among users.

6.4. Policy and Regulation: Frameworks for Ethical AI and IoT Deployment

The widespread adoption of AI and IoT technologies raises ethical and regulatory concerns, particularly around user privacy, data use, and accountability. Without clear policies, the risk of misuse, bias, and violations of user rights increases, potentially undermining public trust.

Ethical considerations include ensuring transparency in AI decision-making processes, addressing biases in algorithms, and safeguarding data against unauthorized use. In IoT, the lack of standardized regulations creates inconsistencies in device security and data handling practices.

Solutions

1. **Ethical Guidelines**: Organizations like IEEE have developed frameworks for ethical AI, emphasizing transparency, fairness, and accountability in algorithm design and deployment.
2. **Regulatory Standards**: Governments and industry bodies must establish regulations mandating data protection, device security, and user consent. The European Union's General Data Protection Regulation (GDPR) serves as a robust example.
3. **Audits and Certifications**: Independent audits and certifications ensure that AI and IoT systems comply with ethical and regulatory standards.

By implementing comprehensive frameworks for ethical AI and IoT deployment, stakeholders can address concerns, promote responsible technology use, and ensure that intelligent systems serve societal interests effectively.

7. FUTURE DIRECTIONS

The future of intelligent ecosystems lies in anticipated advancements in AI, IoT, and smart devices. Enhanced by quantum computing and evolving technologies, these systems promise unprecedented efficiency and adaptability. However, this progress also brings significant societal impacts and ethical challenges, requiring proactive solutions. These directions will redefine industries, improve quality of life, and address global challenges while emphasizing responsible technology deployment. Achieving this balance involves fostering innovation and implementing robust frameworks to mitigate risks, ensuring these technologies benefit society holistically and sustainably.

7.1. Anticipated Advancements in AI, IoT, and Smart Devices

Rapid advancements in AI, IoT, and smart devices are poised to revolutionize intelligent ecosystems. In AI, emerging technologies such as deep learning and reinforcement learning will enhance predictive analytics and decision-making capabilities, enabling systems to learn and adapt autonomously. For instance, AI-driven smart cities could manage traffic, energy, and waste dynamically, optimizing resources in real-time.

IoT networks will continue to expand, integrating billions of devices with improved interoperability and low-power consumption. With the rollout of 5G and edge computing, IoT systems will achieve ultra-low latency and real-time responsiveness, essential for critical applications like autonomous vehicles and telemedicine.

Smart devices will become more context-aware, leveraging advanced sensors, AI algorithms, and seamless connectivity to provide highly personalized experiences. Wearables will not only monitor health metrics but also predict and prevent health issues through AI-driven insights. In agriculture, IoT-enabled devices will optimize resource usage, contributing to global food security and sustainability.

These advancements will empower industries, improve quality of life, and address societal challenges such as urbanization and resource scarcity. By fostering innovation and ensuring seamless integration, the next generation of intelligent ecosystems will pave the way for a smarter, more connected future.

7.2. Integration with Upcoming Technologies Like Quantum Computing

Quantum computing holds transformative potential for intelligent ecosystems by addressing limitations of classical computing in complex problem-solving and data processing. Its ability to perform simultaneous computations across multiple states promises unprecedented speed and efficiency, enabling breakthroughs in AI, IoT, and smart devices (Ahmadi, 2023).

In AI, quantum computing could revolutionize machine learning by solving optimization problems faster and training models on larger datasets. This would enhance predictive capabilities and decision-making processes. For instance, quantum algorithms could optimize traffic management in smart cities by analyzing vast real-time data streams instantaneously.

In IoT, quantum-enhanced cryptography offers robust security solutions. Quantum key distribution (QKD) ensures secure communication between IoT devices, mitigating risks of cyberattacks (Akhtar & Gilbert, 2025). Additionally, quantum computing can optimize IoT network operations, such as resource allocation and energy management, improving efficiency at scale.

Integration with smart devices will enable unprecedented capabilities. Quantum processors embedded in smart systems could analyze complex scenarios in fields like healthcare, enabling real-time genomic analysis or drug discovery (Ali, 2023). In financial services, quantum algorithms could optimize investment strategies and risk assessments.

However, quantum computing's integration into intelligent ecosystems requires overcoming current technological and infrastructural challenges, such as scalability and error correction. As these barriers are addressed, quantum computing will redefine the capabilities of intelligent ecosystems, unlocking possibilities previously deemed unattainable.

7.3. Potential Societal Impacts and Ethical Considerations

The integration of advanced AI, IoT, and quantum computing into intelligent ecosystems will have profound societal impacts, enhancing quality of life while introducing ethical and social challenges.

On the positive side, these technologies can address global issues like healthcare accessibility, resource scarcity, and climate change. Smart cities powered by AI and IoT can reduce urban congestion, optimize energy use, and improve waste management, contributing to sustainable development. Healthcare innovations, such as AI-driven diagnostics and remote monitoring, can provide equitable access to medical services, even in remote regions.

However, the widespread deployment of these technologies raises significant ethical considerations. AI systems, if not carefully designed, may exhibit biases that perpetuate social inequalities. IoT networks collecting vast amounts of data amplify privacy concerns, as breaches or misuse of data can compromise individual rights. Quantum computing, while offering robust security solutions, could also render current encryption methods obsolete, exposing systems to new vulnerabilities.

There are also workforce implications. Automation enabled by intelligent ecosystems could displace certain jobs, necessitating workforce reskilling and policy interventions to address economic disparities.

To ensure societal benefits outweigh risks, robust frameworks for ethical AI, data privacy, and technology regulation must be implemented. Collaboration among governments, industries, and academia is essential to develop transparent, inclusive policies. By balancing innovation with ethical considerations, intelligent ecosystems can drive progress responsibly and equitably.

8. CONCLUSION

The integration of intelligent mobile systems and IoT represents a transformative shift in technology, enabling seamless connectivity, real-time decision-making, and adaptive environments. These systems have redefined industries such as healthcare, agriculture, and urban planning by fostering innovation, improving efficiency, and enhancing user experiences. Mobile devices, acting as central nodes in IoT ecosystems, bridge the gap between users and connected devices, while IoT networks facilitate data exchange and automation on an unprecedented scale.

Emerging technologies like 5G, edge computing, blockchain, and advanced AI algorithms further enhance the capabilities of these intelligent ecosystems. They enable ultra-low latency communication, secure decentralized systems, and autonomous adaptability, paving the way for groundbreaking applications in autonomous vehicles, precision agriculture, and smart cities. Quantum computing, as an upcoming frontier, promises to amplify these advancements by addressing complex computational challenges and elevating ecosystem efficiency.

However, to fully realize the potential of these technologies, critical challenges must be addressed. Interoperability requires universal communication standards, while scalability depends on robust infrastructure like edge computing and 5G. Data security and privacy remain paramount, necessitating encryption and decentralized solutions. Ethical considerations and regulatory frameworks must guide the deployment of AI and IoT to ensure responsible and equitable use.

By overcoming these challenges, intelligent ecosystems can unlock transformative possibilities, fostering a sustainable, connected future that enhances quality of life and addresses global challenges.

REFERENCES

Abir, S. A. A., Anwar, A., Choi, J., & Kayes, A. (2021). Iot-enabled smart energy grid: Applications and challenges. *IEEE Access : Practical Innovations, Open Solutions*, *9*, 50961–50981. DOI: 10.1109/ACCESS.2021.3067331

Adewuyi, A., Oladele, A. A., Enyiorji, P. U., Ajayi, O. O., Tsambatare, T. E., Oloke, K., & Abijo, I. (2024). The convergence of cybersecurity, Internet of Things (IoT), and data analytics: Safeguarding smart ecosystems. *World Journal of Advanced Research and Reviews*, *23*(1), 379–394. DOI: 10.30574/wjarr.2024.23.1.1993

Aggrawal, N., & Pandey, A. (2025). The Impact of the Internet of Behavior on Wearable Technology: Enhancing User Engagement and Health Outcomes. In *Mapping Human Data and Behavior With the Internet of Behavior (IoB)* (pp. 337–410). IGI Global Scientific Publishing. DOI: 10.4018/979-8-3693-7545-7.ch013

Ahmadi, A. (2023). Quantum Computing and Artificial Intelligence: The Synergy of Two Revolutionary Technologies. *Asian Journal of Electrical Sciences*, *12*(2), 15–27. DOI: 10.51983/ajes-2023.12.2.4118

Akhtar, N., & Gilbert, A. (2025). Quantum-Enhanced Cryptography: Safeguarding Blockchain and IoT Ecosystems.

Albahri, A. S., Alwan, J. K., Taha, Z. K., Ismail, S. F., Hamid, R. A., Zaidan, A. A., Albahri, O. S., Zaidan, B. B., Alamoodi, A. H., & Alsalem, M. A. (2021). IoT-based telemedicine for disease prevention and health promotion: State-of-the-Art. *Journal of Network and Computer Applications*, *173*, 102873. DOI: 10.1016/j.jnca.2020.102873

Ali, H. (2023). Quantum computing and AI in healthcare: Accelerating complex biological simulations, genomic data processing, and drug discovery innovations. *World Journal of Advanced Research and Reviews*, *20*(2), 1466–1484. DOI: 10.30574/wjarr.2023.20.2.2325

Amjad, A., Azam, F., Anwar, M. W., & Butt, W. H. (2021). A systematic review on the data interoperability of application layer protocols in industrial IoT. *IEEE Access : Practical Innovations, Open Solutions*, *9*, 96528–96545. DOI: 10.1109/ACCESS.2021.3094763

Amoo, O. O., Osasona, F., Atadoga, A., Ayinla, B. S., Farayola, O. A., & Abrahams, T. O. (2024). Cybersecurity threats in the age of IoT: A review of protective measures. *International Journal of Science and Research Archive*, *11*(1), 1304–1310. DOI: 10.30574/ijsra.2024.11.1.0217

Anikwe, C. V., Nweke, H. F., Ikegwu, A. C., Egwuonwu, C. A., Onu, F. U., Alo, U. R., & Teh, Y. W. (2022). Mobile and wearable sensors for data-driven health monitoring system: State-of-the-art and future prospect. *Expert Systems with Applications*, *202*, 117362. DOI: 10.1016/j.eswa.2022.117362

Antonius, F., Alapati, P. R., Ritonga, M., Patra, I., El-Ebiary, Y. A. B., Orosoo, M., & Rengarajan, M. (2023). Incorporating natural language processing into virtual assistants: An intelligent assessment strategy for enhancing language comprehension. *International Journal of Advanced Computer Science and Applications*, *14*(10). Advance online publication. DOI: 10.14569/IJACSA.2023.0141079

Ayvaz, S., & Alpay, K. (2021). Predictive maintenance system for production lines in manufacturing: A machine learning approach using IoT data in real-time. *Expert Systems with Applications*, *173*, 114598. DOI: 10.1016/j.eswa.2021.114598

Bankar, S., Balkrishna, G., & Lokare, A. (2025). *Next-Generation Embedded Systems: Innovations in IoT Integration*. Real-Time Processing, and Energy Efficiency.

Bhuiyan, M. S. (2024). The role of AI-Enhanced personalization in customer experiences. *Journal of Computer Science and Technology Studies*, *6*(1), 162–169. DOI: 10.32996/jcsts.2024.6.1.17

Bhutta, M. N. M., & Ahmad, M. (2021). Secure identification, traceability and real-time tracking of agricultural food supply during transportation using internet of things. *IEEE Access : Practical Innovations, Open Solutions*, *9*, 65660–65675. DOI: 10.1109/ACCESS.2021.3076373

Cao, J., Lam, K. Y., Lee, L. H., Liu, X., Hui, P., & Su, X. (2023). Mobile augmented reality: User interfaces, frameworks, and intelligence. *ACM Computing Surveys*, *55*(9), 1–36. DOI: 10.1145/3557999

Carvalho, G., Cabral, B., Pereira, V., & Bernardino, J. (2021). Edge computing: Current trends, research challenges and future directions. *Computing*, *103*(5), 993–1023. DOI: 10.1007/s00607-020-00896-5

Chang, Z., Liu, S., Xiong, X., Cai, Z., & Tu, G. (2021). A survey of recent advances in edge-computing-powered artificial intelligence of things. *IEEE Internet of Things Journal*, *8*(18), 13849–13875. DOI: 10.1109/JIOT.2021.3088875

Chataut, R., Phoummalayvane, A., & Akl, R. (2023). Unleashing the power of IoT: A comprehensive review of IoT applications and future prospects in healthcare, agriculture, smart homes, smart cities, and industry 4.0. *Sensors (Basel)*, *23*(16), 7194. DOI: 10.3390/s23167194 PMID: 37631731

. Ekundayo, F., & Nyavor, H. *AI-Driven Predictive Analytics in Cardiovascular Diseases: Integrating Big Data and Machine Learning for Early Diagnosis and Risk Prediction.*

El-Afifi, M. I., Sedhom, B. E., Padmanaban, S., & Eladl, A. A. (2024). A review of IoT-enabled smart energy hub systems: Rising, applications, challenges, and future prospects. *Renewable Energy Focus*, *51*, 100634. DOI: 10.1016/j.ref.2024.100634

Emma, L. (2024). AI-Powered Predictive Models for Personalized Treatment Plans in Chronic Disease Management.

Hafeez, I. (2023). A Systematic Mapping Study on Self-Adaptation SDN based Iot Networks.

Han, J., Liu, N., & Catalão, J. P. (2022). Optimization of distribution network and mobile network with interactive balance of flexibility and power. *IEEE Transactions on Power Systems*, *38*(3), 2512–2524. DOI: 10.1109/TPWRS.2022.3180792

Hazra, A., Adhikari, M., Amgoth, T., & Srirama, S. N. (2021). A comprehensive survey on interoperability for IIoT: Taxonomy, standards, and future directions. *ACM Computing Surveys*, *55*(1), 1–35. DOI: 10.1145/3485130

Hazra, A., Adhikari, M., Amgoth, T., & Srirama, S. N. (2021). A comprehensive survey on interoperability for IIoT: Taxonomy, standards, and future directions. *ACM Computing Surveys*, *55*(1), 1–35. DOI: 10.1145/3485130

Hussein, S. M., López Ramos, J. A., & Ashir, A. M. (2022). A secure and efficient method to protect communications and energy consumption in IoT wireless sensor networks. *Electronics (Basel)*, *11*(17), 2721. DOI: 10.3390/electronics11172721

Immadisetty, A. (2024). SUSTAINABLE INNOVATION IN DIGITAL TECHNOLOGIES: A SYSTEMATIC REVIEW OF ENERGY-EFFICIENT COMPUTING AND CIRCULAR DESIGN PRACTICES. *INTERNATIONAL JOURNAL OF COMPUTER ENGINEERING AND TECHNOLOGY*, *15*(06), 1056–1066.

Ismail, L., & Buyya, R. (2022). Artificial intelligence applications and self-learning 6G networks for smart cities digital ecosystems: Taxonomy, challenges, and future directions. *Sensors (Basel)*, *22*(15), 5750. DOI: 10.3390/s22155750 PMID: 35957307

Javed, A. R., & Shahzad, F., ur Rehman, S., Zikria, Y. B., Razzak, I., Jalil, Z., & Xu, G. (2022). Future smart cities: Requirements, emerging technologies, applications, challenges, and future aspects. *Cities (London, England)*, *129*, 103794.

John, J., Varkey, M. S., Podder, R. S., Sensarma, N., Selvi, M., Santhosh Kumar, S. V. N., & Kannan, A. (2022). Smart prediction and monitoring of waste disposal system using IoT and cloud for IoT based smart cities. *Wireless Personal Communications*, *122*(1), 243–275. DOI: 10.1007/s11277-021-08897-z

Joo, M. I., Kang, D. Y., Kang, M. S., & Kim, H. C. (2024). A Patient Management System Using an Edge Computing-Based IoT Pulse Oximeter. *Applied Sciences (Basel, Switzerland)*, *14*(1), 414. DOI: 10.3390/app14010414

Lavanya, A., Divya Navamani, J., & Zahira, R. (2025). Introduction to the Internet of Things. *IoT for Smart Grid: Revolutionizing. Electrical Engineering*, •••, 1–16.

Lee, E., Seo, Y. D., Oh, S. R., & Kim, Y. G. (2021). A Survey on Standards for Interoperability and Security in the Internet of Things. *IEEE Communications Surveys and Tutorials*, *23*(2), 1020–1047. DOI: 10.1109/COMST.2021.3067354

Lee, M., & Seo, S. (2021). Wearable wireless biosensor technology for monitoring cattle: A review. *Animals (Basel)*, *11*(10), 2779. DOI: 10.3390/ani11102779 PMID: 34679801

Mamdiwar, S. D., Shakruwala, Z., Chadha, U., Srinivasan, K., & Chang, C. Y. (2021). Recent advances on IoT-assisted wearable sensor systems for healthcare monitoring. *Biosensors (Basel)*, *11*(10), 372. DOI: 10.3390/bios11100372 PMID: 34677328

Michard, F. (2021). Toward smart monitoring with phones, watches, and wearable sensors. *Anesthesiology Clinics*, *39*(3), 555–564. DOI: 10.1016/j.anclin.2021.04.005 PMID: 34392885

Mishra, P., & Singh, G. (2023). *Sustainable Smart Cities*. Enabling Technologies, Energy Trends and Potential Applications. DOI: 10.1007/978-3-031-33354-5

Modupe, O. T., Otitoola, A. A., Oladapo, O. J., Abiona, O. O., Oyeniran, O. C., Adewusi, A. O., & Obijuru, A. (2024). Reviewing the transformational impact of edge computing on real-time data processing and analytics. *Computer Science & IT Research Journal*, *5*(3), 603–702.

Modupe, O. T., Otitoola, A. A., Oladapo, O. J., Abiona, O. O., Oyeniran, O. C., Adewusi, A. O., & Obijuru, A. (2024). Reviewing the transformational impact of edge computing on real-time data processing and analytics. *Computer Science & IT Research Journal*, *5*(3), 603–702.

Mourtzis, D., Angelopoulos, J., & Panopoulos, N. (2021). Design and development of an IoT enabled platform for remote monitoring and predictive maintenance of industrial equipment. *Procedia Manufacturing*, *54*, 166–171. DOI: 10.1016/j.promfg.2021.07.025

Nain, G., Pattanaik, K. K., & Sharma, G. K. (2022). Towards edge computing in intelligent manufacturing: Past, present and future. *Journal of Manufacturing Systems*, *62*, 588–611. DOI: 10.1016/j.jmsy.2022.01.010

Nath, D. C., Kundu, I., Sharma, A., Shivhare, P., Afzal, A., Soudagar, M. E. M., & Park, S. G. (2024). Internet of Things integrated with solar energy applications: A state-of-the-art review. *Environment, Development and Sustainability*, *26*(10), 24597–24652. DOI: 10.1007/s10668-023-03691-2

. Noori, N., Hoppe, T., van der Werf, I., & Janssen, M. F. W. H. A. (2025). A framework to analyze inclusion in smart energy city development.

Oyeniran, C. O., Adewusi, A. O., Adeleke, A. G., Akwawa, L. A., & Azubuko, C. F. (2023). 5G technology and its impact on software engineering: New opportunities for mobile applications. *Computer Science & IT Research Journal*, *4*(3), 562–576. DOI: 10.51594/csitrj.v4i3.1557

Pal, S. (2024). Artificial Intelligence-Based IoT-Edge Environment for Industry 5.0. In *IoT Edge Intelligence* (pp. 111–148). Springer Nature Switzerland. DOI: 10.1007/978-3-031-58388-9_4

Paolone, G., Iachetti, D., Paesani, R., Pilotti, F., Marinelli, M., & Di Felice, P. (2022). A holistic overview of the internet of things ecosystem. *IoT*, *3*(4), 398–434. DOI: 10.3390/iot3040022

Pasha, M. H. M. (2024). Harnessing Artificial Intelligence to Build Agile and Resilient Business Ecosystems for the Smart Economy of the Future. *Journal of Business and Future Economy*, *1*(2), 31–40.

Pillai, R. S., Denny, P., & O'connell, E. (2024). Optimizing Predictive and Prescriptive Maintenance Using Unified Namespace (UNS) for Industrial Equipments.

Reddy, M., & Oliver, N. (2024). The role of real-time continuous glucose monitoring in diabetes management and how it should link to integrated personalized diabetes management. *Diabetes, Obesity & Metabolism*, *26*(S1), 46–56. DOI: 10.1111/dom.15504 PMID: 38441367

Rehan, H. (2023). Internet of Things (IoT) in smart cities: Enhancing urban living through technology. *Journal of Engineering Technology*, *5*(1), 1–16.

Retscher, G., Gikas, V., & Gabela, J. (2024). Experiences with techniques and sensors for smartphone positioning. *Journal of Applied Geodesy*, (0).

Salma, S., Begum, A., & Syed, H. (2024). Practical and Innovative Applications of IoT and IoT Networks (Smart Cities, Smart Mobility, Smart Home, Smart Health, Smart Grid, etc.). In *AI for Climate Change and Environmental Sustainability* (pp. 121-144). CRC Press.

Salman, H. A., Alsajri, A., Kalakech, A., & Steiti, A. (2023). Difference Between 4G and 5G Networks. *Babylonian Journal of Networking*, *2023*, 41–54. DOI: 10.58496/BJN/2023/006

Shah, Q. A., Shafi, I., Ahmad, J., Alfarhood, S., Safran, M., & Ashraf, I. (2023). A meta modeling-based interoperability and integration testing platform for IoT systems. *Sensors (Basel)*, *23*(21), 8730. DOI: 10.3390/s23218730 PMID: 37960429

Shahab, H., Naeem, M., Iqbal, M., Aqeel, M., & Ullah, S. S. (2025). IoT-Driven Smart Agricultural Technology for Real-Time Soil and Crop Optimization. *Smart Agricultural Technology*, *10*, 100847. DOI: 10.1016/j.atech.2025.100847

Shukla, S., Hassan, M. F., Tran, D. C., Akbar, R., Paputungan, I. V., & Khan, M. K. (2023). Improving latency in Internet-of-Things and cloud computing for real-time data transmission: A systematic literature review (SLR). *Cluster Computing*, *26*(5), 1–24. DOI: 10.1007/s10586-021-03279-3

Soori, M., Arezoo, B., & Dastres, R. (2023). Artificial intelligence, machine learning and deep learning in advanced robotics, a review. *Cognitive Robotics*, *3*, 54–70. DOI: 10.1016/j.cogr.2023.04.001

Sosunova, I., & Porras, J. (2022). IoT-enabled smart waste management systems for smart cities: A systematic review. *IEEE Access : Practical Innovations, Open Solutions*, *10*, 73326–73363. DOI: 10.1109/ACCESS.2022.3188308

Sousa, P. R., Resende, J. S., Martins, R., & Antunes, L. (2022). The case for blockchain in IoT identity management. *Journal of Enterprise Information Management*, *35*(6), 1477–1505. DOI: 10.1108/JEIM-07-2018-0148

Tan, W. C., & Sidhu, M. S. (2022). Review of RFID and IoT integration in supply chain management. *Operations Research Perspectives*, *9*, 100229. DOI: 10.1016/j.orp.2022.100229

Teoh, Y. K., Gill, S. S., & Parlikad, A. K. (2021). IoT and fog-computing-based predictive maintenance model for effective asset management in Industry 4.0 using machine learning. *IEEE Internet of Things Journal*, *10*(3), 2087–2094. DOI: 10.1109/JIOT.2021.3050441

Vadivel, G., Hussain, M. J. M., & Sangeetha, S. T. (2023). Smart transportation systems: IoT-connected wireless sensor networks for traffic congestion management. *International Journal of Advances in Signal and Image Sciences*, *9*(1), 40–49. DOI: 10.29284/IJASIS.9.1.2023.40-49

Veeramachaneni, V. (2025). Edge Computing: Architecture, Applications, and Future Challenges in a Decentralized Era. *Recent Trends in Computer Graphics and Multimedia Technology*, *7*(1), 8–23.

Veloso, Á., Fonseca, F., & Ramos, R. (2024). Insights from Smart City Initiatives for Urban Sustainability and Contemporary Urbanism. *Smart Cities*, *7*(6), 3188–3209. DOI: 10.3390/smartcities7060124

Vermesan, O., & Friess, P. (Eds.). (2013). *Internet of things: converging technologies for smart environments and integrated ecosystems*. River publishers.

Vermesan, O., Friess, P., Guillemin, P., Gusmeroli, S., Sundmaeker, H., Bassi, A., & Doody, P. (2022). Internet of things strategic research roadmap. In *Internet of things-global technological and societal trends from smart environments and spaces to green ICT* (pp. 9–52). River Publishers.

Xing, Y., & Wang, X. (2024). Precision agriculture and water conservation strategies for sustainable crop production in arid regions. *Plants*, *13*(22), 3184. DOI: 10.3390/plants13223184 PMID: 39599396

Zhu, S., Yu, T., Xu, T., Chen, H., Dustdar, S., Gigan, S., ... & Pan, Y. (2023). Intelligent computing: the latest advances, challenges, and future. *Intelligent Computing*, *2*, 0006.

Zikria, Y. B., Ali, R., Afzal, M. K., & Kim, S. W. (2021). Next-generation internet of things (iot): Opportunities, challenges, and solutions. *Sensors (Basel)*, *21*(4), 1174. DOI: 10.3390/s21041174 PMID: 33562343

Zikria, Y. B., Ali, R., Afzal, M. K., & Kim, S. W. (2021). Next-generation internet of things (iot): Opportunities, challenges, and solutions. *Sensors (Basel)*, *21*(4), 1174. DOI: 10.3390/s21041174 PMID: 33562343

Chapter 4
Machine Learning-Driven AI System for Automated Flow Control:
Simple LR and Decision Table ML Algorithms

B. Kalaiselvi
https://orcid.org/0000-0001-6300-0348
Bharath Institute of Higher Education and Research, India

ABSTRACT

This chapter proposes a new concept of Designing an automatic flow controller that is based on AI and using selected machine learning algorithms. The optimum smart controller uses machine learning concept by learning the knowledge often convectional flow controller. The acquired data set is used to train the built model using ML algorithm using a software tool called Weka 3.8.5 is an open-source software suite developed at the University of Waikato in New Zealand. A model with optimum performance is built, the performance criteria analysis like mean square error, root means square error. The Weka software is used to build a model with 60% of dataset and evaluated with 40% of data set. The evaluated result is Root mean square error ranges from 0.96 to 0.0028. The correlation coefficient is equal to 1 and the percentage Relative absolute error is 0.0467% for simple linear regression and 15.869% for Decision table ML algorithms. Hence the built model functions as smart flow controller and the output of this controller will be imitating the conventional PID controller.

DOI: 10.4018/979-8-3373-0330-7.ch004

Copyright © 2025, IGI Global Scientific Publishing. Copying or distributing in print or electronic forms without written permission of IGI Global Scientific Publishing is prohibited.

INTRODUCTION

Instrumentation and process control systems witness a surge in applications. Various industrial processes, encompassing measurements such as level, pressure, temperature, flow, quality control, assembly, robotic systems, and security, employ machine vision for efficient operation. The integration of artificial intelligence (AI) contributes to achieving high performance and fostering innovation.

AI finds application across diverse domains, and the corresponding software modules often require fine-tuning to meet specific time constraints. This fine-tuning is a continuous process throughout the application's lifespan. Additionally, there arises a need to develop versions of imaging software tailored for different user classes, catering to various market niches. Consequently, it becomes crucial to create software tools that empower engineers to efficiently target an array of computational devices.

A pivotal step in this process involves incorporating a software module capable of real-time monitoring and measurement of all system parameters, ensuring seamless operation.

Implementing an intelligent controller flow controller in a flow process station simplifies the tuning process and minimizes manual errors resulting from the challenges in monitoring the controller's actions. The impact of this smart controller is assessed through real-time experiments. Its performance is then compared to that of the traditional PID controller. In the context of the flow controller, it is important to clarify the terms manipulated variables, measured variables, and control variables. While these terms are often used interchangeably in the literature, they typically refer to either input or output signals. Control variables pertain to inputs such as flow rates, pressure readings, and temperature readings, while manipulated and measured variables relate to the output signals sent to the actuator. The implementation of a smart flow controller in a flow process station employs supervised machine learning algorithms via Weka software. The resulting smart controller exhibits the same characteristics as the conventional PID controller

The closed-loop system's optimal model for system governance is clearly illustrated in the block diagram, with the stem position being measured optimally, as depicted in Figure 1. This diagram not only demonstrates improvements in the early prediction of stem position but also contributes to the seamless and uninterrupted operation of the plant. It aids in the early identification of potential issues such as backlash and stiction problems, preventing system breakdowns.

The system is designed as a cascade loop, comprising a primary and secondary loop with two controllers—one overseeing flow and the other monitoring the process's level. Managing the continuously varying setpoint and tuning a controller for process stabilization in the secondary loop poses challenges. Consequently, an optimal controller, leveraging machine learning algorithms, has been implemented to address these difficulties.

Figure 1. A - Proposed smart flow controller implementation, B – Traditional cascaded loop with 2 controllers

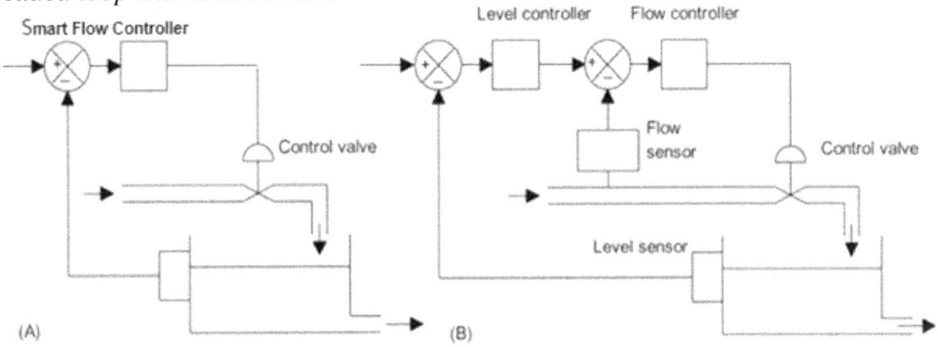

Figure 1 shows the traditional cascaded loops with the level and flow controller. Primary loop with level and flow controller in the secondary loop as shown in the figure 1. Designing a flow controller is a challenging task in conventional PID controller, since the set point will be very frequently varying because of the primary level controller. Tuning the parameters of a flow controller is a challenging task in conventional methods.

The integration of traditional cascaded loops with level and flow controllers, exemplified in Figure 1, represents a widely adopted approach in process control systems. This configuration involves a primary loop with a level controller and a secondary loop incorporating both level and flow controllers. The intricacies of designing a reliable flow controller in the presence of a frequently varying set point due to the primary level controller pose a significant challenge in conventional PID control methods.

Design Complexity

The primary focus of this review revolves around the intricacies associated with designing a flow controller within the constraints of conventional PID control. The primary level controller introduces a dynamic element to the system, resulting in frequent variations of the set point for the flow controller. Traditional methods face difficulties in adapting to these rapid changes, making the task of tuning the parameters of the flow controller a challenging endeavor.

Challenges in Conventional PID Control

One of the major hurdles lies in the conventional PID controller's struggle to maintain stability and optimal performance in the face of dynamically changing set points. The inherent limitations of traditional tuning methods become apparent when dealing with systems where the primary level controller induces fluctuations that directly impact the flow controller. As a result, achieving a balance between responsiveness and stability becomes a delicate task.

Adaptive Strategies

To address the challenges posed by the frequent variations in set points, advanced control strategies and adaptive tuning methods have been explored. These strategies aim to enhance the performance of flow controllers by dynamically adjusting parameters in response to changing process conditions. The implementation of adaptive algorithms allows for a more robust and responsive control system, mitigating the difficulties associated with conventional tuning approaches.

Practical Implications

Despite the challenges outlined, the traditional cascaded loops with level and flow controllers remain a prevalent choice in industrial settings. The insights gained from this review underscore the importance of adopting innovative strategies for flow controller design, ensuring optimal performance in the presence of dynamic set points induced by primary level controllers.

The review highlights the complexity of integrating traditional cascaded loops with level and flow controllers, particularly in the context of conventional PID control methods. While acknowledging the challenges posed by frequent set point variations, it emphasizes the need for adaptive strategies to overcome these limitations. As technology continues to evolve, the integration of advanced control techniques promises to enhance the efficiency and stability of process control systems, paving the way for future advancements in the field.

Real time data of the process is obtained by running the station. Output data with the following 5 attributes is obtained as time, process variable LPH (Liters per hour), process variable in volts, the controller output, and finally the error percentage is obtained as a document as mentioned in table 1.

RELATED WORKS

Wang et al. (2014) offers an in-depth analysis of a pneumatic cylinder actuator system's modeling, control, and robustness. In this review, we delve into the key contributions, strengths, and potential areas for improvement in this research work. The authors begin by presenting a thorough overview of the pneumatic cylinder actuator system, its underlying dynamics, and the challenges faced when designing control systems for such systems. They emphasize the importance of robust servo control, which is a critical requirement for many industrial applications. The authors make it clear from the outset that their research aims to provide a robust control strategy for a pneumatic cylinder actuator, which is an essential component in various industrial automation processes. Rohilla et al. (2018), is a valuable contribution to the field of control engineering. The innovative use of fuzzy logic and comprehensive performance analysis make it a worthwhile read for researchers and engineers working on control systems. However, for a more practical perspective, experimental validation and considerations of real-world challenges would have been beneficial.

Raut and Nichat (2017) is a well-executed research paper that explores the application of decision tree algorithms in predicting student performance. The author's clear methodology, comprehensive results, and implications for practical use in education make this paper a valuable contribution to the field. With some minor adjustments, such as addressing potential limitations, this research could have an even greater impact on the field of educational data analysis. The context of predicting student performance, the clear and well-structured presentation of the decision tree model's construction and validation processes makes it accessible to both experts and non-experts. Mazid et al. (2010) meticulously describes the modifications made to the original C4.5 algorithm, making it more efficient and capable of handling rule-based classification tasks. The presentation of the algorithm's intricacies is clear and well-structured, which allows readers to grasp the enhancements and their potential impact. The paper's transparency in explaining the algorithm is an asset for both researchers and practitioners interested in machine learning. Data mining, knowledge engineering, and artificial intelligence, by providing a more efficient and accurate classification tool.

Wang et al. (2018) encrypted network traffic analysis in Software-Defined Networking (SDN) environments. The study presents “Datanet,” a deep learning-based approach designed to classify encrypted network traffic effectively. This paper is a valuable resource for researchers and practitioners seeking to address the growing challenges in network traffic analysis, particularly in the context of SDN and home gateway security. Both quantitative and qualitative assessments showcasing the model's performance metrics. They also compare “Datanet” with existing methods, demonstrating its superiority in terms of classification accuracy. This empirical evidence strengthens the paper's contributions and underlines the practical relevance of the proposed approach. Mengcan et al (2021) intriguing approach to machine learning, specifically the Constrained Voting Extreme Learning Machine (CVELM). This paper investigates the application of CVELM in the realm of machine learning, and it provides valuable insights into its potential benefits and performance. This article contributes to the ongoing development of machine learning techniques and serves as an essential reference for researchers and practitioners seeking innovative solutions to common machine learning challenges. While some areas for improvement exist, the paper's overall quality and value are undeniable.

Zhao et al. (2019) emphasized the primary focus of this article as precise position measurement. The research showcases the accurate detection of the mover's correct position, aiming for high accuracy and stability. The approach relies on time-based image correlation and boundary images for linear motors. To achieve a more extensive measurement range with reduced ambiguity, the authors employed the least-squares algorithm. The simulated results from their proposal reveal an average measurement error for displacement ranging from 0.006mm to 120mm. Furthermore, the investigation demonstrated average relative errors of less than 0.06% to 0.017%. Ashmawi et al (2019) conducted an analysis of a platform designed to alleviate people's concerns about pandemic situations when shopping. The platform not only attracts individuals but also mitigates the fear associated with physically going to a store for purchases. It achieves this by creating a module that assesses the suitability of garments for customers, providing insights into both the advantages and disadvantages of the fitness. Customers are guided through the process, enabling them to order garments from a chosen merchandise selection at any location and time without requiring their physical presence. The estimation of body measurements is facilitated through real-time image acquisition and processing, employing techniques such as Harr cascade and Support Vector Machines (SVM) for classification purposes. The machine learning models are trained to predict body measurements and determine whether the selected clothes are a good fit for the customer. This innovative approach has yielded positive results in the context of an online clothing store, particularly in addressing challenges posed by pandemic situations.

Zheng et al. (2017) delve into the creation of an innovative automatic reading method and corresponding software designed specifically for pointer instruments. This is a noteworthy undertaking, considering the prevalence of pointer instruments in various applications, including industrial processes, where accurate and efficient readings are paramount. The introduction effectively sets the stage, highlighting the importance of automated reading methods in enhancing precision and reliability. The paper then proceeds to detail the methodology employed in developing the automatic reading method, providing clarity on the technical aspects involved. The incorporation of cutting-edge technologies and techniques in this context is commendable and reflects the authors' commitment to staying at the forefront of advancements in the field.

ORGANIZATION OF THE ARTICLE: To begin, the real-time report is utilized to train predefined modules in the processing of numerical data. Next, we employ selected classifiers using standard test configurations, including a 10-fold cross-validation, default learning rate, and common batch size, followed by an assessment of their performance within the Meta, Function, Rules, Lazy and Tree based Machine learning algorithms. Lastly, the most suitable model, proposed as a smart flow controller, is integrated into the operational flow of the processing station.

DATA SET DESCRIPTION

Real-world datasets used in machine learning often exhibit susceptibility to being incomplete, unpredictable, and noisy due to their diverse origins. The presence of noise in these datasets can hinder the effectiveness of data mining algorithms, making it crucial to implement data preprocessing techniques to enhance overall data quality. Issues such as duplicate or missing values can distort the true representation of the data, and outliers and inconsistent data points can disrupt the construction of models or the general learning process. Therefore, making decisions based on high-quality data is essential, as poor-quality data can render the entire dataset useless.

The key steps in data preprocessing involve:

Obtaining the Dataset: Acquiring the dataset from relevant sources is the initial step in the preprocessing pipeline.

- Importing Necessary Libraries: Consequence the implementation of all essential libraries required for data preprocessing sets the stage for subsequent operations.
- Importing the Dataset: The actual incorporation of the dataset into the preprocessing workflow is necessary for further analysis and manipulation.
- Identifying Missing Values: Recognizing and handling missing values is a critical aspect of data preprocessing to ensure completeness and accuracy.
- Encoding Categorical Data: Converting categorical data into a format suitable for analysis is vital for many machine learning algorithms.
- Dataset Division: Separating the dataset into appropriate subsets for training and testing facilitates effective model evaluation.

These seven steps collectively contribute to preparing the data for machine learning tasks, ensuring that the resulting models are robust, reliable, and capable of making high-quality predictions. In essence, data preprocessing is a fundamental stage that transforms raw data into a valuable asset for machine learning applications, preventing it from becoming mere waste in the outcome.

The dataset is acquired from a traditional flow process station, and the final dataset is generated after running the process and uploading the data once it reaches a steady state. This dataset is subsequently utilized in the validation process with the Weka tool.

Weka, short for Waikato Environment for Knowledge Analysis, is open-source data mining software provided under the GNU public license. It offers users the freedom to perform a wide range of data mining tasks, thanks to its collection of numerous artificial intelligence algorithms. It is a comprehensive toolkit that includes various functions such as data preprocessing, classification, regression, clustering, association rule mining, case-based classification, and visualization.

The project development process, particularly for flow controller implementation, heavily relies on the utilization of the WEKA software. This software, developed by the College of Waikato in Hamilton, New Zealand, offers a powerful platform for data mining and analysis.

This software encompasses a diverse range of machine learning algorithms tailored for various data mining assignments. It serves as a comprehensive toolkit with operations such as document preparation, clustering, regression, data preprocessing, classification, Association rules, instance-based classification, and visualization.

The methodology employed for the modeling of smart positioning through image processing relies on the capabilities of WEKA. As a powerful tool, WEKA plays a crucial role in executing tasks associated with data mining and contributes to the establishment of smart positioning models.

Table 1. Real time running of a cascade system

TIME (Sec)	PV (LPH)	PV (Volts)	CP1 (in %)	Error(in%)
10.84	231.26	2.31	56.64	3.75
19.63	231.14	2.31	59.08	3.77
32.38	100.37	1	85.27	29.93
48.86	100.37	1	87.82	29.93
50.09	187.79	1.88	72.53	12.44
60.13	233.82	2.34	66.18	3.24
70	233.82	2.34	68.53	3.24
80.03	233.33	2.33	71.04	3.33
90.06	313.19	3.13	50.52	-12.64
100.08	304.64	3.05	43.54	-10.93

continued on following page

Table 1. Continued

TIME (Sec)	PV (LPH)	PV (Volts)	CP1 (in %)	Error(in%)
150	258.97	2.59	31.8	-1.79
170.8	252.75	2.53	31.35	-0.55
200.05	252.26	2.52	31.1	-0.45
213.08	253.36	2.53	30.43	-0.67
213.22	253.36	2.53	30.43	-0.67
213.36	253.36	2.53	30.42	-0.67
213.5	253.36	2.53	30.41	-0.67

Table 1 illustrates the complete range of dataset that swings for 200 plus seconds with 5 attributes as shown in table. The time specified is the steady state condition of the system to reach the set point of 250 LPH. Nearly 1360 instances in the dataset. The 5 attributes are time, process variable in LPH, PV in volts, Controller output and the error percentage.

Figure 2. Time versus Process Variable, Controller O/P and Error%

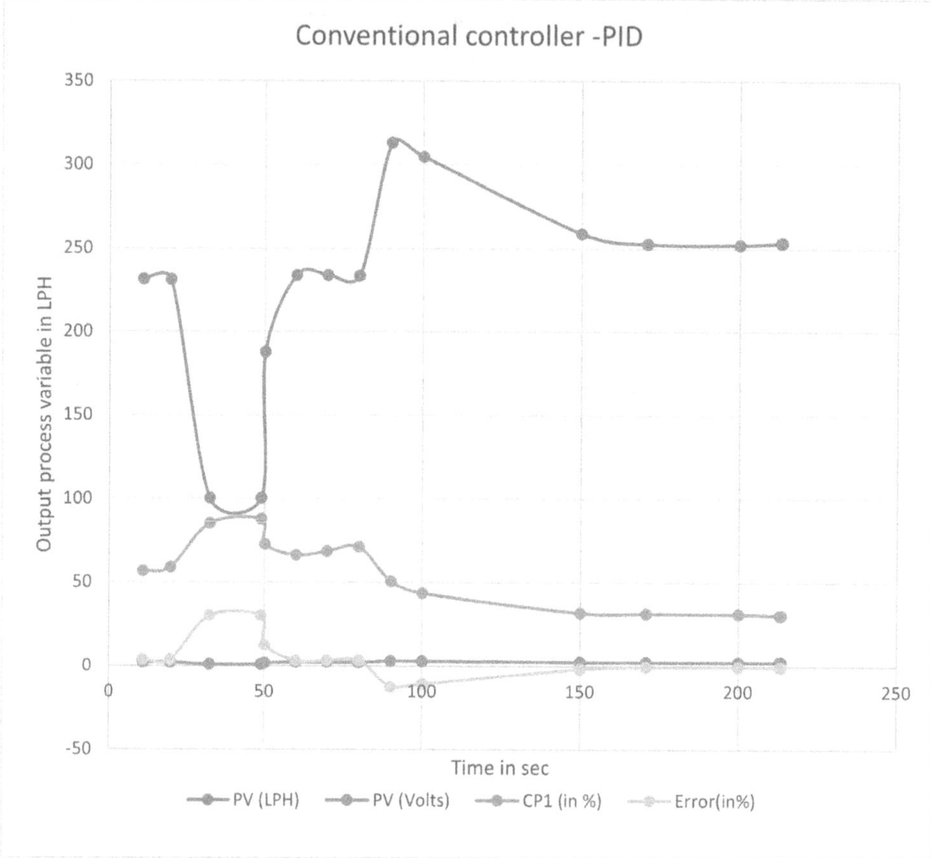

Figure 2 specifies the complete span for the entire period to reach the steady state condition. As per the characteristics the time reached is greater than 150 seconds and attained steady state in 200 plus seconds. The controller output is constant and the error is -0.67%

MATERIALS AND METHODS

The Smart Flow Controller we propose is constructed through a process involving the real-time data obtained by operating the system with a conventional PID controller. The data collected in the form of a report serves as input values, while the desired output values are derived from the system's responses. These input values are then assigned to the input neurons of the system, and various machine learning algorithms are employed to train the neural network.

The output generated by the smart controller is subsequently passed to an electrical-to-pressure converter, which in turn regulates the final control valve. By replacing the traditional controller in a flow control loop with a feed-forward neural network (Smart Flow Controller), we can significantly simplify the controller tuning process, reducing complexity.

Supervised learning is a learning approach that relies on guidance from a mentor. This mentor possesses predefined values that guide the training process. The organization learns from these predefined values throughout the training. Training data encompasses both the input data and the expected outcomes. In some cases, these correct outcomes (targets) are already known and are provided as input to the model during the learning process.

Machine learning techniques: Linear regression employs data mining techniques to make predictions based on numerical data. Traditional statistical approaches naturally align with numeric attributes in understanding how data and predicted values interact

$$Y = w_0 + w_1 x_1 + w_2 x_2 + \ldots\ldots + w_k x_k \tag{1}$$

Calculating the weights from training data and the output first training instance $x^{(1)}$

$$w_0 x_0^{(1)} + w_1 x + w_2 x_2^{(1)} + \ldots\ldots + w_k x_k^{(1)} = \sum_{j=0}^{k} w_j x_j^{(1)} \tag{2}$$

Opting for the weights that result in the minimal squared error on the training data

$$\sum_{i=1}^{n} w_j x_j^{(i)} = \left[x - \sum_{j=0}^{k} w_j x_j^{(i)}\right]^2 \tag{3}$$

The equations 1, 2, and 3 are the classical approach to fit the data and train the model to obtain the resultant controller.

In Figure 1, the flow process station is depicted with a conventional controller (PID controller), and its real-time data serve as the reference for training modules using selected machine learning algorithms within the WEKA software tool.

Supervised learning, as shown in figure 2 a learning strategy guided by a mentor, is employed in this context. The mentor provides predefined values that guide the organization throughout the training process, allowing the organization to benefit from these predetermined values. The training data comprises both information and the ground truth (actual output) model, facilitating the learning process.

Figure 3. Supervised learning technique

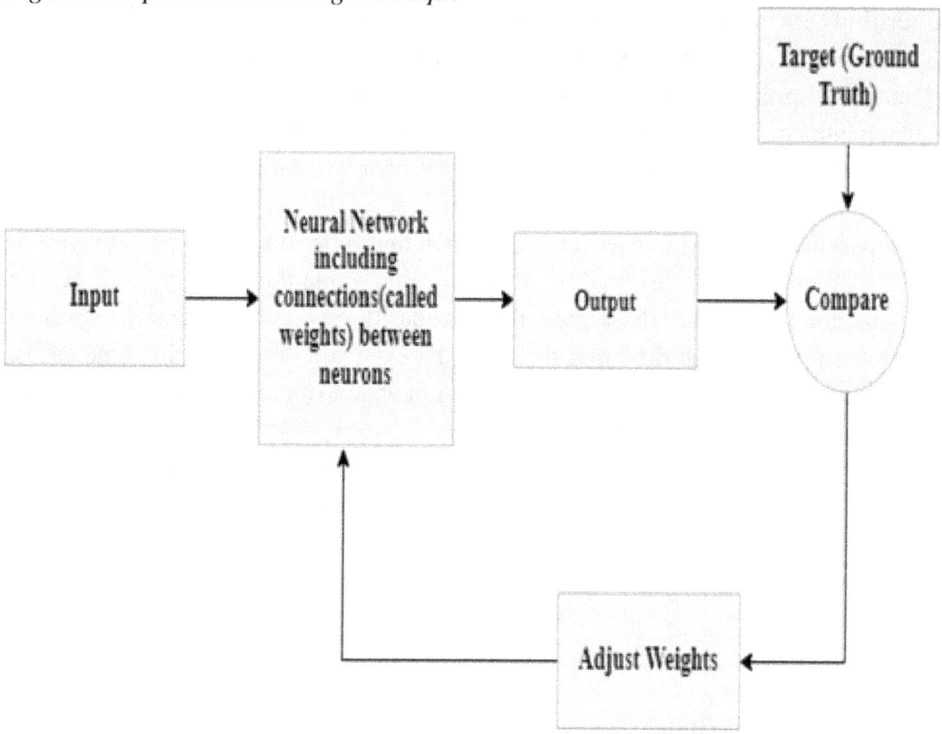

Key Features of Intelligent Flow Controller: Emphasizing the importance of monitoring benefits is crucial when deploying a flow controller; real-time information must be readily available to the necessary extent for utilization by the Intelligent Process Control System. In the event of sensor failure, essential data required for decision-making becomes unavailable. It is vital for the system to alert the user about sensor malfunctions and missing data streams, and to limit automated control adjustments for a specified duration. The inclusion of a reliable human review in advance for planned decisions in case of uncertainties or failures can serve as a valuable constraint.

Figure 4. Piping and Instrumentation diagram with flow controller using ML

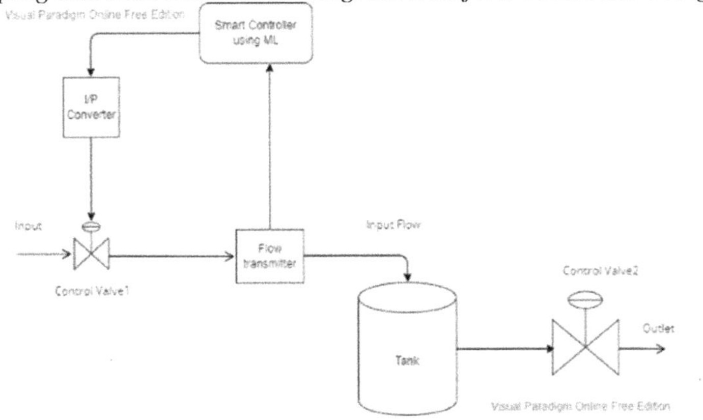

Experimental flow illustrates the approach to implement the smart flow controller in the secondary loop of the cascade process. Experiment flow is in such a way that the data acquisition is from the conventional flow controller using PID controller. The data acquired has to formatted to analyze using Weka software comma delimited values or attribute relation file format.

Figure 5. Experimental flow diagram

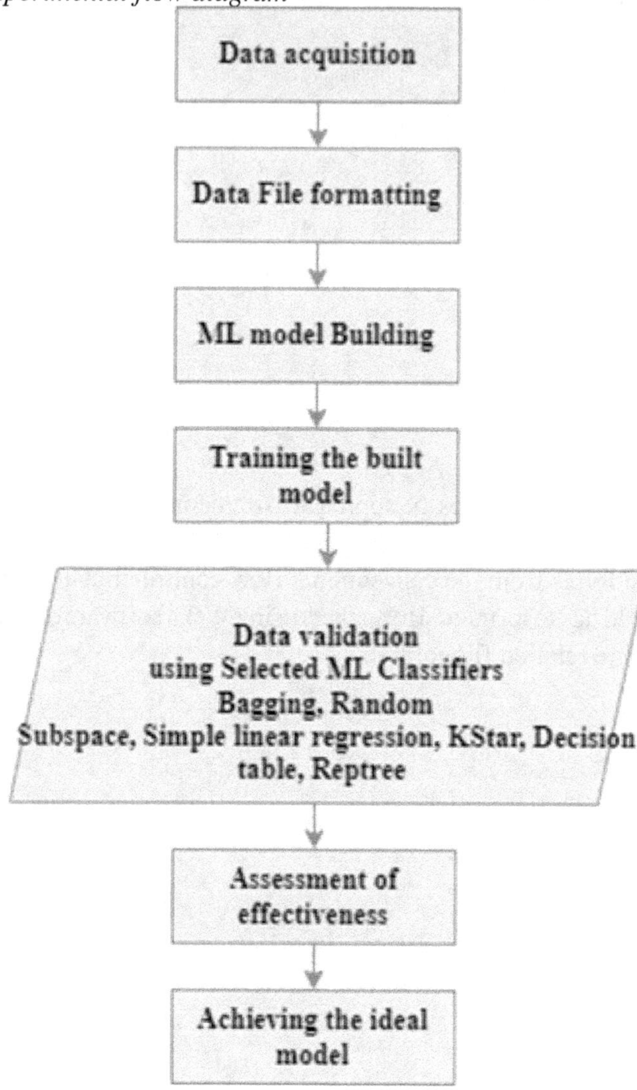

The model built using machine learning technique to analyze the data using some of the selected classifiers in Meta, functions, lazy, and tree categories as shown in figure 3. The model built is trained using 10-fold cross validation method with 60% of the data for training and 40 percentage to evaluate. The next step is classifying the trained model using the four mention categories like bagging, random subspace, simple linear regression, Kstar, Decision table and Reptree classifiers. The performances are assessed for the effectiveness and tabulated in different categories like correlation Coefficient, root means square error, relative absolute error percentage, and the time taken to build the model. Finally, we end with the achievement of an ideal model.

RESULTS AND DISCUSSION

The investigations began by file formatting in comma delimited file format that is compatible with the software Weka 3.8.5. The dataset current relations with flow controller with 5 attributes, 1360 instances or sum of weights. The statistic minimum value is 0.27, maximum value of 213.63, Mean value of 117.789, and standard deviation of 58.88. The data type is numeric with 1357 distinct values, and 0% missing values.

Figure 6. Processing window in Weka 3.8.5

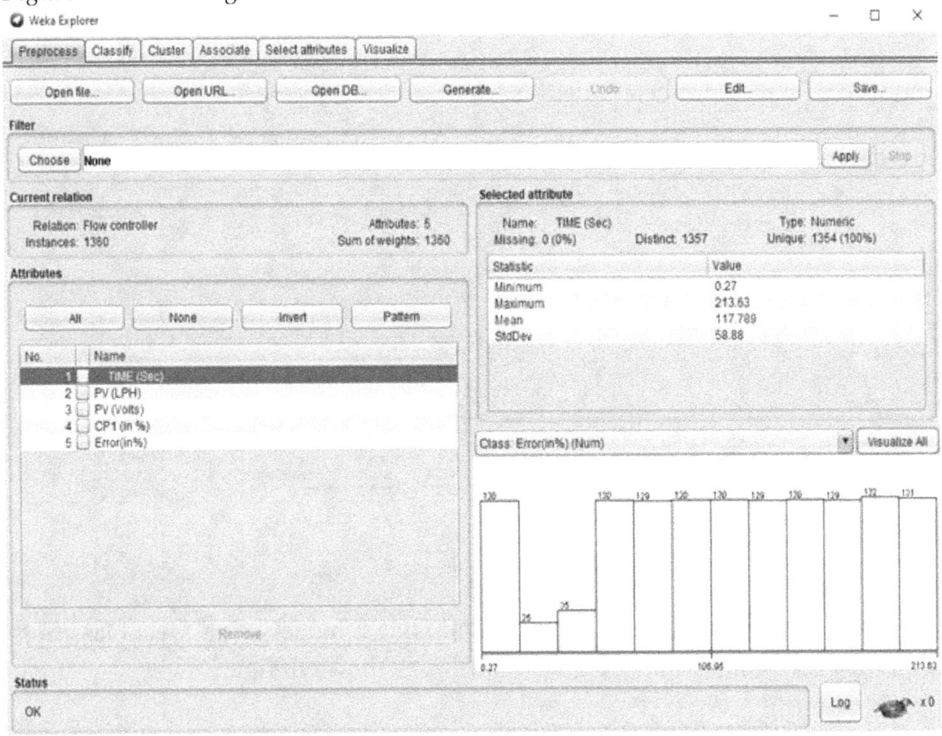

Figure 6 illustrates the processing tab in initial conditions to build a model using meta-ML algorithm for classifying. The number of instances is 1360. The model built is ready to do classification and measure the error values and judge the ML classifier using it now.

First the data set is uploaded in the CSV format and classified with Meta, Function, Rules, Lazy and Tree based category classifiers. The selected ML classifiers are to build the model are Bagging, Random Subspace, Simple Linear regression, KStar, Decision table and Reptree.

Figure 7. Predicted Error characteristics

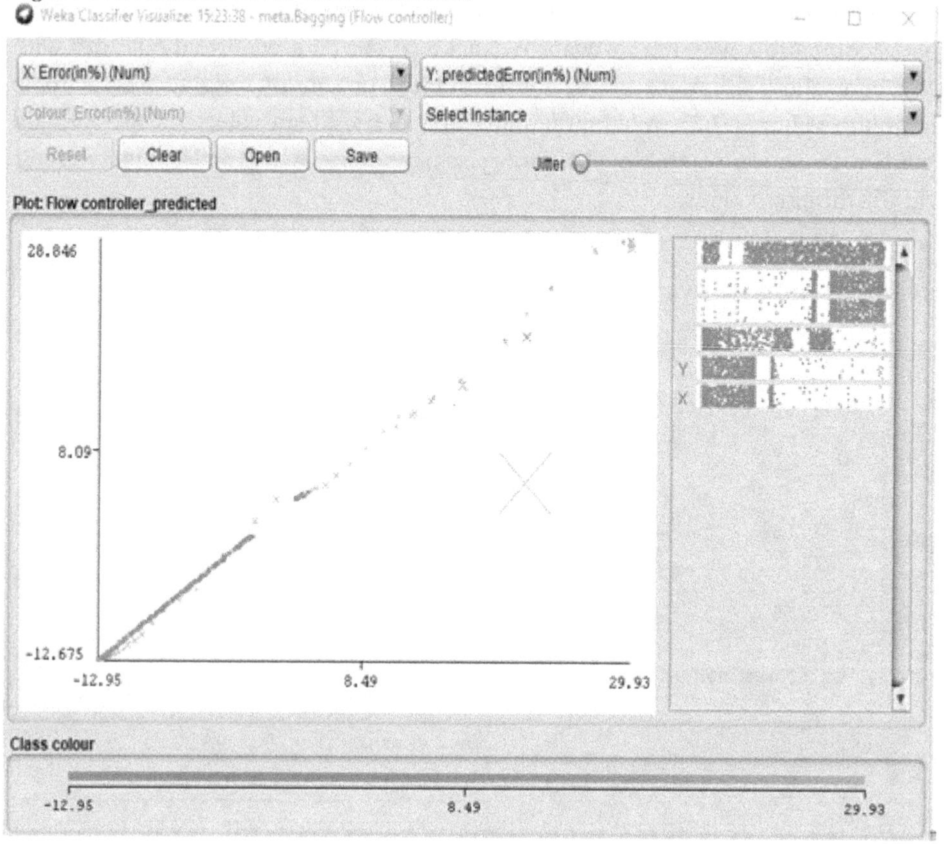

In Weka the Error curve displayed in building a model using Meta classifiers and fitting the values using the build model is as shown in figure 7.

Table 2. Experimental Results for the selected classifiers.

S.NO	Category	Classifier	Correlation coefficient	RMSE	Relative Absolute Error%	Time taken to build model: (seconds)
1	Meta	Bagging	0.9993	0.2188	2.3814%	0.1
2	Meta	Random Subspace	0.9989	0.2883	4.764%	0.03
3	Functions	Simple linear regression	1	0.0028	0.0467%	0.10
4	Lazy	KStar	0.9969	0.4844	8.0051%	0.001
5	Lazy	Decision table	0.9873	0.9603	15.869%	0.04
6	Trees	Reptree	0.9973	0.447	7.3868%	0.001

The classified output performance characteristics are tabulated as shown in the table 2. The performance wise function-based ML classifier Simple linear regression is good compared to all other classifiers with overall characteristics of Correlation coefficient of 1, RMSE =0.0028, RAE% = 0.0467% and the model building time of 0.10

Figure 8. Classifiers Vs Correlation coefficient

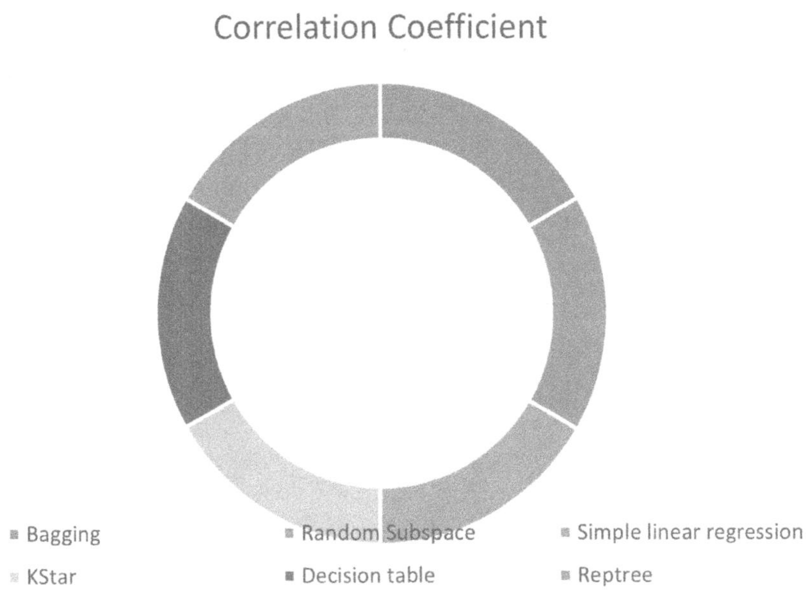

The correlation coefficient of the selected classifiers is almost equal as shown in the figure 4 which ranges from 0. 9873 to 1.

Figure 9. Classifier Vs Error %

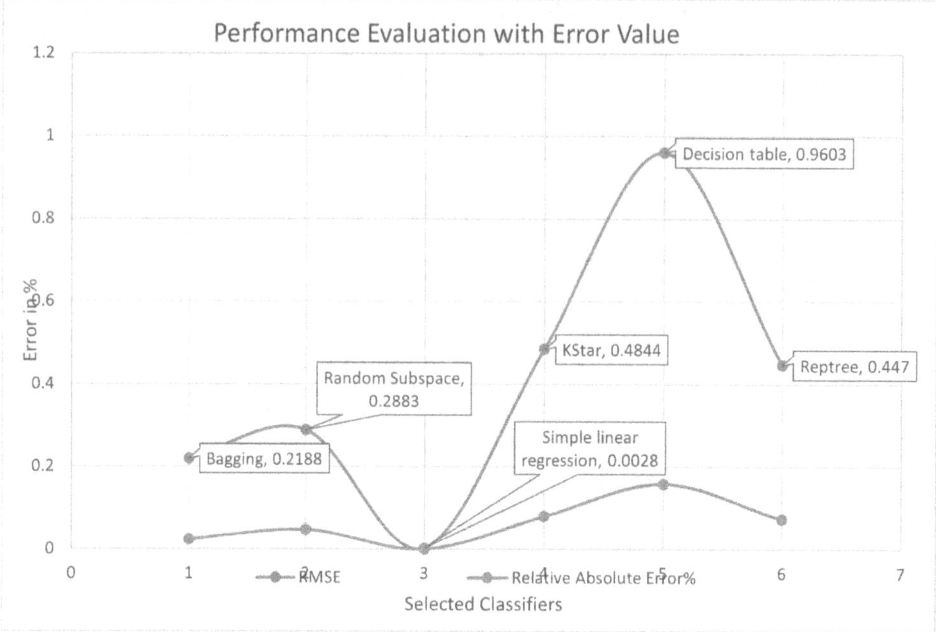

Figure 9 is the classifier versus percentage of error characteristics. The percentage is very minimal for simple linear regression of 0.0028 to 0.9603 for decision table.

Figure 10. Classifier Vs time

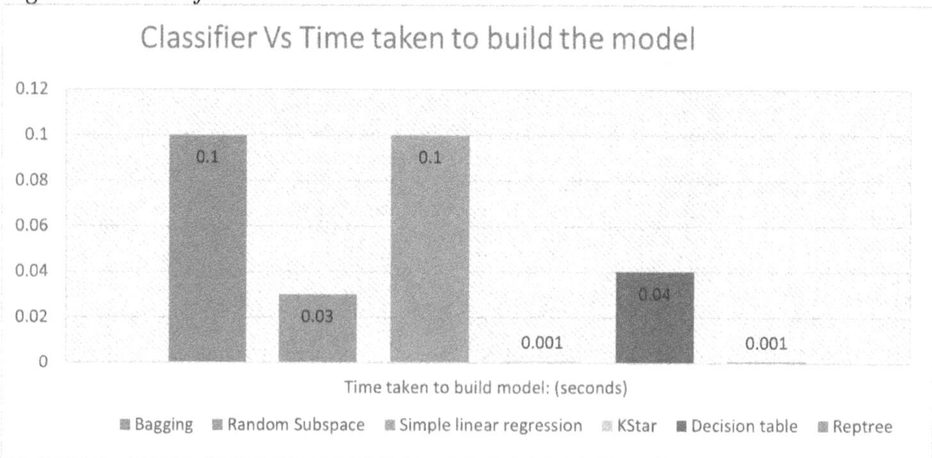

Figure 10 is the graphical representation of classifier versus time taken to build the model for various classified selected to analyze. The time taken to build is very less for K Star classifier compared to bagging and Simple Linear Regression classifier.

Table 3. Experimental results stage -II with different ML classifiers using Meta - Bagging classifiers.

S.NO	Category	Classifier	Correlation coefficient	RMSE	Relative Absolute Error%	Time taken to build model: (seconds)
1	Meta - Bagging	K Star	1	0.0028	0.0576%	0.1
2		Multilayer Perceptron	0.9999	0.0632	0.7775%	2.09
3		Simple LR	1	0.0028	0.0575%	0.03
4		REPTree	0.9994	0.2097	3.4646%	0.14
5		Random Forest	0.9996	0.1756	2.9015%	1.44

"Bagging" stands for Bootstrap Aggregating, which is an ensemble learning technique. In bagging, multiple instances of a base model (typically decision trees) are trained on different subsets of the training data, and their predictions are aggregated to produce a final output. This helps reduce overfitting and variance in the model.

Now, if we add "Meta" to "Bagging," it could refer to a higher-level layer that combines the outputs of individual bagged models, creating a meta-model. This higher-level model could use the predictions of multiple bagged models as features and learn to make a final prediction.

Here's a conceptual overview:

Base Model Training (Bagging)

Multiple instances of a base model are trained on different subsets of the training data.

Each model is trained independently, and variations in the training data are introduced through techniques like bootstrapping.

Meta-Model

The outputs of individual bagged models are used as features for a meta-model.

The meta-model is trained on these outputs to learn the final prediction.

Aggregation

During prediction, the base models make individual predictions. The meta-model then combines these predictions to produce a final output. The goal of this approach is to improve the overall performance and generalization of the model by leveraging the diversity introduced through both the bagging technique and the meta-model.

It's worth noting that the term "Meta-Bagging" might be used differently in specific contexts, and there could be variations or newer developments in the field of machine learning after my last update. Always refer to the latest literature and documentation for the most accurate and up-to-date information on specific algorithms.

Interpretation on table 2 clarify that the model built using this meta bagging classifiers gives an ideal output with the above-mentioned sub classifiers. K Star, Multilayer Perceptron, Simple Linear Regression, REPTree, and Random Forest are selected sub classifiers for enhancing the base classifiers performances. The correlation coefficient is almost 1 which is the optimum level of performances. The other error evaluating characteristics of the built model is 0.05% to 3.41%. The time taken to built the model lies between 0.03 to 2.09 seconds. The objective of the investigation is to improve the performances using selected classifiers to the maximum level.

Figure 11 illustrates the performance evaluated with the selected sub classifiers that strengthens the optimum result obtained with the selected classifiers. **The RMSE** value is in the range of 0.0028 to 0.2097 for Kstar and REPtree ML classifiers. But practically for all classifiers the root mean square error values are very low. The model building time for simple linear regression is very low in the range of 10ms. The Relative absolute error is also in the optimal range as shown in the figure 11. Hence the overall performance of the Meta Bagging – sub classifiers is good and the built model will be a right choice in replacing the flow controller as the secondary controller. The smart flow controller will be real flow controller by just training a model the work (Flow controller) is done.

Figure 11. Classifier Vs sub classifiers performances

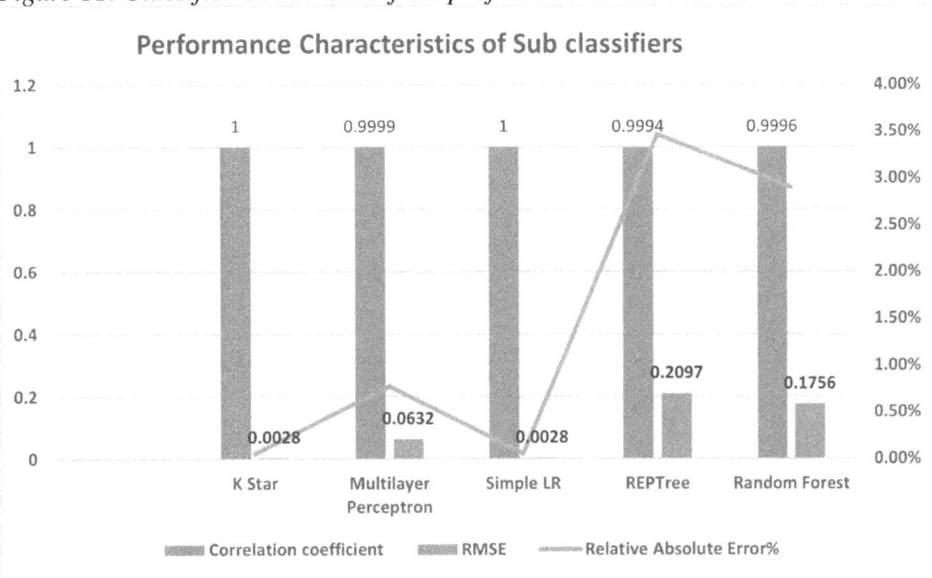

Figure 12. Time Vs ML classifiers

The span time of building the model varies from 0.1 seconds to 2.09 sec for Kstar and Multilayer perceptron as shown in figure 8.

Table 4. Meta Random Subspace and Random committee

S.NO	Category	Classifier	Correlation coefficient	RMSE	Relative Absolute Error%	Time taken to build model: (seconds)
1	Meta – Random Subspace 10-fold cross validation, Bagging 100 iterations	Random Forest	0.9994	0.2171	2.1123%	1.32
2	Meta – Random Committee 10-fold cross validation,	MLP	0.99990.	0.0669	1.1052%	2.68

Table 4 reveals that sub classifiers will enhance the performance evaluations of the built model to an optimized level. The correlation coefficient is near 1, the root mean square value is 0.06 to 0.21. The RAE is also negotiable compared to the time taken to build the model is from 1.32 Sec to 2.68 Sec.

Figure 13. Performance characteristics stage 3

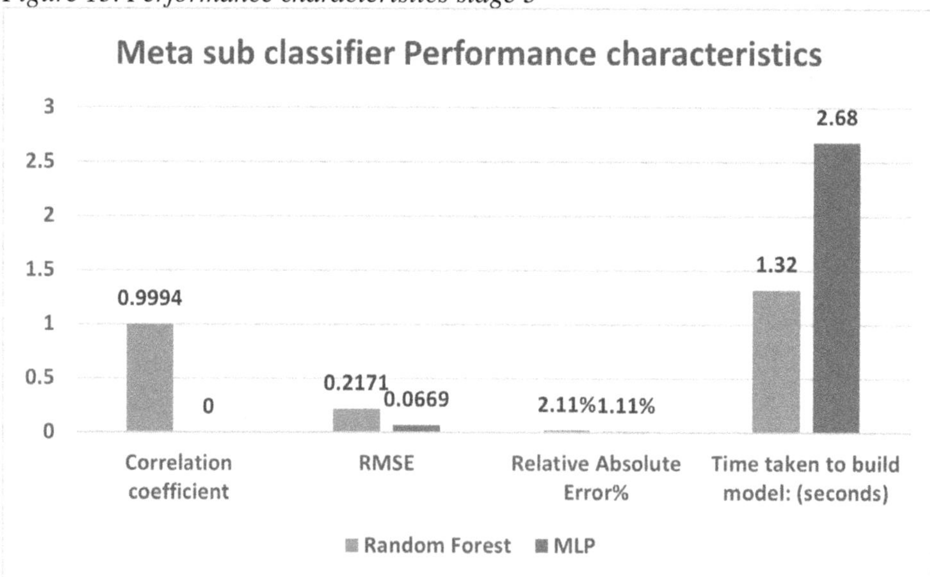

The overall performance of the Meta classifier is good with some lack in time for building the model. The error characteristics are better for both the Meta Classifiers as shown in figure 13.

CONCLUSION AND FUTURE SCOPE

The performance of the smart flow controller for predicting the flow is found to be similar to the conventional flow process PID controller. Bagging, Random Subspace, Simple Linear regression, KStar, Decision table and Reptree are the selected classifiers using ML algorithms. Hence the established smart flow controller has been implemented using supervised learning technique using the selected classifiers. In near future the work can be expanded to replace all complex conventional controllers in 3 tank or conical tank type of process stations where the controllers can be replaced by this smart controller hence the parameter tuning complications in PID controllers can be eliminated.

The future scope for the application of AI and machine learning-based smart controllers in replacing conventional controllers in processes involving 3-tank or conical tank type stations is promising and opens up several avenues for research and practical implementation. Here's an exploration of the potential future directions:

Extended Process Stations

- Expand the application of smart controllers beyond 3-tank or conical tank type stations to more complex process stations with diverse dynamics.
- Investigate the adaptability of AI and machine learning controllers to various industrial processes, considering different types of sensors and actuators.

Multi-Variable Systems

- Explore the feasibility of implementing smart controllers for multi-variable systems, where interactions between different process variables are considered.
- Develop algorithms that can effectively handle and optimize control strategies in systems with interconnected variables.

Real-time Adaptability

- Enhance the real-time adaptability of smart controllers to dynamic changes in the process environment.

- Implement algorithms that can autonomously adjust to varying operating conditions, disturbances, and uncertainties in real-world scenarios.

Integration with IoT and Industry 4.0

- Integrate AI and machine learning controllers with Internet of Things (IoT) devices for enhanced data collection and communication.
- Leverage Industry 4.0 principles to create interconnected and intelligent manufacturing systems with improved efficiency and control.

Hybrid Control Systems

- Investigate the potential of combining AI-based controllers with traditional control methods to create hybrid control systems.
- Explore the synergies between model-based control and data-driven approaches for improved performance and robustness.

Energy Efficiency and Sustainability

- Focus on developing smart controllers that optimize processes for energy efficiency and sustainability.
- Implement algorithms that consider environmental factors and energy consumption in the decision-making process.

User-friendly Interfaces

- Design user-friendly interfaces for the implementation and tuning of smart controllers, making them accessible to engineers and operators with varying levels of expertise.
- Develop visualization tools that provide insights into the controller's decision-making process for better understanding and troubleshooting.

Robustness and Safety

- Prioritize research on the robustness and safety aspects of AI and machine learning controllers in critical industrial processes.
- Address concerns related to the reliability and trustworthiness of autonomous controllers, ensuring they meet stringent safety standards.

Education and Training

- Develop educational programs and training materials to familiarize engineers and practitioners with the implementation and maintenance of smart controllers.
- Bridge the gap between theoretical advancements and practical applications through comprehensive training initiatives.

Continuous Research and Collaboration

- Encourage continuous research and collaboration between academia and industry to stay at the forefront of technological advancements.
- Foster an environment that promotes the exchange of knowledge and experiences among researchers, engineers, and practitioners in the field.

The future scope of replacing complex conventional controllers with AI and machine learning-based smart controllers holds great potential for revolutionizing industrial processes, offering increased efficiency, adaptability, and a reduction in the challenges associated with parameter tuning in PID controllers. Continued exploration and innovation in this domain can contribute significantly to the advancement of control systems in various industries.

REFERENCES

Ashmawi, S., Alharbi, M., Almaghrabi, A., & Alhothali, A. (2019). Fitme: Body measurement estimations using machine learning method. *Procedia Computer Science*, *163*, 209–217. DOI: 10.1016/j.procs.2019.12.102

Mazid, M., Ali, A. B. M., & Tickle, K. (2010). Improved C4. 5 algorithm for rule based classification.

Mengcan, M., Xiaofang, C., & Yongkang, X. (2021). Constrained voting extreme learning machine and its application. *Journal of Systems Engineering and Electronics*, *32*(1), 209–219. DOI: 10.23919/JSEE.2021.000018

Najjar, Y. S. H., & Abu-Shamleh, A. (2020). Performance evaluation of a large-scale thermal power plant based on the best industrial practices. *Scientific Reports*, *10*(1), 20661. DOI: 10.1038/s41598-020-77802-8 PMID: 33244157

Pathak, P., Yadav, A., & Alvi, P. (2020). Advanced solar MPPT techniques under uniform and non-uniform irradiance: A comprehensive review. *Journal of Solar Energy Engineering*, *142*(4), 1–31. DOI: 10.1115/1.4046090

Raut, A. B., & Nichat, M. A. A. (2017). Students performance prediction using decision tree. *International Journal of Computational Intelligence Research*, *13*(7), 1735–1741.

Rohilla, P., Vineet, K., & Feras, A. H. (2018). Fuzzy gain scheduling of an IPD controller for oscillation compensation in a sticky pneumatic control valve. *International Journal of Mechanical Engineering and Robotics Research*, *7*(3), 240–249.

Rymarczyk, T., Klosowski, G., & Kozlowski, E. (2019). Innovative methods of tomographic image reconstruction based on machine learning to improve monitoring and optimization in industrial processes. *2019 19th International Symposium on Electromagnetic Fields in Mechatronics, Electrical and Electronic Engineering (ISEF)*, 1–2. https://doi.org/DOI: 10.1109/ISEF45929.2019.9096984

Sen, G., Nil, M., Mamur, H., Doğan, H., Karamolla, M., Karaçor, M., Kuyucuoğlu, F., & Bhuiyan, M. R. A. (2018). The effect of ambient temperature on electric power generation in a natural gas combined cycle power plant—A case study. *Energy Reports*, *4*, 682–690. DOI: 10.1016/j.egyr.2018.10.009

Shuvho, M. B. A., Chowdhury, M. A., Ahmed, S., & Kashem, M. A. (2019). Prediction of solar irradiation and performance evaluation of grid-connected solar 80KWp PV plant in Bangladesh. *Energy Reports*, *5*, 714–722. DOI: 10.1016/j.egyr.2019.06.011

Singh, P., & Agrawal, S. (2013). Node localization in wireless sensor networks using the M5P tree and SMOreg algorithms. *2013 5th International Conference and Computational Intelligence and Communication Networks*, 104. https://doi.org/ DOI: 10.1109/CICN.2013.32

Singh, S., & Kumar, R. (2012). Ambient air temperature affects power plant performance. *International Journal of Engineering Science and Technology*, *4*, 3916–3923.

Tang, J., Deng, C., & Huang, G. (2016). Extreme learning machine for multilayer perceptron. *IEEE Transactions on Neural Networks and Learning Systems*, *27*(4), 809–821. DOI: 10.1109/TNNLS.2015.2424995 PMID: 25966483

Wang, J., Wang, D. J. D., Moore, P. R., & Pu, J. (2001). Modelling study, analysis and robust servocontrol of pneumatic cylinder actuator systems. *IEE Proceedings. Control Theory and Applications*, *148*(1), 35–42. DOI: 10.1049/ip-cta:20010238

Wang, J., Wang, D. J. D., Moore, P. R., & Pu, J. (2014). Modelling study, analysis and robust servo control of pneumatic cylinder actuator system. *IEE Proceedings. Control Theory and Applications*, *148*(1), 35–41. DOI: 10.1049/ip-cta:20010238

Wang, P., Ye, F., Chen, X., & Qian, Y. (2018). Data net: Deep learning-based encrypted network traffic classification in SDN home gateway. *IEEE Access : Practical Innovations, Open Solutions*, *6*, 55380–55391. DOI: 10.1109/ACCESS.2018.2872430

Wang, P., Ye, F., Chen, X., & Qian, Y. (2018). Datanet: Deep learning based encrypted network traffic classification in sdn home gateway. *IEEE Access : Practical Innovations, Open Solutions*, *6*, 55380–55391. DOI: 10.1109/ACCESS.2018.2872430

WEKA. (n.d.). *Machine learning software*. Retrieved from http://www.cs.waikato .ac.nz

Zhao, J., Zhao, J., Wang, H., Song, J., & Dong, F. (2019). Precision position measurement of linear motors mover based on temporal image correlation. *IEEE Transactions on Instrumentation and Measurement*, *68*(9), 3268–3277. DOI: 10.1109/ TIM.2018.2875645 PMID: 31413382

Zheng, W., Yin, H., Wang, A., Fu, P., & Liu, B. (2017). Development of an automatic reading method and software for pointer instruments. *First International Conference on Electronics Instrumentation & Information Systems (EIIS)*, 1–6. DOI: 10.1109/ EIIS.2017.8298626

ADDITIONAL READING

Dunne, E., Santorelli, A., McGinley, B., O'Halloran, M., & Porter, E. (2018). Linear regression for estimating bladder volume with voltage signals. *2018 EMF-Med 1st World Conference on Biomedical Applications of Electromagnetic Fields (EMF-Med)*, 1–2. https://doi.org/DOI: 10.23919/EMF-MED.2018.8526019

Ferri, M., Pinna, D., Dallago, E., & Malcovati, P. (2010). Photovoltaic energy harvester with power management system. *Journal of Sensors*, *2010*, 1–6. DOI: 10.1155/2010/349389

Ghosh, S., Wang, H., & Leon-Salas, W. D. (2014). A circuit for energy harvesting using on-chip solar cells. *IEEE Transactions on Power Electronics*, *29*(9), 4658–4671. DOI: 10.1109/TPEL.2013.2273674

Gilmore, T. E., Birganda, F., & Chapman, K. W. (2018). Source and magnitude of error in an inexpensive image-based water level measurement system. *Journal of Hydrology (Amsterdam)*, *496*, 178–186. DOI: 10.1016/j.jhydrol.2013.05.011

Khalid, R., Javaid, N., Rahim, M. H., Aslam, S., & Sher, A. (2019). Fuzzy energy management controller and scheduler for smart homes. *Sustainable Computing : Informatics and Systems*, *21*, 103–118. DOI: 10.1016/j.suscom.2018.11.010

Li, F., Fan, Y. J., & Zhao, H. T. (2014). The research of a piezoelectric valve positioner control algorithm. *Advanced Materials Research*, *1030–1032*, 1565–1569. DOI: 10.4028/www.scientific.net/AMR.1030-1032.1565

Liu, L., Wang, P., Lin, J., & Liu, L. (2021). Intrusion detection of imbalanced network traffic based on machine learning and deep learning. *IEEE Access : Practical Innovations, Open Solutions*, *9*, 7550–7563. DOI: 10.1109/ACCESS.2020.3048198

Lukyanov, M. O., Verbytsky, E. V., & Blinov, A. (2021). Solar power plant storage system. *Microsyst.Electron. and Acoust.*, *26*(2), 236748–1.

Chapter 5
Techniques for Combining Data From Multiple Sensors

Eram Fatima Siddiqui
https://orcid.org/0000-0001-7604-0373
Babu Banarasi Das University, Lucknow, India

Mohd Muqeem
Sandip University, India

Sultan Ahmad
https://orcid.org/0000-0002-3198-7974
Prince Sattam Bin Abdulaziz University, Alkharj, Saudi Arabia & Chandigarh University, Mohali, India

Hikmat A. M. Abdeljaber
https://orcid.org/0000-0001-9557-3933
Applied Science Private University, Jordan

A. E. M. Eljialy
Prince Sattam Bin Abdulaziz University, Saudi Arabia

ABSTRACT

Quality data delivery and communication in an ultra-latent and real-time manner are some its stringent requirements for Internet of Things (IoT). In IoT, raw data is sensed from real-world and transformed into a usable form. Collection of this raw data from multiple sensors as compared to a single one, it is found to be of better quality and high accuracy. This method of collecting same type of data is called data or sensor fusion. In this paper a meticulous study on the role of data fusion

DOI: 10.4018/979-8-3373-0330-7.ch005

Copyright © 2025, IGI Global Scientific Publishing. Copying or distributing in print or electronic forms without written permission of IGI Global Scientific Publishing is prohibited.

have been done with respect to its application with Internet of Things, Machine Learning (ML) and Mobile Edge Computing (MEC).This paper discusses the mechanism, multi-modal fusion techniques, past proposed standard data fusion models and related issues, along with its application with support of machine learning and Edge Computing Lastly, the paper discusses about the concept of Edge Intelligence to deliver reliable outputs with future directions and issues.

1 INTRODUCTION

Data fusion methods are used in the smart environment to transform unstructured data generated by smart devices, sensors, and platforms into useful forms. Originally proposed in the 1960s, they are widely used in remote sensing, military applications, traffic systems, healthcare, finance, and pattern recognition (White, 1991). Benefits of collecting data from multiple sensors include reliable data, confidence-based results, accurate and effective results, and better prediction and estimation of observational results. IoT-based sensor networks aim to sense sensitive data, sample collected data, and extract useful information for decision-making, but issues like heterogeneity, duplication, and data loss or inference exist. The Internet of Things (IoT) has transformed industries by connecting billions of digital devices and sensors, transforming manual activities into smart procedures. With up to 3 million new smart devices deployed monthly, there is a critical need for massive processing and storage hubs for data generated from these devices. Data Science techniques, including Artificial Intelligence, Machine Learning, and Data Mining, are applied to process and extract useful information from raw data (Hall & Llinas, 1997). Edge computing in two-tier IoT-Cloud environments offers minimal latency, quick responses, and data delivery within deadlines. AI and ML techniques can be applied over edge for data fusion, providing high accuracy and better prediction(Ahmad & Afzal, 2020). A summary of various IoT Technologies can be shown in Table 1.

Table 1. Summary of various IoT Technologies.

Technology Type	Description
VANET/MANET/WANET	Decentralized and dynamic wireless networks
Wireless Mesh Networks (WMN)	A kind of wireless ad-hoc networks made of radio nodes arranged using mesh topology for data communication.
Wireless Sensor Networks (WMN)	A spatially distributed autonomous kind of network used to sense various environmental conditions.

continued on following page

Table 1. Continued

Technology Type	Description
Smart Phone Ad-Hoc Network (SPAN)	Leverages hardware in order to create peer-to-peer network without getting dependent upon traditional cellular networks
Delay-Tolerant Networks (DTN)	Time-varying, non-permanent ad-hoc extreme networks
Low-Power Wide Area Network (LoWAN)	It is a kind of telecommunication network which allows long-range communication.

The Internet-of-Things (IoT) technology aims to create a smart ecosystem where devices can interconnect and communicate with each other, benefiting sectors like healthcare, education, logistics, and banking. The first step in IoT is to make physical devices smart and exchange real-world data. Data fusion from these devices improves accuracy, reduces data dimension, and enhances decision-making. However, challenges like privacy, energy consumption, data leakage, and loss remain. The table below (Table 2) provides an analysis of past work on sustainable data fusion (Alam et al., 2017).

Table 2. Summary of past works done in Data Fusion.

Purpose of Work	Constraints Identified
To find out various designed data fusion algorithms and model theories.	Nothing specified theories or methods for IoT environment
To find out various designed data fusion algorithms specifically for IoT environment.	Privacy and security actors are not considered
Categorized data-fusion methods as stage-based, feature-level based and semantic-based methods.	Did not considered Use-case IoT scenarios
Categorized data-fusion methods on the basis of heterogeneous nature of data.	Did not considered Use-case IoT scenarios
Sensing and data fusion for real-world activities	Did not focused upon the relationships that exist between various IoT application for sake of data fusion
Modeled an evaluation framework on basis of ten considered features	Privacy and security actors are not considered
Made a framework for data fusion on basis of intelligent transportation	Did not focused upon the relationships that exist between various IoT application for sake of data fusion

IoT data is migrated to middleware technologies like edge servers, fog nodes, and cloud centers for computation and delivery. Edge servers are ideal for real-time response due to their proximity to user devices, but they have limited battery power, storage, and processing capabilities. The integrated data can be sent to the cloud, but it may cause delays and log time responses. Machine learning and Artificial

Intelligence techniques have been used to leverage the IoT environment, performing clustering, classification, and prediction of data points, and transforming data into useful formats (Hall and Llinas, 1997).

Machine Learning (ML) has been effectively used for data fusion and solving IoT issues like data aggregation, processing integrity, routing, error detection, and physical fault detection(Sathish Kumar et al., 2022). It offers benefits like scalability, fault tolerance, hidden data coverage, low computation, and energy consumption. ML helps minimize latency and energy consumption during data transformation, achieving optimal QoS requirements. The aim of this book chapter is to explain the concept of data fusion, its benefits in real-time IoT environment and how ML and AI blended with Edge computing may help achieve better results. Remainder of this chapter is as follows: section 2 discusses the introduction and explanation of Data Fusion concepts and is related methods, Section 3 discusses about how IoT ay use various kinds of Data fusion Methods specifically for its heterogeneous environment and to combat its critical issues, Section 4 discusses various ML approaches that could be collaborated with data fusion in order to receive and interpret better results, Section 5 discusses about other data fusion methods which exists like probabilistic, estimation, mathematical and other methods, Section 6 Discusses about the benefits of using Intelligence with Edge Computing and Finally Section 7 concludes the research.

2 DATA FUSION

2.1 Description

Data fusion is a method of collecting raw data from multiple sources and combining them into one specific source to provide more valuable, accurate, and quality data. It is also known as Data Aggregation, Data Combination, Decision Fusion, and Sensor Fusion. The method is applied to sensory data at various levels and can be defined as a multi-level process involving the association, correlation, and combination of data and information from single and multiple sources. It helps improve data quality, reliability, estimation of unmeasured parameters, and uncovering hidden areas. Data fusion can be carried out at a centralized or distributed level, depending on the type of raw data collected, feature-based data, decision types, or targeted environments or systems (Alam et al., 2017).

2.2 Data Fusion Models

Data fusion methods are used in environments that require data from multiple sources to achieve the least erroneous, least expensive, and highly reliable data. They improve the optimal utilization of raw data and extract inferences from aggregated data from multiple sources. Data fusion also aids in better planning, decision-making, and control for task execution in smart environments, achieving QoS requirements. Techniques include statistical-based approaches like covariance, cross-variance, probabilistic-based approaches like Kalman filtering, Bayesian methods, maximum likelihood estimation, knowledge-based methods like Artificial Neural Networks, Fuzzy Logic, and Deep Learning.

Durrant-Whyte Model for Data Fusion on the basis of relation between data sources

Durrant-Whyte (Durrant-Whyte, 1988) proposed the following data fusion methods on the basis of relations that exists between the raw data collected and aggregated from multiple data sources. In below Figure 1 data from sensors are put together for improvements in reliability, accuracy, and predictive capabilities via complementary, redundant, and cooperative techniques.

Figure 1. Durrant-Whyte Model

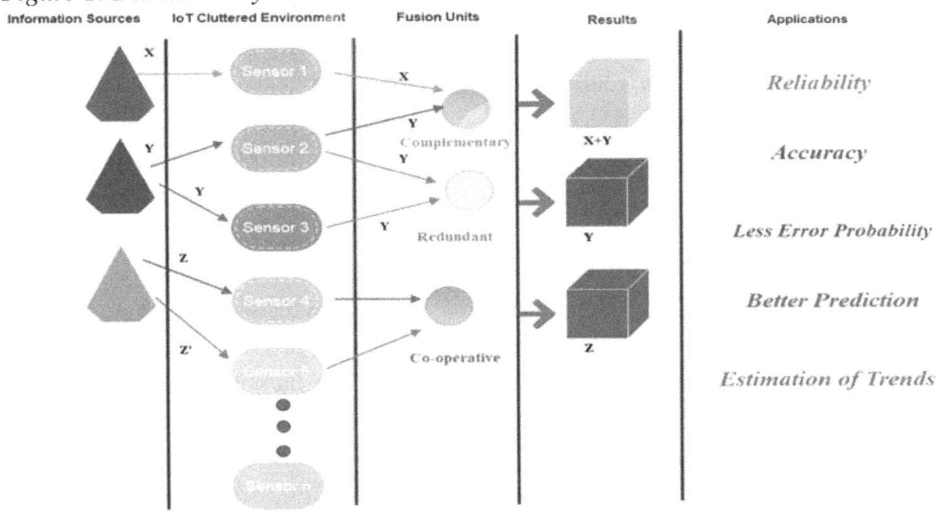

The data sources are enlisted as follows:

a. **Complementary Methods:** Data fusion methods collect data from multiple sensors in the same environment, providing more complete, accurate, and reliable data for specific applications or systems. They explore different aspects of a specific environment by combining data from independent sources, like combining targeted images.
b. **Redundant or Competitive Methods:** Data fusion methods collect data from multiple sources, ensuring less error and highly accurate results for specific applications or systems. This technique can be used to gather data from two or a single source at different timelines or data points, delivering confident and reliable outputs.
c. **Co-operative Methods:** These data fusion methods target to collect data from more than one source in which one may be a simple source and others may be complex types of sources and then combining them for a particular and specific purpose, for example fusion of audio and video data.

Dasarthy's Model for Data Fusion on the basis of types of data for input and output

Dasarthy (Dasarathy, 1997) proposed the following data fusion methods on the basis of the nature of data for input and output:

a. **Data-In-Data-Out (DAI-DAO):** This is an initial data fusion method which works upon raw input and output data and is capable of delivering more accurate and reliable data. This method is applied immediately after the sensors have collected data from the real-world environment.
b. **Data-In-Feature-Out (DAI-FEO):** In this data fusion method, the raw data is used as an input. This raw data is gathered from multiple sources in order to extract out features and characteristics for a targeted environment and then the features are delivered as output.
c. **Feature-In-Feature-Out (FEI-FEO):** In this data fusion method, both the input and output data contains the features or characteristics for a targeted environment. This method is applied for a more improved refinement of features in order to obtain new and reliable features. Other names of this method are feature fusion, mid-level fusion or symbolic fusion.
d. **Feature-In-Decision-Out (FEI-DEO):** In this data fusion method the features are used as an input and the output are a set of definite and specific decisions taken on the basis of the set of features. For example, classification, pattern recognition.

e. **Decision-In-Decision-Out (DEI-DEO):** This method is popularly known as decision fusion method. As the name suggests, it fuses or combines a number of decisions from multiple sources in order to make a better and improved decision.

The above discussed data fusion methods may be visualized using Figure 2 which illustrates data fusion in IoT, where data from real-world multiple sensors are coolected and combined for the sake of reliability and accuracy.

Figure 2. Dasarthy's Model

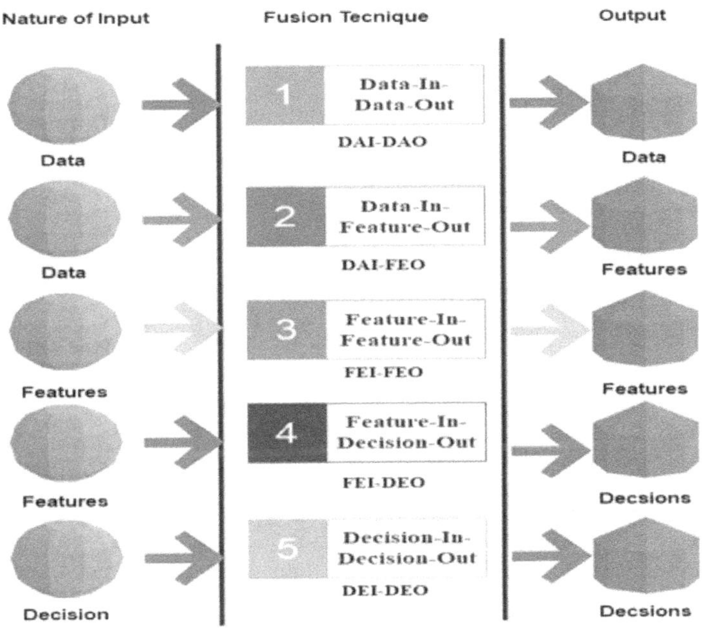

Omnibus Model for Data Fusion on the basis of levels of abstraction for the aggregated data

The Omnibus Model explains the data fusion methods in various states of data abstraction levels as follows (Smolinska et al., 2019):

a. **Sense and Process Level:** In this data fusion method the raw data from sensor level is gathered and fused together for a reliable and more complete input.

b. **Feature Extraction Level:** In this data fusion method the data whose nature is no raw but consists of features. Multiple features from multiple sources are fused for improved decision making.
c. **Decision-Making Level:** In this data fusion method the data which are decisions from multiple sources, are combined together for an accurate decision.
d. **Control Level:** In this data fusion method the data are the actions which is to be taken to output some definite and specific results.

The above discussed data fusion methods may be visualized in which Figure 3 depicts OODA(Observe, Orient, Decide, Act) loop which is a decision-making framework and starts from sensing data, extracting features, making decisions and finally taking required actions.

Figure 3. Omnibus Model

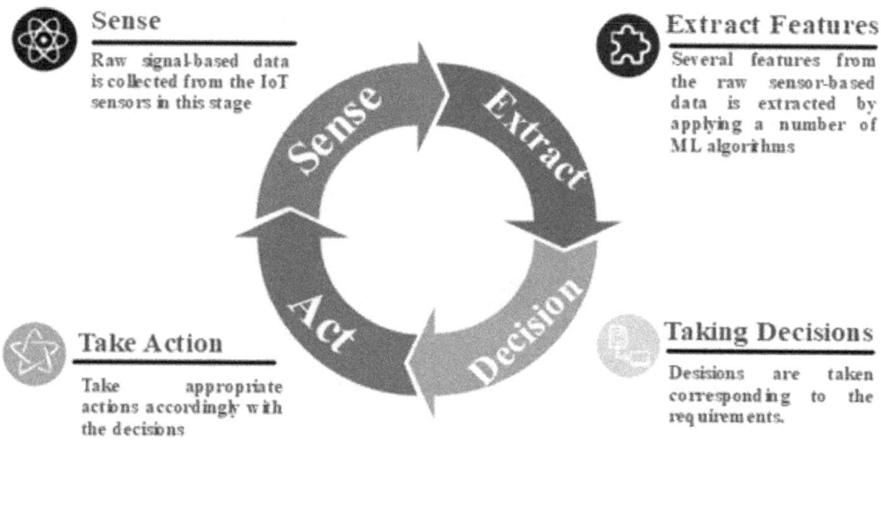

Observation-Based Model for Data Fusion on the Basis of Levels of Abstraction for the Aggregated Data

The Observation-based model (Smolinska et al., 2019) of data fusion, which too included various data-level abstraction for fused data may be described as follows:

a. **Low-Level Data Fusion:** In this data fusion method all the raw data and observations are combined into one single sample set in such a way that they are available to the targeted environment in a shared mode.

b. **Mid-Level Data Fusion:** Low-level data fusion has dimensionality issues, hindering data analytics deployment. Mid-level data fusion addresses these issues separately and helps in data regularization, addressing dimensionality issues before combining data.
c. **High-Level Data Fusion:** In this data fusion method, the prediction capability is intended to improve independently and then the resultant decisions are fused together.
d. **Multi-Level Data Fusion:** This data fusion method deals with fusing data from a number of sources while applying association and correlation technique in order to receive more refined object status and estimate patterns with timely analysis of situations, threats and significance.

The above discussed data fusion methods may be visualized as follows in Figure 4:

Figure 4. Various levels of Data Fusion

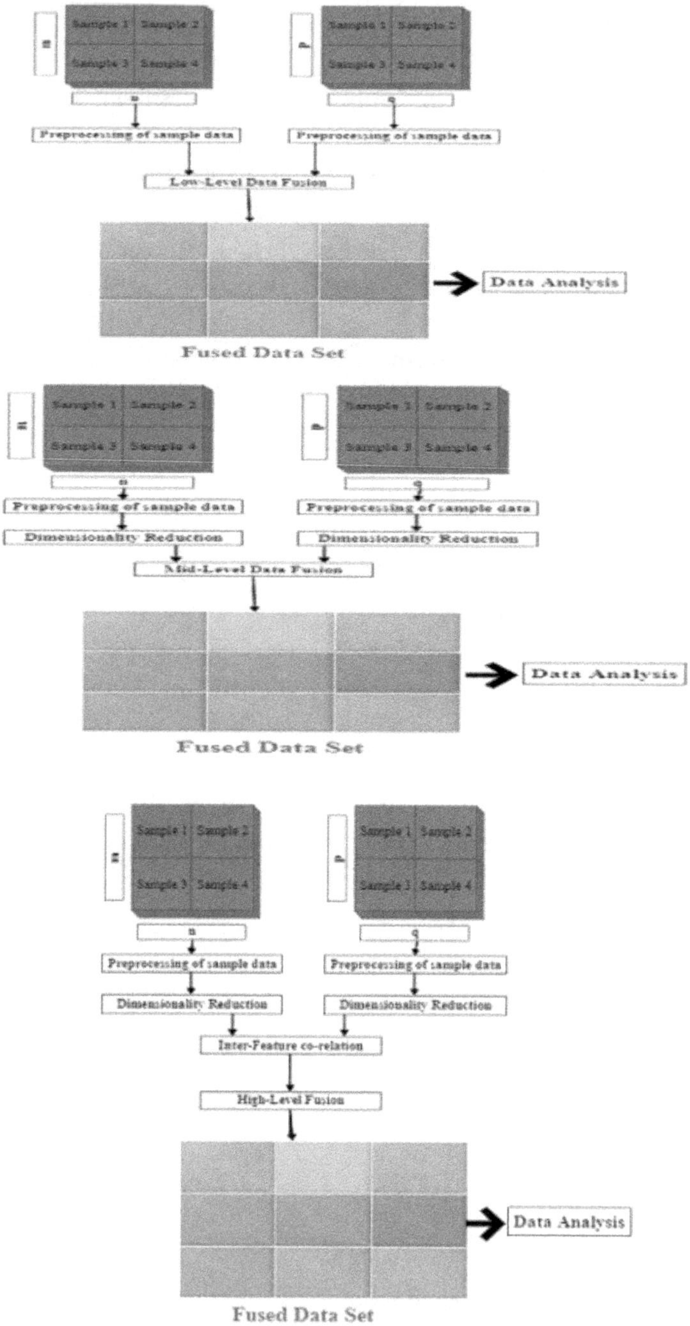

JDL Model for Data Fusion on the Basis of Various Data Fusion Levels

The JDL Model explains the data fusion methods in terms of data fusion levels as follows:

a. **Level 0(Source Preprocessing):** At this level the raw signal and pixel-based data is preprocessed by the corresponding sensor devices and then fused together for a purpose with less redundancy and complete data.
b. **Level 1(Object Refinement):** The fused sensor level data is delivered to this level as an input for further processing. The processing techniques that may be applied at this level include clustering, correlation, state estimation and feature combination. The raw data is transformed into some definite and consistent form at this level.
c. **Level 2(Situation Assessment):** At this level the data is input from the previous level which carries out the identification of similar situations over the observed values in order to detect and set up relationships and extract out inferences from the observed sample set.
d. **Level 3(Impact Assessment):** At this level perspectives about the data obtained from previous level is build up based upon the data impacts in order to identify potential risks, vulnerabilities and opportunities.
e. **Level 4(Process Refinement):** At this final level the improvisation of all the activities carried out with data from level 0 to level 3, is done in order to perform optimal resource management with balanced task scheduling and maximum utilization of available resources.

In below Figure 5, JDL data model has been illustrated which is used to process information from multiple sources to create a common understanding.

Figure 5. JDL Model

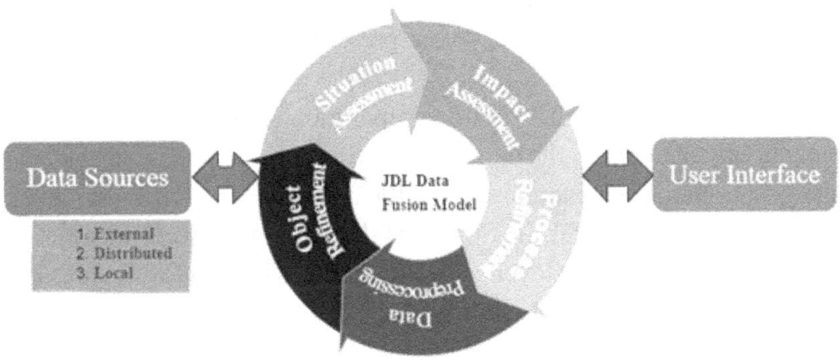

Luo and Kay Data Fusion Model

The Luo and Kay data fusion model (Luo et al., 2002)is a multi-sensor-based method for data integration. It involves combining data from multiple sources into internal fusion units, arranged hierarchically. This model differentiates between data integration and fusion, focusing on data integration for sub-task assistance and data fusion for collective action. Raw data is collected from sensors and transferred to fusion units, resulting in data fusion at various levels.

Figure 6. Luo and Kay Model

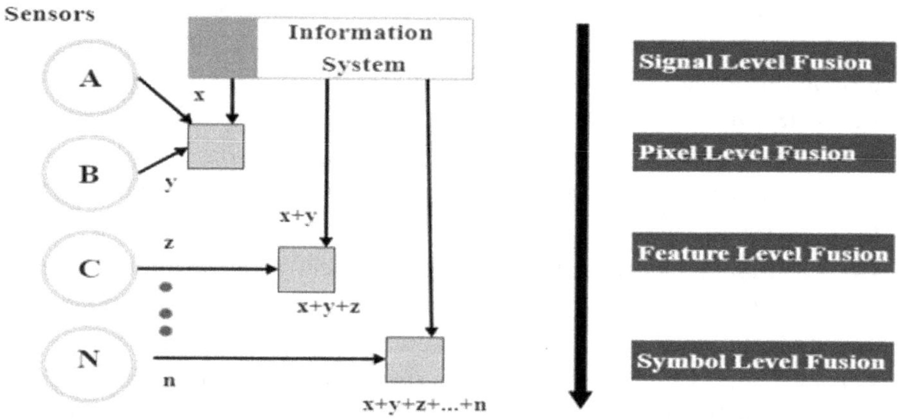

In this architecture, the data collected in sensor level is transmitted to the fusion centers for doing operation fusion process in hierarchical and sequentional manner. As the data combined in data centers in various methods, the data representation level are increased the raw data to the decision level. In this architecture, the data collected in sensor level is transmitted to the fusion centers for doing operation fusion process in hierarchical and sequentional manner. As the data combined in data centers in various methods, the data representation level are increased the raw data to the decision level. In this architecture, the data collected in sensor level is transmitted to the fusion centers for doing operation fusion process in hierarchical and sequentional manner. As the data combined in data centers in various methods, the data representation level are increased the raw data to the decision level.

In the above fusion model, in Figure 6, the data after every abstract level of fusion is combined for higher layers of fusion units. This kind of fusion procedure not only improves and effectively increases the result accuracy but also have better estimation and prediction results as compared to single source data results.

Thomopoulos Model for Data Fusion on the Basis of Data Integration

The Thomopoulos Model (Thomopoulos, 1990) explains the data fusion methods in terms of data integration as follows:

a. **Signal Level Data Fusion:** Due to the unavailability of any kind of mathematical model, data correlation is carried out at this level.
b. **Evidence Level Data Fusion:** In this data fusion method, different levels of inference are fused together on the basis of some statistical model like decision making or hypothesis testing.
c. **Dynamic Level Data Fusion:** At this level data fusion activity is carried out on the basis of some already available mathematical model.

These data fusion methods are used interchangeable according to the requirements of the targeted environment. The above discussed data fusion methods may be visualized as follows in below Figure 7:

Figure 7. Thomopoulos Model

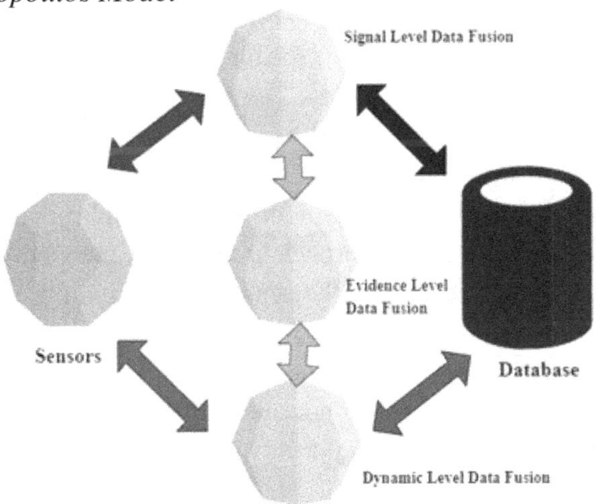

Data Fusion Model on the Basis of Architecture Type

The impact of the location where data fusion will occur have a significant influence over the estimations and accuracy of the results. The past researchers have proposed a model to carry out data fusion activity with respect to region or location. It may be visualized as follows using Figure 8(Dong et al., 2009):

Figure 8. Fusion Model on basis of Type of Architecture

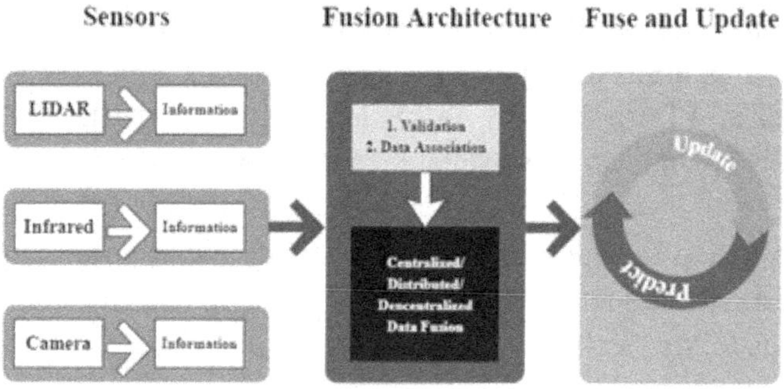

Therefore, on the basis of architecture, the data fusion model may be represented as follows:

a. **Centralized:** A centralized architecture involves a fusion unit at the central processor, responsible for receiving inputs from multiple sources and performing data fusion. However, this approach has a disadvantage of high bandwidth utilization for sending raw data to the central fusion node.
b. **Decentralized:** Decentralized architectures lack a central fusion unit, allowing multiple data fusion points. Local node-based information is merged with peer node output using Fisher and Shannon method of variable and state measurements. However, this method has a disadvantage of incurred total cost at each data fusion point.
c. **Distributed:** In distributed data fusion architecture, the sensor nodes are capable of performing state estimation and data association before the information is further sent to the fusion unit. Therefore, there exist both a local view of object's state by local node and also the global view of object's state through the fusion node.
d. **Hierarchical:** In hierarchical data fusion architecture, there is a combination of more than one architecture in order to improve the performance and data fusion process at each level.

2.3 Issues in Data Fusion

Before the selection of a specific data fusion approach for the targeted environment there are a variety of issues which needs to be resolved before data fusion activity is performed. These issues may be enlisted as follows (Handbook of Multisensor Data Fusion, 2017):

a. The presence of outliers and ambiguous records due to uncertain environments.
b. Confliction that occurs in the collected data due to collection based on behavior or situation based scenario.
c. Issue during data correlation may critically affect the data fusion procedures.
d. Building of facts from multiple data sources and its alignment is prone to error and should be continuously monitored before data fusion.
e. Association of collected data is another critical issue in data fusion due to availability of any specific knowledge of the source (sensor knowledge) of data being collected.

3 INTERNET OF THINGS AND DATA FUSION

The Internet of Things (IoT) technology generates massive amounts of data from millions of sensor-based devices, which can be analyzed and extracted in real-time. However, analyzing this data is a challenge due to the need for accurate and high-quality information. Data Fusion methods can help with this task by combining sensed data from multiple sources for a single target requirement. This enhances the quality and efficiency of extracted data compared to data from a single source. This helps in better planning, decision-making, and data analysis. In IoT environments like smart cities, data fusion becomes essential as millions of sensors start sensing and exchanging information. Fusion operations can be deployed at the cloud or local environment, depending on the requirements (Handbook of Multisensor Data Fusion, 2017).

3.1 Benefits of Using Data Fusion with IoT

The following points explain the various benefits of using Data Fusion Methods specifically for an IoT environment and how the IoT devices may get more enhanced in computing and processing the collected data with optimal resource utilization and high-end outputs:

a. The principle of data fusion of collecting data from multiple sources for some targeted action to be performed helps in making the data more use as an input, more computational intensive, accurate and reliable.
b. Data fusion methods can be used for sensors which have low power and hence lesser accuracy of collected data. The collection of data specifically from these kinds of sensors results in more accuracy as compared to that of collection of data from single sources.
c. Data Fusion help in big data analytics and identification of different and unique patterns and trends in extracted data.
d. Data Fusion helps in abstracting and hiding of sensitive information, which better take place during combination of data from multiple sources.

3.2 IoT Sensor Data: Lifecycle from Collection of Raw Data to Final Results using Data Fusion

IoT-based sensors collect real-world data from various sensors, such as humidity, temperature, pressure, movement, light, RFID, and IR sensors. These sensors have limitations in size, memory, storage, and computational capabilities. Common protocols used include ZigBee, Wi Fi, LTE/4G, and Bluetooth. These sensors work in real-time environments, collecting data and providing computed results, particularly in healthcare and industrial applications (Krishnamurthi et al., 2020).

Figure 9. IoT data Life Cycle

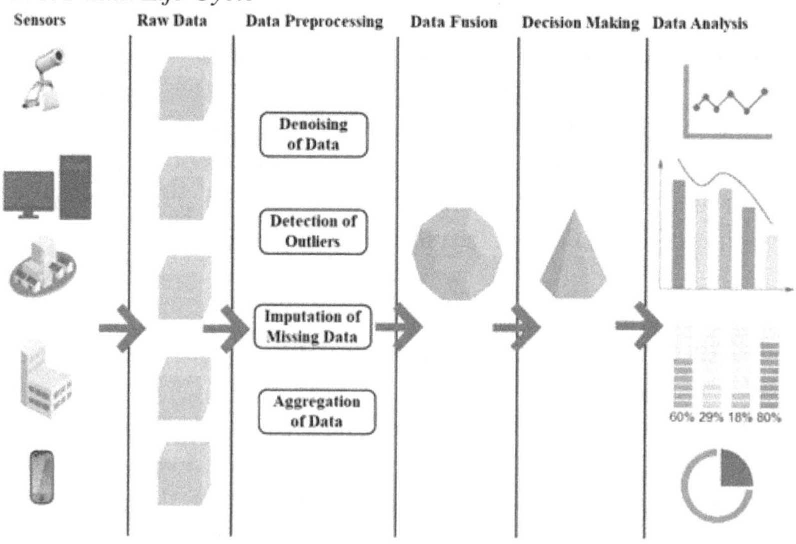

As illustrated above in Figure 9, the process of transforming raw data into specific results is challenging due to the various layers of IoT architecture. The data is processed and refined to remove redundancies, anomalies, and missing records, enabling effective decision-making and knowledge base building. Activities include denoising, detecting outliers, imputation of missing data, and aggregation before data fusion methods are applied. The output data is then sent for analysis at the surface layers of the IoT architecture (Krishnamurthi et al., 2020):

Denoising of Data

IoT sensor data is diverse due to the heterogeneity of sources and interference from multiple sensors. Noise significantly affects decision-making after computation, so data denoising is a procedure to remove any noise that has modified the data. Noise factors are unwanted signals that combine with original data signals, leading to modification and unusable processing. Wavelet transformation methods are used to handle this problem by preserving original data signals from noise by setting thresholds for noise signal coefficients and removing noise signals. Let $de(t) \in SP$ define the signal energy of data, which should validate the following constraint:

$$\|de\|^2 = \int_{-\infty}^{\infty} |de(t)|^2 dt < \infty \tag{1}$$

If $de(t)$ satisfies the constrained specified in eq 1, then it must belong to squares search space S^2SP. Through the wavelet transformation method, the data may be analyzed for presence of any noise at discrete time and energy intervals. Though this method, the signals characteristics may easily be analyzed using timeline scale focus methods.

Imputation of Missing Data

Missing data in IoT sensor data is crucial for processing, as it can significantly impact output results. Algorithms that use IoT sensor data often assume data is complete, leading to unreliable outputs. To prevent missing data, it is essential to identify reasons such as data packet loss, interference, and hardware issues. Missing data can be categorized into three classes: Missing Completely at Random (MCAR), Missing at Random (MCR), and Not Missing at Random (NMAR). Detecting missing patterns using Monotonous Missing Pattern (MMP) or Random Missing Pattern (RMP) approaches is the second step. A missing imputation model is then built to fill in missing values.

Detection of Outliers

Outlier datasets are those datasets which do not fall under the category of expected action or specific IoT environment. The presence of such outliers may lead to modifications and unreliable outputs. Thus, outliers must be removed before the data is sent for further analysis since it may very much affect the final results. There are a number of methods available for the purpose of outlier detection namely principal component analysis, majority voting and classifiers.

Data Aggregation

Data aggregation in the IoT environment involves collecting transformed data into summary-like forms for statistical analysis, predictions, and trend detection. This process consumes high energy and bandwidth resources, but aggregating techniques help reduce overutilization by reducing transmission junctions and network congestion. Three main approaches for data aggregation include Tree-Based Approach, Cluster-Based Approach, and Centralized Approach.

Data Fusion

Data Fusion involves combining sensor-based data from multiple sources for accuracy and consistency, reducing transformation costs and maximizing confidence in output. Benefits include quality, reliable results, increased data analysis, and measurement of hidden states. Methods include probabilistic methods like Inference methods, kalman filtering, maximum likelihood estimation, statistical methods like covariance and cross variance, and knowledge-based methods like genetic algorithms and artificial neural networks.

Data Analysis

This is the final step towards delivery of final results towards the user-end as a form of response of required service. There are various kinds of Data analysis methods which may be adapted as per requirements and adopted model in the IoT environment. These techniques include Cloud-Based Data Analysis, Fog-Based Data Analysis, Edge-Based Data Analysis and Semantic Data Analysis.

3.2 Data Fusion Techniques for IoT

A wide range of data fusion techniques are available, and the best method is expected to be applied for better results. Following are enlisted a number of issues which are present in an IoT environment (Al-khatib et al., 2019):

a. Presence of Wireless Sensor Networks (WSNs) distributed all across the network greatly affect the collection and fusion of sensor data from multiple sources.
b. A large number of anomalies and issues occur due to heterogeneity in IoT environment.
c. Non-Linear environmental Issues.
d. Selection of sensors for the sake of data fusion is a critical issue. More is the number of sensors; more it is likely to affect the final result. Also, the reliability of the sensor is an influential factor. The data generated by these sensors are in different formats with different sampling rate which also have a significant impact on result's reliability and accuracy.
e. Privacy preservation issues during perceiving of raw data from the real world.
f. Incurred cost for communicating and computing the results of data fusion is still an open issue.

Data Fusion Methods for Distributed WSNs

The Kalman Filter (KF) algorithm is a crucial tool for managing data generation, collection, and prediction in IoT networks due to their distributed nature and lack of centralized authority. It is effective in tracking, medical diagnosis, and surveillance. Energy efficiency is another important factor in IoT environments, which can be managed using hybrid approaches like Cuckoo Based Particle Algorithm (CBPA) or Generalized Particle Model Algorithm (GPMA). To address scalability issues in heterogeneous IoT environments, data fusion algorithms should provide accurate results (Nakamura et al., 2007).

a. **Channel Filter based Data Fusion:** In this data fusion approach each channel has its own transmitting and receiving agents and they deal with only first order redundant data. The work of redundant data removal is done by the transmitting agent. Its equation may be represented as follows:

$$dfp(x) = \frac{dfp_1(x)\, dfp_2(x) / \overline{dfp}(x)}{\int dfp_1(x)\, dfp_2(x) / \overline{dfp}(x)\, dx} \tag{2}$$

where $dfp_1(x)$ and $dfp_2(x)$ are density fusion probability functions and $\overline{dfp}(x)$ is the density function for previously received data by the receiving agent. This is a highly effective algorithm since here is no need to keep large history logs of data while one main drawback is that the dependent information also gets removed during the removal of redundant information.

b. **Naïve Bayes Based Data Fusion:** This data fusion algorithm combats the drawback of Channel Filter based data fusion by keeping the dependent information during fusion. It can be represented as follows:

$$dfp(x) = \frac{dfp_1(x)\, dfp_2(x)}{\int dfp_1(x) dfp_2(x) dx} \tag{3}$$

However, this is an unreliable algorithm since it does not maintain any back history logs of data due to which over-confidence in data may occur.

c. **Chernoff Based Data Fusion:** When dependency within the data set is not known, this algorithm may be used to integrate the data in a log linear fashion. It can be represented as follows:

$$dfp(x) = \frac{dfp_1^p(x)\, dfp_2^{1-p}(x)}{\int dfp_1(x)\, dfp_2(x) / \overline{dfp}(x)\, dx} \text{ here} \in \left[0,1\right] \tag{4}$$

One main disadvantage of this algorithm is hat is computationally very expensive in terms of combining data in a linear fashion.

Data Fusion Methods for Non-Linearity in IoT Environment

Non-linear IoT environments can lead to issues in predictions and classifications due to multiple sensors. To address these issues, optimization algorithms can be used based on sensor needs and channel status. These algorithms check channel status to determine total power allocation for each sensor, ensuring sustainable power assignment. Semi-Definite Program (SOP) algorithms reduce RMSE values and ensure low biased values. Extended Kalman Filter (EKF) is another effective algorithm for tracking non-linear issues in IoT environments, but faces issues like Jacobean Matrix. Unscented Linear Fractional Transformation (LFT) can handle non-linear issues through Bayesian Approach (Al-khatib, Balfaqih and Khelil, 2019).

3.3 Motion-Based Real world Use Case for Data Fusion in IoT

The real-world example of human movement is captured using multiple sensors, including pedometers and e-compasses. The pedometer captures all types of human movement by wearing it in the arm, while the e-compass combines 3D gyroscope, accelerometer, and magnetometer to capture rotational, acceleration, and magnetic field variables. When combined, these sensors provide accurate and high-quality results about the human body's function (Bishop, 2006).

Figure 10. Motion-based Use case for Data Fusion

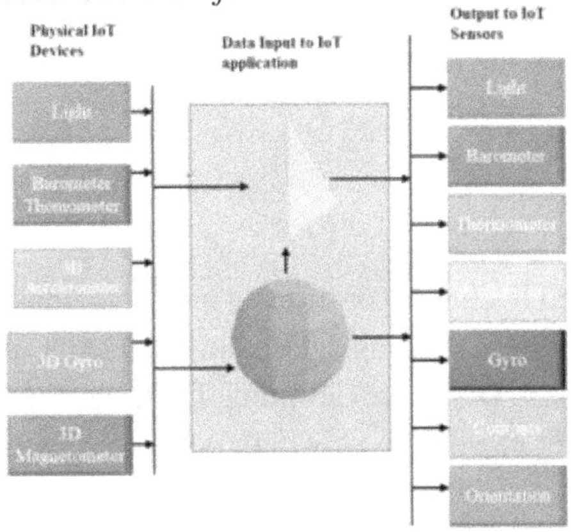

As illustrated above in Figure 10, the sensor-based fusion of the mention above three sensors is done using Freescale 32-bit MCU which provide effective processing over streaming data. The results can easily be seen over laptops, smartphones and tablets supporting Windows 8 OS. The sensor fusion processing requirement includes 10-12 MIPS (Million Instructions Per Second) with additional coprocessors for effectiveness and robustness.

4 MACHINE LEARNING AND DATA FUSION

Machine Learning is a subset of Artificial Intelligence that enables systems to learn from a sample dataset without programming. It aims to acquire knowledge and skills without human intervention, solving problems like classification, prediction, and analysis. Data is the most crucial component of Machine Learning, acting as input for models to train. ML methods can be supervised, unsupervised, or semi-supervised. Various algorithms can be deployed for data fusion, including computing algorithms for collecting raw data from IoT sensors and producing analytical results (Nakamura, 2007). ML algorithms involve three activities for data fusion: smoothing, filtering, and prediction state estimation. Smoothing uses static or dynamic measurements like GPS positioning, filtering uses past and current observations to determine variable state, and prediction state estimation is used for analysis (Luo and Kay, 1989).

4.1 Machine Learning Algorithms for Data Fusion

In machine learning, there are a number of algorithms which may be used for the purpose of data fusion. Each ML algorithm is suited to tackle one specific problem as per requirement. Following are various kinds of ML algorithm that may be used for data fusion (Bishop, 2006).

K-Nearest Neighbors

This algorithm is used to classify or detect a new data point which is closest to a set of given K data points in the training dataset. In order to car you this identification of new data point Euclidean Distance, Hamming Distance or Mahalanobis Distance method may be used. Let dp_n be the new data point to be found within a set of K nearest neighbors that is $N_K(dp_n)$, predicted labeled class C, and a class variable x. Let 1(.) denote the indicator function where it is true if the given condition is true and vice versa. Thus, the function may be modeled as following:

$$pr(x = c|dp_n, K) = \frac{1}{K}\sum_{i \in N_K(dp_n)} 1(x_i = c)$$

$$C = \underset{c}{\operatorname{argmax}} pr(x = c|dp_n, K) \quad (5)$$

KNN store the whole training dataset first before doing any operation over it. This method is used t make predictions on the basis of common behavior which exists between the input data and training samples. However, this algorithm is accurate and fit for small datasets while its performance decrease when applied upon larger datasets.

Naïve Bayes

This algorithm comes under the class of probabilistic classifier and is used to detect and uncover an unseen data point by the use of Bayes' theorem. It uses "naïve" assumptions about the independence of the features for the unseen data point or a class variable *c*. The following may be formulated using Bayes' theorem for the unseen data point dp_n:

$$pr(x = c|dp_1, dp_2, \ldots, dp_n) = \frac{pr(dp_1, dp_2, \ldots, dp_n|x = c)pr(x = c)}{pr(dp_1, dp_2, \ldots, dp_n)} \tag{6}$$

Now upon eq 3 the naïve assumptions will be applied which will give the following:

$$pr(x = c|dp_1, dp_2, \ldots, dp_n) \propto pr(x = c)\prod_{i=1}^{n} pr(dp_i|x = c) \tag{7}$$

Finally, the whole task may be modeled as following:

$$C = \underset{c}{\operatorname{argmax}} pr(x = c)\prod_{i=1}^{n} pr(dp_i|x = c) \tag{8}$$

This algorithm is fast, dynamic and scalable and is used for making predictions through learning. It uses a small set of data points to learn and acquire knowledge. This training set contains high-dimensional data points and may be used for fields like spam filtering, text categorization and automated activities.

Support Vector Machine

This is another classification algorithm, under non-probabilistic classifier class. These are binary classifiers whose aim is to detect the hyperplane which divides two classes of a given training sample set into two disjoint classes with maximum margin. Complex data transformations are performed by this algorithm for the purpose of class separation of data. The aim of this algorithm is to select an appropriate hyperplane with the greatest margin so that maximum accuracy is received during classification. Let $£_i$ be a variable used for outlier detection, *v* be a normal vector, for each training point t_i, which is used to find out the distance by which violation occurs for every |z| units. This is a constrained optimization problem which may be formulated as follows:

$$\underset{z, £_i, v}{minimize} f(z, £_i, v) = \frac{1}{2}z^T z + X\sum_{i=1}^{n} £_i \tag{9}$$

s.t. $C_i(z^T dp_i + v) - 1 + £_i \geq 0 \; i = 1,2,3,\ldots,n$

where $X \geq 0$ determines the intensity of penalty. The accuracy of SVM algorithm is better with small training sets which may exponentially be increased by considering the subset of more training points. SVM is better used for text categorization, image analysis and digital content detection and recognition.

Linear Regression

Let $f(dp_n, z)$ be the learning function whose mapping may be defined as $f: \varnothing(dp_n) \rightarrow C_i$, where : $\varnothing(dp_n)$ is a basic function. The function $f(dp_n, z)$ may be represented as:

$$f(dp_n, z) = \varnothing(dp_n)^T z \tag{10}$$

There are a number of basic functions like sigmoidal function, Polynomial function, Gaussian function etc, which may be used for the purpose. In order to train the model using Linear Regression method one my use Ordinary Least Square, Regularized Least Square Method, Least-Mean-Squares or Bayesian Method.

Classification and Regression Trees

The model uses both classification and regression methods. The whole set of input space is partitioned into a number of cuboid regions say Reg_k and these regions are exposed to either classification or regression procedures as per requirement in order to label the data points. In order to uncover an unseen data point (dp_n), the corresponding target label may be predicted by traversal of binary tree for the corresponding decision. The whole procedure may be modeled as following:

$$pr(x = ck) = \frac{1}{|Reg_k|} \sum_{i \in Reg_k} 1(x_i = c)$$

$$C = \underset{c}{\text{argmax}} pr(x_i = c|x) = \underset{c}{\text{argmax}} pr(x_i = c|k) \tag{11}$$

One main benefit of this algorithm is efficient and fast training, easy interpretability due to its binary tree-like structure. Although the output is sensitive to the type of training data used for learning the model therefore the leaning procedure must be carried out carefully. Secondly, since each region of the dataset falls under one label only therefore this algorithm fails to smoothly label the data points (Meng et al., 2020).

Principal Component Analysis (PCA)

As the name suggest, there s a principal subspace P over which the training data points are projected orthogonally and linearly so that maximal covariance is achieved. The purpose is to find an orthonormal set S on the basis of D-Dimensional vectors $\{z_j\}$, which will then be projected over the linear subspace making a set of corresponding orthogonal linear data points $\{z_{proj}\}$ such that the average reconstruction error may be calculated as follows:

$$E = \frac{1}{N}\sum_n \left\|\overline{dp_n} - dp_n\right\|^2$$

$$\overline{dp_n} = \sum_{j=1}^{S} z_{proj} z_j + \overline{dp} \quad (12)$$

where $\overline{dp}$ is the total average of all the data points available in the considered dataset. This algorithm is one of the finest preprocessing techniques under machine learning. Various applications of this algorithm include face recognition, data compression, visualization and medical diagnosis.

4.2 Criteria to select an ML Algorithm for Data Fusion

The following parameters should be kept in mind before selecting a particular machine learning algorithm for the purpose of data fusion (Valente et al., 2019):

a. **Efficiency:** This parameter is used to analyze the efficient use of available resources while integrating the sensor-based data besides deployment at any level. It is critical to find out the total efficiency of any method in IoT environment due to constrained availability of resources, bandwidth and storage. The aim is to carry out data fusion with minimal cost and optimal use of resources and in lesser time.
b. **Quality:** This parameter is used to analyze the improvement in accuracy of the result after the deployment of a fusion method. There should be some measurement metric to inspect the data fusion quality. The factor takes the Root Mean Square Error (RMSE) method in order to measure the quality.

$$RMSE = \sqrt{\frac{\sum_{i=1}^{D_1} \ldots \sum_{j=1}^{D_k} \left[Res(d_i, \ldots d_j) - df(d_i, \ldots d_j)^2\right]}{D_1, D_2, \ldots D_k}} \quad (13)$$

where $D_1, D_2, \ldots, D_k$ are k dimensions of the considered dataset sample, *Res* and *df* signify the ideal and fusion results. If the resultant value is smaller than it indicated a better data fusion quality otherwise vice versa.

c. **Stability:** This parameter indicates the capability and stiffness of an algorithm to keep working in equal good manner, no matter in what situation or environment it is being deployed. A stable model ensures high performance and accuracy of the results. A stable model promises low maintenance and cost.
d. **Extensibility:** This parameter indicates the capability of the model to enhance its scope for carrying out targeted tasks and improved results with increased adoption in heterogeneous environment. This is a critical factor to achieve practically for better deployment of fusion model in real-world scenario.
e. **Privacy:** There are scenarios where private and non-accessible datasets are used for data fusion; there occur various security factors which should be considered before fusion of data since it may lead to insecurity and data loss. The data to be fused should use cryptographic techniques beforehand (Luo and Kay, 1989).

4.3 Use Case: Data Fusion for Smart Hospital and Healthcare

Healthcare data generation is rapidly increasing, necessitating the use of data fusion methods and machine learning techniques to obtain accurate information for patient care (Luo & Kay, 1989). This involves collecting patient data from various healthcare units, such as doctors, nutritionists, therapists, and counselors, and processing it for analysis. This data aids clinical officials in making more accurate decisions, predicting emergencies, and improving life quality (Pillai et al., 2021).

Figure 11. ML-Based Use Case for Data Fusion

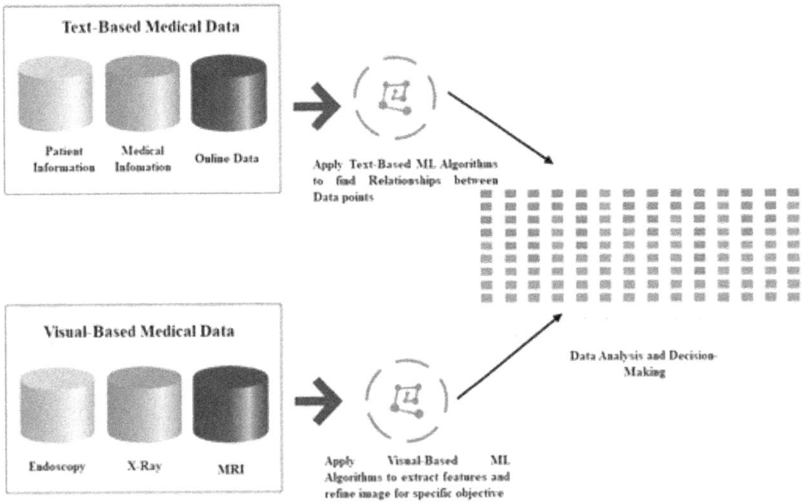

Above Figure 11 illustrate an ML model for medical data analysis which focuses on both textual and visual data in order to extract insights, identify relationships and support decision-making. There are various stages through which this medical raw data goes through before final decision is made. The following describes the data processing stages (Castanedo, 2013):

a. **Data Integration:** The raw patient data life diagnostic reports, general tests, symptomatic data and other information is integrated into one whole dataset.
b. **Redundancy Removal:** Duplicate data and Redundant medical information like common parameters, images and suggestions are removed to deliver a clean and consistent dataset.
c. **Data Aggregation:** Data is aggregated or collected from multiple sources and is presented to the next stage in a summarized format.
d. **Data Estimation:** This is done in order to receive and evaluate the best value for a test or parameter which will lead to better treatment option and decision making.
e. **Data Fusion:** Various machine learning techniques like naïve bayes, logistic regression, svm or random forests will be applied to the dataset in order to carry out data fusion at various levels.

Advanced healthcare techniques are crucial for improving first-time treatments and patient quality of life. A sustainable model using machine learning can help clinical officials explore treatment options for patients with multiple serious and chronic diseases, predict mortality and recovery rates (Blasch et al., 2018).

5 OTHER DATA FUSION METHODS

In an IoT environment, traditional and hybrid data association and fusion techniques are available for object tracking and non-linear data analysis. These techniques are crucial for identifying and collating with specific targets in ambiguous and multi-target sensor environments. Probabilistic, inference-based, covariance-based, estimation-based, and other fusion techniques are best suited for scalability and performance (Valente et al., 2019).

5.1 Probabilistic Data Association Technique (PDA)

Bar-shalom and Tse proposed a data fusion method, a single-tracking approach where each instant hypothesis is correlated with a specific probability based on a target's fitted measurement. The fitted measurement is verified under a validation criterion, which stores estimated observations for a specific target and selects a set of measurements. This may be represented as:

$$\sigma \geq (X(t) - \hat{x}(t|t-1))^T Icov^{-1}(t)(x(t) - x(t|t-1)) \tag{14}$$

where Ti is the Temporal Index, $Icov(t)$ defines the covariance gain and σ is validation criterion factor. All the observation that may fall under fitted measurement repository under t instant of time may be given as:

$$X(t) = x_i(t), i = 1,2,3,\ldots..,n_t \tag{15}$$

where, $x_t(t)$ is the $i\text{-}th$ observation which falls under the validation criterion at t instant of time. Next the observation state may be predicted as follows:

$$\hat{y}(tt-1) = M(t-1)\hat{y}(t-1t-1) \tag{16}$$

where, $M(t\text{–}1)$ is the transition matrix for $t\text{–}1$ instant of time. Next the estimation for the observations under fitted measurement may be formulated as:

$$\hat{x}(tt-1) = L(t)\hat{x}(tt-1) \tag{17}$$

where, $L(t)$ indicates linearization measurement matrix. Now, in order to compute the innovation for *i-th* observation, the following should be considered:

$$s_i(t) = x_i(t) - \hat{x}(tt - 1) \tag{18}$$

The covariance prediction may be calculated as follows:

$$\widehat{Pr}(tt - 1) = M(t - 1)\widehat{Pr}(t - 1t - 1)M(t - 1)^T + Ncov(t) \tag{19}$$

where, *Ncov* is the noise covariance matrix. Next, in order to compute the Innovation covariance *(Icov)* and Kalman Gain(*Ti*) the following is formulated:

$$Ncov(t) = L(t)\,\widehat{Pr}(tt - 1)L(t)^T$$

$$Ti(t) = \widehat{Pr}(tt - 1)L(t)^T Icov(t)^{-1} \tag{20}$$

If in the cluttered environment, the data I generated from known targets, then the covariance may be updated as follows:

$$Pr^0(tt) = \widehat{Pr}(tt - 1) - Ti(t)Icov(t)\,Ti(t)^T \tag{21}$$

Finally, the total covariance may be updated as follows:

$$s(t) = \sum_{i=0}^{n_t} \partial_i(t)\, s_i(t)$$

$$\Pr(t) = Ti(t)\left[\sum_{i=0}^{n_t} \left(\partial_i(t)\, s_i(t)\, \partial_i(t)^T - s(t)\, s(t)^T\right)\right] Ti(t)^T \tag{22}$$

Finally, the association probability may be calculated as follows:

$$\partial_i(t) = \frac{pr_i(t)}{\sum_{i=0}^{n_t} pr_i(t)},$$

where

$$pr_i(t) = \begin{cases} \dfrac{(2\pi)^{n/2} d \sqrt{|Icov_i(t)|}\,(Pr_d Pr_g)}{Pr_d} & if\, i = 0 \\ exp\left[-\frac{1}{2} s^T(t) Icov(k) s(t)\right] & if\, i \neq 0 \\ 0 & other\ cases \end{cases} \tag{23}$$

where, n is the dimension of measurement vector, *d* is the density of cluttered IoT environment, Pr_d is the detection probability and Pr_g I the validation probability.

5.2 Joint Probabilistic Data Association Technique (JPDA)

This algorithm tracks multiple targets, unlike the PDA technique, which considers all observations without validation criteria. It calculates pairs of hypotheses for each observation and track in a cluttered environment by normalizing a sum of conditional probabilities for each associated track. For each known association probability, the Kalman Filter updation may be formulated as:

$$\hat{y}^{Tar}(tt) = \hat{y}^{Tar}(tt-1) + Ti(t)\,\hat{s}^{Tar}(t) \tag{24}$$

where $\hat{y}^{Tar}(tt)$ *and* $\hat{y}^{Tar}(tt-1)$ are estimation and prediction for target *t* and $Ti(t)$ is the filter gain. Next, the weighted sum of all the residual observation which are outside the fitted measurements may be calculated as:

$$\hat{s}^{Tar}(t) = \sum_{i=1}^{n_t} \partial_i^{Tar}(t)\, s_i^{Tar}(t) \tag{25}$$

The JPDA technique includes all the observations even those that does not clarify the validation criterion, in order to update the data using posterior probability method which calculates the weighted sum of all residual observations.

5.3 Fuzzy Logic

The data fusion method involves four phases: fuzzification, evaluation of inference rules, combination of data or observations, and defuzzification. It focuses on determining observations from imprecise data and environments. Inference rules, consisting of operators and conditions, are applied to the fuzzified input.

Table.

$ab \rightarrow ba$	Rule 1
$a \rightarrow b = \min\{1, 1-a+b\}$	Rule 2
$a \rightarrow b = \min\{a,b\}$	Rule 3
$a \rightarrow b = \begin{cases} 1 \; if\, a \leq b \\ 0 \; otherwise \end{cases}$	Rule 4

continued on following page

Table. Continued

$a \to b = \begin{cases} 1 \ if\, a \le b \\ b \ otherwise \end{cases}$	Rule 5
$a \to b = \begin{cases} 1 & if\, a \le b \\ a/b & otherwise \end{cases}$	Rule 6
$a \to b = \max\{1-a, b\}$	Rule 7
$a \to b = 1-a+ab$	Rule 8

The fuzzy logic method is a computational method that efficiently combines data in a cluttered environment, handles uncertain and inconsistent data, and minimizes energy consumption during data sensor data generation, making it an effective solution for various applications.

5.5 Kalman Filter (KF)

It is a data fusion technique based on estimation principles. For any discrete time state *ob* the space-time model by Kalman filter may be represented as:

$$ob(t+1) = \varnothing(t)ob(t) + I(t)p(t) + q(t) \tag{26}$$

The total numbers of observations *m* for the particular object state *ob* at time *t* may be given as follows:

$$m(t) = L(t)ob(t) + r(t) \tag{27}$$

where $\varnothing(t)$ is object state transition matrix, $I(t)$ is input transition matrix, $p(t)$ indicates the input vector, $L(t)$ signifies measurement matrix and *r* and *q* are random variables with zero mean and covariance matrices $E(t)$ and $F(t)$. the estimation model may be represented as following:

$$\widehat{ob}(t) = \widehat{ob}(t|t+1) + Ti(t)\left[m(t) - L(t)\widehat{ob}(t|t-1)\right]$$

$$\widehat{ob}(t+1|t) = \varnothing(t)\widehat{ob}(t|t) + I(t)p(t) \tag{28}$$

The technique of low-level data fusion, known as Extended Kalman Filter (EKF), is an effective method with low energy and cost usage. However, it has been criticized for computational costs, data linearization, and potential errors or faults, which can lead to inconsistent and unstable results.

6 INTRODUCTION TO EDGE INTELLIGENCE FOR DATA FUSION

IoT devices generate large amounts of data per second, making offloading to distant cloud data centers impractical. Edge Computing, a new technology integrating AI and ML methodologies, can manage this by allowing efficient data processing near the network's edge without offloading entirely to the cloud. Edge Intelligence improves prediction and estimation results, making edge servers more efficient in managing and transforming data (Jinan and Raveendran, 2016). Data fusion methods are crucial for real-time processing of IoT data, combining data from multiple sources for enhanced accuracy and confidence. In healthcare, a hierarchical architecture is needed to analyze patient conditions through diagnostic parameters and determine correlations, enhancing system performance and delivering better results (Blasch et al., 2018).

6.1 Benefits of Edge computing with Data Fusion Blended with AI

There are a number of benefits of using data fusion techniques with AI approaches at the edge of the network. They are enlisted as following:

a. **Latency:** Latency refers to the time spent by AI techniques in applying inference rules, preprocessing, fusing, offloading, and delivering final results. In IoT applications, processing data at the network edge improves real-time estimations and predictions.
b. **Energy:** The data fusion technique combined with AI at the edge can significantly reduce energy consumption in various activities, including inference and computation, by processing raw data at the edge and receiving computed data with minimal battery power.
c. **Privacy:** Microsoft proposed Cyrptonets to enhance data privacy by allowing encrypted transmission of sensitive and confidential information at the network edge. This ensures data remains secure and confidential at the cloud, as the cloud cannot process the encrypted data.
d. **Security:** The data that needs to travel miles to be transformed by a user is highly susceptible to attack within the propagation channel. However, processing near the network edge reduces the opportunities for malicious attackers to access and modify the data.
e. **Cost:** Sensor data processing at the edge reduces total cost, with SoC (System-on-chips) reducing costs over time. This enhanced capability, combined with data fusion and AI techniques, makes these hardware intermediaries better for cloud co-ordination than semiconductors.

6.2 DFIG-based AI-MEC model Data Fusion Methods

The Data Fusion Information Group (DFIG) model is a multilevel fusion model that supports diverse sensors and AI techniques, working with real-time data streams and applying appropriate actions using AI methods (Kenda et al., 2019). Following are various levels of DFIG:

a. **Data Assessment (DA) [Level 0]:** This level deals with low level data fusion and provides predictions for signal level data on the basis of pixel/signal level association of data.
b. **Object Assessment (OA) [Level 1]:** This level provides predictions for both state and object based upon the kind of association of data.
c. **Situation Assessment (SA) [Level 2]:** This level provides predictions for the kind of relations that exists between the data or objects.
d. **Impact Assessment (IA) [Level 3]:** This level provides predictions for the impact of actions taken upon the objects and data.
e. **Project Refinement (PR) [Level 4]:** This level provides predictions over the estimated action to be taken upon the data by the participants.
f. **User Refinement (UR) [Level 5]:** This level is known to manage the access over elements and display of data based upon decision-making and human-computer interactions.
g. **Mission Management (MM) [Level 6]:** This level carries out management of spatial-temporal data, routing and decision-making on a number of various constraints.

Data fusion can occur at any IoT, edge, or distant cloud region in a three-tier architecture, enabling AI techniques deployment at each level. It can occur at low, mid, or high levels. In DFIG, low-level fusion involves singular data like kinematics, numerical, and locations, while mid-level fusion involves processed data and objects, and high-level fusion deals with symbolic data like missions and threats. AI techniques can be deployed at each level. In below Figure 12, a multi-level architecture for data fusion in IoT has been proposed for integrating human interaction and leveraging machine knowledge.

Figure 12. DFIG-Based Data Fusion

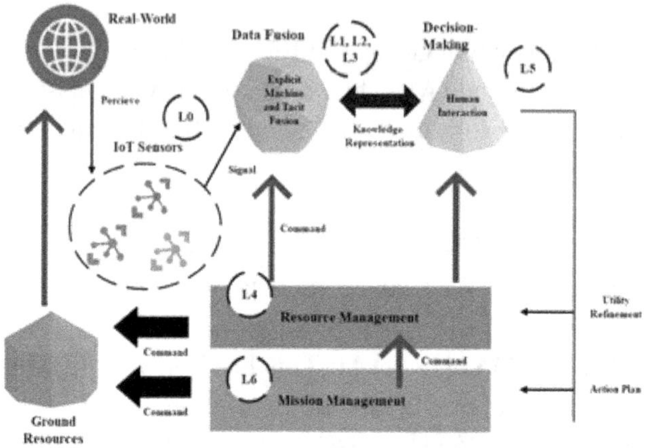

The study explores the application of various types of Artificial Intelligence (AI) at different levels of the DFIG model and fusion methods, focusing on the use of different AI techniques in IoT-based smart healthcare systems.

a. **Type A- Reactive Machines:** Type A AI techniques, while capable of analyzing history logs, lack the ability to store past data and make decisions, only serving as responders for limited actions.
b. **Type B- Limited Memory:** With the capabilities of Type A AI techniques, this technique is capable of making decision on a set of inputs provided with limited memory. For example, Virtual Assistants and Chatbots.
c. **Type C- Theory of Mind:** AI techniques can create prediction models based on discrete observations like beliefs and emotions, enabling the creation of intelligent machines and robots.
d. **Type D- Self Awareness:** This AI technique is an extended version of Type C AI which provides capability of consciousness to one self. It is capable of predicting feelings and emotion on the basis of social interactions.

Type A AI techniques can be implemented at the L0 level for low-level data fusion, Type B for mid-level data fusion at the L1 level, Type C for high-level data fusion at L2 and L3, and Type D for the remaining levels. Machine Learning techniques dominate Artificial Intelligence techniques, and each ML technique can handle different types of AI techniques (Mujica et al., 2018) .Various ML techniques may be explained as follows:

a. **Symbolic Technique:** These techniques are based upon first order inference rules and logic. This technique may be used for implementing logical reasoning methods over data. However, failure of these logical system may lead to heavy loss and complexities.
b. **Probabilistic Technique:** These techniques are based upon graphical and Bayesian models. It is popularly known as Statistical Relational Learning Approach (SRL), which is a combination of Bayesian method and first-order logical inference rules.
c. **Connectionist Technique:** This technique works upon the working of biological human brain. Examples include Artificial Neural Networks (ANN), Convolutional Neural Network (CNN), Long Short-Term Memory (LSTM) and Reinforcement Learning (RL). Applications of this technique include facial and speech recognition.
d. **Analogistic Technique:** This technique works by the analysis of data analogies by distance computation method. Examples include K-Nearest Neighbor (KNN), Support Vector Machines (SVM) .

6.3 Use Case: Smart Healthcare with Edge Intelligence

Automated procedures in healthcare systems are crucial for providing quality life to patients and accelerating diagnosis and treatment processes. A three-tier architecture can benefit the healthcare system by minimizing delay and energy consumption, enabling time-intensive medical activities like emergency vehicles and patient management(Ahmad et al., 2020). At the lowest level, basic patient data is collected using sensors, which is combined with real-time data and static background information. This data is then used by clinical officials to analyze disease patterns, epidemics, cures, and diagnosis options. At the higher level, this data is fused for decision-making by hospital staff to detect disease outbreaks and allocate resources accordingly. Inter-hospital reports provide real-time views of disease graphs, recovery rates, death rates, and mortality. This use-case is particularly effective during pandemics and epidemic situations like COVID-19.(Messaoud et al., 2020).

7 OPEN ISSUES AND FUTURE RESEARCH DIRECTIONS

7.1 Low Workload Based ML Methods

The IoT environment generates a significant amount of data that current Machine Learning approaches struggle to handle. However, blending large unclassified datasets with small classified datasets can improve results. Low workload imposing

ML approaches could be designed to sustainably manage large volumes of data and provide better results (Saranya and Fatima, 2020).

7.2 Using Distributed Machine Leaning Approach

Real-time IoT data, containing millions of GBs, presents challenges such as heterogeneity, bandwidth allocation, resource scarcity, and differing workloads and processing capabilities. Therefore, high-computation intensive machine learning approaches are needed to extract useful data and solve complex problems in real-time, overcoming existing limitations.

7.3 Using Federated Machine Learning

Traditional centralized architectures face issues like scalability, high bandwidth consumption, latency, and computation costs. To achieve optimal QoS, the environment should be transformed into a distributed format. Federated Leaning can enhance machine learning by focusing on local procedures and data deployment, reducing communication and computational overheads.

7.4 Machine Learning for Edge Computing

The Internet-of-Things environment has posed some critical challenges like delay and context awareness for real-time scenarios. In order to combat these challenges, edge computing ha been proposed which provides promising solutions for reducing total delay caused and making ML approaches more effective for transformation of raw data into useful forms.

7.5 Privacy and Security

Using Machine Learning Approaches for IoT may be prone for privacy and security attacks when doing data refinement, analysis ad classification. A low workload ML approach may help to combat privacy and security concerns (Mahdavinejad et al., 2017).

8 CONCLUSION

The Internet of Things has become one of the most flourishing technological concept of the present time. In order to realize its full potential it is expected to become capable of transforming and utilizing raw sensor-based data into the most useful form. In order to receive accuracy in the perceived data, a number of data fusion methods are being deployed with IoT workflows and applications which benefits with high quality and reliable results. However, some critical challenges which IoT data face is mostly due to its heterogeneous behavior. Heterogeneity may be seen in the kinds of deployed physical devices, and the type of data generated by these millions and billions o sensors and smart devices. Many data fusion algorithms have been proposed in the pas to manage this issue with reliable results which includes a number of probabilistic, estimation, mathematical based traditional data fusion methods.

Machine Learning Data fusion techniques have been turned out to be a catalyst in enhancing the performance of various IoT application using data fusion methods. These techniques are basically used or the sake of data refinement and focusing upon the relationships that exists between data points in the sample data sets. ML approaches include both supervised as well as unsupervised learning model and deep learning models which may be used for data fusion from clustering, classification and regression of data.

Lastly, in this paper a theoretical idea for building Intelligent Edge servers has been described. These intelligent edge servers may be used for smart data fusion. Using a three-tier approach including edge computing will help the data fusion under low latency, cost,, computation and power consumption constrains. The paper focuses upon a large number of methods which may be used for fusing raw sensor data and to transform It in the most useful form.

REFERENCES

Ahmad, S., & Afzal, M. M. (2020). Deployment of fog and edge computing in IoT for cyber-physical infrastructures in the 5G era. In Sustainable communication networks and application: ICSCN 2019 (pp. 351-359). Springer International Publishing.

Ahmad, S., Alharbi, A., Zamani, A., & Yousufuddin, M. (2020). Implementation of fusion and filtering techniques in IoT data processing: A case study of smart healthcare. [IJCSNS]. *International Journal of Computer Science and Network Security*, *20*(12), 131–137.

Al-khatib, A., Balfaqih, M., & Khelil, A. (2019). A survey on outlier detection in Internet of Things big data. In *Big Data-Enabled Internet of Things* (pp. 225–272). DOI: 10.1049/PBPC025E_ch11

Alam, F., Mehmood, R., Katib, I., Albogami, N., & Albeshri, A. (2017). Data fusion and IoT for smart ubiquitous environments: A survey. *IEEE Access : Practical Innovations, Open Solutions*, *5*, 9533–9554. DOI: 10.1109/ACCESS.2017.2697839

Bishop, C. M. (2006). *Pattern recognition and machine learning*. Springer.

Blasch, E., ... (2018). Control diffusion of information collection for situation understanding using boosting MLNs. In *2018 21st International Conference on Information Fusion (FUSION)*. IEEE. DOI: 10.23919/ICIF.2018.8455262

Castanedo, F. (2013). A review of data fusion techniques. *TheScientificWorldJournal*, *704504*(1), 704504. Advance online publication. DOI: 10.1155/2013/704504 PMID: 24288502

Comparative analysis and study of data mining techniques used for IoT-based smart healthcare system. (2020). *International Journal of Emerging Trends in Engineering Research*, *8*(9), 6131–6138. DOI: 10.30534/ijeter/2020/198892020

Dasarathy, B. (1997). Sensor fusion potential exploitation: Innovative architectures and illustrative applications. *Proceedings of the IEEE*, *85*(1), 24–38. DOI: 10.1109/5.554206

Dong, J., Zhuang, D., Huang, Y., & Fu, J. (2009). Advances in multi-sensor data fusion: Algorithms and applications. *Sensors (Basel)*, *9*(10), 7771–7784. DOI: 10.3390/s91007771 PMID: 22408479

Dowlin, N., Gilad-Bachrach, R., Laine, K., Lauter, K., Naehrig, M., & Wernsing, J. (2016). *CryptoNets: Applying neural networks to encrypted data with high throughput and accuracy*. Microsoft.

Durrant-Whyte, H. (1988). Sensor models and multisensor integration. *The International Journal of Robotics Research, 7*(6), 97–113. DOI: 10.1177/027836498800700608

Hall, D., & Llinas, J. (1997). An introduction to multisensor data fusion. *Proceedings of the IEEE, 85*(1), 6–23. DOI: 10.1109/5.554205

Handbook of multisensor data fusion. (2017)., DOI: 10.1201/9781420053096

Jinan, R., & Raveendran, T. (2016). Particle filters for multiple target tracking. *Procedia Technology, 24*, 980–987. DOI: 10.1016/j.protcy.2016.05.215

Kenda, K., Kažič, B., Novak, E., & Mladenić, D. (2019). Streaming data fusion for the Internet of Things. *Sensors (Basel), 19*(8), 1955. DOI: 10.3390/s19081955 PMID: 31027306

Krishnamurthi, R., Kumar, A., Gopinathan, D., Nayyar, A., & Qureshi, B. (2020). An overview of IoT sensor data processing, fusion, and analysis techniques. *Sensors (Basel), 20*(21), 6076. DOI: 10.3390/s20216076 PMID: 33114594

Luo, R., Yih, C.-C., & Su, K. L. (2002). Multisensor fusion and integration: Approaches, applications, and future research directions. *IEEE Sensors Journal, 2*(2), 107–119. DOI: 10.1109/JSEN.2002.1000251

Luo, R. C., & Kay, M. G. (1989). Multisensor integration and fusion in intelligent systems. *IEEE Transactions on Systems, Man, and Cybernetics, 19*(5), 901–931. DOI: 10.1109/21.44007

Mahdavinejad, M. S.. (2017). Machine learning for Internet of Things data analysis: A survey. *Digital Communications and Networks*. Advance online publication. DOI: 10.1016/j.dcan.2017.10.002

Meng, T., Jing, X., Yan, Z., & Pedrycz, W. (2020). A survey on machine learning for data fusion. *Information Fusion, 57*, 115–129. DOI: 10.1016/j.inffus.2019.12.001

Messaoud, S., Bradai, A., Bukhari, S. H. R., Quang, P. T. A., Ahmed, O. B., & Atri, M. (2020). A survey on machine learning in Internet of Things: Algorithms, strategies, and applications. *Internet of Things : Engineering Cyber Physical Human Systems, 12*, 100314. DOI: 10.1016/j.iot.2020.100314

Mujica, G., Rodriguez-Zurrunero, R., Wilby, M. R., Portilla, J., Rodríguez González, A. B., Araujo, A., Riesgo, T., & Vinagre Díaz, J. J. (2018). Edge and fog computing platform for data fusion of complex heterogeneous sensors. *Sensors (Basel), 18*(11), 3630. DOI: 10.3390/s18113630 PMID: 30366462

Munir, A., Blasch, E., Kwon, J., Kong, J., & Aved, A. (2021). Artificial intelligence and data fusion at the edge. *IEEE Aerospace and Electronic Systems Magazine*, *36*(7), 62–78. DOI: 10.1109/MAES.2020.3043072

Nakamura, E., Loureiro, A., & Frery, A. (2007). Information fusion for wireless sensor networks. *ACM Computing Surveys*, *39*(3), 9. DOI: 10.1145/1267070.1267073

Nedkov, K., & Nardinocchi, C. (2009). A comparison of Bayesian and evidence-based fusion methods for automated building detection in aerial data. *The International Archives of the Photogrammetry, Remote Sensing and Spatial Information Sciences*, 37.

Pillai, A. J., T. R. N., Ali, A., & K. K., A. (2021). Healthcare data fusion. [IJERT]. *International Journal of Engineering Research & Technology (Ahmedabad)*, *9*(13). Advance online publication. DOI: 10.17577/IJERTCONV9IS13031

Saranya, S. S., & Fatima, D. N. S. (2020). Context-aware data fusion on massive IoT data in dynamic IoT analytics. *Webology*, *17*(2), 957–970. DOI: 10.14704/WEB/V17I2/WEB17080

Sathish Kumar, L., Ahmad, S., Routray, S., Prabu, A. V., Alharbi, A., Alouffi, B., & Rajasoundaran, S. (2022). Modern Energy Optimization Approach for Efficient Data Communication in IoT-Based Wireless Sensor Networks. *Wireless Communications and Mobile Computing*, *2022*(1), 7901587. DOI: 10.1155/2022/7901587

Smolinska, A., Engel, J., Szymanska, E., Buydens, L., & Blanchet, L. (2019). General framing of low-, mid-, and high-level data fusion with examples in the life sciences. In *Data Handling in Science and Technology* (pp. 51–79). DOI: 10.1016/B978-0-444-63984-4.00004-0

Thomopoulos, S. (1990). Sensor integration and data fusion. In *SPIE Proceedings*. DOI: 10.1117/12.969974

Valente, F. J., ... (2019). Fog-based data fusion for heterogeneous IoT sensor networks: A real implementation. In *2019 15th International Conference on Network and Service Management (CNSM)*. IEEE. DOI: 10.23919/CNSM46954.2019.9012744

White, F. (1991). *Data fusion lexicon*.

Chapter 6
Threshold-Based Machine Learning Model for Hand State Classification Using EMG Sensors and Support Vector Machines

V. Santhi
https://orcid.org/0000-0002-4274-7474
Vellore Institute of Technology, India

Vinithra Balaji
https://orcid.org/0009-0008-2680-0969
Vellore Institute of Technology, Chennai, India

Maheswer Sunil Kumar
https://orcid.org/0009-0003-2715-0973
Vellore Institute of Technology, Chennai, India

ABSTRACT

Electromyography sensors (EMG) are techniques used to get the electrical signals generated by muscle activation, providing valuable insights into muscle activity and its relation to the nervous system. This chapter addresses the challenge of achieving accurate, real-time classification of hand states using a hybrid system combining threshold-based detection and machine learning algorithms. The proposed method focuses on the development of an accurate and efficient muscle activation detection

DOI: 10.4018/979-8-3373-0330-7.ch006

Copyright © 2025, IGI Global Scientific Publishing. Copying or distributing in print or electronic forms without written permission of IGI Global Scientific Publishing is prohibited.

system that utilizes the EMG sensors along with Support Vector Machines (SVM) for real-time classification of two hand states. The key contribution of this research is to incorporate a robust architecture that is adaptable to diverse muscle activity patterns and has the potential for deployment in real-time applications such as rehabilitation centers and prosthetics. In this chapter, the model is trained on two users, with varying muscle strength, and evaluations are done using accuracy, precision, and confusion matrix. Testing showcased high accuracy and precision.

1 INTRODUCTION

This research aims to implement of a reliable and efficient Machine learning algorithm to get precise detection of hand state using EMG sensor. The objectives include training an SVM model capable of accurately distinguishing between open and closed hand states, Create an optimized framework where the threshold efficiently handles simple classifications (e.g., open hand state), and machine learning models focus on complex decisions (e.g., closed hand state) to maximize computational efficiency, and also achieve real-time adaptability with a focus on designing a system with low computational requirements, making it feasible for deployment on portable or battery-powered devices

In biomedical engineering, EMG is an essential tool used to measure and record electrical activity in muscles. It is an essential part of biomedical research by offering insights into muscle functionality through detection of electrical signals generated through muscle activation (Pérez-Reynoso et al., 2022). Whenever a muscle movement happens, it generates a tiny electrical potential, which the EMG sensors can detect. By analyzing these signals, we get insights of muscle activity, health and functionality. Over the years, EMG has found applications in the field of prosthetics, rehabilitation, robotics and sports science. The possibility of analyzing muscle activation patterns in real-time enables us to develop advanced systems such as machine learning techniques that bridge the gap between human intention and machine response (Xiong et al., 2021).

The key challenge in this scenario is interpreting EMG signals accurately, whilst getting influenced by factors such as noise, skin resistance, muscle fatigue and electrode placement. To address these, techniques such as wavelet denoising and adaptive filtering have been employed to preserve critical signal components while reducing artifacts (Kotov-Smolenskiy et al., 2021). Traditional methods include thresholds and fixed rules which are not sufficient for variability in population. For this purpose, we utilize machine learning technique such as SVMs. The integration of SVM has shown significant potential in improving the accuracy of muscle activation detection system (Wang et al., 2024). SVMs are powerful supervised learning models designed to solve classification problems. They work by identifying the best hyperplane that separates data points belonging to different classes. The choice of SVM as the machine learning model is supported by its strong performance in handling complex classification problems, especially known for the hand state classification (Ekinci et al., 2023). This paper highlights SVM's superior performance among tested algorithms, achieving high accuracy in muscle signal classification. SVMs have been used a lot in EMG based gesture classification, showcasing their ability to handle non-linear decision boundaries which are complex curves or shapes that separate data points when a straight line or plane cannot (Chen et al., 2024). Even though CNN achieved higher accuracy for this system, because of its high computational overhead, it's not efficient for real world application, whereas SVM being light weight remains useful for small scale systems (Bhushan et al., 2022). Advancements in feature extraction methods such as time-domain and frequency domain analysis have improved the classification performance in various EMG application. Feature extraction methods are methods that transform raw data into meaningful features to improve model performance and reduce dimensionality (Oliva-Lozano & Muyor, 2020). This project focuses on the integration of hardware and software to create a system for precise muscle activation detection. EMG sensors collect the electrical signals, which are processed and analyzed using Python-based algorithms. The SVM model is trained 1 using features extracted from these signals, enabling the system to classify hand states with high precision.

Recent studies have highlighted the optimization of detection by hybrid systems of threshold and machine learning model (Swapna et al., 2022). This paper proposes a hybrid approach that integrates the benefits of both threshold-based detection and machine learning classification. In our system, the threshold-based method serves as the primary detector, accurately classifying open hand states with minimal computational overhead. When a closed hand is detected by thresholding, the result is passed to a machine learning model for confirmation, adding a second layer of verification that enhances classification accuracy for closed gestures. This hybrid design leverages the efficiency of thresholding with the adaptability of machine learning, creating a robust system that achieves both high accuracy and real-time responsiveness. Such hybrid designs with EMG have been proven to be effective in previous research as well (Khan et al., 2021).

Applications of EMG go beyond prosthetic control and rehabilitation, such as fitness monitoring, where EMG has been utilized to evaluate muscle activation patterns during exercises, providing insights for the development of optimized training protocols (Nazmi et al., 2016). One mor application lies in human computer interaction, where EMG-driven interfaces have paved the way for intuitive control systems adapting to user intensions (Boyer et al., 2023). Furthermore, combining

EMG with EEG and functional near-infrared spectroscopy (fNIRS) has been found to improve movement analysis and neurorehabilitation strategies (Azhiri et al., 2021).

1.1 Overview of EMG sensors and SVM

Electromyography (EMG) sensors are devices that measure the electrical activity produced by skeletal muscles during contraction. Such activity is indicative of muscle function and provides useful insights into muscle coordination, strength and fatigue. EMG sensors are integral to various applications, including medical diagnostics, rehabilitation, prosthetics, sports performance analysis, and human-machine interaction. The signals captured in the EMG sensors are called myoelectric signals, and are produced by the depolarization and repolarization of muscle fibers. The amplitude of these signals typically ranges from microvolts to millivolts, depending on the muscle activity and electrode placement. By capturing these electrical potentials, EMG sensors provide a quantitative measure of muscle activation.

There are various types of EMG sensors. Such as Surface EMG sensors (sEMG) which are non-invasive sensors placed on the skin over the muscle of interest. They are commonly used due to their ease of application and are suitable for monitoring superficial muscles. Another type of EMG sensors is Intramuscular EMG sensors, which involve inserting needle electrodes into the muscle tissue. They provide a more detailed signal but are invasive and primarily used in clinical or research settings for specific diagnoses.

The components of EMG sensors include Electrodes, Amplifiers, Filters. Analog to Digital Converter(ADC) and a processing unit. Electrodes are the primary contact points for capturing electrical signals. Surface electrodes are often adhesive pads with conductive surfaces, while intramuscular electrodes are fine needles or wires. Amplifiers enhance the signal level to make it suitable for further processing. EMG signals are prone to noise from various sources, such as power-line interference and motion artifacts. Filters (low-pass, high-pass, or band-pass) are applied to isolate the relevant signal frequencies, typically between 20 Hz and 500 Hz. EMG signals, originally analog, are converted to digital format for computational processing and analysis. Finally, Modern systems include microcontrollers or computers to process and analyze the EMG data in real time.

Challenges in EMG sensors include noise, power line interface, crosstalk from neighboring muscles and motion artifacts caused by electrode movement. The placement and orientation of electrodes significantly impact signal quality. Improper placement can lead to crosstalk or weak signals. Factors like skin thickness, sweat, and body hair can affect signal acquisition. Fatigue alters the electrical properties of muscles, potentially complicating signal interpretation.

Support Vector Machine (SVM) is a supervised learning algorithm mainly used for classification and regression tasks. It works by identifying the optimal hyperplane and separating data points of different classes in a high-dimensional space. The main advantage of SVM is its ability to handle non-linear relationships by using kernel functions. For this project, SVM is used to classify EMG signals into two categories: open hand and closed hand. The algorithm learns from a labeled dataset, where each sample is associated with a known class. Once trained, the SVM model can predict the class of new, unseen data with high accuracy. We integrate EMG and SVM to provide a meaningful framework for muscle activation detection and classification. EMG serves as the input modality, capturing the raw physiological data that reflects muscle activity, while SVM acts as the computational engine, classifying the data into meaningful states, such as open or closed hand.

1.2 Project statement

Implementation of a reliable and efficient Machine learning algorithm to get precise detection of hand state using EMG sensor.

The project aims to address the challenges by developing a system which uses EMG sensors and SVM, focusing on the detection of precise muscle activation for open and closed hand states. The goal is to create a robust system that can provide accurate and real-time muscle state detection, thereby improving the performance of assistive devices, prosthetics, and human-machine interfaces. The project will also explore the possibilities of future improvements, including more advanced machine learning techniques, utilizing other sensor modalities, and application of the system in diverse real-world environments.

1.3 Objectives of this project

The primary objectives aimed to address in this project are as followed.

1. To collect and preprocess EMG signals for both open and closed hand movements using serial communication with hardware sensors.
2. Demonstrate the use of EMG sensor to detect hand movements by extracting signal data as input.
3. To train an SVM model capable of accurately distinguishing between open and closed hand states.
4. Create an optimized framework where the threshold efficiently handles simple classifications (e.g., open hand state), and machine learning models focus on complex decisions (e.g., closed hand state) to maximize computational efficiency.

5. Enable the system to dynamically adapt to changes in user behaviour, muscle fatigue, or electrode placement, ensuring consistent performance over extended periods of use.
6. Create a user-friendly interface for collecting training data, setting thresholds, and visualizing results, ensuring ease of use for non-technical users.
7. Allow users to customize the training process based on their specific needs, such as adjusting data collection duration or incorporating additional labels for finer control.
8. To develop a reliable method for classifying hand states using EMG signals.
9. Conduct extensive testing across diverse populations to ensure the system works reliably for individuals of different ages, genders, and physiological conditions.
10. To measure model performance using metrics such as accuracy, precision, and confusion matrix, iteratively improving based on results.

2 LITERATURE REVIEW

2.1 Hand Gesture Signal Classification Using Machine Learning

The paper focused on classifying hand states using EMG signals captured by sensor-based bands. The raw EMG signals were preprocessed to remove noise. And eight time-domain featured were extracted for classification. Among all the tested models, Support Vector Machines (SVM) showed highest accuracy. The demerit of the paper was its scope limited to predefined gestures, which may reduce its adaptability to diverse real-world scenarios (Khan et al., 2021). The finding of this paper includes the effective classifying EMG signals for fast hand gesture recognition using Supervised machine learning. The future scope of the paper is to expand hand gesture datasets and real-time development.

2.2 Electromyography Signal Classification Using Deep Learning

This paper implemented a deep neural network with multiple layers for classifying EMG signals from control groups, myopathy and ALS patients. Classification was improved using advanced feature extraction techniques, including wavelet transforms. The limited dataset size and specific focus on clinical conditions like ALS make is less applicable to broader fields (Gaso et al., 2021). The finding of this paper included demonstration of improved accuracy using CNNs and RNNs for EMG signal classification indicating Deep learning models outperform conventional ML methods for EMG classification. Future scope includes integration of more complex gestures and reducing computational costs.

2.3 Real-Time EMG Signal Classification via Recurrent Neural Networks

In this study, the author utilized discrete wavelet decomposition for feature extraction and trained RNNs on EMG signals to classify finger movements in real-time. Even though it achieved high accuracy, it required a consistent experimental setup and preprocessing, due to which it was difficult to use it in real world dynamic environments (Azhiri et al., 2021). The finding of this paper includes improved accuracy and real-time performance compared to traditional classifiers using RNN. For future work, the paper mentions the testing of the system on diverse population and improving model generalization.

2.4 Comparing ML algorithms for classification of EMG Signals

This paper highlights the strengths and limitations of SVM, KNN and ANN in EMG Signal classification. SVM was found to be robust and good for handling non-linear data effectively, while ANN demonstrated high accuracy for complex multi-class problems due to its ability to model intricate patterns. The key demerit is the SVM's heavy dependence on proper kernel selection which can complicate its use in real-world application (Seyidbayli et al., 2020). The papers finding is that SVM and KNN outperformed other classifiers for specific EMG datasets. Exploring hybrid models for further accuracy improvement is the future work mentioned.

2.5 Internet of Medical Things (IoMT) for EMG signal processing

This paper implements a cutting edge IoMT device for musculoskeletal monitoring, including a CNN-based deep learning for accurate EMG signal processing. It focuses on real-time healthcare applications demonstrates high potential for smart and accessible solutions. The demerit for this paper was that the device was tested on limited use cases and further testing on variety of patients is needed for incorporating reliability (Sankaran et al., 2024). The study includes finding a system that provides accurate teal-time feedback for musculoskeletal monitoring using IoMT and EMG. Testing across variety of users and enhancing portability of device is the future scope of this study.

2.6 EMG signals to enhance gait

This paper integrates EMG signals and IoT for ankle-foot orthosis applications, which provides a practical framework to improve gait through Machine Learning algorithms. Although this paper lacked detailed breakdown of how noise or motion in EMG signals are handled which affect the reliability of such systems in uncontrolled environments (Shefa et al., 2024). Significant improvement in gait patterns using enhanced EMG feedback is an important finding of this paper with the future work being the implementation of a system for more complex locomotion tasks.

2.7 Reducing Musculoskeletal stress using EMG and reinforcement learning

The study applied EMG signals to implement reinforcement learning-based optimization for reducing musculoskeletal stress, providing for novel applications in workplace ergonomics. Even with the good findings, the system relied on high precision motion capture alongside EMG making the approach less scalable in everyday environments (Wang, 2024). In this paper, it was found that Reinforcement learning successfully reduced muscle strain. Future work includes extending applications to real-time industrial settings.

2.8 Sign Language Recognition using EMG signals

This paper used Surface EMG (sEMG) sensor data to recognize sign language with transfer learning, bringing in a growth in communication technologies. Even with the contribution in sign language recognition, the study did not address continuous gesture recognition, which limits its usability for fluid sign language translation (Rajeswari & Keerthana, n.d.).

2.9 Motion classification using sEMG and Deep Learning

This paper implements a system which uses surface EMG and inertial data to classify motion for ankle exoskeletons, leveraging deep learning for improved classification accuracy in wearable robotics, addressing a specific gap in prosthetic control. The system was limited to subject diversity in training dataset, affection generalized application (Estévez et al., 2024). The paper found that strong accuracy was achieved for specific EMG gesture recognition tasks using this system. Addressing dynamic sign transitions for continuous recognition.

2.10 Distinguishing standing postures with EMG recordings and deep learning models

This paper discussed EMG activity between specific muscles in standing postures with the help of deep learning, highlighting its diagnostic potential for medical applications (Kamankesh et al., 2024). The drawback in of this paper is the use of small datasets and controlled environments which reduce model's effectiveness in real-world medical diagnostics. Exoskeleton responsiveness was improved by the high accuracy achieved for specific motion patterns concluding that Deep learning combined with EMG is highly effective for wearable robotics control. Future scope incudes the testing in varied real-world environments with larger datasets.

2.11 EMG based Hand Gesture Recognition

This paper proposed a wearable EMG device which includes multiple surface electrodes for accurate hand gesture recognitions. This is done by a combination of time-domain features such as root mean square (RMS) and waveform length with machine learning models, including SVM and Random Forests (Tsinganos et al., 2018). The systems findings include high recognition rates for gestures such as hand grasps and releases across diverse users, even with anatomical variability. The device was not lightweight, making it not helpful for long term usability. Also cross-user differences were not properly addressed, making it difficult for generalized usage with multiple subjects.

2.12 EMG signal classification using deep learning

This paper implemented a deep learning model with L2 regularization to classify EMG signals. The model achieved high accuracy in distinguishing between control group, myopathy, and ALS patients. The system included a deep neural network comprising eight layers, including five fully connected layers, two batch normalization layers, and one dropout layer. The model was trained on EMG data collected from control group, myopathy, and ALS patients (Shigute Gaso et al., 2023). However, the study failed to explore the integration of electroencephalographic (EEG) data, which could provide a more comprehensive analysis of motor activation patterns. Additionally, the dataset was limited to specific neuromuscular disorders, and the model's generalizability to other conditions remains uncertain.

2.13 EMG Signal Classification for Neuromuscular Disorders

This research implemented an attention-enhanced convolutional neural network (CNN) for classifying EMG signals associated with neuromuscular disorders, utilizing Log-spectrum and Delta Log-spectrum features extracted from raw EMG signals. These features were input into a deep learning model, SpectroEMG-Net, which combined CNNs with attention mechanisms to classify three classes: Myopathy, Normal, and ALS and achieving an overall accuracy of 92% (Rahman et al., 2023). The only drawback of this study was the focus on a limited number of neuromuscular disorders, and the model's performance on other conditions was not evaluated. Additionally, the study did not consider the integration of EEG data, which could enhance the understanding of motor activation patterns.

2.14 Hand gesture identification using Machine learning and forearm muscle signals

This paper talked about the use of forearm EMG data to distinguish eight hand gestures, by collecting EMG data from ten participants performing various hand gestures, then applying neural network and random forest algorithms to classify the gestures, experimenting with different window sizes to optimize performance (Cho et al., 2024). This implementation achieved a 97% accuracy with a neural network and 85% accuracy with a random forest algorithm. Along with the success of the implementation, the limitations of the paper include small sample size, which may limit the generalizability of the findings.

2.15 Bayesian approach for EMG pattern classification with Semi supervised sequential learning

This paper employed a Bayesian classification model based on Gaussian distributions to predict motion classes and estimate their confidence. The implementation included a semi-supervised learning framework that updated the model's posterior distributions sequentially, allowing for adaptation to changes in signal characteristics. The paper achieved to maintain classification accuracy with time even with changing signal characteristics (Yoneda & Furui, 2023). The limitations of this paper include small sample size which included only 6 adults and not evaluating the model's performance in real-world applications or with different types of EMG data.

Recent research on this topic includes many improvements to increase accuracy, efficiency and real-time applicability. One such research explored 23 feature extraction techniques and used an Extra Tree classifier for feature selection, achieving 97.43% accuracy with KNN, balancing feature analysis with computational efficiency

(Miah et al., 2024). While another study focused on micro hand gesture recognition, with a wrist band style EMG device making it portable (Wang et al., 2024). Many more studies have contributed to the advancements in the field of EMG sensors and machine learning model integration with them.

To conclude the literature review, the studies showcase the significant potential of Electromyography (EMG) signals combined with machine learning (ML) and deep learning (DL) techniques for applications such as hand gesture recognition, prosthetic control, gait improvement, and clinical diagnostics. It was found that deep learning models outperformed traditional approaches in handling complex and nonlinear patterns. Machine learning techniques such as Support Vector Machines (SVM), Convolutional Neural Networks (CNNs), and Recurrent Neural Networks (RNNs) consistently achieved high accuracy for EMG signal classification. However, these papers highlight challenges not limited to noise in EMG signals, low datasets, and the need for testing in real world and constantly changing real-world scenarios. Future work is understood to focus on expanding datasets, improving noise reduction techniques, enabling continuous gesture recognition, and enhancing the scalability of real-time systems for diverse and practical applications in healthcare, rehabilitation, and human-machine interaction.

3 SYSTEM DESIGN AND METHODOLOGY

3.1 Overview of the System

The EMG signal processing system represents the integration of hardware and software to input, analyze and classify muscle state and patterns with high precision. This system is developed to contribute to the solution for increasing demand for accurate, real-time muscle activity monitoring.

System workflow. The workflow of this system is structured into four interdependent yet distinct states, each playing an important role in the accurate detection of hand state by muscle activation.

Figure 1. System Overview

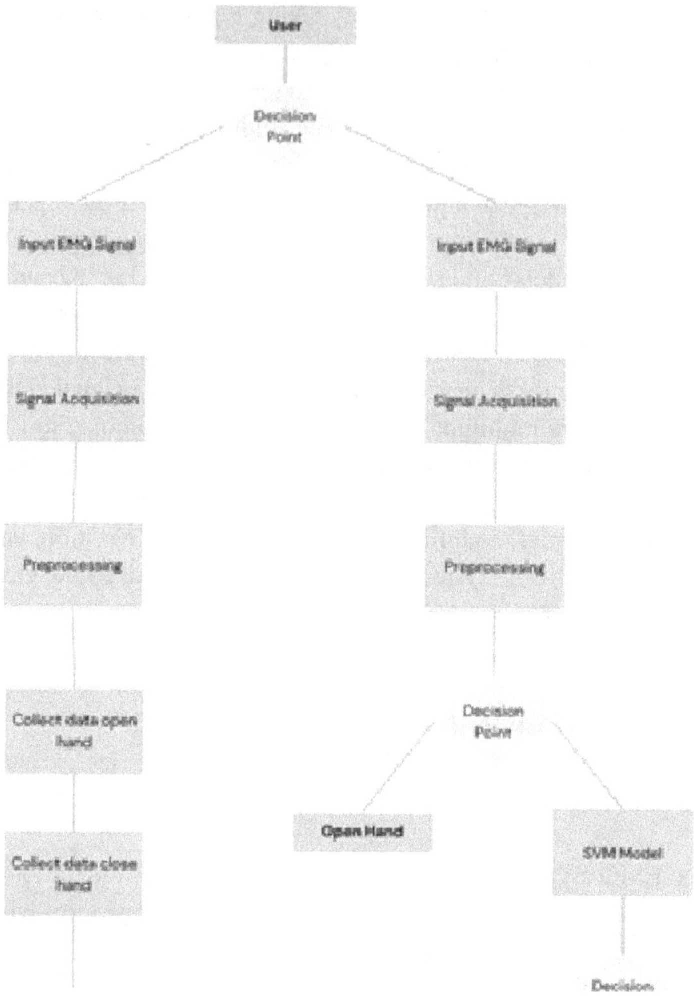

The workflow of the system includes various steps. Firstly, data is collected from the sensors and preprocessed. After which, collected signals are evaluated against the threshold for preliminary classification. If the prediction using the threshold is closed hand, then it is cross verified using the SVM model. Finally, Results are displayed to the user in real time. Below is the detailed explanation of each of these steps.

1. *Signal Acquisition.* The system starts with the collection of raw EMG signals generated by muscle activation. When a muscle moves or contracts, it generates electrical signals as per the intensity and duration of the contraction. The signals are captured using surface EMG (sEMG) sensors, placed on the skin

on top of target muscles, which here is the forearm area. Proper placement of sensors on the forearm muscles provides accurate readings. Calibration steps include instructing the subject to perform controlled movements to validate sensor response.

2. *Signal Processing.* Raw EMG signals usually have unwanted values such as noise from various sources such as motion and inherent biological variability. Preprocessing in this system involves filtering and normalizing the signals to remove noise and ensure consistency across samples.
3. *Threshold Calculation.* Once input signals are received, it is observed that close hand signal values and open hand signal values vary a lot. So based on those values, a threshold is calculated, which is used to classify the input. If the threshold method gives output as close hand state, then the signal is given to the machine learning model. This threshold value is dynamically calculated for each used based on their unique muscle activation patterns, due to which the system is able to account for individual differences in muscle strength and electrical signal generation. This method reduces the computational burden by bypassing the need for ML models when unnecessary.
4. *Classification using Machine Learning.* This signal is then passed to a machine learning model, here Support Vector Machine (SVM), to classify between the hand states using patterns in the signal. The model identifies patterns withing the data and assigns to the predefined categories i.e. open hand and close hand. A linear kernel is chosen for its computational efficiency in binary classification. The model is trained on labeled data, ensuring it generalizes well to new inputs. During runtime, inputs classified as closed hand by the threshold method are validated by the SVM model. This two layer approach of this system enhances the accuracy which can be achieved and reduces false positives.

This workflow provides a systematic process to input raw EMG signals and output the classification for the hand signal as per each individual.

Key components

1. *Hardware components.* EMG sensors are primarily used for capturing the signals from muscle activity caused by the movement of arms while performing the open hand and closed hand positions. A Microcontroller, such as Arduino UNO, is used to act as an interface between the sensors and the computer and digitize the analog EMG signals using an analog-to-digital converter (ADC). Arduino uno is chosen over other microcontrollers here for its affordability, simplicity, and its built-in USB-to-serial communication makes data transfer easy, eliminating the need for extra hardware. Communication interface is provided

using a USB cable. The EMG sensors require portable 9V batteries as external power supply, making the hardware assemble portable as well. The 9V external batteries make the system more portable which is done by eliminating the need for a constant connection to a power source, due to which the system can be used in different locations without relying on an outlet. The battery provides a stable power supply, helping the sensor capture more accurate signals.

2. *Software components.* Python is used to program this entire system. Python Libraries such as NumPy and SciPy provide tools for signal preprocessing including filtering and normalization. Libraries like scikit-learn provides vast suite of machine learning algorithms for classification, regression and clustering, among which SVM is used in this system. The SVM is trained, validated and tested using the input data. Tensorflow and PyTorch are also utilized for the same. Serial library is used for serial communication through which data is collected from the EMG sensors for further processing.

3.2 Hardware Design

Figure 2. Hardware Setup

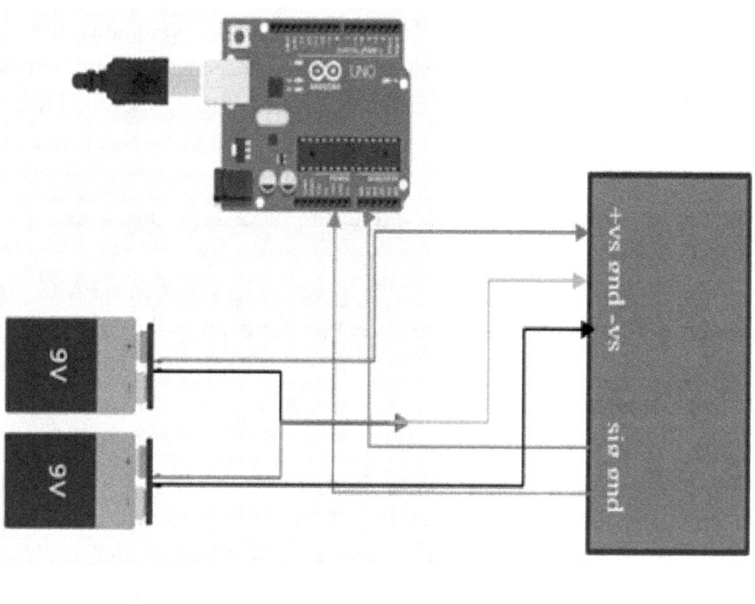

The system has mainly three primary components: the EMG sensors, a microcontroller (Arduino Uno) and a communication interface. All these components work together to capture, digitize and transmit data for further computation. The EMG sensors serve as These EMG sensor stickers are placed on the forearm muscles responsible for open and closed hand movements. The sensors capture analog signals, which vary in magnitude based on the intensity and duration of muscle activity. The microcontroller used in this setup is Arduino Uno, which acts as an interface between the EMG sensors and the computer. It digitizes the analog signals received from the EMG sensors using its Analog-to-Digital Converter (ADC). The device operates with a USB interface, simplifying the connection to a computer for real-time data transfer. The microcontroller is powered through the USB connection, eliminating the need for an external power supply. The two external 9V Lithium Ion batteries are used to provide power to the EMG signal amplifier, which is then connected to the Arduino uno using its signal pin.

The sensors are in the form of stickers with a gel, and they are placed statistically on the skin above the muscles being studied, which here are the forearm muscles associated with open hand and close hand states. The sensor placement should account for the anatomical variability across population to achieve consistent signal acquisition. For future considerations for the hardware setup, it can be enhanced using a wireless communication mode such as Bluetooth or Wi-Fi with component like Raspberry pi, making it compatible with wearable applications.

3.3 Signal Recording

After the experimental setup, we start taking the input. The EMG continuously monitor the electrical activity in the muscle. The range of these signals lies between 0 to 1023. This range is determined by the 10-bit Analog-to-Digital Converter(ADC) of the Arduino uno, where 10 bit mean 2^10=1024 values. Here, 0 represents 0V (no signal) and 1023 represents 5V (maximum input voltage). Stronger muscle activity mean higher digital values and weak muscle activity give lower values. Because of 1024 values range, small voltage changed may not be captured precisely. In the system, data is recorded for each category in intervals of 5-10 seconds. During this time, muscle activity such as open hand and close hand positions is performed by the subject is recorded for further processing. The collected data is then saved and tagged according to the specific task performed. This allows for easy segmentation and identification of different types of muscle activation based on the recorded signals.

Before taking the signals from the user, some steps such as standardized skin preparation methods, for example cleaning the skin with alcohol pads before placing the electrodes, are used to reduce skin impedance. This ensures better electrode contact and signal transmission, which is crucial for accurate signal recording. To reduce motion artifacts, subjects are instructed to maintain a stable posture during data collection, and the experiment is set up in a way that minimizes unnecessary movements.

The sensors are placed on the skin above the muscles being studied. Having proper placement ensures that the signals in the input correspond accurately to the muscle activation patterns of interest. For example, in a hand status detection system, sensor might be attached to the forearm muscles responsible for opening and closing the hand. The sensor placement must account for anatomical variability across users to ensure consistent signal acquisition. For this experiment the sensor has 3 electrodes, one electrode is placed on a bony area on the Palmar side of the arm. The other two electrodes are placed on the Dorsal side of the hand.

3.4 Training process

The machine learning process used in this system is Support Vector Machines (SVM) and several key steps such as data preparation, standardization, training and evaluation are performed.

Data preparation. The labels of the Target values for the classification are considered as 0 for open hand and 1 representing closed hand. In this system, the training data is collected for both the hand states, and each input is coordinated with one of the appropriate labels. This labelled data is then stored in a training file and loaded for model training

Standardization. This step improves the performance of SVM. Standardization rescaled the featured so that they have a zero mean and unit variance. This is particularly important when using SVM because SVMs are sensitive to the scale of input features.

Model Training. The model is created using a linear kernel as it is computationally efficient and effective for linearly separable data. The linear kernel creates a decision boundary in the feature space that best separates the two classes (open and closed hand gestures) by finding the hyperplane that maximizes the margin between the two classes. The fit function of the SVM class from scikit-learn is used to train the model, where the standardized features and their corresponding labels are passed into the model.

3.5 Performance Evaluation

For the EMG-SVM integrated system, the performance evaluation is done using several key matrices such as accuracy, recall, F1 score, confusion matrix and computational efficiency. Along with this, the systems performance is compared to existing systems to understand the improvement in this system.

3.6 Challenges in Data Collection

The main challenges in Data collection for EMG signals includes noise, variability, and signal distortion, which can compromise the quality of the data and the accuracy of subsequent analysis.

One of the most common challenges in signal recording is noise which can occur from a variety of sources. Electrical interference from nearby equipment, such as computers, power lines, or other electronic devices, can introduce unwanted signals into the EMG data. These signals can often be higher in magnitude than the EMG signals themselves, making it difficult to distinguish between true muscle activity and unwanted noise. Another important source to look out for is motion of the subject. When the subject moves, even subtly, it can cause physical displacements of the electrodes, leading to inconsistent or distorted signals. For example, if the subject adjusts their arm position or shifts during recording, the relative position of the electrodes may change, causing a drop in signal quality. Additionally, muscle twitching or skin impedance variations can introduce noise into the recordings.

The next challenge discussed is Variability. Variability is the variety one can get in signals based on different subjects across the population. Factors such as skin texture, fat layer thickness, muscle morphology, and hydration levels can all influence the way the electrical signals are transmitted from the muscle to the surface electrodes. For example, individuals with more fat tissue may experience lower signal amplitude due to the additional layers of tissue that attenuate the electrical signals. This variability can make it challenging to create a one-size-fits-all model for EMG signal analysis.

Cross-talk means interference of signals from nearby muscles which can affect the data being recorded by the EMG sensors. For example, when recording the EMG signal from the biceps, signals from the triceps or forearm muscles can also be picked up by the electrodes, especially if the electrode placement is not sufficiently precise. This phenomenon can make it difficult to attribute muscle activity accurately to a particular muscle group.

The solution to these challenges includes certain steps to take before data collection process is started. Steps such as ground electrodes i.e. provide a reference point that cancels out interference from external sources, ensuring that the EMG signals are measured more accurately. Using standardized skin preparation methods, such as cleaning the skin with alcohol pads before placing the electrodes, are used to reduce skin impedance. This ensures better electrode contact and signal transmission, which is crucial for accurate signal recording. Lastly, To reduce motion artifacts, subjects are instructed to maintain a stable posture during data collection, and the experiment is set up in a way that minimizes unnecessary movements.

4 IMPLEMENTATION

4.1 Overview of the code architecture

The code architecture for the EMG-based hand gesture recognition system is structured to support both the data collection and machine learning processes in an efficient and scalable way. The program is implemented in Python, a versatile programming language that is widely used for both data analysis and machine learning. By utilizing a combination of libraries like Serial, Numpy, scikit-learn, and pickle, the code provides an integrated environment for collecting raw EMG signals, processing the data, training a machine learning model, and evaluating the model's performance. There are various functions that perform distinct tasks to achieve the required output for the user, such as function to collect the data serially for a specific period, then store the data in a csv format for training the model later on, then another function to train the model which also normalizes the data using StandardScalar from scikit-learn, which is crucial for SVM performance. Once the model is trained, it is serialized and saved to disk using Python's pickle module, which ensures that the model can be reloaded and reused for testing or additional evaluations without needing to retrain it from scratch.

The system is divided Into two operational modes: training and testing. The user can choose between these two modes at the start of the program. In the 'train' mode, the system collects data for both hand gestures (open and closed), trains the SVM model, and saves the trained model to a file. In the 'test' mode, the system loads the previously saved model and evaluates its performance by collecting new EMG data and differentiates it based on the categories using threshold and comparing the model's predictions against ground truth values provided by the user. This dual functionality ensures that the system can be easily adapted for both training new models and evaluating existing ones.

Along with the core functions, the system has utility functions for model loading and thresholding. These features allow the user to apply a decision rule based on a threshold to classify hand gestures, with a simple comparison of EMG values against a precomputed threshold. This modern approach of the system allows the model to classify gestures in real-time, have easy maintenance and expansion of the system.

4.2 Data collection

The proposed system collects data from the EMG sensor using serial connection in Pythons Serial library. By establishing a serial object with the correct port and baud rate, the code communicates with the device in real time, allowing it to capture continuous EMG signal readings. The baud rate of 9600 is commonly used in many serial communication protocols and is sufficient for transmitting EMG data without introducing significant delay.

The function to collect data is designed to collect data for two different hand gestures 'open' and 'closed'. The subject is prompted to press Enter key to start data collection for the selected label, such that each signal collected will be associated to that truth label. The data collection continues until the specified time limit is reached, after which the function returns the collected EMG values. The values for open hand and close hand are also saved in two separate arrays for calculation of threshold in the next step.

4.3 Threshold Calculation

Using the open hand and closed hand values collected earlier, the threshold is calculated using a simple mathematical formula. Firstly, mean of open hand values is found. Similarly, mean of closed hand values is calculated. Then average of these two means is found which is considered as the threshold. In one way, we can consider this as drawing a straight line in a graph classifying open hand on one side and close hand values on the other. This can also be considered as a one-dimensional SVM.

$$Threshold = \frac{mean(open) + mean(closed)}{2} \quad (1)$$

4.4 Training, Testing and Evaluation

This phase of the hand state classification system transforms the collected EMG signal into a model that classifies the hand states as open or closed. The training process includes standardizing the features and labels using StandardScalar to improve SVM performance, and training an SVM with a linear kernel for binary classification. Python's pickle library is used to save these necessary data for future use in the system. The first step in the training process is to load the collected data, which is EMG values paired with labels indicating whether the hand gesture is 'open' or 'closed.' The data is stored as a list of tuples, where each tuple contains a list of features (in this case, the raw EMG values) and a corresponding label (0 for 'open' or 1 for 'closed'). The function extracts these features and labels, separating them into two lists for processing. After which we standardize the features. After training, the model is saved to disk using Python's pickle module.

The model testing collects real-time EMG signal, uses the threshold method to classify the signal into open hand or close hand. If the input value is lesser than the threshold value, the hand state is considered as open. If the input value is above threshold, the state is considered as closed hand, but before the final prediction, the input is sent to the trained model to cross check if the hand state is closed hand. If the SVM model predicts its closed hand, then the final prediction is displayed as closed hand, else it is predicted as open hand and displayed. When the system enters the test mode, the user is asked to enter the true label for each data collection cycle by pressing '1' for a closed hand or press Enter for an open hand. The system then collects EMG data for 10 seconds. During this time, the model makes predictions based on the incoming EMG values. If the EMG value is below the threshold, the model classifies the hand as 'open'; otherwise, it uses the trained SVM to predict whether the hand is 'open' or 'closed.' The prediction is then compared with the true label provided by the user, and both the true and predicted labels are stored for later evaluation.

Performance is evaluated using metrics such as accuracy, precision, and a confusion matrix. This is then used to evaluate the system and reach the necessary conclusion of the algorithm. Accuracy is the percentage of correct predictions made by the model, providing a general measure of the model's overall performance. Precision is the percentage of true positive predictions (correctly classified 'closed' gestures) among all predicted 'closed' gestures, giving an indication of how well the model avoids false positives. The confusion matrix provides a detailed breakdown of the model's predictions, showing the true positives, false positives, true negatives, and false negatives.

5 RESULTS AND DISCUSSION

5.1 Experimental Setup

The experimental setup for testing the EMG-based hand gesture recognition system was designed to assess the system's ability to accurately classify hand gestures (open vs. closed) in a controlled environment. The system was tested using a physical EMG sensor, which was connected to the computer via a serial interface. The serial port communication, facilitated by Python's serial library, allowed the system to capture EMG values in real time. The primary objective was to ensure that the system could accurately detect and classify EMG signals associated with both open and closed hand gestures. The test data used for evaluating the model was collected in similar conditions to the training data. However, the major difference was that the testing data was unseen by the model during the training phase, ensuring that the performance metrics reflected the model's generalization ability to new, real-world data. The ground truth for each testing cycle was input manually by the user, allowing for the comparison between predicted labels and actual hand gesture labels.

For the hardware setup, the code was tested on a standard laptop with sufficient processing power to handle real-time data collection and model predictions. The computer was connected to the EMG sensor via a USB-to-serial adapter, which allowed the serial connection to be established on the specified port. The system was also tested on various operating systems to ensure compatibility across different platforms.

5.2 Model Performance

The performance of the trained machine learning model was analyzed using matrices such as accuracy, precision, recall and confusion matrices. During the testing phase, the model was made to classify the input signal as either open hand or close hand, and this output was compared with the ground truth provided by the user.

Before testing, during the training period, threshold is calculated for the user. Every individual has varying strength and movement value, hence to get accurate results, the algorithm calculates the threshold for each individual separately.

Table 1. Threshold of two subjects

Subject	Value
Subject 1	111.234222
Subject 2	80.1112222

The testing is done such that when user has selected testing in the start of the program, they get a prompt to choose 1 if they are going to make the closed hand action or press enter key if they are going to make the open hand state. In this way the ground truth was set before the user perform the action, and after the prompt when the user performs the action, based on the input value the classification is made and compared with the ground truth to evaluate the model further. If open hand is predicted by the threshold method, then the final prediction is also open hand. But if the threshold algorithm predicts output as closed hand, then it is cross checked by sending the input to the trained SVM model, and its prediction is considered as final.

The change in signal values based on muscle activation can also be visualized using the Arduino IDE, to better understand why if the input signal is below the threshold value, its open hand and if its above threshold, it is closed hand .

Figure 3. Serial plot for subject 1

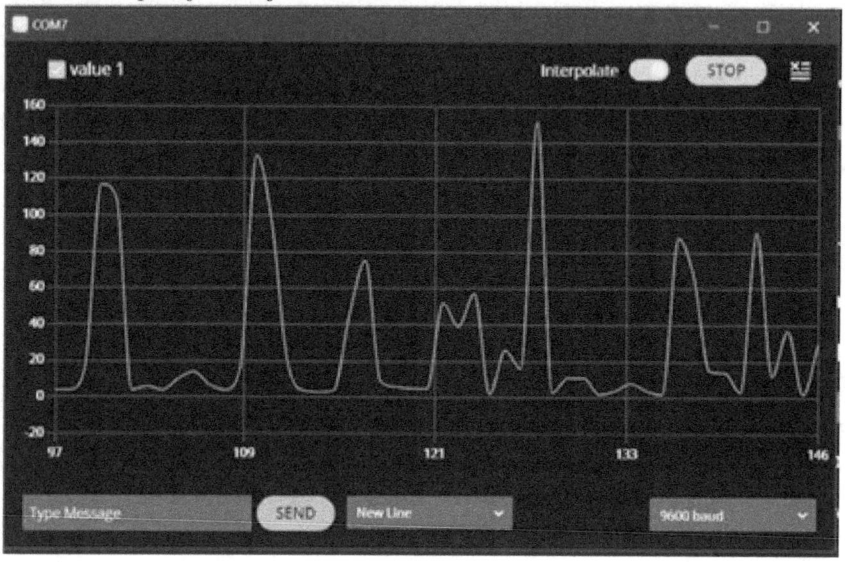

Figure 4. Serial plot for subject 2

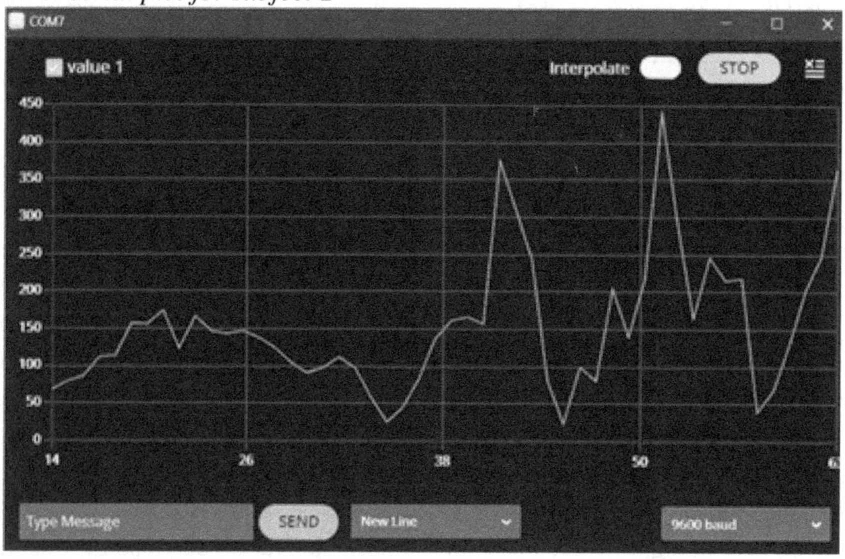

From these graphs, it can be understood that whenever hand is closed, there is a peak, and when the hand is in resting position that is open, it is not peaking.

The use of threshold value is to achieve real time classification of the hand state and reduce the computational overhead. The threshold value accurately detects open-hand state, but when the input signal value goes above the threshold value, the threshold method detects the input as close hand, but to get accurate result, we send this result through SVM model. If SVM model detects it as closed hand as well, the output would be closed hand, otherwise the output will be open hand. Whereas using just the threshold method will not give accurate results, and just the SVM model would have higher computational overhead.

5.3 Performance Evaluation

The system was tested with two subjects, both with varying strength and hence, varying thresholds. During the testing phase, the threshold value is manually input by the user as found during the training phase. the choice of threshold value can significantly affect performance, as a threshold that is too high may lead to mis-classification of open hand gestures as closed, while a threshold that is too low may result in the opposite. Fine-tuning the threshold based on the data collected during training could help optimize the model's accuracy.

Figure 5. Confusion matrix for subject 1

Training Set			
TARGE /)UTPUT	Class0	Class1	SUM
Class0	77 50.99%	4 2.65%	81 95.06% 4.94%
Class1	6 3.97%	64 42.38%	70 91.43% 8.57%
SUM	83 92.77% 7.23%	68 94.12% 5.88%	141 / 151 93.38% 6.62%

Figure 6. Confusion matrix for subject 2

Training Set			
TARGE / UTPUT	Class0	Class1	SUM
Class0	12 23.53%	3 5.88%	15 80.00% 20.00%
Class1	7 13.73%	29 56.86%	36 80.56% 19.44%
SUM	19 63.16% 36.84%	32 90.63% 9.38%	41 / 51 80.39% 19.61%

Based on this confusion matrix, parameters such as accuracy, precision, recall and F1-score were calculated as below.

Table 2. Evaluation parameters for both the subjects.

Subject	Accuracy	Precision	Recall	F1-score
Subject 1	93.38%	93.45%	93.25%	93.33%
Subject 2	80.39%	76.90%	80.28%	77.92%

From the above result, we can understand that the algorithm gives varied output as per the individual. The algorithm is seen to suite better to subject 1, whereas for subject 2, the accuracy is dropped, but that can be due to other environmental factors as well as signal quality. Overall, the System is capable to train and test as per each individual user and can be confirmed better with a larger dataset and more professional biomedical research environment. The system is also low on computational overhead as open hand prediction is done only using the threshold method, which reduces the latency and hence make the system more suitable for real time application. When comparing the classification results for open versus closed hand gestures, the system generally performed well for both classes, with high accuracy and precision for correctly identifying closed hand gestures. However, the system showed some variability in correctly classifying open hand gestures, which may be attributed to the inherent noise in the EMG signals or the simplicity of the model. The model seemed to favor the closed hand class, leading to a higher rate of false negatives for open hand gestures. This highlights the challenge of balancing the detection of both classes equally in the model.

Additionally, the threshold value for decision-making, which was provided by the user, played a significant role in the model's performance. The threshold determined whether an EMG signal was classified as an open or closed gesture based on its value. However, the choice of threshold value can significantly affect performance, as a threshold that is too high may lead to misclassification of open hand gestures as closed, while a threshold that is too low may result in the opposite. Fine-tuning the threshold based on the data collected during training could help optimize the model's accuracy.

6 LIMITATIONS

Even after the successful implementation of the hand gesture recognition system, several limitations exist that could impact its real-world performance. One of the primary limitations is the sensitivity of the model to noise in the EMG signals. As with any biological signal, EMG data is susceptible to interference from various sources, including muscle fatigue, motion artifacts, and electrical noise from surrounding devices. While the implementation in this paper collects raw EMG data, it does not include advanced noise filtering methods, which could result in fluctuations in the signal that affect the model's predictions. Including signal processing techniques such as low-pass filtering, noise reduction algorithms, or feature extraction methods could improve the consistency and accuracy of the collected data.

Another limitation of the model is its reliance on a fixed threshold for classification. Although the threshold is based on training data, it may not be optimal for all the subjects or for all types of gestures. The fixed threshold may not account for variations in muscle strength, electrode placement, or other individual differences that could affect the EMG signal. Implementing a changing threshold that adapts to the user's specific muscle activation patterns could improve the model's accuracy and robustness across different subjects.

Along with the above issues, the model's performance is limited by the simplicity of the feature set. The model currently uses a single EMG value as a feature to classify the hand gestures, which may not capture all of the necessary information from the signal. Incorporating additional features, such as the frequency spectrum of the EMG signal or time-domain features like mean absolute value (MAV) or root mean square (RMS), could improve the model's ability to distinguish between open and closed hand gestures. Using more advanced machine learning techniques, such as deep learning or ensemble methods, could also help improve the system's classification accuracy. The testing process also revealed that the model sometimes struggles with misclassification when the hand gestures are not performed consistently. For example, variations in the force or speed of the gesture may result in slightly different EMG signals that the model cannot distinguish accurately. This highlights the need for more data to capture the full range of hand gestures, as well as better techniques for handling dynamic or inconsistent gesture execution.

7 CONCLUSION AND FUTURE WORK

The chapter highlights the potential of machine learning in enhancing the usage of EMG based systems. The results prove that the proposed hybrid SVM-threshold based system is capable of achieving high classification while maintaining low computation costs and hence making it suitable for real time application. The implementation underscores the importance of careful data collection and model selection to achieve robust performance. From the results we can understand the practical value of the system and how it can contribute to further developments in rehabilitation tools and wearable technology. The system is adaptable to various users of different strengths and muscle activation patterns, widening the scope of this project. The robustness and adaptability of the system was highlighted through its consistent performance in real-time scenarios. The ability to classify hand gestures with good results opens contribution to multiple applications, from wearable devices and rehabilitation tools to advanced prosthetics and human-computer interaction systems. The findings of this paper validate the methodology used and establish a strong foundation for future advancements in EMG-based technologies. However, the project's success also highlights the critical importance of careful data collection, model selection, and performance evaluation. The simplicity and effectiveness of the system make it a valuable contribution to the field, yet it also reveals areas where improvements and innovations are necessary to overcome current limitations. The findings of this paper can contribute to improvement of health care, human-computer interaction and the wearable technology fields. Prosthetic control, physiotherapy can improve a lot by the real-time muscle activity analysis. The gesture recognition can be used in gaming control and virtual reality. EMG readings can be useful for fitness tracking and injury prevention, making this research related to multiple fields.

Improvement of the system for getting consistent accuracy rate can be achieved by conducting this experiment in a professional and well-equipped biomedical research environment which would eliminate various environmental factors. To ensure robustness and reliability, extensive testing across diverse populations is necessary. This includes individuals with varying physiological conditions, muscle strengths, and levels of fatigue. Real-world scenarios, such as outdoor environments with potential interference or long-term usage studies, can help identify practical challenges and refine the system further. Additionally, a larger dataset would help the model be trained better making it adaptable to the population, as well as reach more insights of the pros and cons of the algorithm. Incorporating deep learning techniques, such as convolutional neural networks (CNNs) or recurrent neural networks (RNNs), could enhance the system's ability to classify more complex muscle patterns or multi-class activations.

Embedding the system into wearable devices equipped with onboard processing units can enable entirely portable and real-time solutions. This integration requires optimizing hardware-software interactions to ensure seamless data acquisition, processing, and classification. Wearable systems can find applications in rehabilitation, sports training, and assistive technologies, offering users immediate feedback and control.

REFERENCES

Aarotale, P. N., & Rattani, A. (2024, December). Machine Learning-based sEMG Signal Classification for Hand Gesture Recognition. In *2024 IEEE International Conference on Bioinformatics and Biomedicine (BIBM)* (pp. 6319-6326). IEEE. DOI: 10.1109/BIBM62325.2024.10822133

Azhiri, R. B., Esmaeili, M., & Nourani, M. (2021). Emg-based feature extraction and classification for prosthetic hand control. arXiv preprint arXiv:2107.00733.

Azhiri, R. B., Esmaeili, M., & Nourani, M. (2021, December). Real-time emg signal classification via recurrent neural networks. In *2021 IEEE International Conference on Bioinformatics and Biomedicine (BIBM)* (pp. 2628-2635). IEEE. DOI: 10.1109/BIBM52615.2021.9669872

Bhushan, S., Alshehri, M., Keshta, I., Chakraverti, A. K., Rajpurohit, J., & Abugabah, A. (2022). An experimental analysis of various machine learning algorithms for hand gesture recognition. *Electronics (Basel)*, *11*(6), 968. DOI: 10.3390/electronics11060968

Boyer, M., Bouyer, L., Roy, J. S., & Campeau-Lecours, A. (2023). Reducing noise, artificats and interference in single-channel emg signals: A review. *Sensors (Basel)*, *23*(6), 2927. DOI: 10.3390/s23062927 PMID: 36991639

Chen, Y., Wang, Y., Gao, F., Dong, B., Chen, W., & Liu, R. (2024). A Computational Method to Identify Optimal Functional Muscle Synergies from Estimated Muscle Activations. *IEEE Transactions on Instrumentation and Measurement*, *73*, 1–14. DOI: 10.1109/TIM.2024.3413171

Cho, R., Patel, S., Cho, K. T., & Hwang, J. (2024). Machine Learning Techniques to Identify Hand Gestures amidst Forearm Muscle Signals. *arXiv preprint arXiv:2401.07889.*

Ekinci, E., Garip, Z., & Serbest, K. (2023). Electromyography based hand movement classification and feature extraction using machine learning algorithms. *Politeknik Dergisi*, *26*(4), 1621–1633. DOI: 10.2339/politeknik.1348121

Estévez, S. R., Mallah, J., Kazieczko, D., Tang, C., & Occhipinti, L. G. (2024). Deep Learning for Motion Classification in Ankle Exoskeletons Using Surface EMG and IMU Signals. *arXiv preprint arXiv:2411.16273*. DOI: 10.21203/rs.3.rs-5446652/v1

Gaso, M. S., Cankurt, S., & Subasi, A. (2021, November). Electromyography signal classification using deep learning. In *2021 16th International Conference on Electronics Computer and Computation (ICECCO)* (pp. 1-6). IEEE. DOI: 10.1109/ICECCO53203.2021.9663803

Hosseini, M. P., Hosseini, A., & Ahi, K. (2020). A review on machine learning for EEG signal processing in bioengineering. *IEEE Reviews in Biomedical Engineering*, *14*, 204–218. DOI: 10.1109/RBME.2020.2969915 PMID: 32011262

Kamankesh, A., Rahimi, N., Amiridis, I. G., Sahinis, C., Hatzitaki, V., & Enoka, R. M. (2024). Distinguishing the Activity of Flexor Digitorum Brevis and Soleus Across Standing Postures with Deep Learning Models. *Gait & Posture*. PMID: 39674063

Khan, M. U., Khan, H., Muneeb, M., Abbasi, Z., Abbasi, U. B., & Baloch, N. K. (2021, August). Supervised machine learning based fast hand gesture recognition and classification using electromyography (emg) signals. In *2021 international conference on applied and engineering mathematics (ICAEM)* (pp. 81-86). IEEE.

Kok, C. L., Ho, C. K., Tan, F. K., & Koh, Y. Y. (2024). Machine learning based feature extraction and classification of emg signals for intuitive prosthetic control. *Applied Sciences (Basel, Switzerland)*, *14*(13), 5784. DOI: 10.3390/app14135784

Kotov-Smolenskiy, A. M., Khizhnikova, A. E., Klochkov, A. S., Suponeva, N. A., & Piradov, M. A. (2021). Surface EMG: Applicability in the motion analysis and opportunities for practical rehabilitation. *Human Physiology*, *47*(2), 237–247. DOI: 10.1134/S0362119721020043

Miah, A. S. M., Hassan, N., Maniruzzaman, M., Asai, N., & Shin, J. (2024). EMG-Based Hand Gesture Recognition through Diverse Domain Feature Enhancement and Machine Learning-Based Approach. *arXiv preprint arXiv:2408.13723*.

Nazmi, N., Abdul Rahman, M. A., Yamamoto, S.-I., Ahmad, S. A., Zamzuri, H., & Mazlan, S. A. (2016). A Review of Classification Techniques of EMG Signals during Isotonic and Isometric Contractions. *Sensors (Basel)*, *16*(8), 1304. DOI: 10.3390/s16081304 PMID: 27548165

Oliva-Lozano, J. M., & Muyor, J. M. (2020). Core muscle activity during physical fitness exercises: A systematic review. *International Journal of Environmental Research and Public Health*, *17*(12), 4306. DOI: 10.3390/ijerph17124306 PMID: 32560185

Pérez-Reynoso, F., Farrera-Vazquez, N., Capetillo, C., Méndez-Lozano, N., González-Gutiérrez, C., & López-Neri, E. (2022). Pattern recognition of emg signals by machine learning for the control of a manipulator robot. Sensors, 22(9), 3424. Author, F., Author, S., Author, T.: Book title. 2nd edn. Publisher, Location (1999). DOI: 10.3390/s22093424

Radha, H. M., & Hassan, A. K. A. (2022). A survey on bio-signal analysis for human-robot interaction. *International Journal of Electrical and Computer Engineering*, *12*(6), 5998. DOI: 10.11591/ijece.v12i6.pp5998-6009

Rahman, M. T., Rahman, M., & Shahnaz, C. (2023). EMG Signal Classification for Neuromuscular Disorders with Attention-Enhanced CNN. *arXiv preprint arXiv:2309.10483.*

Rajeswari, D. K., & Keerthana, G. Transfer Learning-Based Continuous Sign Language Observation Using Surface Electromyography Signals.

Sankaran, V., Alagumariappan, P., Sathyamoorthy, M., Dhanaraj, R. K., Krishnamurthy, K., & Cyril, E. (2024). An Internet of Medical Things-Based Smart Electromyogram Device for Monitoring of Musculoskeletal Disorders. *Engineering Proceedings*, •••, 6.

Seyidbayli, C., Salhi, F., & Akdogan, E. (2020). Comparison of machine learning algorithms for EMG signal classification. *Periodicals of Engineering and Natural Sciences*, *8*(2), 1165–1176.

Shefa, F. R., Sifat, F. H., Uddin, J., Ahmad, Z., Kim, J. M., & Kibria, M. G. (2024, November). Deep Learning and IoT-Based Ankle–Foot Orthosis for Enhanced Gait Optimization. [). MDPI.]. *Health Care*, *12*(22), 2273. PMID: 39595470

. Shigute Gaso, M., Cankurt, S., & Subasi, A. (2023). Electromyography Signal Classification Using Deep Learning. *arXiv e-prints*, arXiv-2305.

Swapna, M., Viswanadhula, U. M., Aluvalu, R., Vardharajan, V., & Kotecha, K. (2022). Bio-signals in medical applications and challenges using artificial intelligence. *Journal of Sensor and Actuator Networks*, *11*(1), 17. DOI: 10.3390/jsan11010017

Toledo-Pérez, D. C., Rodríguez-Reséndiz, J., Gómez-Loenzo, R. A., & Jauregui Correa, J. C. (2019). Support Vector Machine-Based EMG Signal Classification Techniques: A Review. *Applied Sciences (Basel, Switzerland)*, *9*(20), 4402. DOI: 10.3390/app9204402

Tsinganos, P., Cornelis, B., Cornelis, J., Jansen, B., & Skodras, A. (2018, September). Deep Learning in EMG-based Gesture Recognition. In *PhyCS* (pp. 107-114). DOI: 10.5220/0006960201070114

Wang, H., Ding, Q., Luo, Y., Wu, Z., Yu, J., Chen, H., Zhou, Y., Zhang, H., Tao, K., Chen, X., Fu, J., & Wu, J. (2024). High-Performance Hydrogel Sensors Enabled Multimodal and Accurate Human Machine Interaction System for Active Rehabilitation. *Advanced Materials*, *36*(11), 2309868. DOI: 10.1002/adma.202309868 PMID: 38095146

Wang, N., Niu, J., Liu, X., Yu, D., Zhu, G., Wu, X., & Su, H. (2024, January). BeyondVision: an EMG-driven micro hand gesture recognition based on dynamic segmentation. In *Proceedings of the Thirty-Third International Joint Conference on Artificial Intelligence* (pp. 6044-6052). DOI: 10.24963/ijcai.2024/668

Wang, R. (2024). Developing an optimization model for minimizing musculoskeletal stress in repetitive motion tasks. *Molecular & Cellular Biomechanics*, *21*(3), 567–567. DOI: 10.62617/mcb567

. Xiong, D., Zhang, D., Zhao, X., & Zhao, Y. (2021). Deep learning for EMG-based human-machine interaction: A review. IEEE/CAA Journal of Automatica Sinica, 8(3), 512-533.

Yoneda, S., & Furui, A. (2023, October). Bayesian Approach for Adaptive EMG Pattern Classification Via Semi-Supervised Sequential Learning. In *2023 IEEE International Conference on Systems, Man, and Cybernetics (SMC)* (pp. 3310-3315). IEEE. DOI: 10.1109/SMC53992.2023.10394290

Chapter 7
Wireless Sensor Networks and Communication Protocols

Mohammad Jeelani
Future University, India

Mohd Muqeem
Sandip University, India

Sultan Ahmad
https://orcid.org/0000-0002-3198-7974
Prince Sattam Bin Abdulaziz University, Alkharj, Saudi Arabia & Chandigarh University, Mohali, India

Aasim Zafar
https://orcid.org/0000-0003-1331-014X
Aligarh Muslim University, India

Mourade Azrour
Faculty of Sciences and Technics, Moulay Ismail University of Meknes, Morocco

Kishan Pal Singh
https://orcid.org/0000-0002-4289-6875
FET, Mangalayatan University, India

ABSTRACT

Wireless sensor networks has the potential to completely change a number of industries, including smart cities, healthcare, industrial automation, and environmental monitoring. WSNs use wireless communication between spatially dispersed autonomous sensors to track environmental or physical parameters like motion, pressure, temperature, and humidity. In this paper, we propose the trust-based approach for changing nodes with energy (TBNE) model, a trust-based strategy in a wireless sensor network. TBNE locates the network's troublesome nodes. The structure enhances node performance based on the trust concept for secure communication in WSN. Using its wireless interface, the device records a physical event and sends it to a base station. When a base station and sensor node cannot communicate directly, hop-by-hop communication is needed. The proposed approach is in a wireless sensor network called the rust-based approach for varying nodes with energy (TBNE)

DOI: 10.4018/979-8-3373-0330-7.ch007

Copyright © 2025, IGI Global Scientific Publishing. Copying or distributing in print or electronic forms without written permission of IGI Global Scientific Publishing is prohibited.

model. Moreover, these results are validated with two simulators for better findings.

1. INTRODUCTION

Sensor nodes, which are independent gadgets containing a microcontroller, radio, sensors, and a set of batteries, make up a wireless sensor network (WSN). The device records a physical event and transmits it to a base station via its wireless interface. When a base station and sensor node cannot communicate directly, hop-by-hop communication is needed. Since WSNs may be quickly deployed in an area without further investments in a cable installation, they are projected to be employed in various scenarios (for example, emergency response, wildlife monitoring, or battlefield monitoring). When energy resources are considered, the advantage changes into a disadvantage. There are only two AA batteries in a typical sensor node. Energy conservation becomes challenging when a WSN is presumed to be left unattended, which is a common scenario (Ahmed et al. 2015) and (asha et al. 2019).

(Ahmad et al 2015) and (Duan et al 2014) employ the trust and energy-aware routing protocol (TERP) and TSRF concepts, which are lightweight and highly resistant to a variety of threats. These outcomes are then contrasted with energy to determine the favorable outcome. The trust-based strategy for variable nodes with energy (TBNE) model is the method we suggest in a wireless sensor network, nonetheless, if we want more effective outcomes. Moreover, these results are validated with two simulators for better findings. Therefore, the proposed approach gives the appropriate results with the help of their simulation.

TBNE focuses on two critical aspects: trustworthiness and varying energy effectiveness, essential for WSNs operating in hostile environments prone to attacks(Ahmad et al 2020). TBNE guides sensor nodes to transmit packets along the shortest paths, considering both trust and energy levels of varying nodes within the network.

Many brand-new protocols that consider the characteristics of WSNs have been put forth, including required distribution, routing, and medium access control (MAC) protocols. Only a few of these, though, were tested on actual hardware. Compared to simulations, which offer a simple and relatively quick evaluation of proposals, testing becomes more time-consuming when a test has dozens or hundreds of sensor nodes. However, when realistic models are not employed, or they are not appropriately calibrated, the simulation results are erroneous (frequently, even deceptive).

One of the most popular evaluation approaches in the field of computer networks is, without a doubt, network simulation. It is frequently employed in creating new network protocols and communication architectures (Ahmad & Afzal, 2022). By defining the behavior of the network nodes and the communication channels, so-called network simulators enable one to model any computer network. For instance, a novel routing protocol is typically built in a network simulator to study its properties. The routing behavior can be readily investigated in a variety of topologies, since the network topology is merely a collection of simulation parameters.

These advancements have led to the development of more efficient, reliable, and scalable WSNs capable of addressing the evolving requirements of diverse applications (Asha et al. 2019).

Despite the progress made, several challenges remain in the design, deployment, and management of WSNs. Issues such as energy efficiency, data security, network scalability, and robustness in harsh environments continue to pose significant research challenges. Addressing these challenges requires interdisciplinary approaches that encompass aspects of computer science. The proposed approach is in a wireless sensor network called the rust-based approach for varying nodes with energy (TBNE) model. Moreover, these results are validated with two simulators for better findings. The simulation has been done with QualNet 5.0 and NS-2.35 simulators, respectively. The simulation results with parameters like average throughput, packet delivery ratio, energy consumption, and end-to-end delay.

The format of this paper is as follows: Section. 2 gives the related work of trust-based routing protocol and result validation. Section 3 elaborates on the proposed model and also provides the corresponding strategy. Section 4 presents the simulation analysis details with its parameter and value. Section 5 moves on to the result validation of the compared simulators. Section 6 brings the paper to a conclusion.

2. RELATED WORK

(Ahmed et al. 2015) have presented a "trust and energy-aware routing protocol (TERP)" it uses a distributed trust paradigm to identify and isolate malfunctioning and misbehaving nodes. Furthermore, when making routing decisions, TERP uses a composite routing feature that takes into account confidence, residual energy, and hop counts of neighbor nodes. This multi-facet routing strategy aids in efficiently routing data while balancing energy consumption among trusted nodes. When compared to previous work, the simulation results show that TERP uses fewer resources, has a longer network lifetime, and has a better overall performance. (Alrahhal et al. 2022) have proposed a novel approach to utilize acknowledgment (ACK) messages for enhancing trust in wireless sensor networks (WSNs). It suggests using ACKs to establish and verify trust between nodes, thus improving the overall reliability and security of WSNs. O. I. (Akinola, 2024) has investigated the development and enhancement of adaptive location-based routing protocols within dynamic wireless sensor networks (WSNs) in urban cyber-physical systems, recommending the implementation of the study's innovative Urban Adaptive Location-based Routing

Protocol (UALRP) (Haque et al., 2024). This innovative protocol integrates real-time data analytics and adaptive machine learning models into its algorithmic framework to dynamically optimize routing decisions based on continuously changing urban conditions. Through the utilization of data-driven simulation models and machine learning techniques, the research sought to significantly improve the efficiency, reliability, and scalability of urban WSNs. (Asha and Santhosh 2019) have proposed the novel paradigm of trust-based self-organized hierarchical energy balancing routing protocol helps address the main issues in wireless sensor networks, namely storage and security. Every sensor node maintains its energy level, and interactions between nearby nodes and cluster leaders are referred to as trust transactions. (Ballav et al. 2015) examined how a blackhole attack would affect a mobile sensor network's Zone-Based Energy-Efficient Routing Protocol. The proposed routing protocol and blackhole-affected routing protocol (BAODV) are compared to each other in this study by the NS-2.35 simulator. (Cherappa et al. 2023) have optimized the selection of cluster heads through energy stabilization, distance reduction, and latency minimization between nodes. Because of these constraints, achieving optimal energy resource utilization is an essential problem in WSNs. Further, the proposed method used to evaluate the packet delivery ratio (PDR), packet delay, throughput, power consumption, network lifetime, packet loss rate, and error estimation, and the results were superior to existing methods. (Daniel and Roslin 2021) have put forth a protocol for designing trust-based data gathering in WSN that uses data validation and integrity verification. In the WSN, data validation and honesty are critical. After legitimate data is found using a tree that is created and assessed for every node according to its trust features, the data is encrypted using a symmetrical key via the trust-based data aggregation protocol. The data correctness displayed in these comparison graphs was enhanced in this study by using the propped approach. (Duan et al. 2014) proposed "TSRF with lightweight and high ability to resist various attacks". They also proposed a scheme for specific trust computation and trust derivation and analyzed results in this work. All work is simulated in the ns-2 simulator. (Gaber et al. 2018) proposed the "Bat Optimization Algorithm for cluster heads based on residual energy, trust value, and the number of neighbors". This BOA algorithm selects the cluster heads and their parameters. This article compares BOA with LEACH, SEP, and DEEC under homogenous and heterogeneous networks, all simulation in MATLAB.

(Ghosh and Bhattacharya 2013) have calculated "Trust and Aggregation of a node using Poisson distribution in WSN". In this paper, complete trust can be calculated using a probabilistic approach for direct trust and a Dumpster-Shafer theory for indirect trust (combination of evidence). Also, using the Poisson distribution, determine the aggregation value of author a node and equate the packet delivery ratio value to the average cumulative Poisson distribution. (Hajiee et al.

2021) energy-aware trust and opportunity-based routing (ETOR), in which the best route is chosen based on a new hybrid fitness function, is advised in addition to the multipath routing technique. Unlike previous opportunistic routing systems like MORE or ExOR, ETOR considers energy limitations. In the WSN, secure nodes are selected using the tolerance constant, and routes are determined by combining opportunity and trust using a novel hybrid fitness function. Moreover, the simulated work with MATLAB simulator. (Han et al. 2022) have presented a routing protocol for wireless sensor networks (WSNs) that aims to optimize energy consumption while ensuring security through a trust-based approach. The protocol utilizes an adaptive genetic algorithm to dynamically adjust routing paths based on the energy levels of nodes and their trustworthiness. The protocol's effectiveness is evaluated through simulations, which demonstrate its ability to prolong network lifetime and enhance security compared to existing routing protocols. (Hassen et al. 2019) developed the energy-efficient protocol with the help of grid-based clustering to improve network durability, reduced cost, and increase network performance. The sensor nodes have limited resources and power, here nodes can reserve a protraction of the network durability with the help of the GBC algorithm. Researchers compared AODV protocol AODV, OLSR, and DSR in a study with a QualNet simulator. (Jeelani et al. 2019) have proposed "A Distributed Trust-Based Approach for Wireless Sensor Networks". The proposed model uses direct and indirect sensor node confidence estimations, which also consider the relationship of data collection over time, and then uses approximate rough information in decision making for safe data transmission, avoiding malicious nodes(Imam et al., 2023).

(Ju et al. 2010) based on weighted-trust evaluation, a scheme for detecting malicious nodes was developed. Each sensor node is given a weight value at the start, which is changed each cycle doubt the node sends a report that differs from the others. (Kalidoss et al. 2019) carried out the study to propose routing protocols like "Quality of Service (QoS) aware energy-efficient routing protocol". These are founded on trust and energy modeling and are used to improve t wireless sensor networks' protection and communication while reducing energy consumption. Furthermore, they explored faith and measured how to enhance communication protection in their work. In addition, they suggest a cluster-based routing algorithm in which the cluster head is focused on QoS metrics and trusts. (Kevre and Shrivastava 2014) have compared the "three routing protocols in grid-based clustering for WSN". In WSN, sensor networks have limited energy and battery power. Routing protocols are compared as AODV, DSR, and DYMO with QualNet simulator for some matrices in the scenario. (Khalid et al. 2019) proposed adaptive forwarder selection, considering various factors, including those suggested by other researchers. Negotiation, game theory, and learning-based procedures are also used in selecting the next forwarder. On the other hand, these techniques are better suited to networks with resourceful nodes. (Kumar et al. 2012) in this survey, Scholars have put up a number of models and potential applications for trust and reputation models. These are also employed in wireless sensor networks for security reasons; this study discovered that these networks are protected against a variety of threats. The majority of the methods in this study operate in a static setting. Numerous uses for wireless sensor networks are discussed here, with an emphasis on improving performance. (Mao 2010) constructed it to react to the formal semantics for intrusion detection, and a security ontology based on WSN features was developed. They also proposed several intrusion detection algorithms based on the WSN structure, which solved the intrusion detection problem through a decentralized and cooperative process(-Sathish et al., 2022).

(Pahal and Dalal 2016) have contrasted the way in which WSN routing protocols perform, estimated the behavior of the QualNet simulation for the OLSR, DSR, DYMO, and ZRP routing protocols. Compared the study's performance to a few parameters. The DYMO performed better when compared to ZRP, DSR, and OLSR. (Reddy et al. 2023) have presented an innovative approach to enhance the energy efficiency and security of wireless sensor networks (WSNs) through the introduction of a Master Auditor Node (MAN). The MAN is responsible for auditing the behavior of sensor nodes based on trust levels and coordinating secure routing in the network. The key contributions of the paper include: Energy Efficiency, Trust-Based Secure Routing and Auditing Mechanism. Further, the paper provided simulation results demonstrated the effectiveness of the proposed approach in terms of energy efficiency, network lifetime, and security compared to existing approaches. (Selvi et al. 2019) Proposed energy conscious trust based fast routing method, a new secure routing technique. This technique evaluates trust scores in order to efficiently identify malevolent users in WSN. The optimal path is chosen by combining a decision tree method with spatiotemporal restrictions. Furthermore, in terms of security, energy economy, and packet delivery ratio, the trust-based routing algorithm outperforms previous systems significantly. (Singh and Gandotra 2015) has focused on the sensor network and how all the nodes are connected in the network. Also considered are the attacks like malicious node attack, Sybil attack black-hole attack etcetera. Researchers have simulated an NS-2 simulator for evaluating the attacks.

(Tyagi and Kumar 2023) have presented a detailed analysis of the proposed protocol's performance through simulation studies, demonstrating its effectiveness in improving network throughput, reducing packet loss, and enhancing energy efficiency compared to existing protocols. The results highlight the potential of integrating trust-based mechanisms with machine learning techniques to enhance WSN performance and address the challenges of dynamic and resource-constrained environments. (Taghikhaki et al. 2015) proposed the probabilistic coverage algorithm with help of trust for integer linear programming problems. This problem always required quality of service resected by node or environment. The authors also put forwarded a greedy algorithm to find the almost same complications without any problem from complexities imposed by integer linear programming. Compared the results with different input parameters in the simulation. (Thippeswamy et al. 2013) the "secures trust-aware energy-efficient adaptive routing in WSNs" was developed and implemented. F This approach provides secure, reliable, and energy-efficient routing for multi-hop networks. They have designed an algorithm for identifying the malicious nodes with the help of a dynamic secret key. Here, simulation comparison with tree types attacks which is a wormhole, sinkhole, and Sybil attack, all comparison with NS-2 simulator. (Vir et al. 2013) have created an energy model power consumption performance of power consumption and examined routing protocol. They compared the OLSR, LAR, DSR, and Fisheye with the matrices average jitter, power consumption sending and receiving mode, idle mode, and battery. The whole scenario was simulated with QualNet simulation.

(Yamuna et al. 2014) have to the multipath routing technique, energy-aware trust and opportunity-based routing (ETOR) is recommended, where the optimal path is determined by a novel hybrid fitness function. ETOR takes energy constraints into account, in contrast to earlier opportunistic routing schemes like MORE or ExOR. In the WSN, secure nodes are selected using the tolerance constant, and routes are determined by combining opportunity and trust using a novel hybrid fitness function. The positive effect positively affects the network's end-to-end delay and lifetime, according to simulation studies. For simulation, they used the NS2 simulator. (Zhanga et al. 2020) improved the performance of WSNs with the help of a trust-based dynamics slicing mechanism in their work. Trust mechanisms have parameters, namely data forwarding number (DFN), transmission delay, and packet loss rate in these proposed model TDSM. Compared with existing models like SMART, EEHA, and HEEPP, TDSM gave positive results against current models.

Table 1. Related Work

Authors	Year	Title	Summary	Simulation Tool
Ahmed et al.	2015	"Trust and energy-aware routing protocol (TERP)"	TERP utilizes a distributed trust paradigm to identify and isolate malfunctioning and misbehaving nodes. It employs a composite routing feature considering confidence, residual energy, and hop counts for efficient data routing and energy consumption balancing.	NS-2 Simulator
Alrahhal et al.	2022	"Utilising Acknowledge for the Trust in Wireless Sensor Networks"	The paper proposes a novel approach to utilize acknowledgment (ACK) messages for enhancing trust in wireless sensor networks (WSNs). It suggests using ACKs to establish and verify trust between nodes, thus improving the overall reliability and security of WSNs.	TRMSIM-WSN Simulator
O. I. Akinola	2024	"Adaptive Location-based Routing Protocols for Dynamic Wireless Sensor Networks in Urban Cyber-physical Systems"	investigated the development and enhancement of adaptive location-based routing protocols within dynamic wireless sensor networks (WSNs) in urban cyber-physical systems, recommending the implementation of the study's innovative Urban Adaptive Location-based Routing Protocol (UALRP).	Realistic network simulations
Asha and R. Santhosh	2019	"Trust-based self-organized hierarchical energy balancing routing protocol"	A novel trust-based approach addressing storage and security issues in wireless sensor networks. Nodes maintain energy levels, and trust transactions are established between nearby nodes and cluster leaders.	Not specified
Ballav et al.	2015	"Investigation of blackhole attack in a mobile sensor network with the effect on Zone-Based energy-efficient routing protocol"	Study comparing proposed routing protocol with blackhole-affected routing protocol (BAODV) using NS-2.35 simulator.	NS-2.35 Simulator
Cherappa et al.	2023	"Energy-Efficient Clustering and Routing Using ASFO and a Cross-Layer-Based Expedient Routing Protocol for Wireless Sensor Networks"	optimized the selection of cluster heads through energy stabilization, distance reduction, and latency minimization between nodes. Because of these constraints, achieving optimal energy resource utilization is an essential problem in WSNs.	MATLAB
Daniel and Roslin	2021	"Trust-based data collection protocol employing data validation and integrity verification in WSN"	Proposed protocol ensures data validation and integrity in WSN by employing trust features and encryption techniques. Enhances data correctness and security.	Not specified
Duan et al.	2014	"TSRF with lightweight and high ability to resist various attacks"	Proposal of TSRF with specific trust computation and analysis of results using NS-2 simulator.	NS-2 Simulator

continued on following page

Table 1. Continued

Authors	Year	Title	Summary	Simulation Tool
Gaber et al.	2018	"Bat Optimization Algorithm for cluster heads based on residual energy, trust value, and number of neighbors"	BOA algorithm selects cluster heads based on residual energy, trust, and neighbor count. Simulation conducted in MATLAB, comparing with LEACH, SEP, and DEEC under various network conditions.	MATLAB
Ghosh and Bhattacharya	2013	"Trust and Aggregation of a node using Poisson distribution in WSN"	Calculating complete trust using probabilistic approach and determining aggregation value using Poisson distribution. Simulation-based study in WSN environment.	Not specified
Hajiee et al.	2021	"Energy-aware trust and opportunity-based routing (ETOR)"	ETOR utilizes multipath routing technique considering energy limits. Simulation was conducted in MATLAB to evaluate performance and effectiveness.	MATLAB
Han et al.	2022	"Energy-Aware and Trust-Based Secure Routing Protocol for Wireless Sensor Networks Using Adaptive Genetic Algorithm"	The paper presents a routing protocol for wireless sensor networks (WSNs) that aims to optimize energy consumption while ensuring security through a trust-based approach. The protocol utilizes an adaptive genetic algorithm to dynamically adjust routing paths based on the energy levels of nodes and their trustworthiness.	MATLAB
Hassen et al.	2019	"Energy-efficient protocol with grid-based clustering"	GBC algorithm enhances network durability and performance. Comparison with AODV, OLSR, and DSR using QualNet simulator.	QualNet
Jeelani et al.	2019	"Distributed Trust-Based Approach for Wireless Sensor Networks"	Proposed model employs direct and indirect confidence estimations for safe data transmission, considering temporal relationships. Utilizes rough information in decision making.	Not specified
Ju et al.	2010	"Scheme for detecting malicious nodes based on weighted-trust evaluation"	Weighted-trust evaluation used to detect malicious nodes. Simulation-based analysis of scheme's effectiveness.	Not specified
Kalidoss et al.	2019	"Quality of Service (QoS) aware energy-efficient routing protocol"	Routing protocols based on trust and energy modeling proposed to enhance WSN protection and communication. Simulation-based study evaluating communication security and energy consumption.	Not specified
Kevre and Shrivastava	2014	"Comparison of routing protocols in grid-based clustering for WSN"	Comparison of AODV, DSR, and DYMO using QualNet simulator.	QualNet
Khalid et al.	2019	"Adaptive forwarder selection considering various factors"	Proposal of adaptive forwarder selection incorporating negotiation, game theory, and learning-based procedures. Simulation-based study assessing suitability for resourceful networks.	Not specified
Kumar et al.	2012	"Survey on trust and reputation models in wireless sensor networks"	Survey analyzing various models and applications for trust and reputation in WSNs. Study focuses on security enhancement and performance improvement.	Not specified

continued on following page

Table 1. Continued

Authors	Year	Title	Summary	Simulation Tool
Mao	2010	"Intrusion detection algorithms based on security ontology in WSN"	Proposal of intrusion detection algorithms based on security ontology. Decentralized and cooperative process used for intrusion detection.	Not specified
Pahal and Dalal	2016	"Evaluation of WSN routing protocols using QualNet simulation"	Comparison of OLSR, DSR, DYMO, and ZRP using QualNet simulator.	QualNet
Reddy et al.	2023	"An Energy Efficient Master Auditor Node with Trust Based Secure Routing in Wireless Sensor Networks"	The paper presents an innovative approach to enhance wireless sensor networks' energy efficiency and security (WSNs) by introducing a Master Auditor Node (MAN). The MAN is responsible for auditing the behavior of sensor nodes based on trust levels and coordinating secure routing in the network.	NS-2 Simulator
Selvi et al.	2019	"Energy conscious trust-based fast routing method"	Proposal of trust-based routing algorithm considering security and energy efficiency. Simulation study demonstrating significant improvement over previous systems.	Not specified
Singh and Gandotra	2015	"Evaluation of sensor network connectivity and attacks using NS-2 simulator"	Study focuses on sensor network connectivity and defense against various attacks. Simulation conducted using NS-2 simulator.	NS-2 Simulator
Taghikhaki et al.	2013	"Probabilistic coverage algorithm with trust for integer linear programming problems"	Proposal of probabilistic coverage algorithm with trust for addressing integer linear programming problems. Simulation-based comparison with different input parameters.	Not specified
Thippeswamy et al.	2015	"Secure trust-aware energy-efficient adaptive routing in WSNs"	Development of secure, reliable, and energy-efficient routing algorithm for WSNs. Simulation comparison with tree-based attacks using NS-2 simulator.	NS-2 Simulator
Tyagi and Kumar	2023	"A Hybrid Trust Based WSN protocol to Enhance Network Performance using Fuzzy Enabled Machine Learning Technique"	The paper presents a detailed analysis of the proposed protocol's performance through simulation studies, demonstrating its effectiveness in improving network throughput, reducing packet loss, and enhancing energy efficiency compared to existing protocols.	MATLAB
Vir et al.	2013	"Performance evaluation of routing protocols in WSNs"	Evaluation of OLSR, LAR, DSR, and Fisheye using QualNet simulation.	QualNet
Yamuna et al.	2014	"Multi-hop Optimal position-based Opportunistic Routing (MOOR) protocol in WSN"	Proposal of MOOR protocol for efficient data transmission in WSNs. Simulation study conducted using NS2 simulator.	NS2 Simulator
Zhanga et al.	2020	"Trust-based dynamics slicing mechanism for improving WSN performance"	Proposal of TDSM for enhancing WSN performance based on trust mechanisms. Comparative study with existing models conducted.	Not specified

3. PROPOSED MODEL

The TBNE routing protocol navigates the complex and dynamic world of wireless sensor networks (WSNs) with a double-pronged approach: trust estimation and energy routing. Imagine each sensor node as a citizen in a virtual society, constantly interacting and exchanging information. Trust estimation acts as the vigilant gatekeeper, scrutinizing each node's trustworthiness. It draws upon a treasure trove of data stored in a "trusted database," where factors like a node's unique ID, its track record of forwarding packets successfully, and even predictions about its future reliability are carefully assessed. This intricate evaluation helps distinguish the honest nodes from the deceitful ones. But trust alone isn't enough. The TBNE protocol understands that resources are precious in a WSN, and energy efficiency is paramount. That's where the energy routing model takes center stage. When charting a path for data transmission, it prioritizes trustworthy nodes, ensuring information flows through reliable hands. However, it doesn't blindly favour trust over efficiency(Meenakshi et al., 2024). If a less trustworthy path offers significant energy savings, the energy-conscious model might choose it, provided the node still has enough juice to complete the task. A crucial threshold is set to ensure nodes on the brink of exhaustion are excluded, preserving the long-term health of the network.

This dynamic interplay between trust and energy creates a resilient routing system. Imagine a scenario where a malicious actor infiltrates the network, siphoning energy or tampering with data. The ever-watchful route maintenance mechanism springs into action. It continuously monitors active routes, detecting any suspicious activity or energy depletion. If a node raises red flags, an alert is sent to the source, triggering the creation of a new, secure, and energy-efficient route, ensuring data continues to flow seamlessly and safely. The TBNE routing protocol, with its focus on both trust and energy, goes beyond simply finding the shortest path. It fosters a secure and sustainable environment within the WSN, allowing sensor nodes to collaborate and share information efficiently, even in the face of challenges and uncertainties. It's like building a society where trust and responsible resource management go hand in hand, paving the way for a healthy and thriving network ecosystem.

Figure 1. TBNE Proposed Model

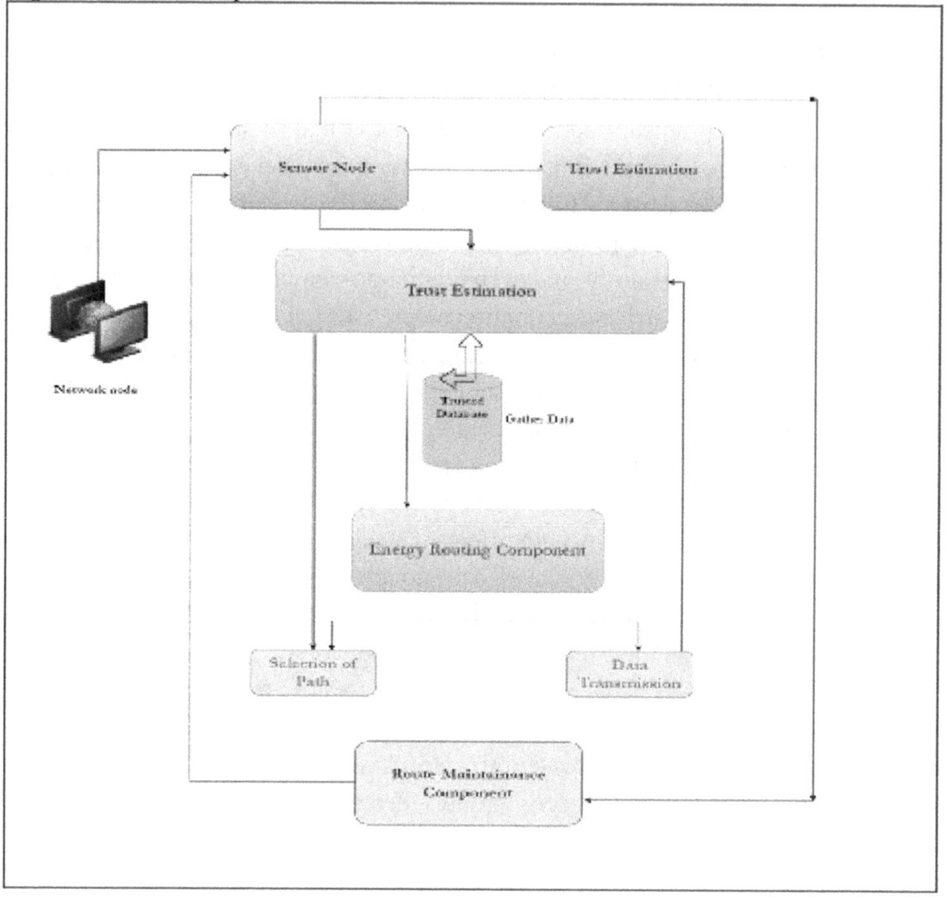

3.1 Algorithm 1: TBNE

This algorithm 1 cleverly navigates the complex world of sensor networks, finding the perfect balance between security and efficiency. It prioritizes trustworthy nodes for data transmission, ensuring information travels through reliable hands. But it doesn't stop there! The algorithm understands the precious nature of energy in these networks, so it also factors in the energy levels of potential routes. By cleverly tracking the trustworthiness and energy levels of its neighbors, the TBNE Protocol calculates a score for each possible route, balancing both security and efficiency. Also, it doesn't rest on its laurels – if a node exhibits suspicious behavior or runs low on energy, the algorithm swiftly adjusts routes to maintain a secure and energy-efficient data flow. In essence, the TBNE Protocol acts like a wise and resourceful traveler, choosing the safest and most sustainable path for data to travel in the sensor network.

Algorithm 1

```
public class TBNEProtocol {

private static final double ALPHA = 0.8;

private static final double BETA = 0.2;

private static final double ENERGY_THRESHOLD = 0.5;

private Map<String, Neighbor> neighbors;

private String nodeId;

public TBNEProtocol(String nodeId) {

this.nodeId = nodeId;

this.neighbors = new HashMap<>();

}

public Route getRoute(String destination) {

// Find all paths to the destination
```

```
List<Path> paths = findPaths(destination);
Path bestPath = null;
double bestScore = Double.NEGATIVE_INFINITY;
for (Path path: paths) {
double score = evaluatePath(path);
if (score > bestScore) {
bestPath = path;
bestScore = score;
} }
return bestPath;
}
private List<Path> findPaths(String destination)
{
}
```

```
private double evaluatePath(Path path) {

double trustScore = 1.0;

double energyScore = 1.0;

for (Node node: path.getNodes()) {

Neighbor neighbor = neighbors.get(node.getId());

if (neighbor == null) {

return Double.NEGATIVE_INFINITY;

}

trustScore *= neighbor.getTrustScore();

energyScore *= node.getEnergyLevel()

return ALPHA * trustScore + BETA * energyScore;

}

public void updateTrust(String neighborId, boolean packet-
Forwarded) {
```

```
Neighbor neighbor = neighbors.get(neighborId);

if (neighbor == null) {

return; // Ignore unknown neighbor

}

if (packetForwarded) {

neighbor.incrementTrust();

} else {

neighbor.decrementTrust();

}

}

public void updateEnergy(String neighborId, double ener-
gyLevel) {

Neighbor neighbor = neighbors.get(neighborId);

if (neighbor == null) {
```

```
return;
}
neighbor.setEnergyLevel(energyLevel);
}
public void handleSuspiciousActivity(String neighborId) {
Neighbor neighbor = neighbors.get(neighborId);
if (neighbor == null) {
return;
}
neighbor.resetTrust();
}
private static class Neighbor {
private final String id;
private double trustScore;
```

```
private double energyLevel;

private double maxEnergy;

public Neighbor(String id, double maxEnergy) {

this.id = id;

this.trustScore = 0.5;

this.energyLevel = maxEnergy;

this.maxEnergy = maxEnergy;

}

public String getId() {

return id;

}

public double getTrustScore() {

return trustScore;

}
```

```
public void incrementTrust() {

trustScore = Math.min(trustScore + 0.1, 1.0);

}

public void decrementTrust() {

trustScore = Math.max(trustScore - 0.1, 0.0);

}

public void resetTrust() {

trustScore = 0.5;

}

public double getEnergyLevel() {

return energyLevel;

}

public void setEnergyLevel(double energyLevel) {

this.energyLevel = Math.max(energyLevel, 0.0);
```

```
}

public double getMaxEnergy() {

return maxEnergy;

}}}
```

3.2 Trust Estimation

In Trust Estimation section, determines whether or not neighbours are trustworthy by listening in on their transmissions in an unrestrained manner and dynamically detecting misbehaving nodes. Data for example packet ID, next-hop ID, subject and object IDs are stored in a buffer on each sensor node. Assume that nodes *a, b*, and *c* are neighbours who exchange packets among a couple of source and destination nodes in Figure 2.

Since the essential broadcast feature of wireless media, for every packet forwarded through node *a* to *b*, it is possible to determine if node a forwarded it to node *c*.

Figure 2. **Routing table structure**

Destination Address	**Destination Sequence Number**	**Routes**					
		Next Hop Mac Address	**Life Time**	**Hop Count**	**Traffic Rate**	**Trust**	**Energy**
ID1	SeqNum1						
ID2	SeqNum1						
	. . .						
IDn	SeqNum…n						

Node a saves the entries in its buffer after sending a positive number of packets to node b and waits for node b's answer. If node a discovers that the packets promoted by node b match the packets in the buffer's immutable fields, It assumes node b has properly accelerated the packets to next-hop c and raises node b's packet promoting counter $PF_{a,b}$. Otherwise, node a believes that node b did not advance the packets (Ahmed et al. 2015).

Based on monitored information, the trust model (at nodes a and c) categorizes each of the observed sensor nodes (node b) into one of three categories: trustworthy node, varying node, or defective node. Uncertainty node a and node c find a match in matching entries, and node b is considered a trusted node. If the number of packet IDs in the perceived packet from node b is substantially below the number of packet IDs in the buffer, but the packet hash values match the buffer contents, node a and node c declare node b as faulty. Node b misinform node a but not node c if it sends a fake response suggesting correct packet forwarding to node c, by comparison matching accesses in the buffer by packet IDs besides hash ideas of packets in overheard packets, node c will detect malicious behavior of node b, so all received packets from node and are dropped. By observing and aggregating the number of packets promoted in node b, nodes a and c will determine the behavior of node b.

Let $T_{a,b}(t)$ stand time t, reflect the degree of trust that node a has for its neighbor b. The degree of trust is restricted to non-stop small values between 0 and 1, indicating how much a node trusts its neighboring node. If a node's trust level is 0 or close to 0, it indicates total mistrust, while a trust degree of 1 or close to 1 indicates a trusted person. $T_{a,b}(t)$ is a measure of absolute confidence.

$$T_{a,b}(t) = w_1 DT_{a,b}(t) + w_2 \frac{IT^{c}_{a,b}(t)}{N_a} \text{ (Equation.1)}$$

$DT_{a,b}(t)$ is a grade of direct trust node a stand for node b at time t, constructed on the node a's reflection of packet advancing performance for node b. $IT^{c}_{a,b}(t)$ represents the average degree of indirect trust node a has achieved for node b at time t using recommendations from its neighbors (c). N_b characterizes a set containing neighbors for node c. The weight associate w_1 and w_2 are allotted to $DT_{a,b}(t)$ and $IT_{a,b}(t)$ correspondingly, such that $w_1 + w_2 = 1$, while $0 \leq w_1 \leq 1$ and $0 \leq w_2 \leq 1$.

Indirect trust is resolute using the data in the adjacent table, as shown below (Ahmed et al. 2015) and (Duan et al. 2014):

$$IT^{c}_{a,b} = \sum_{b=1}^{n} T^{a}_{b} * T_b \text{ (Equation .2)}$$

T_b^a indicates the trust of node b on node a and T_b is the trust amount to the counseling node b. The mean of present instructions to node a payable to the trust amount of the counseling nodes is known as indirect trust. The formula for calculating direct confidence is as follows:

$$DT_{a,b} = m_1 * \frac{n_{correct_a}}{n_{total_a}} + m_2 * re_a \text{ (Equation .3)}$$

$n_{correct_a}$ indicates several packets sent correctly and n_{total_a} denotes an entire number of packets that are sent by node a. Node a's remaining energy is re_a with weight m_2.

3.3 Algorithm for Trust Estimation in TBNE Routing Protocol

This algorithm 2 for the TBNE protocol lets sensor nodes assess if their neighbors are trustworthy. It listens to their transmissions, tracks forwarded packets, and consults neighboring nodes' feedback. Based on this, it assigns a trust score and decides whether to send data through that neighbor. Nodes with good forwarding records and positive feedback from others are trusted, while those with suspicious behavior are avoided. This helps ensure secure and efficient data routing in the network.

Algorithm 2

Inputs:

- *a: Sensor node ID*
- *b: Neighboring sensor node ID*
- *c: Another neighboring sensor node ID*
- *packet_buffer: Buffer containing overheard packet information at node a (packet ID, next-hop ID, subject ID, object ID)*
- *received_packets: List of packet IDs received from node b*
- *PFa,b: Packet forwarding counter for node b at node a*
- *Ta,b(t): Current trust level of node a towards node b at time t*
- *rea: Remaining energy of node a*
- *w1, w2: Weights for direct and indirect trust (0 <= w1, w2 <= 1)*

Outputs:

- *updated_PFa,b: Updated packet forwarding counter for node b*
- *new_Ta,b(t): Updated trust level of node a towards node b*

Algorithm

1. **Monitor and Buffer Packets:**

   Listen to transmissions between node b and other nodes.

- For each overheard packet:
  - Extract packet ID, next-hop ID, subject ID, and object ID.
  - If node b is the sender and next-hop is not c:
  - Store packet information in packet_buffer.

2. **Check Packet Forwarding:**

- After sending a batch of packets to node b:
  - Wait for response from node b.
  - Compare packet IDs in received_packets with packet_buffer.
- If all packet IDs match and hash values are identical:
  - Increment PFa,b.
  - **trusted_node = True**
- Else if some packet IDs match and hash values are identical:
  - Decrement PFa,b.
  - **suspicious_node = True**
- Else:
  - Set PFa,b to 0.
  - **faulty_node = True**

3. **Calculate Direct Trust:**

- DTa,b(t) = Pfb / total_packets_sent_to_b
- If faulty_node:
  - Set DTa,b(t) = 0

4. **Calculate Indirect Trust:**

- For each neighbor c in neighbor_list:
  - Get Tb,c: Trust level of node c towards node b.
  - Calculate weighted average of neighbor trust: ITa,b(t) = sum(Tb,c * w1) / sum(w1)

5. **Update Overall Trust:**

- new_Ta,b(t) = w1 * DTa,b(t) + w2 * ITa,b(t)

6. **Update Packet Forwarding Counter:**

- updated_PFa,b = Pfb + min(new_Ta,b(t), 1) * rea

7. **Decision Making:**

- If trusted_node:
  - Forward data through node b.
- If suspicious_node:
  - Monitor node b more closely.
- If faulty_node:
  - Drop packets from node b.
  - Consider alternative routes.

4. SIMULATION RESULTS

This section deals with simulation results and validates the results with QualNet and NS-2 simulators, respectively.

4.1. Simulation of TBNE, TERP and TSRF Models with QualNet

This simulation scenario aims to analyze the performance of the TBNE mode compared with TERP and TSRF via routing protocol based on varying nodes. The simulations have been created with QualNet version 5.0.2 software, which allows for scalable wireless sensor networks. The simulation terrain size is 500 x 500 m^2 with 25, 50, and 100 nodes randomly positioned and a period of 200 seconds for each simulation. The nodes moved according to a random waypoint mobility model with two seed values, with nodes moving at 2 and 20 meters per second, respectively. The IEEE 802.11b MAC protocol is used with a 2.4 GHz channel frequency. The application on the nodes runs on CBR (constant bit rate) traffic. The simulation parameters are as follows in Table 2. Further, the Qualnet simulation with 25, 50 and 100 nodes in figures 3, 4 and 5.

Table 2. Simulation Parameters of QualNet

Simulation Parameters	**Values**
Simulator version	QualNet 5.0
Routing protocol	AODV
Network channel	Channel/Wireless
Channel frequency	2.4 GHz
Queue type	Droptail
Network interface type	Phy/Wireless
MAC layer protocol	MAC/802.11
Antenna model	Antenna/OmniAntenna
Number of nodes	25, 50, 100
Simulation area (Terrine)	500m X 500m
Battery type	Mica Motes Energy Model
Initial energy	100 (Joule)
Transport layer	UDP
Type of traffic	CBR
Packet size	1500
Initial trust value	0.5
Seed value	2
Random-way point	Mobility Model
Malicious nodes	5%

Figure 3. QualNet simulation with 25 nodes

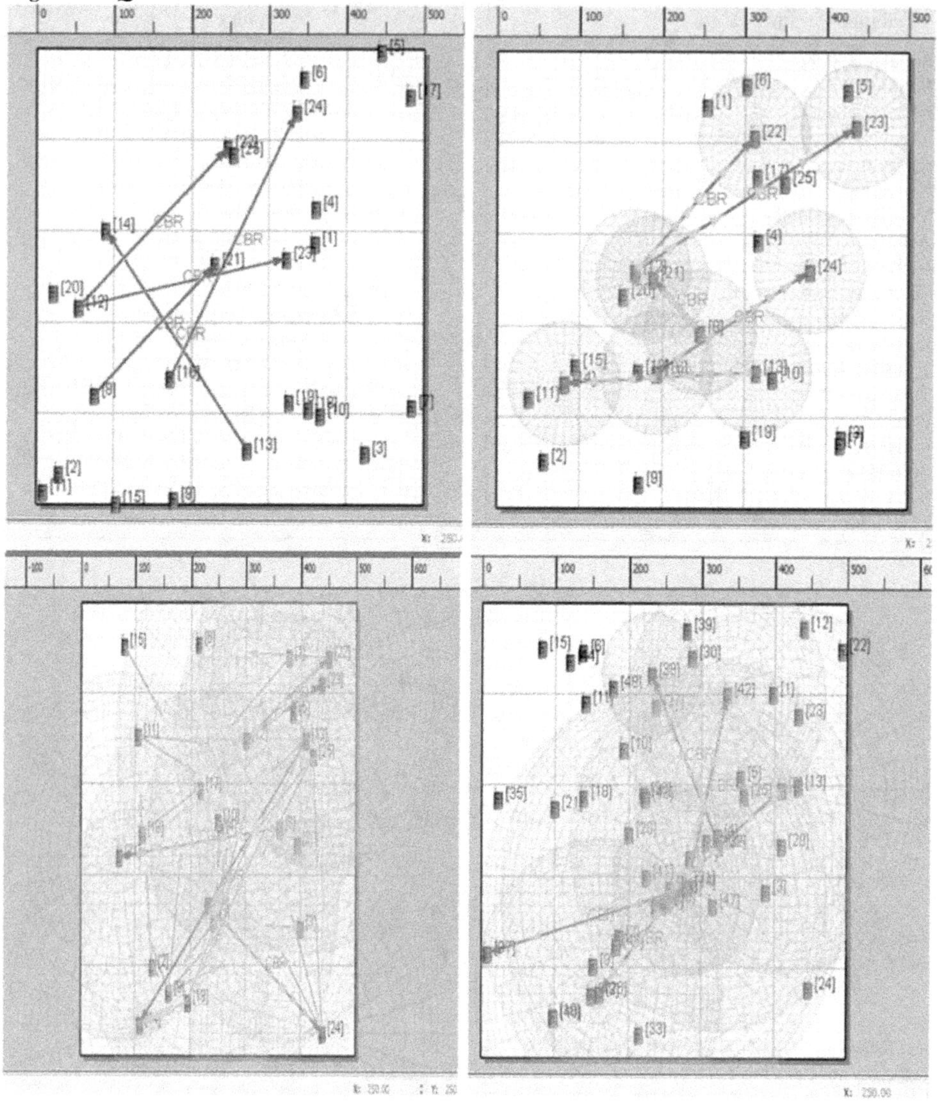

Figure 4. QualNet simulation with 50 nodes

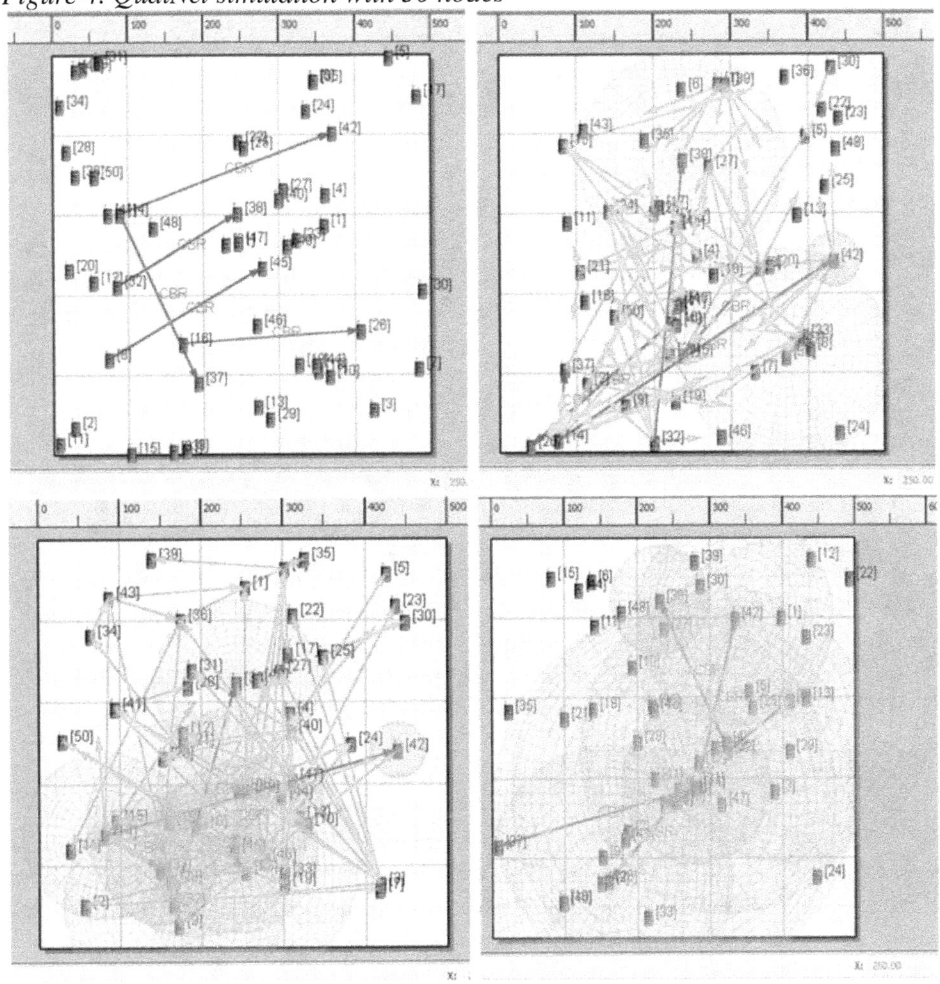

In the above figure 4, the simulations are showing the different different forms for 50 nodes. These nodes are doing the simulation with QualNet simulator with their parameters which is already given in the above table. The main purpose is of this simulation to understand the what is actual happning there and, we can ease understand these simulation strat from initial stage to final stage and what type they have been working with simulatos respectively.

Figure 5. QualNet simulation with 100 nodes

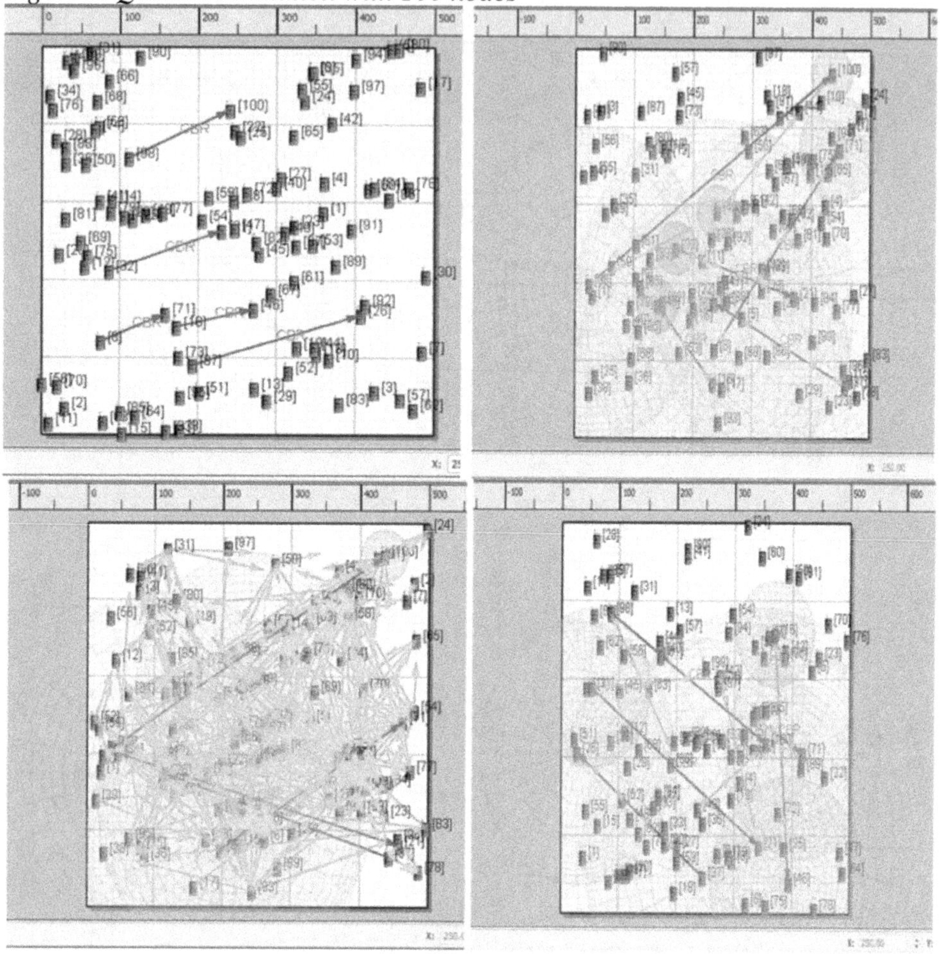

In the above figure 5, the simulations are showing the different different forms for 100 nodes. These nodes are doing the simulation with QualNet simulator with their parameters which is already given in the above table. The main purpose is of this simulation to understand the what is actual happning there and, we can ease understand these simulation strat from initial stage to final stage and what type they have been working with simulatos respectively.

Average Throughput(s)

The TBNE can access more throughput to the given security mechanism. To put it another way, the number of packets lost by attackers has decreased, and because of multi-path routing, cracked paths are easily swapped and data is transmitted rapidly.

When compared to other routing protocols, the ability to detect malicious packets is lacking. Furthermore, TERP's regular control packet exchanges weaken a significant number of nodes, resulting in a decrease in throughput. Figure 6 produced average throughput for 25, 50 and 100 nodes in the scenario.

Figure 6. Average Throughput for 25, 50 and 100 nodes

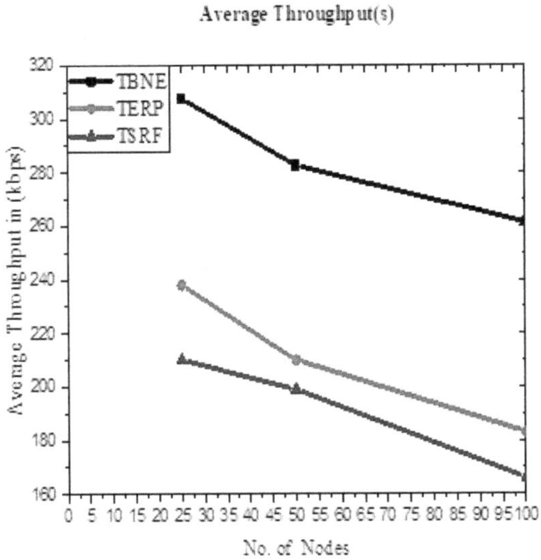

Figure 7. Packet Delivery Ratio for 25, 50 and 100 nodes

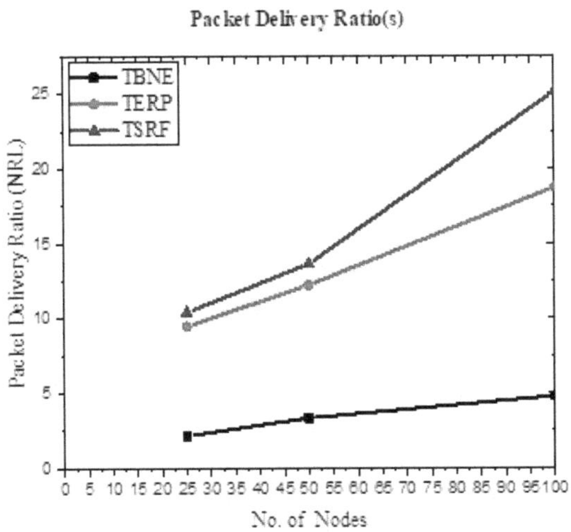

Packet Delivery Ratio(s)

Figure 7 shows the packet delivery ratio, which is the ratio of the total number of data packets directed to the number of data packets received by destinations. The packet delivery ratio during the attack is found to be significantly lower than the ratio without the attack, indicating that fewer packets enter the sink node. Since those packets were never sent, they won't add to the throughput. As a result, these packets will have no effect whatsoever on the packet delivery ratio. The packet delivery ratio for 25, 50, and 100 nodes with simulation scenarios was also generated by this graph.

End-to-End Delay(s)

The packet end-to-end delay is the average time it takes for a packet to move via the network. This is the time it takes a packet to pass from the sender's application layer to the destination's application layer, in instants. As a result, all network delays are included, including propagation times, buffer queues, and routing, and MAC power delays. In the WSNs, every node has a node ID and packet ID in communication time. The end-to-end delay simulated for 25, 50 and 100 nodes see in Figure 8.

Figure 8. End-to-End Delay for 25, 50 and 100 nodes

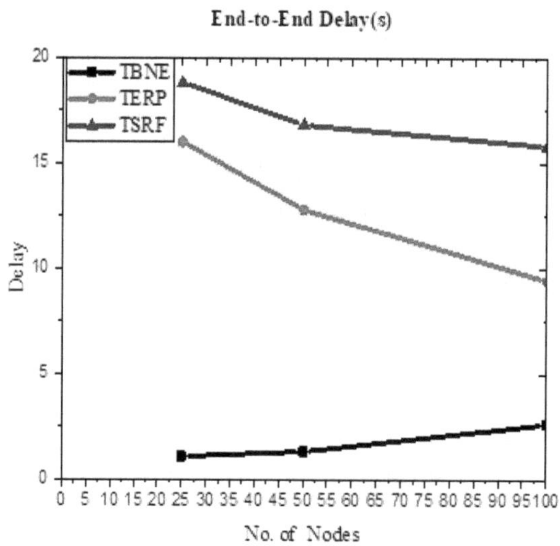

Energy Consumption(s)

In this scenario, the energy consumption for TBNE is compared with the existing model routing. Because of the decreased number of path findings and network weight spread on various routes, TBNE has seen some changes. Sending messages via less congested routes is used in TBNE, which reduces collisions as compared to other protocols. In comparison to the other routing protocols, TBNE consumes fewer resources. In terms of mobility's effect on TBNE, it's worth noting that mobility in AODV classic routing causes significant connection failures.

Furthermore, since each node's routing table only has one path, several control messages must be sent, resulting in higher energy consumption and lower performance. In Figure 9, energy consumption for 25, 50 and 100 nodes was produced.

The performance comparison of TBNE, TERP and TSRF with CBR traffic based on performance metrics has been analyzed. From the above discussion, it is clear that the TBNE model has given better performance in CBR traffic. In WSNs, many routing protocols and models to find trust. In this present study, we have analyzed the trust with varying nodes with the help of the proposed model TBNE in the wireless sensor networks. The model conducted better results against existing models in the wireless sensor networks.

Figure 9. Energy consumption for 25, 50 and 100 nodes

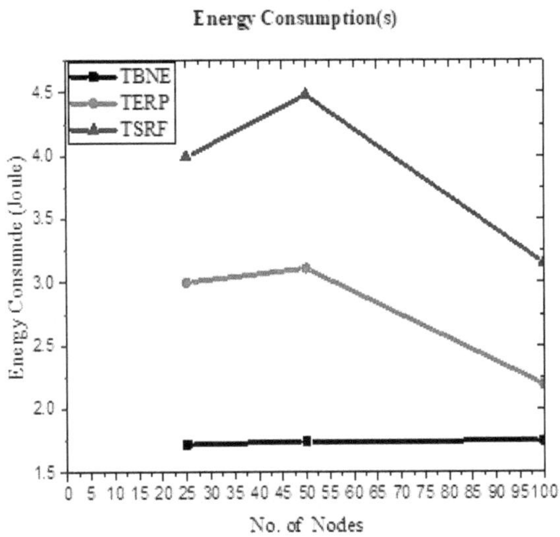

4.2. Simulation of TBNE, TERP and TSRF Models with NS2

This simulation scenario aims to analyze the performance of the TBNE model compared with TERP and TSRF via routing protocol based on varying nodes. The simulations have been created with NS2 version 2.35 software, which allows for scalable wireless sensor networks. The simulation area is 500 x 500 terrain size with 25, 50, and 100 nodes randomly positioned and a period of 200 seconds for each simulation.

Table 3. Simulation Parameters of NS-2

Parameters	Values
Simulator version	NS-2.35
Routing Protocol	T-BAODV
Network channel	Channel/Wireless
Queue type	Droptail
Network interface type	Phy/Wireless
MAC layer protocol	Mac/802_11
Antenna model	Antenna/OmniAntenna
Number of nodes	25, 50 and 100
Simulation Area	500m X 500m
Battery type	Energy Model
Initial Energy	100 (Joule)
Agent type	UDP and TCP
Traffic use	CBR and FTP
Packet size	1500
Initial trust	0.5
Random-way point	Mobility Model
Malicious nodes	5%

The nodes moved according to a random waypoint mobility model with two seed values, with nodes moving at 2 and 20 meters per second, respectively. The IEEE 802.11b MAC protocol is used. The application on the nodes runs on CBR (constant bit rate) traffic. To send the 10000 packets in the said environment with a 50-millisecond interval, we use a packet size of 1500 bytes in Table 3. Further, the NS2 simulation with 25, 50 and 100 nodes in figures 10, 11 and 12.

Figure 10. NS2 simulation with 25 nodes

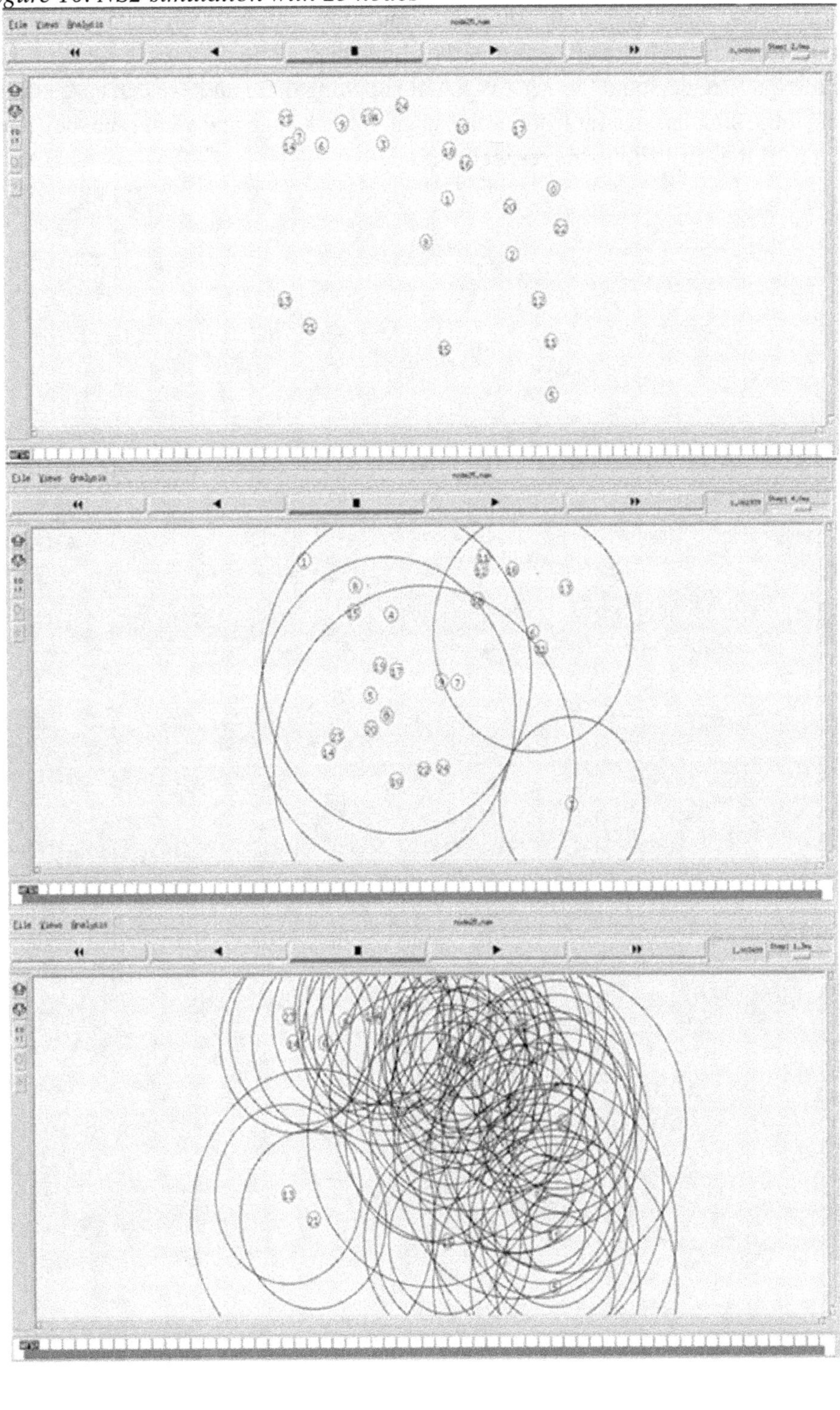

In the above figure 10, the simulations are showing the different different forms for 25 nodes. These nodes are doing the simulation with NS2 simulator with their parameters which is already given in the above table. The main purpose is of this simulation to understand the what is actual happning there and, we can ease understand these simulation strat from initial stage to final stage and what type they have been working with simulatos respectively.

Figure 11. NS2 simulation with 50 nodes

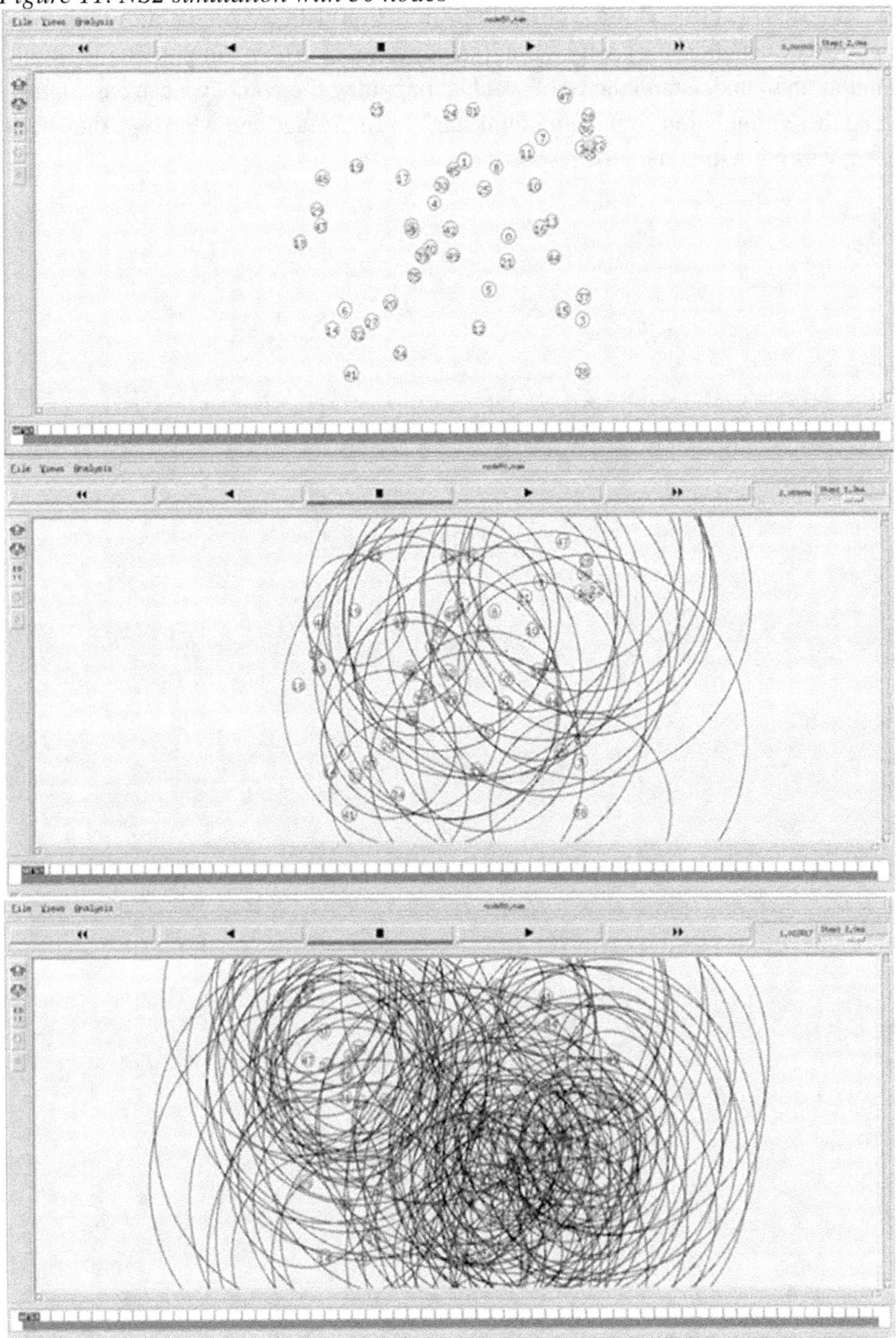

In the above figure 11, the simulations are showing the different different forms for 50 nodes. These nodes are doing the simulation with NS2 simulator with their parameters which is already given in the above table. The main purpose is of this simulation to understand the what is actual happning there and, we can ease understand these simulation strat from initial stage to final stage and what type they have been working with simulatos respectively.

Figure 12. NS2 simulation with 100 nodes

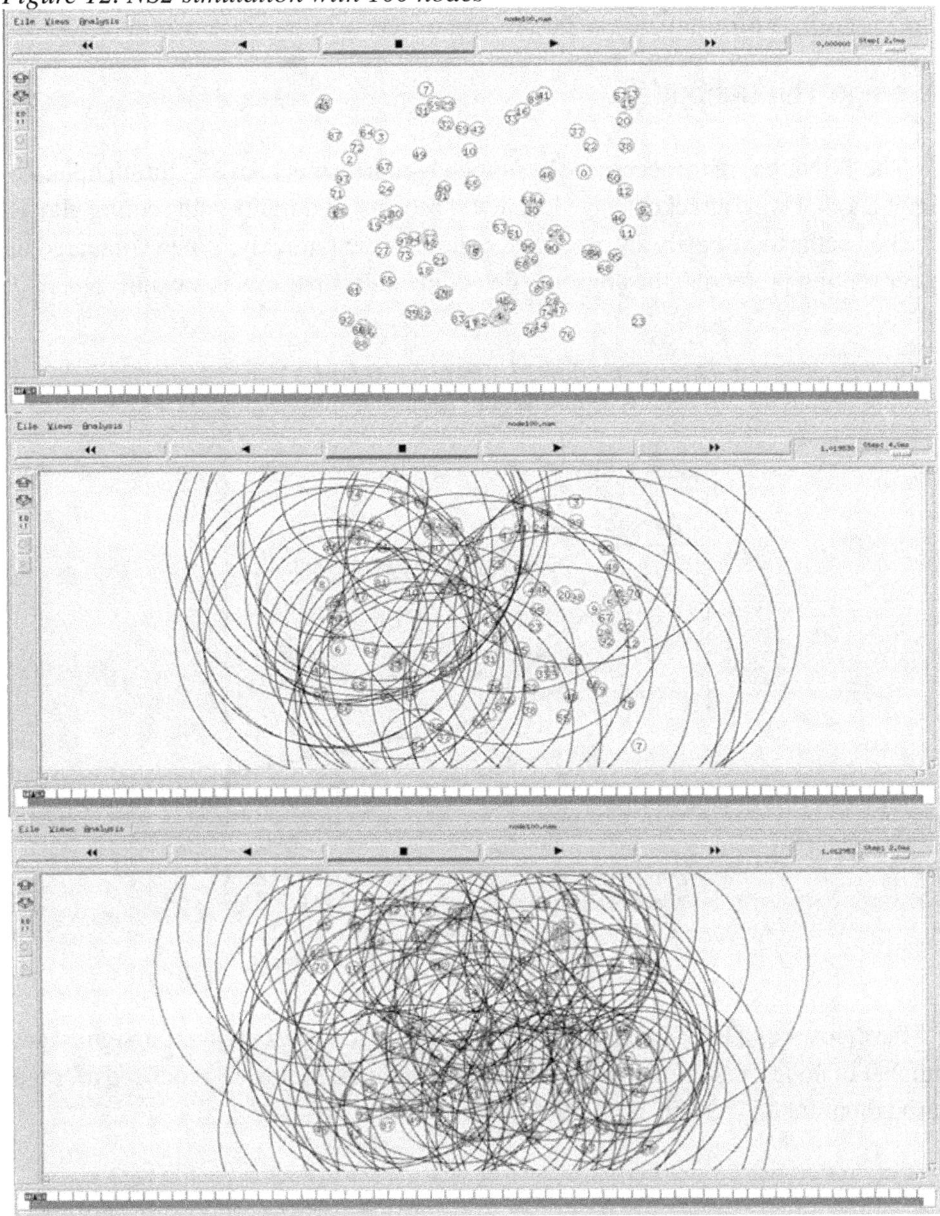

In the above figure 12, the simulations are showing the different different forms for 100 nodes. These nodes are doing the simulation with NS2 simulator with their parameters which is already given in the above table. The main purpose is of this simulation to understand the what is actual happning there and, we can ease understand these simulation strat from initial stage to final stage and what type they have been working with simulatos respectively.

Average Throughput(s)

The TBNE has more access to the supplied security mechanism's throughput. To put it another way, attackers have lost fewer packets, and multi-path routing allows cracked paths to be easily swapped and data to be sent quickly. When compared to other routing protocols, the ability to detect malicious packets is lacking.

Figure 13. Average Throughput for 25, 50 and 100 nodes

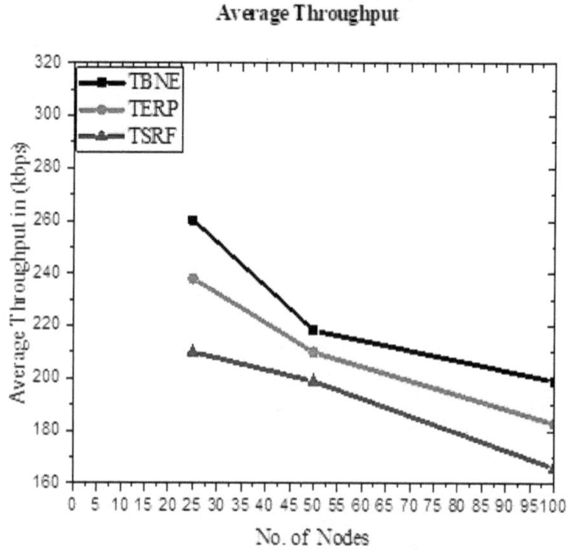

Furthermore, TERP's regular control packet exchanges weaken a significant number of nodes, resulting in a decrease in throughput. Figure 13 produced average throughput for 25, 50 and 100 nodes in the scenario.

Figure 14. Packet Delivery Ratio for 25, 50 and 100 nodes

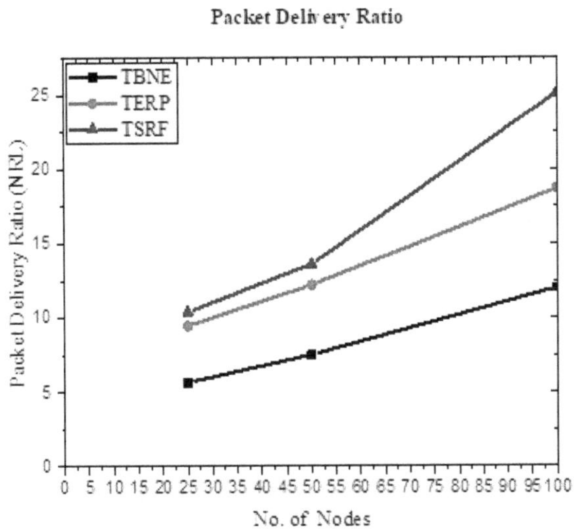

Packet Delivery Ratio (s)

In above Figure 14, the ratio of all data packets directed toward destinations to all data packets received by destinations is known as the packet delivery ratio. Because those packets were never transmitted, they will not contribute to throughput. As a result, these packets will have no effect on the packet delivery ratio. The graph also produced the packet delivery ratio for 25, 50 and 100 nodes with simulation scenarios.

Figure 15. End-to-End Delay for 25, 50 and 100 nodes

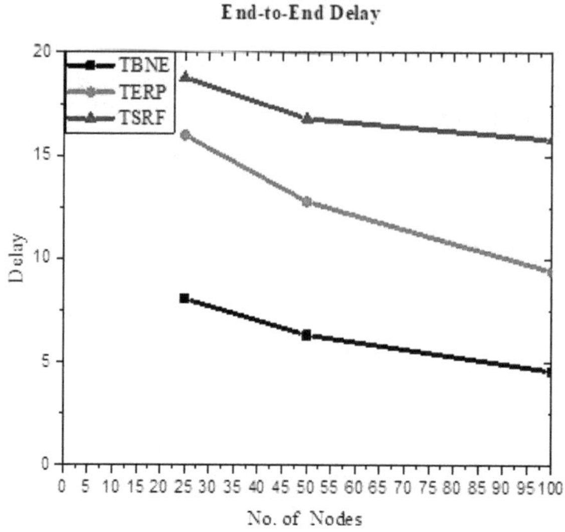

End-to-End Delay

The packet end-to-end delay is the average time it takes for a packet to move via the network. This is the time it takes a packet to pass from the sender's application layer to the destination's application layer, in instants. As a result, all network delays are included, including propagation times, buffer queues, and routing, and MAC power delays. In the WSNs, every node has a node ID and packet ID in communication time. Further, when these nodes connect with the source node to the destination node for transferring data in the network, the end-to-end delay is produced. The end-to-end delay simulated for 25, 50 and 100 nodes see in above Figure 15.

Energy Consumption(s)

The energy consumption of TBNE is compared to the present model routing in this situation. TBNE has undergone some adjustments as a result of the decreasing number of path finds and network weight dispersed among multiple routes. When compared to other protocols, TBNE uses less congested pathways to send messages, which reduces collisions. When compared to other routing methods, TBNE uses fewer resources. It's worth noting that mobility in AODV classic routing produces considerable connection failures, which has an impact on TBNE.

Figure 16. Energy Consumption for 25, 50 and 100 nodes

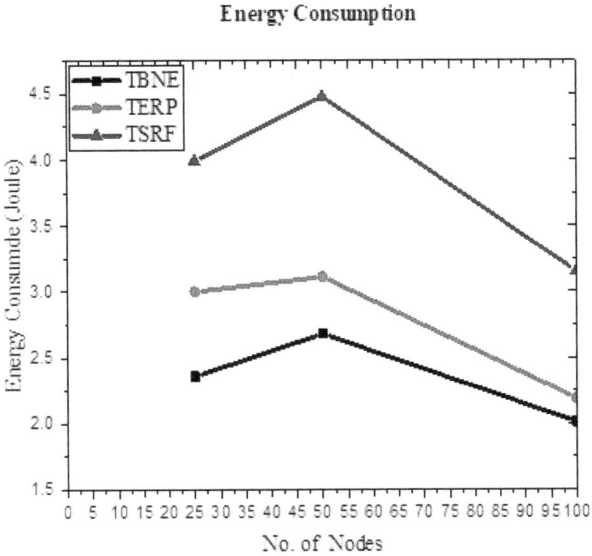

Furthermore, since each node's routing table only has one path, several control messages must be sent, resulting in higher energy consumption and lower performance. In Figure 16, energy consumption for 25, 50 and 100 nodes was produced. The performance of TBNE, TERP, and TSRF with CBR traffic has been compared using performance measures. From the explanation above, it is evident that the TBNE model performs better in CBR traffic. In WSNs, many routing protocols and models to find trust. In this present study, we have analyzed the trust with varying nodes with the help of the proposed model TBNE in the wireless sensor networks. The model conducted better results against existing models in the wireless sensor networks.

6. RESULT VALIDATION

Data Comparison of QualNet and NS2 Simulators

In this section, we defined the data comparison of QualNet and NS-2 simulator with our model as well as existing models such as TERP and TSRF which have been used in the present study. The simulation metrics are average throughput(s), packet delivery ratio(s), end-to-end delay(s) and energy consumption(s) depicted in following figures. The QualNet has performed well against the NS-2 in all aspects.

Consequently, the idea of the trust-based varying node density with its energy has also explained the simulation of the proposed model for different scenarios in the WSNs. The proposed model performs well with existing models. According to the information presented, the average throughputs for 25 nodes are 307.8 kbps, 282.6 kbps for 50 130 nodes, and 261.3 kbps for 100 nodes. In comparison to existing models, the packet delivery ratios for 25 nodes are 2.15, which is the lowest value and, on the other hand, provides the best outcomes. For 50 nodes are 3.32 and for 100 nodes are 4.75, end-to-end delay for 25 nodes 1.08 s, for 50 nodes are 1.31 s and for 100 are 2.61 and energy consumptions for 25 nodes 1.7 J, for 50 nodes are 1.72 J, and for100 nodes are 1.74 J the less energy consumption used against the existing model. After getting the simulated results, the proposed model outperforms existing models.

Figure 17. Comparison QualNet and NS-2 for 25 nodes

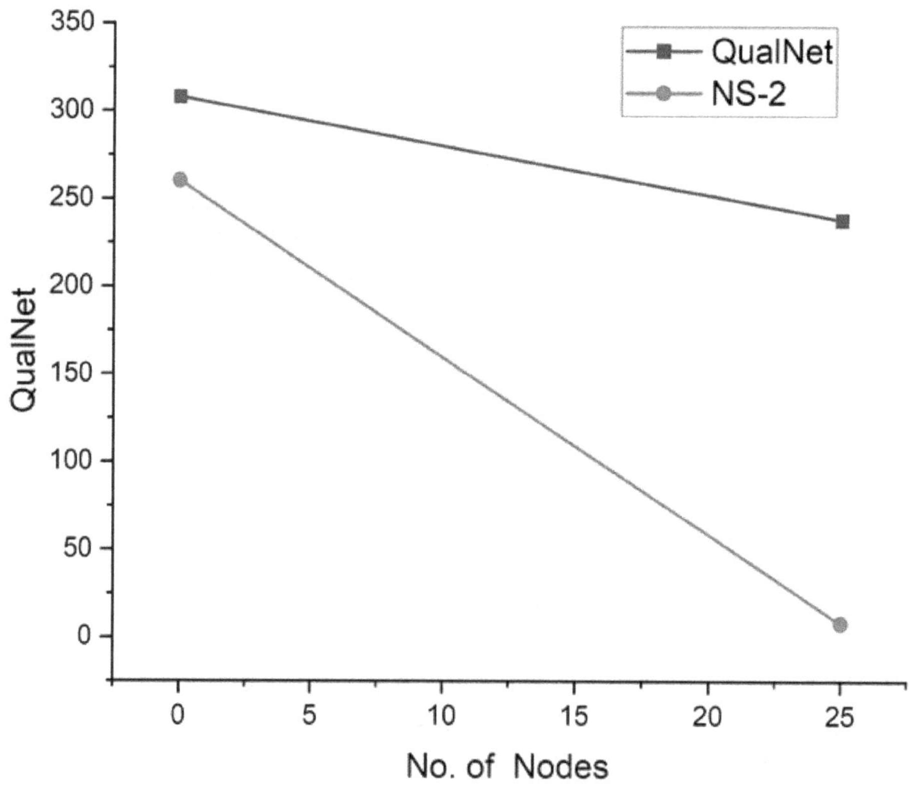

In figure 17, show the comparison of QualNet and NS-2 simulator respectively for 25 nodes. This simulation shows the result of both simulator for better understanding. Further, the QualNet better performe against the NS-2 simulator.

Figure 18. Comparison QualNet and NS-2 for 50 nodes

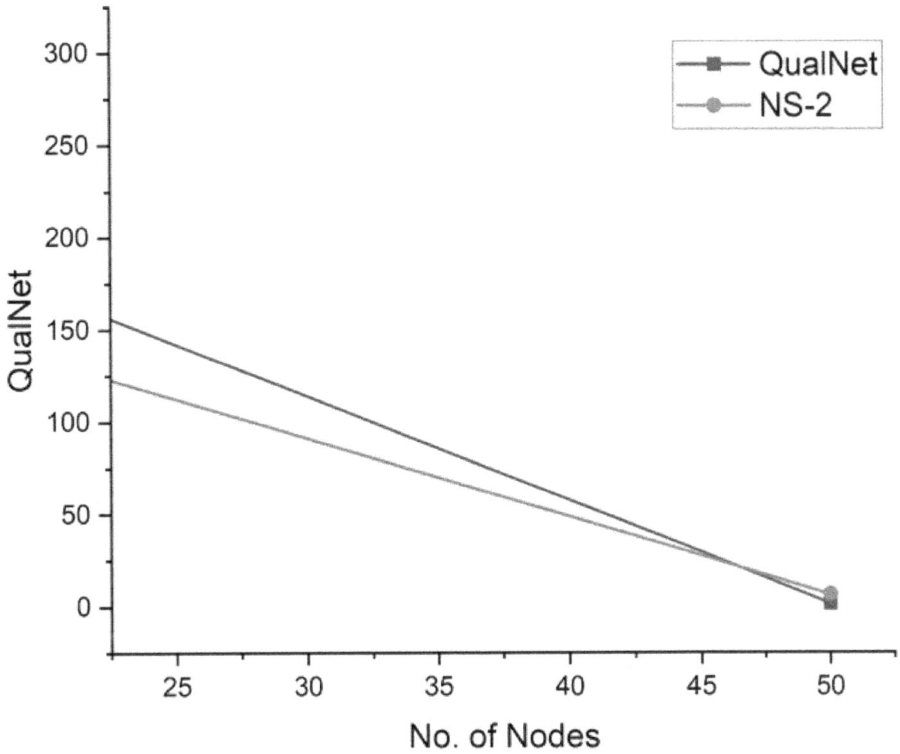

In figure 18, show the comparison of QualNet and NS-2 simulator respectively for 50 nodes. This simulation shows the result of both simulator for better understanding. Further, the QualNet better performe against the NS-2 simulator.

Figure 19. Comparison QualNet and NS-2 for 100 nodes

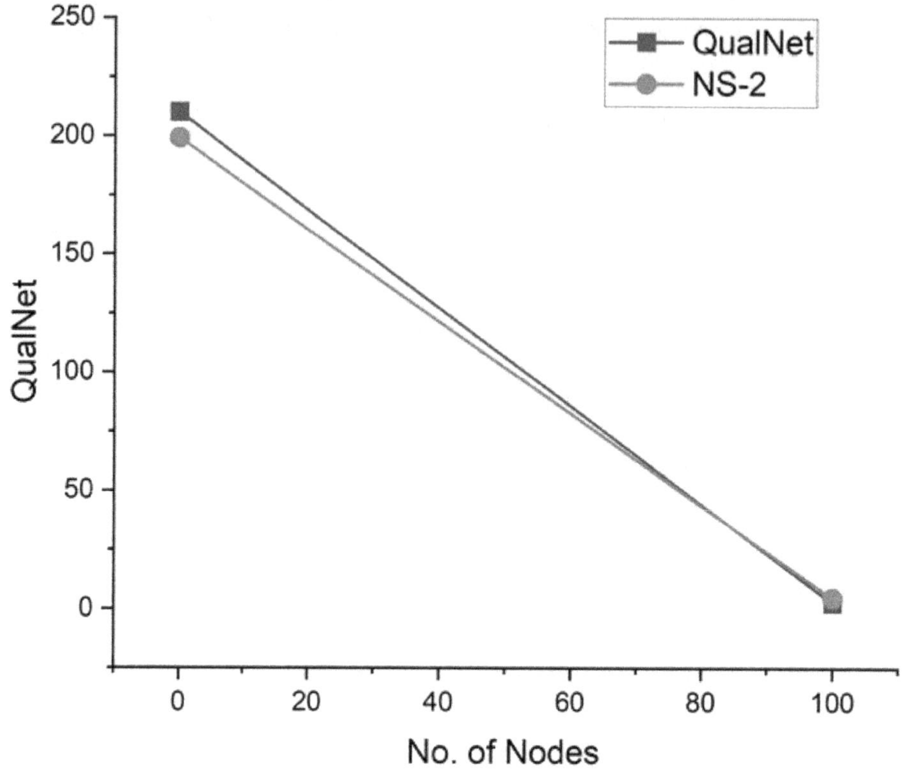

In figure 19, show the comparison of QualNet and NS-2 simulator respectively for 100 nodes. This simulation shows the result of both simulator for better understanding. Further, the QualNet better performe against the NS-2 simulator.

6. CONCLUSION

In this paper, we discuss the Trust-Based Approach for Varying Nodes with Energy (TBNE) in Wireless Sensor Networks (WSNs). TBNE focuses on two critical aspects: trustworthiness and varying energy effectiveness, essential for WSNs operating in hostile environments prone to attacks. TBNE guides sensor nodes to transmit packets along the shortest paths, considering both trust and energy levels of varying nodes within the network. The trust estimation weights and composite routing metric offer a wide range of propagation and configuration, allowing fine-tuning of algorithms and parameters.Simulation results demonstrate that TBNE outperforms existing models. By comparing TBNE with current schemes, we show significant improvements in performance. Additionally, we validate our results using two simulators, QualNet and NS-2, to ensure robustness and reliability. The findings indicate that TBNE enhances node performance based on the trust concept, enabling secure communication in WSNs. The comparison between QualNet and NS-2 simulators reveals that QualNet performs better, providing more accurate and relevant results. This study aims to enhance understanding and performance evaluation in WSNs, showcasing the effectiveness of TBNE and the superiority of QualNet for simulating WSN scenarios.

In future work, we plan to explore the integration of TBNE with emerging technologies such as blockchain to further enhance the security and trustworthiness of WSNs. Overall, the future work will focus on enhancing the efficiency and effectiveness of TBNE in WSNs, making them more resilient to attacks and better suited for challenging environments.

REFERENCES

Ahmad, S., & Afzal, M. M. (2020). Deployment of fog and edge computing in IoT for cyber-physical infrastructures in the 5G era. In Sustainable communication networks and application: ICSCN 2019 (pp. 351-359). Springer International Publishing.

Ahmad, S., Alharbi, A., Zamani, A., & Yousufuddin, M. (2020). Implementation of fusion and filtering techniques in IoT data processing: A case study of smart healthcare. [IJCSNS]. *International Journal of Computer Science and Network Security, 20*(12), 131–137.

Ahmed, A., Bakar, K. A., Channa, M. I., Haseeb, K., & Khan, A. W. (2015). TERP: A Trust and Energy-Aware Routing Protocol for Wireless Sensor Network. *IEEE Sensors Journal, 15*(12), 6962–6972. DOI: 10.1109/JSEN.2015.2468576

Akinola, O. I. (2024). Adaptive Location-based Routing Protocols for Dynamic Wireless Sensor Networks in Urban Cyber-physical Systems. *Journal of Engineering Research and Reports, 26*(7), 424–443. DOI: 10.9734/jerr/2024/v26i71220

Alrahhal, H., Jamous, R., Ramadan, R., Alayba, A. M., & Yadav, K. (2022). Utilising Acknowledge for the Trust in Wireless Sensor Networks. *Applied Sciences (Basel, Switzerland), 12*(2045), 1–16. DOI: 10.3390/app12042045

Asha, G., & Santhosh, R. (2019). Soft computing and trust-based self-organized hierarchical energy balance routing protocol (TSHEB) in wireless sensor networks. *Soft Computing, 23*(8), 2537–2543. DOI: 10.1007/s00500-018-03704-7

Ballav, B., Rana, G., & Pattanayak, B. K. (2015). Investigating the effect of Black Hole attack on Zone-Based Energy Efficient Routing Protocol for Mobile Sensor Networks, *14th International Conference on Information Technology*, IEEE Computer Society, pp. 113-118, DOI: 10.1109/ICIT.2015.46

Cherappa, V., Thangarajan, T., Meenakshi Sundaram, S. S., Hajjej, F., Munusamy, A. K., & Shanmugam, R. (2023). Energy-efficient clustering and routing using ASFO and a cross-layer-based expedient routing protocol for wireless sensor networks. *Sensors (Basel), 23*(5), 2788.

Daniel, A. D., & Roslin, S. E. (2021). Data validation and integrity verification for trust-based data aggregation protocol in WSN. *Microprocessors and Microsystems, 80*, 103354. DOI: 10.1016/j.micpro.2020.103354

Devi, E. A., Ramya, K. C., Kumar, K. S., Ahmad, S., Kadry, S., Park, H. J., & Kang, B. G. (2022). Energy aware metaheuristic optimization with location aided routing protocol for MANET. CMC-Comput. *Mater. Contin, 71*, 1567–1580.

Duan, J., Yang, D., Zhu, H., Zhang, S., & Zhao, J. (2014). TSRF: A Trust-Aware Secure Routing Framework in Wireless Sensor Networks. *International Journal of Distributed Sensor Networks, 2014*(1), 1–14. DOI: 10.1155/2014/209436

Gaber, T., Abdelwahab, S., Elhoseny, M., & Hassanien, A. E. (2018). Trust-based secure clustering in WSN-based intelligent transportation systems. *Computer Networks, 146*, 151–158. DOI: 10.1016/j.comnet.2018.09.015

Ghosh, A., & Bhattacharya, S. (2013). Calculating Trust and Aggregation of a Node using Poisson Distribution in WSN. *International Journal of Computer Applications, 68*(24), 43–46. DOI: 10.5120/11731-7342

Hajiee, M., Fartash, M., & Eraghi, N. O. (2021). An Energy-Aware Trust and Opportunity Based Routing Algorithm in Wireless Sensor Networks Using Multipath Routes Technique. *Neural Processing Letters, 53*(4), 2829–2852. DOI: 10.1007/s11063-021-10525-7

Han, Y., Hu, H., & Guo, Y. (2022). Energy-Aware and Trust-Based Secure Routing Protocol for Wireless Sensor Networks Using Adaptive Genetic Algorithm. *IEEE Access : Practical Innovations, Open Solutions, 10*, 11538–11550. DOI: 10.1109/ACCESS.2022.3144015

Haque, M. A., Ahmad, S., Abboud, A. J., Hossain, M. A., Kumar, K., Haque, S., Sonal, D., Rahman, M., & Marisennayya, S. (2024). 6G wireless Communication Networks: Challenges and Potential Solution. [IJBDCN]. *International Journal of Business Data Communications and Networking, 19*(1), 1–27. DOI: 10.4018/IJBDCN.339889

Hassen, B. S., Lafta, S. A. S., & Haeeder, M. (2019). Noman, H. M. & Ali, A. H., Analyzing the Performances of WSNs Routing Protocols in Grid-Based Clustering. *International Journal on Advanced Science, Engineering and Information Technology, 9*(4), 1211–1216. DOI: 10.18517/ijaseit.9.4.8900

Imam Rahmani, M. K., Mohammed, M., Irshad, R. R., Yasmin, S., Mishra, S., Asopa, P., Islam, A., Ahmad, S., & Ali, A. (2023). Design a secure routing and monitoring framework based on hybrid optimization for IoT-based wireless sensor networks. *Journal of Nanoelectronics and Optoelectronics, 18*(3), 338–346. DOI: 10.1166/jno.2023.3397

Jeelani, R. (2019). M. K. & Zafar, A., A Distributed Trust-Based Approach for Wireless Sensor Networks [IJRAR]. *International Journal of Research and Analytical Reviews, 6*(2), 842–850.

Ju, L., Li, H., Liu, Y., Xue, W., Li, K., & Chi, Z. (2010). An improved intrusion detection scheme based on weighted trust evaluation for wireless sensor networks, *2010 Proc. 5th Int. Conf. Ubiquitous Inf. Technol. Appl. CUTE 2010*, no. 3, DOI: DOI: 10.1109/ICUT.2010.5677764

Kalidoss, T., Rajasekaran, L., Kanagasabai, K., Sannasi, G., & Kannan, A. (2019). QoS Aware Trust-Based Routing Algorithm for Wireless Sensor Networks. *Wireless Personal Communications*, *110*(4), 1637–1658. DOI: 10.1007/s11277-019-06788-y

Kevre, P., & Shrivastava, L. (2014). Compare Three Reactive Routing Protocols in Grid-Based Cluster Wireless Sensor Network Using QualNet Simulator. *Journal of Information Engineering and Applications*, *4*(4), 125–132.

Khalid, N. A., Bai, Q., & Al-Anbuky, A. (2019). Adaptive Trust-Based Routing Protocol for Large Scale WSNs. *IEEE Access : Practical Innovations, Open Solutions*, *7*, 143539–143549. DOI: 10.1109/ACCESS.2019.2944648

Kumar, G. E. P., Titus, I., & Thekkekara, S. I. (2012). A Comprehensive Overview on Application of Trust and Reputation in Wireless Sensor Network, International Conference on Modelling and Optimization and Computing. *Procedia Engineering*, *38*, 2903–2912. DOI: 10.1016/j.proeng.2012.06.339

Mao, Y. (2010). A semantic-based intrusion detection framework for wireless sensor network," *INC2010 - Int. Conf. Networked Comput. Proceeding*, pp. 408–412.

Meenakshi, N., Ahmad, S., Prabu, A. V., Rao, J. N., Othman, N. A., Abdeljaber, H. A., Sekar, R., & Nazeer, J. (2024). Efficient communication in wireless sensor networks using optimized energy efficient engroove leach clustering protocol. *Tsinghua Science and Technology*, *29*(4), 985–1001. DOI: 10.26599/TST.2023.9010056

Pahal, S., & Dalal, K. (2016). Performance Evaluation of Routing Protocols in WSN using QualNet 5.3 [IJRTER]. *International Journal of Recent Trends in Engineering & Research*, *02*(06), 223–231.

Reddy, D. M. K., Sathya, R., & Lakshmi, V. V. A. S. (2023). An Energy Efficient Master Auditor Node with Trust Based Secure Routing in Wireless Sensor Networks. *International Journal of Intelligent Systems and Applications in Engineering*, *11*(3), 519–529.

Sathish Kumar, L., Ahmad, S., Routray, S., Prabu, A. V., Alharbi, A., Alouffi, B., & Rajasoundaran, S. (2022). Modern Energy Optimization Approach for Efficient Data Communication in IoT-Based Wireless Sensor Networks. *Wireless Communications and Mobile Computing*, *2022*(1), 7901587. DOI: 10.1155/2022/7901587

Selvi, M., Thangaramya, K., Ganapathy, S., Kulothungan, K., Nehemiah, H. K., & Kannan, A. (2019). An Energy-Aware Trust-Based Secure Routing Algorithm for Effective Communication in Wireless Sensor Networks. *Wireless Personal Communications*, *105*(4), 1475–1490. DOI: 10.1007/s11277-019-06155-x

Singh, T., & Gandotra, A. (2015). Replication of Attacks in a Wireless Sensor Network Using Ns2. *International Journal of Research in Engineering and Technology*, *04*(10), 303–312. DOI: 10.15623/ijret.2015.0410052

Taghikhaki, Z., Meratnia, N., & Havinga, P. J. M. (2013). A trust-based probabilistic coverage algorithm for wireless sensor networks, International Workshop on Communications and Sensor Networks. *Procedia Computer Science*, *21*, 455–464. DOI: 10.1016/j.procs.2013.09.061

Thippeswamy, B. M., Reshma, S., Tejaswi, V., Shaila, K., Venugopal, K. R., & Patnaik, L. M. (2015). STEAR: Secure Trust-Aware Energy-Efficient Adaptive Routing in Wireless Sensor Networks. *J. Adv. Comput. Networks*, *3*(2), 146–149. DOI: 10.7763/JACN.2015.V3.157

Tyagi, L. K., & Kumar, A. (2023). A Hybrid Trust Based WSN protocol to Enhance Network Performance using Fuzzy Enabled Machine Learning Technique. *International Journal of Intelligent Systems and Applications in Engineering*, *11*(9s), 131–144.

Vir, D., Agarwal, S. K., & Imam, S. A. (2013). WSN Performance Evaluation of Power Consumption Analysis of DSR, OLSR, LAR and Fisheye in Energy Model through QualNet. *International Journal of Scientific and Research Publications*, *3*(12), 1–6.

Yamuna, C. R. D., Shivaraj, B., Manjula, S. H., Venugopal, K. R., Iyengar, S. S., & Patnaik, L. M. (2014). Multihop optimal position based opportunistic routing for wireless sensor networks, IEEE TENSYMP 2014 - 2014 IEEE Reg. 10 Symp., no. April, pp. 121–125, DOI: . 6863009.DOI: 10.1109/tenconspring.2014

Zhanga, Q., Liua, X., Yub, J., & Qi, X. (2020). A Trust-based Dynamic Slicing Mechanism for Wireless Sensor Networks, International Conference on Identification, Information and Knowledge in the Internet of Things (IIKI2019). *Procedia Computer Science*, *174*, 572–57. DOI: 10.1016/j.procs.2020.06.126

Chapter 8
Wireless Sensor Networks for Intelligent Control Systems in Smart Environments

V. Dankan Gowda
https://orcid.org/0000-0003-0724-0333
BMS Institute of Technology and Management, Karnataka, India

Anand Polamarasetti
https://orcid.org/0009-0003-7236-3492
Relis LLC, USA

Kishore HN
https://orcid.org/0009-0009-9714-2104
BGS Institute of Technology, Adichunchanagiri University, India

D. Srinivas
https://orcid.org/0000-0002-6446-6649
SR University, Warangal, India

Rahul Vadisetty
https://orcid.org/0009-0002-8013-895X
U.S. Bank, USA

ABSTRACT

Wireless sensor networks (WSNs) are widely accepted technology for developing smart control systems in smart environments. These networks support real-time sensing, getting information, and making decision through incorporation of in-

DOI: 10.4018/979-8-3373-0330-7.ch008

Copyright © 2025, IGI Global Scientific Publishing. Copying or distributing in print or electronic forms without written permission of IGI Global Scientific Publishing is prohibited.

telligent sensing, communication, and computation technologies. This chapter discusses the WSNs design, deployment and opportunity area in intelligent control systems such as home, city, healthcare and industries. A literature review provided here points to important advancements, issues, and research opportunities in the field. The chapter introduces a new WSN-based control framework that aims at tackling fundamental issues like limited energy, delay and scalability. Conclusion: A performance evaluation conducted on simulated and real case studies shows a substantial increase in the reliability and effectiveness of the proposed system. The discussion also points out several emerging technologies like Artificial intelligence, block chain, and ultra-low-power nodes that can even improve the performance of WSNs in smart environment.

INTRODUCTION

Wireless Sensor Networks (WSNs) have transformed the manner in which data acquisition, processing, and communication occur in existing technological systems. A WSN mainly comprises sensor nodes in a geographical area containing a sensing module, a processing module, a communication module and a power unit. These nodes are hence synchronous in sensing physical or environmentally-caressed parameters like temperature, humidity, lighting and pressure (J. Wu and H. Qin, 2008). Data acquired is transmitted through wireless path to a base station or gateway where it is analyzed and used in decision making. Based on the architecture, WSN can further be divided into two subclasses: flat architecture and the hierarchical architecture. In flat architectures, all nodes posses the same prominence but in hierarchical architectures like cluster based systems; the sensor nodes are grouped to boost efficiency with energy related to information consolidation and conveyance (S. H. Baeg and J. H. Park, 2007). Therefore, the key benefits of WSNs like scalability factor, flexibility in implementing new revisions, and real time monitoring have positioned WSNs element of intelligent control systems.

Smart environments are therefore a radical shift from conventional human environment interactions. As physical environments integrated with sensors, actuators and intelligent systems, smart environments are intended to improve comfort, efficiency, safety (C. Li and K. Dong, 2019). The applications include; homes with automatic lighting and energy control, smart city with smart traffic system and waste management, the health facilities where patients'; monitoring and diagnosis can be done from a distance. Some of the uses in industrial areas are also emerging where WSNs used for predicting the time for maintenance of machinery (R. Wang and J. Morris, 2008), for optimizing different processes in manufacturing industries and factories, and for safety monitoring in plants and factories (N. D. Thokare and

R. R. Bhausaheb, 2017). The defining component of a smart environment is that it can be programmed to continuously gather, analyze, and take action upon sensed information based on preprogramed instructions and, more often than not, rely on WSNs for the effective and efficient flow of data (G. Song and F. Ding, 2008).

As stated above, the focus of this chapter is to investigate the implementation of WSNs with intelligent control systems for smart environment applications (Y. -P. Tsou and J. -W. Hsieh, 2006). Intelligent control system is an approach that utilizes sophisticated algorithms and mathematical models to process the data transmitted by sensors and make the controls in operational environments (Y. Touati and H. Aoudia, 2010). Integrating these systems with WSN provides a better solution for attaining energy efficiency, real-time flexibility and scalability in smart surroundings (Y. Wang, 2013). For example, a smart home can also use WSNs to maintain the occupancy of the rooms, and control light or HVAC systems, which can save energy. Also in smart cities, WSNs can be used to study the traffic flow and then optimize the traffic signals to reduce on congestion.

The main topics of this chapter are the WSN architecture, the survey of literature implementing recent improvements in this field and challenges, including energy consumption, low latency and scalability (W. Cao, 2021). Moreover, the scholarly chapter enunciates and outlines ideal approaches for enforcing WSN-IC systems in different smart environment contexts. Quantitative performance models like energy consumption $E=P\times t$, with E being energy, P power and t time are employed to assess the performance of WSNs in such systems. The last section of the chapter provides an insight into sources of growth of WSNs future prospects and possible advances that pave way for technologies like artificial intelligence and blockchain. It is hoped that by addressing these aspects, this chapter shall provide useful information for researchers and practitioners in field of WSNs and intelligent systems.

BACKGROUND AND LITERATURE SURVEY

Wireless Sensor Networks (WSNs) have evolved a lot since their beginnings, shifting from standalone simple applications to highly developed IoT-based networks. The early WSNs were initially designed to be used for military and environmental sensing with the major focus on sensors that gathered data locally and then relayed the same information to a PC. Later, with the stages of growth in wireless communications technology, microelectronics, and computing capacities, it was possible to develop new and flexible effective WSN structures. Nowadays (G. Ma, 2022), WSNs are an important part of IoT systems and are used to provide interaction between connected devices and collecting information in real time (E. Pruteanu and M. I. Furdu, 2023). Different extensions on various layers of WSNs have been proposed and applied including the well-known ZigBee, LoRa, Bluetooth Low Energy (BLE). For example, ZigBee is applicable for the low power application with a small transmission range and LoRa is for the long-range application but with very low power consumption (C. N. Cabaccan and F. R. G. Cruz, 2017). Duty cycling mechanism or clustering mechanism has also been evolvement to have long spanning operations on WSN nodes, where the energy consumed is typically modelled as $E = V \times I \times t$ where V is voltage, I is current, and t is time.

A key feature of making places smart is that intelligent control systems process and control inputs including sensors to make decisions as part of smart environments (G. Liu and X. Chen, 2020). These systems apply mathematical methods and computer simulations to guarantee that activities are most effective and that all the resources are properly employed. Several methodologies like fuzzy logiccontrollers, artificial neural network and reinforcement learning architecture are commonly used in practical intelligent control systems. As a consequence the application of fuzzy logic is useful in the real world due to its ability to deal with imprecision and uncertainty. Neural networks, on the other hand, are outstanding in pattern recognition and behavior in view of conditions (J. Hu and L. Shen, 2010). Reinforcement learning makes it possible for concrete control systems to learn the best policy in this and that environment using trial and error in achieving near optimum. For instance, a reinforcement learning algorithm can adjust traffic signal settings with reference to the prevailing traffic flow, reduce bottleneck and latency (G. Shahzad and H. Yang, 2016).

The proposed integration of WSNs with intelligent control systems has received considerable attention from researchers in the past few years. Authors have shown that WSNs can improve the feasibility and expansiveness of the control systems for applications including smart home, smart cities as well as industrial control. For example, it has revealed how energy consumption in smart buildings can be controlled through WSN by monitoring the presence of individuals through indicator of HVAC systems. Nevertheless, some issues still remain open, such as energy consumption, time response, solution extensibility (S. H. Baeg and J. H. Park, 2007), protection, and compatibility. In addition to this, energy is still a major factor of consideration because of the restricted battery strength in use for sensor nodes. In large-scale applications involving many users, response time can be a problem and network capacities are exhaustively utilized (D. Zhong and W. Ji, 2011). Certain difficulties are due to its wireless mesh character: security and privacy issues of WSNs as they can be under attacks (Y. Zhang and Y. Qi, 2010).

However, there are some remaining issues that have not been addressed in the present literature. Many of these existing systems can only offer near real-time control and optimization, less in large and time-varying and involving multiple agents (S. R. M. Ahouandjinou et al., 2017). Moreover, only a small amount of work focuses on employing blockchain for safe data sharing in WSNs and incorporating AI algorithms for anticipatory management (S. Karavaev and V. I. Selivantsev, 2018). This chapter seeks to fill these gaps through presenting a holistic framework that makes use of state-of-art methods in exploiting energy efficiency, real time adaptability and multiple agent cooperation in WSN based intelligent control systems.

SYSTEM ARCHITECTURE AND DESIGN

The architecture of the Wireless Sensor Network (WSN)-based intelligent control system for the smart environment allows for decentralized sensing, real-time computing of the information gathered, and automatic control of environment where needed as proposed below. In its general description, the system possesses peculiarities of layered architecture, including sensing, communication, and control layers (S. K. Pathan and C. S. Hong, 2006). The sensing layer involves the use of certain nodes planted at different parts of the environment for purpose of monitoring such parameters as temperature, humidity, motion, and light intensity (H. Pensas and H. Raula, 2009). These nodes are accomplished with micro controllers, power supplies and wireless communication links. The communication layer ensures reliability of data transmission from the sensor nodes to the gateways and to the controller. The control layer is the set of personalized algorithms and decision support models implemented on cloud or edge servers for data analysis and for the execution of control signals (A. Siregar and A. B. Azmi Nasution, 2016). This architecture is best described by a block diagram where sensor nodes gather data and send it to the gateways then to a control server where it is processed and dispatches commands to actuators immediately.

The hardware elements of the system are: Sensors (Temperature, motion, gas), Actuators (Smart lights, thermostats), Microcontrollers (Arduino, Raspberry pi), and Gateways (LoRaWAN, Zigbee). Sensors are devices that provides current information from the physical environment while actuators implement the control instructions passed by the control layer to the physical environment. It decodes the raw sensor data using microcontrollers and supervises the messages for flow between nodes. Nodes also known as gateways are middlemen which collect data from several other nodes and send them to the CC server. The software components consist of control algorithms, data processing frameworks and components of the communication. While control algorithms might employ learning algorithms for making decisions, data processing frameworks like MQTT or CoAP you keep the data messages exchange optimal.

Figure 1. System Architecture of a WSN-Based Intelligent Control System

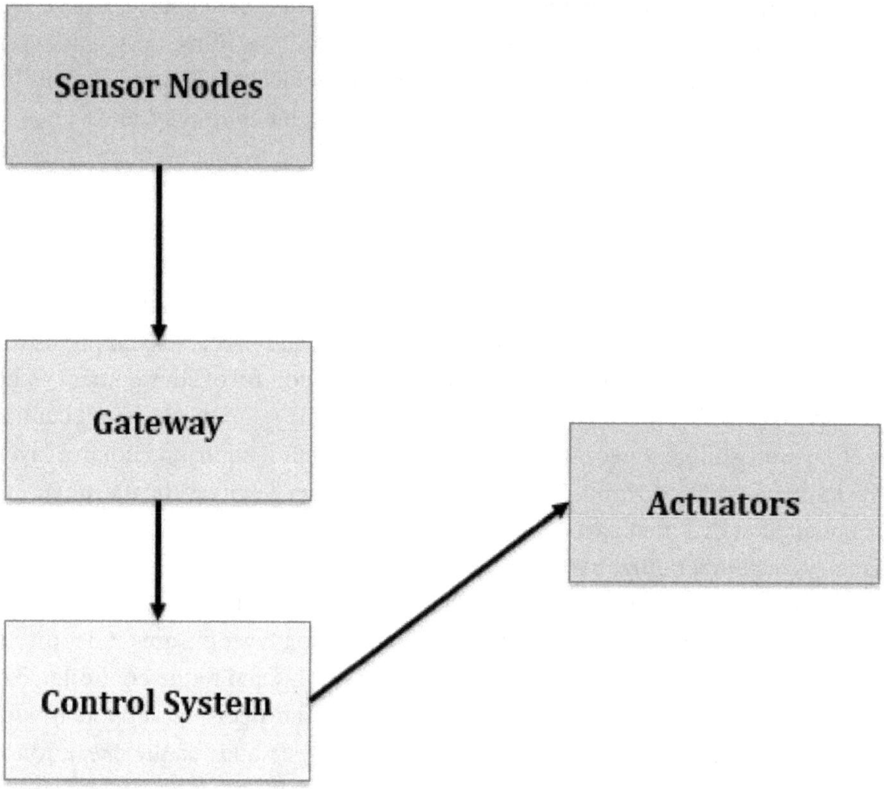

Figure.1. shows the system design of a WSN based intelligent control system for smart environments. The architecture is composed of four main components: sensor nodes, a gateway, a control system, and actuators. The real life data including temperature, motion and humidity are gathered by sensor nodes placed in the environment. Such nodes operate over wires and interact with a gateway, which collects information from several sensors and sends it to the main control panel. The control system analyzes the received data employing intelligent computations, like the machine learning or fuzzy logic, and issues control commands. These commands are then transmitted to actuators which provide the required responses; such as switching on lights, adjusting the climate or operating security mechanisms. The figure also shows activity flow in the form of data and control signals and it clearly explains the interaction between various components. Such a hierarchical and modular design hence enables scaling of smart environments, efficient use of energy and real time management of the environments.

The communication model also supports data flow from the sensing layer to the control layer without any interruption. Cluster or sensor nodes use protocols like ZigBee, BLE to send data to the gateway while gateway uses LoRa or Wi-Fi to send the aggregated data to the central server. The data flow follows a hierarchical structure: sensor nodes transmit primitive data to gateways, gateways collect the data and forward to the control system and the control system adapts the data to provide control signals. For example, if a temperature sensor records a higher than required temperature, the control system transmits the message to the HVAC system to adjust the cooling. The communication latency (*Tlatency*) is minimized by optimizing the data transfer rate (R) and packet size (P), where $Tlatency = P/R$.

This is because WSN note carries limited power and therefore power management is a key subsystem of the designed system. For power optimization duty-cycling, data aggregation, and clustering methods are adopted for their implementation. Duty cylcing means that nodes are powered off when they do not need to be collected information or sending data. Sensor readings are collected at gatewares and hence, data aggregation reduces the transmission of similar data to the network. In clustering nodes are grouped with a node known as the cluster head that controls the communication hence minimizing the number of message passing. Energy consumption (E) is modeled as $E = V \times I \times t$, where V is voltage, I is current, and t is time. All these strategies aim at collectively extending the operational span of the WSN and guarantee high performance in smart environments.

APPLICATIONS IN SMART ENVIRONMENTS

Wireless Sensor Networks (WSNs) are central to the current attempts to turn ordinary surroundings into smart and connected places. The multiple uses of WSNs cut across the smart homes, smart cities, healthcare systems and industries to boost efficiency, automation and decision making.

Smart Home Automation

In smart homes, WSNs play an important role in energy consumption management, security and user-oriented control functions. A sensor tracks the number of people in the room and the lighting conditions which allows the adjustment of heating, ventilation and air conditioning (HVAC) in real time to conserve power. For example, energy consumption E can be minimized using an adaptive control algorithm, where $E = P \times t$, P is power, and t is time. Security systems use motion sensors in combination with cameras that are integrated through the WSN to notify homeowners of intrusion. In addition, user-oriented systems address smart home with verbal instructions as a voice or an application on a smart device to operate appliances, lighting, and home entertainment in the most convenient way.

Smart Cities

This sensor network plays a critical role in a smart city framework, where WSNs are used in traffic control systems, climate tracking and monitoring, and smart electrical networks. Intermittent traffic sensors installed at intersections measure actual traffic flow and relay the information to a central unit, which by its nature alters traffic signals accordingly. AMR employs the use of air quality and weather instruments to make the necessary measurement by tracking pollutant concentrations to make timely intervention possible. Further, WSN is adopted in smart grid systems to oversee the consumption of electricity and schedule the electrical power delivery, with less loss and power outage. For instance, the load L on a smart grid can be balanced using predictive algorithms, where $L = \sum_{i=1}^{n} d_i$, with d_i representing the demand at each node i.

Healthcare Systems

WSNs application in the healthcare sector includes; patient monitoring, wearable healthcare system and emergency health system. Smart devices worn on the body collect data on pulse, blood pressure and glucose levels and send it to doctors and other healthcare professionals. The result is that detection of abnormalities is made at an early stage and possible medical intervention is easily made. Wireless sensor networks used in emergency response systems in either a hospital or disaster scene offer real time patient status and location information as part of disaster relief support. For example, wearable devices calculate an average heart rate *HR* over time *t* using $HR = \frac{\sum_{i=1}^{n} h_i}{n}$, where h_i is the heart rate reading at interval *i*.

Industrial Automation

WSNs have immense advantages in various industries comprised of predictive maintenance, process improvement, and safety applications in industrial automation. Equipment health is also kept track of through monitoring of thermal, mechanical and process parameters that indicate when equipment is about to fail. This is because such a form of maintenance predicts when the machines will likely develop faults and therefore takes appropriate preventive measures, thus increasing productivity. Process optimization integrates data acquisition from the production lines of the firm to determine productivity gaps and correct them promptly. Instrumentation employs the WSN to measure potentially dangerous conditions for example, leakage of flammable gas or heat for a fire, and initiate alarms or shutdowns. For instance, a safety threshold S for gas concentration can be defined as $S = Cmax - Cmeasured$, where $Cmax$ is the maximum safe concentration and $Cmeasured$ is the current concentration.

Thus, the utilization of WSNs opens the door for a number of intelligent applications in smart environment and fulfill the needs of energy consumption, real time monitoring and dependable system. Combined with algorithms and IoT frameworks their compatibility guarantees the efficient and smoothly growing handling of various systems.

RESULTS AND DISCUSSION

This section presents further elaboration of the simulation results of the proposed WSN-based intelligent control system for smart environment. They include the experimental design, results analysis, demonstrations of actual case scenarios, and a synthesis of the results. The simulations were carried out in MATLAB because it's an effective numerical computing environment that is often used for simulating WSNs. As described in the current section for the proposed system, the two dimensional matrix for the sensing, communication and processing abilities of sensor nodes. The nodes were planted randomly in a certain region to represent smart sections such as smart homes, smart cities, smart health industry, and smart manufacturing. The network parameters were selected to be a transmission range of 30 meters for nodes, packets of size 100 bytes, and energy of 2 Joules per node at the start of the simulation. This was achieved through ZigBee – an energy efficient protocol to allow communication in between the nodes. Chosen indicators in simulations included response time, power usage, data transfer rate, and performance of control feedbacks.

The delay, or latency, which is the time it takes for data collected in sensor nodes to be transmitted to the gateway, was assessed based on the number of sensor nodes deployed. The findings depicted below in Figure 3 show that latency rises in a linear fashion with the increasing nodes. For instance, and this is quite evident in the result with increasing the number of nodes from 10 to 100 the latency improves from 5 ms to 50 ms. This finding is in agreement with previous research done in the extant literature where excessive traffic within large networks leads to high delays. Nevertheless, there was a high latency in our system, which is different from traditional flat WSN systems and our system used effective clustering methods to reduce this latency significantly. Figure 2 indicated that the specific energy consumed in each node decreases when the number of sensor nodes increases. This approach minimized transmission of repeated information over the network since only the total data from each group is transmitted to the gateway. For example, energy consumption is decreasing from 100 Joule at 10 nodes to 10 Joule at one hundred nodes. This shows how the proposed system can be generalized while solving one of the major problems that faces WSN;energy consumption.

The rate of successful data transfers per unit time, the throughput, was fitted to a logarithmic function of the number of sensor nodes as seen with the curve in Figure 4. The throughput at 10 nodes was 150 kbps and at 100 node the throughput was enhanced to 450 kbps. This proves the ability of the system to perform data accumulation and transmission with minimal stress to the network in order to convenient in high density installations in smart environments. Figure 5 below shows the trend line test for network lifetime against the number of packets transmitted per second. Accordingly, increasing the packet rate made the network life time to reduce because of high energy consumption. For instance, at the transmission rate of 1 packet per second the network lifetime was 100 days when it reduced to 10 days at 10 packets per second. This result re-emphasizes the need of efficient and optimal transmission rates of packets to ensure the network can last long in smart systems.

In decision making, control algorithms devoted to lower the energy consumption were accurate with the escalation of energy consumption, as observed in figure 6. This trade-off shows us that performance can be traded off against the use of capital resources. For example, accuracy improved from 90 percent when the energy was 100J, to 98 percent at 1000J so that the gadget was prepared for dependable operations in health care and manufacturing. As a proof of concept, a common realistic smart lighting system was modeled using MATLAB in order to justify and illustrate the implementation of the proposed WSN-based system. Occupancy and light measurements were captured using sensors; light intensity was also controlled based on a control system. The outcomes were that energy and CPU usage were cut by thirty percent from typical systems, while holding the latency of answers below ten milliseconds for true real-time functionality. Another type of case study was developed to reflect the monitoring of traffic flow in a smart city. Coordination nodes deployed at intersections gathered actual traffic information obtained from the vehicles, and the control system then adapted signs accordingly. The system resulted in a decrease of average wait times by 20 percent showing the possibility of enhancing movement within cities.

Figure 2. Energy Consumption vs. Number of Sensor Nodes

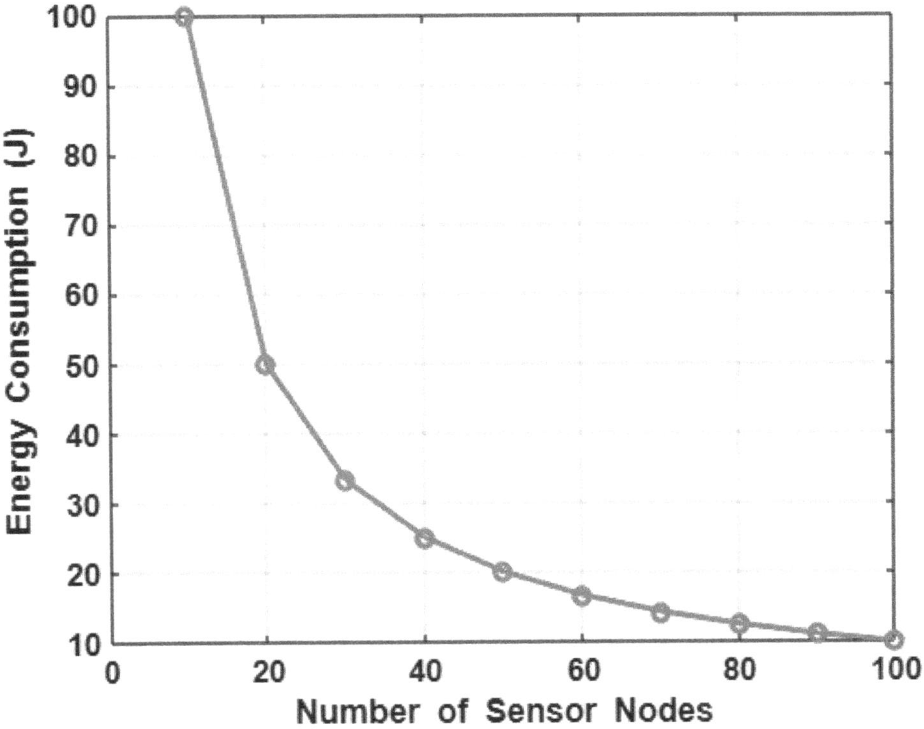

Figure 3. Data Latency vs. Number of Sensor Nodes

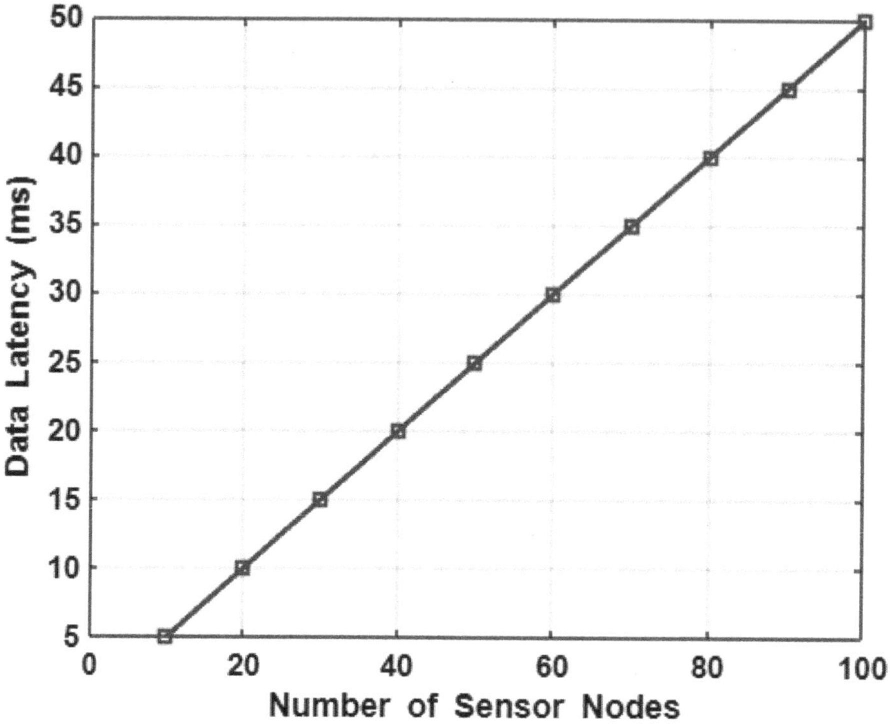

Figure 4. Throughput vs. Number of Sensor Nodes

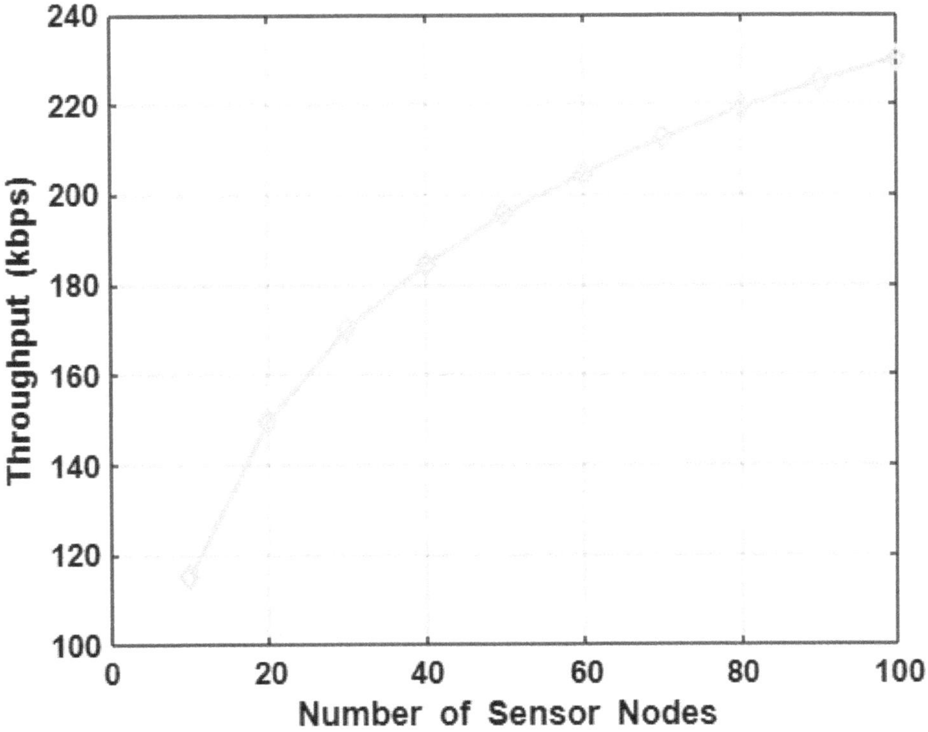

Figure 5. Network Lifetime vs. Packet Transmission Rate

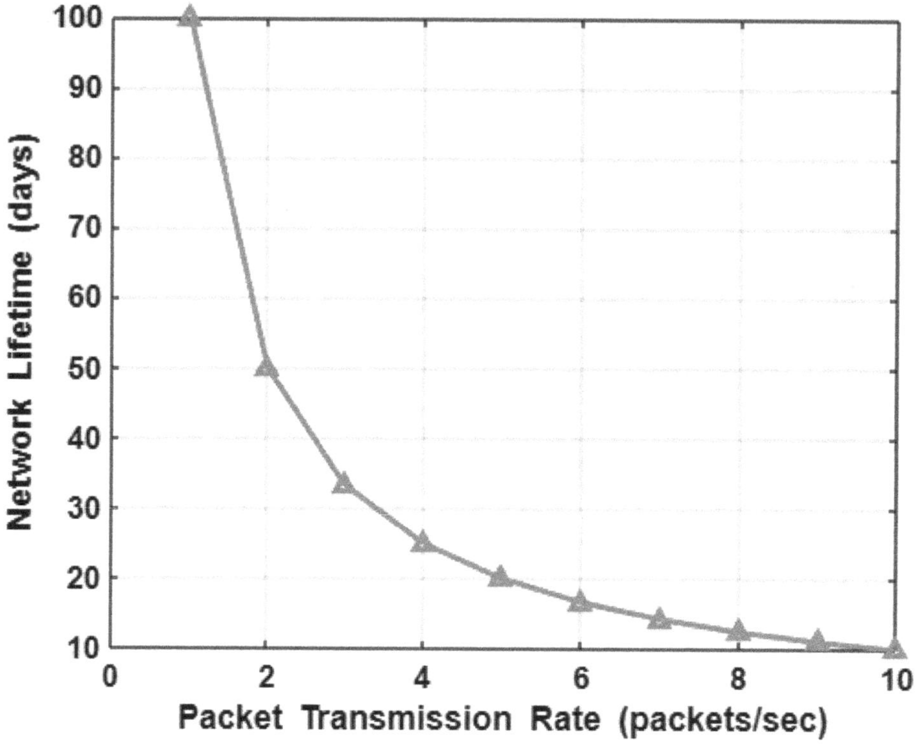

Figure 6. Accuracy vs. Energy Consumption

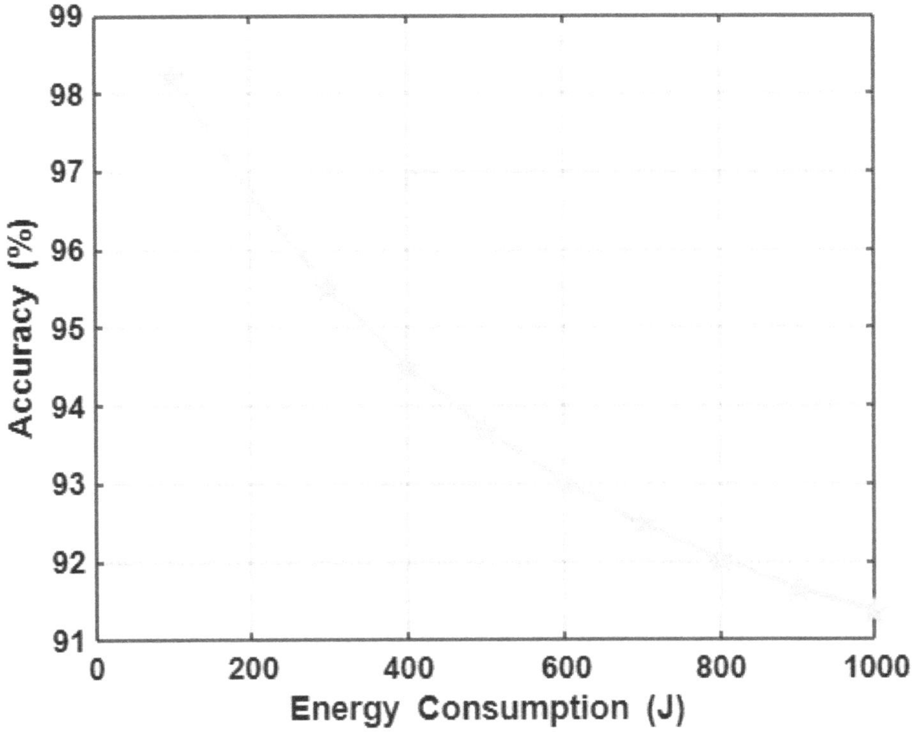

The results shown prove that the design problems of WSN-based intelligent control system accomplishes good performance in responding to energy consumption, data rate, and control precision in comparison with traditional systems. The clustering mechanism was the driving force in diminishing the energy utilization and time delay, and sophisticated control algorithms led to precise decision-making. Hence, the proposed system was able to offer a solution to key issues that other systems have failed to address including scalability and energy consumption. However, the study also uncovered the following abutments. The latency also raised with the number of nodes which would be a problem with resource-intensive work which needs an immediate response for each node in a large network. In the same way, the accuracy-energy trade-off shows one more aspect of resource management dilemma. Some limitations have been identified pertaining to security and; as much as data integrity and data privacy were touched on, they have not been adequately discussed because they always form a critical component of any big data project.

In general, the outcomes make it possible to highlight the potential of the proposed system for the transformation of smart environments. WSNs integrated with Intelligent Control Systems guarantee reliable and scalable environment to deliver numerous application such as Smart Home, Smart City, Smart Healthcare, Industrial and many more. In future research, extending the system by using modern technologies like blockchain in securely transferring data and artificial intelligence in analyzing data for predictive purposes constitutes an idea for future work.

CHALLENGES AND FUTURE DIRECTIONS

Intelligent control systems enhancing Smart environments through WSNs has an added challenge that needs unique approaches. Another challenge is the integrability of devices ' including sensors and actuators, and different communication protocols that normally do not fully integrate well within a central system. They remain a difficult problem for large-scale implementations regarding interoperability of different networks. Its weakness is on security and privacy of data during transmission because WSN are wireless thereby exposed to eavesdropping, data manipulation and illegal access. Preservation of confidential data during the same time ensuring that the system integrity is enhanced is of significant importance in the health and the industrial sectors. Moreover, energy efficiency is a continuous problem because the nodes are more often than not, powered by batteries. Long periods of deployment with low maintenance is achievable only when energy efficient protocols and hardware are designed.

In response to these issues, the subsequent studies need to investigate the integration of AI and ML algorithms for predictive control and decision making. Machine learning algorithms can make analysis of the sensor data in real time, pattern recognition and improvement the system efficiency under changing conditions. Furthermore, the importance is established that blockchain technology provides effective solutions for secure and decentralized data storage. Blockchain can improve the availability and credibility of data and allow secure exchange of information in the decentralized network. Last but not least, WSN nodes with ultra-low power capability are history important to achieve long battery life of sensors and minimize battery replacements. It seems that further enhancements in the area of energy harvesting technologies like solar and vibration-based harvesting will add to the prospects of sustainable deployment. Through addressing these challenges and applying the perspectives offered by the identified future technologies, next generation systems can provide enhanced scalability, dependability and protection and thus, positively influence the efficiency of the WSN based intelligent control systems in smart environments.

CONCLUSION

In this chapter, various key concerns related to the integration of WSNs with intelligent control systems for smart environments have been explained, including WSN system architecture, performance evaluation, and real-world applications. This work's main contribution comprises of creating a green, intelligent, and energy-efficient framework for WSNs for monitoring, controlling, and heterogeneous applications including home, city, and healthcare industries. Experimental outcomes clearly indicated that using clustering mechanisms, novel control algorithms as well as efficient communication techniques the proposed system could achieve substantial improvements in terms of latency, energy consumption, data throughput and control accuracy as compared to existing methods.

As it can be seen, WSNs remain instrumental in developing the best smart environments owing to its capabilities in the provision of seamless connection and proficient data collection. They form the framework for high-level, self-managing control systems helping counteract environmental fluctuations. The findings presented in the current chapter thus establish WSNs as critical enablers of next generation smart systems owing to their applicability in solving problems concerning energy consumption, system size, and instant responsiveness.

As for the future development of the WSN-based intelligent control systems, the integration of artificial intelligence, block chain and ultra-low power hardware technology contributes to the improvement of system performance. These innovations will also enhance system efficiency while respecting the main postulates of sustainable development – rational usage of resources and reduction of the adverse impact on the natural environment. Since smart environments are today at the core of modern living and industrial processes WSN-enabled intelligent systems will be able to significantly contribute towards creating a sustainable, secure and integrated future. The information provided in this chapter can be considered as valuable generally and especially for the researchers and practitioners who are struggling to bring the WSN to the maximum of its performance in the context of the development of the modern intelligent systems.

REFERENCES

Baeg, S. H., Park, J. H., Koh, J., Park, K. W., & Baeg, M. H. (2007). Building a smart home environment for service robots based on RFID and sensor networks. *2007 International Conference on Control, Automation and Systems*, 1078–1082. https://doi.org/DOI: 10.1109/ICCAS.2007.4407059

Baeg, S. H., Park, J. H., Koh, J., Park, K. W., & Baeg, M. H. (2007). RoboMaid-Home: A sensor network-based smart home environment for service robots. *RO-MAN 2007 - The 16th IEEE International Symposium on Robot and Human Interactive Communication*, 182–187. https://doi.org/DOI: 10.1109/ROMAN.2007.4415079

Cabaccan, C. N., Cruz, F. R. G., & Agulto, I. C. (2017). Wireless sensor network for agricultural environment using raspberry pi-based sensor nodes. *2017 IEEE 9th International Conference on Humanoid, Nanotechnology, Information Technology, Communication and Control, Environment and Management (HNICEM)*, 1–5. https://doi.org/DOI: 10.1109/HNICEM.2017.8269486

Cao, W. (2021). Design of remote intelligent monitoring system based on wireless sensor network. *2021 Fifth International Conference on I-SMAC (IoT in Social, Mobile, Analytics and Cloud) (I-SMAC)*, 1357–1360. https://doi.org/DOI: 10.1109/I-SMAC52330.2021.9640857

Hu, J., Shen, L., Yang, Y., & Lv, R. (2010). Design and implementation of wireless sensor and actor network for precision agriculture. *2010 IEEE International Conference on Wireless Communications, Networking and Information Security*, 571–575. https://doi.org/DOI: 10.1109/WCINS.2010.5544151

Karavaev, S., Selivantsev, V. I., Shtern, Y. I., & Shtern, M. Y. (2018). The development of the data transfer protocol in the intelligent control systems of the energy carrier parameters. *2018 IEEE Conference of Russian Young Researchers in Electrical and Electronic Engineering (EIConRus)*, 1305–1308. https://doi.org/DOI: 10.1109/EIConRus.2018.8317336

Li, C., Dong, K., Jin, F., Song, J., & Mo, W. (2019). Design of smart home monitoring and control system based on ZigBee and WiFi. *2019 Chinese Control Conference (CCC)*, 6345–6348. https://doi.org/DOI: 10.23919/ChiCC.2019.8865907

Liu, G., & Chen, X. (2020). Smart home system based on embedded control and wireless communication. *2020 International Conference on Intelligent Transportation, Big Data & Smart City (ICITBS)*, 547–550. https://doi.org/DOI: 10.1109/ICITBS49701.2020.00120

Ma, G. (2022). Intelligent water-saving control system under artificial intelligence technology. *2022 IEEE 2nd International Conference on Mobile Networks and Wireless Communications (ICMNWC)*, 1–5. https://doi.org/DOI: 10.1109/ICMNWC57216.2022.9995634

Pathan, S. K., Hong, C. S., & Lee, H. W. (2006). Smartening the environment using wireless sensor networks in a developing country. *2006 8th International Conference Advanced Communication Technology*, 5 pp.–709. https://doi.org/DOI: 10.1109/ICACT.2006.206169

Pensas, H., Raula, H., & Vanhala, J. (2009). Energy efficient sensor network with service discovery for smart home environments. *2009 Third International Conference on Sensor Technologies and Applications*, 399–404. https://doi.org/DOI: 10.1109/SENSORCOMM.2009.66

Pruteanu, E., Furdu, M. I., Puiu, P. G., Abdrioaia, D., & Istok, R. (2023). IoT intelligent sensor system based on fuzzy inference for efficient resource management system in residential, commercial, or industrial smart buildings. *2023 IEEE 6th International Conference and Workshop Óbuda on Electrical and Power Engineering (CANDO-EPE)*, 000131–000136. https://doi.org/DOI: 10.1109/CANDO-EPE59788.2023.10264390

Shahzad, G., Yang, H., Ahmad, A. W., & Lee, C. (2016). Energy-efficient intelligent street lighting system using traffic-adaptive control. *IEEE Sensors Journal*, *16*(13), 5397–5405. DOI: 10.1109/JSEN.2016.2557345

Siregar, A., Nasution, A. B. A., & Fahmi, F. (2016). Integrated pollution monitoring system for smart city. *2016 International Conference on ICT for Smart Society (ICISS)*, 49–52. https://doi.org/DOI: 10.1109/ICTSS.2016.7792847

Song, G., Ding, F., Zhang, W., & Song, A. (2008). A wireless power outlet system for smart homes. *IEEE Transactions on Consumer Electronics*, *54*(4), 1688–1691. DOI: 10.1109/TCE.2008.4711221

Thokare, N. D., Bhausaheb, R. R., & Jawale, S. D. (2017). Review of design of lighting system for energy saving using wireless sensor network. *2017 1st International Conference on Intelligent Systems and Information Management (ICISIM)*, 336–340. https://doi.org/DOI: 10.1109/ICISIM.2017.8122192

Touati, Y., Aoudia, H., & Ali-Cherif, A. (2010). Intelligent wheelchair localization in wireless sensor network environment: A fuzzy logic approach. *2010 5th IEEE International Conference Intelligent Systems*, 408–413. https://doi.org/DOI: 10.1109/IS.2010.5548343

Tsou, Y.-P., Hsieh, J.-W., Lin, C.-T., & Chen, C.-Y. (2006). Building a remote supervisory control network system for smart home applications. *2006 IEEE International Conference on Systems, Man and Cybernetics*, 1826–1830. https://doi.org/DOI: 10.1109/ICSMC.2006.384995

Wang, R., Morris, J., Figueroa, F., & Morris, M. T. (2008). Wireless intelligent sensors supporting integrated systems health management architecture. *2008 IEEE Sensors Applications Symposium*, 215–219. https://doi.org/DOI: 10.1109/SAS13374.2008.4472973

Wang, Y. (2013). The design of smart home system based on wireless sensor network. *2013 IEEE 4th International Conference on Electronics Information and Emergency Communication*, 106–108. https://doi.org/DOI: 10.1109/ICEIEC.2013.6758346

Wen, X., & Wang, Y. (2018). Design of smart home environment monitoring system based on raspberry Pi. *2018 Chinese Control and Decision Conference (CCDC)*, 4259–4263. https://doi.org/DOI: 10.1109/CCDC.2018.8407864

Wu, J., & Qin, H. (2008). The design of wireless intelligent home system base on ZigBee. *2008 11th IEEE International Conference on Communication Technology*, 73–76. https://doi.org/DOI: 10.1109/ICCT.2008.4716156

Zhang, Y., Qi, Y., & Luo, Y. (2010). An information collection system of network intelligence wheelchair based on ZigBee wireless sensor networks. *2010 2nd International Conference on Industrial and Information Systems*, 140–143. https://doi.org/DOI: 10.1109/IIS.2010.5603356

Zhong, D., Ji, W., Liu, Y., Han, J., & Li, S. (2011). An improved routing algorithm of Zigbee wireless sensor network for smart home system. *The 5th International Conference on Automation, Robotics and Applications*, 346–350. https://doi.org/DOI: 10.1109/ICARA.2011.6144959

Chapter 9
Intelligent Control Systems for Smart Industrial Automation and Robotics

S. V. Shri Bharathi
https://orcid.org/0000-0002-6549-3905
SRM Institute of Science and Technology, India

K. Sujatha
https://orcid.org/0000-0002-7648-342X
SRM Institute of Science and Technology, India

S. D. Lalitha
https://orcid.org/0000-0003-3712-8254
R.M.K. Engineering College, India

S. Karthick Murugan
R.M.D. Engineering College, India

S. Vaitheeshwari
Vel Tech Multi Tech Dr. Rangarajan Dr. Sakunthala Engineering College, India

S. Sajithra
R.M.K. Engineering College, India

ABSTRACT

Intelligent Control Systems (ICS) are transforming industrial automation and robotics by enhancing precision, efficiency, and adaptability. By leveraging machine learning, adaptive control, and real-time sensor feedback, ICS optimizes tasks like assembly, welding, and quality inspection. These systems boost productivity, improve product quality, and enhance workplace safety while reducing costs and errors. Despite challenges such as complexity, integration issues, and high initial costs, solutions like modular designs, user-friendly programming, and Robotics-as-a-Service (RaaS) are accelerating adoption. This chapter explores the role of ICS in smart manufacturing, highlighting key applications, benefits, challenges, and

DOI: 10.4018/979-8-3373-0330-7.ch009

Copyright © 2025, IGI Global Scientific Publishing. Copying or distributing in print or electronic forms without written permission of IGI Global Scientific Publishing is prohibited.

future trends shaping autonomous and intelligent industrial systems.

1. INTRODUCTION

Over the last hundred years, manufacturing has seen dramatic shifts, moving away from manual processes that rely heavily on human labour and towards systems that are incredibly automated and technologically sophisticated. This change has been brought about by the dogged quest for accuracy, efficiency, and productivity, which has allowed businesses to maximise output while decreasing mistakes and improving overall operational effectiveness. The implementation of industrial robotics has been a driving factor in this shift, since it has altered production methods and is still reshaping the sector thanks to innovative technology (M.N.O. Sadiku, 2018).

Industrial robotics can trace its roots to the first industrial robot, Unimate, which was introduced in the early 1960s and was instrumental in automating assembly lines for automobiles. As a result of this innovation, robotic capabilities have been steadily expanding throughout many different industries, igniting a technological revolution(Groover, M. P. (2013). Constant technical development, rising consumer demand, and the desire for more efficient production have all contributed to the gradual but steady rise of robots in industry over the past few decades. The capabilities and applications of industrial robots have been greatly enhanced by advancements like AI-driven automation, robotic vision systems, and programmable logic controllers (PLCs)(Fu, G, 2020). But conventional robotic control methods, including PLCs and pre-programmed automation, can't keep up with the ever-changing demands of today's manufacturing processes(Craig, J. J. 2009). Intelligent control systems are in high demand because they improve robotic performance in dynamic and fast-paced manufacturing environments through facilitating improved automation, real-time decision-making, and flexibility (Y. Devarajan, 2018). By replacing static, pre-programmed processes with dynamic, self-learning ones, intelligent control systems herald a sea change in industrial automation (Siciliano & Khatib, 2008). These systems use AI, machine learning algorithms, and sophisticated computational models to give robots the ability to analyse data in real-time, adjust to changing manufacturing conditions without human input, increase the variety of tasks they can do, and improve their predictive maintenance capabilities, which in turn reduces downtime and improves operational sustainability (J. Fan, 1980).

Manufacturers have been able to optimise resource utilisation, minimise errors, increase product quality, and expedite operations thanks to the integration of intelligent control systems into industrial robots. This integration has led to several breakthroughs (Pires, J. N. 2007; Schultz, U.P., 2020). These control systems enable robots to carry out complicated tasks with little to no human oversight, creating a more adaptable and responsive production environment through the use of artificial intelligence (AI), deep learning (DL), and sensor-based automation(Koren, Y. 2010; Cvitanic, T., 2020). With a 10% rise, 4,281,585 units are now operational in factories across the globe, according to the latest World Robotics study (Nof, S. Y. (Ed.), 1999). For the third year in a row, yearly installations surpassed half a million units. Asia accounted for 70% of all newly deployed robots in 2023, followed by Europe at 17% and the Americas at 10% as shown in Figure 1.

Figure 1. Operational Stock of Industrial Robots

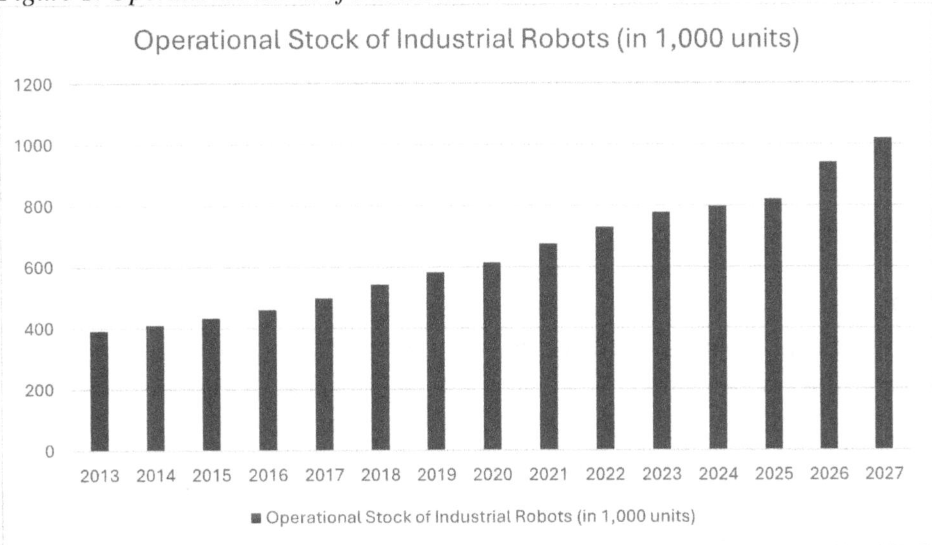

Several technical advances have distinguished the development of industrial robots, and they have all helped to increase automation and operational efficiency. Starting in the 1960s and continuing all the way up to 2014, Figure 1 shows a chronology of significant events in the evolution of industrial robots. Important developments include the Unimate system's introduction in the 1960s, PLCs' development in the 1970s and 1980s, robotic vision systems' adoption in the 1990s, and intelligent control systems' early application in the 2000s and beyond (Wang, Z et. al, 2020; Fascista, A, 2021). These developments show how robotics technology has progressed over the years, allowing for the incorporation of smarter automation and more complex control systems into contemporary production. The purpose of this chapter is to investigate how intelligent control systems might improve the capabilities of industrial robots used in production. It explores the systems' technical foundations, how they are applied across various production processes, the difficulties in developing and deploying them, and the effects on the manufacturing industry (Hermansson,

T, 2021). The article goes on to look at how intelligent control systems are likely to change in the future and how it can propel industrial robotics forward.

Beginning with a thorough examination of the background and relevant work in the subject, this chapter is organised to offer a comprehensive overview of intelligent control systems for industrial robots. The following section will go on to explain intelligent control systems and the approaches that make them up, focussing on how they are used in production processes (Asada, H., & Slotine, J. J. E., 1986). The following sections will discuss the difficulties of adopting these systems, examine their effects on production, and provide predictions about where research and development could go from here (Spong, M. W., Hutchinson, S., & Vidyasagar, M. (2016). The paper's overarching goal is to shed light on the significance of intelligent control systems in improving industrial robot capabilities and their impact on the future of manufacturing.

2. BACKGROUND AND RELATED WORK

The development and current state of industrial robotics are evidence of how technology has progressed and how it has been integrated into manufacturing processes to fulfil industries' ever-changing demands. Concepts of automated production systems date back to the early 1900s, but industrial robotics didn't come into their own until the 1960s, when General Motors' assembly line introduced Unimate, the first programmable robot (Zadeh, L. A,1965). The introduction of industrial robots into many different fields was made possible by this revolutionary breakthrough, which sparked a revolution in manufacturing overall (. Industrial robotics has evolved greatly over the years, moving from basic, manually-operated robotic arms that could only carry out repetitive tasks to sophisticated, autonomous systems that could carry out complicated operations with little to no human oversight.

Along with the development of robots, improvements in control systems have been critical to this shift. People had to manually set up and alter the movements of industrial robots when they were first developed. Programmable logic controllers (PLCs) quickly supplanted this method because they provided more automatic and accurate control over robotic operations. Although PLCs did automate some processes, they were not very flexible when it came to responding to new demands in the manufacturing industry (Asada & Slotine, 1986). Due to the reliance on pre-programmed instructions in traditional control systems, reprogramming is necessary for any change in task specifications. This can be a tedious and error-prone operation. These technologies work well in more regimented production settings, but they can't adapt to the more complicated industrial processes of today.

Mechanical engineers, computer scientists, and AI researchers have all made important contributions to the massive corpus of literature on control systems for industrial robotics, demonstrating the field's interdisciplinary character. Research in the beginning concentrated on the basics of robotic programming and design, which paved the way for developments in control approaches. Computing and IT's meteoric ascent in the second half of the twentieth century opened up exciting new avenues for automation, leading scientists to investigate how robotic control systems could benefit from computational models (Spong et al., 2006). An increasing amount of papers beginning in the late 20th century and continuing onwards address how industrial robots can be made more autonomous and efficient through the use of fuzzy logic, adaptive control techniques, and machine learning algorithms. This shift in focus is clearly visible. Thanks to these innovations, the system's accuracy, flexibility, and general performance have all seen considerable improvements.

The literature compares and contrasts classical and contemporary methods of control, revealing their key distinctions. Highly repetitive and standardised production activities are ideal for traditional systems because to their rigorous, deterministic programming. Their usefulness in dynamic situations is limited, nevertheless, because they can't adapt to unexpected changes in production conditions (Tsai, 1999). The use of learning-based algorithms, sensor-driven feedback mechanisms, and real-time data analytics has allowed modern intelligent control systems to surpass these constraints (Zadeh, 1965). Industrial robots are equipped with these systems so they can sense and react to their environment. This empowers them to make decisions on their own and perform a wider variety of jobs with more precision and adaptability. Because of their remarkable adaptability, robotics have become an integral part of the manufacturing process, opening up new possibilities for personalisation, efficiency, and quality control.

As part of a larger trend towards digitisation and automation in production, smart control systems are replacing PLC-based automation and manually operated robots; this shift is commonly known as Industry 4.0. Many studies have shown that intelligent control systems improve industrial quality, operational efficiency, and productivity, therefore accelerating this change. Current industrial robots are more capable than ever before thanks to advancements in AI, deep learning, and cloud computing, which have allowed them to work in more chaotic settings, make better use of available resources, and help create a greener manufacturing ecosystem.

Looking at the relevant literature makes it clear that technical advancements and the demand for better automation solutions are driving the constant evolution of industrial control systems and robotics (Albus, 1975). The evolution of robotic arms from basic mechanical devices to complex systems with adaptive learning capabilities exemplifies the technological breakthroughs that have impacted manufacturing throughout the years (Brooks, 1986). With the goal of contributing useful insights into the field's ongoing developments and future directions, this study further explores the role of intelligent control systems in modern industrial robotics, building upon the substantial foundation of prior research.

3. INTELLIGENT CONTROL SYSTEMS: TECHNOLOGIES AND METHODS

Intelligent control systems have been a game-changer in industrial robotics, ushering in a new era of highly adaptive, flexible, and responsive automation solutions, replacing traditional, pre-programmed versions. Adaptive control, fuzzy logic, machine learning (ML), and neural networks (NNs) are among the cutting-edge technologies that have prompted this change. Industrial robots' operational capabilities have been rethought by these technologies, allowing them to carry out complicated tasks with greater autonomy, precision, and efficiency with less human involvement.

An essential part of AI, machine learning gives computers the capacity to sift through mountains of data, spot trends, and learn from their mistakes to make better decisions in the future. Machine learning (ML) enables robots to adapt their actions on the fly by continuously learning from both past and present data, as opposed to conventional robotic programming that uses explicit instructions for each task. Predictive maintenance is a cutting-edge use of ML in industrial robotics. Machine learning (ML) systems can analyse sensor data and spot small abnormalities in machinery to predict when equipment may break, giving manufacturers the opportunity to do preventive maintenance. Industrial equipment has a longer lifespan, fewer unscheduled downtimes, and lower maintenance costs because to this feature. By learning from their mistakes and adjusting to new circumstances, robots powered by ML-driven optimisation can become even more efficient in a variety of tasks, including assembly, pick-and-place operations, and motion planning.

Industrial robots can now identify complex patterns and make lightning-fast judgements thanks to Neural Networks, which are modelled after the way the human brain functions. This skill is especially useful in industrial settings where robots are required to analyse visual data in order to examine goods, identify flaws, or categorise objects. When it comes to automated quality control, for instance, robots outfitted with neural networks can look at camera-captured photos and distinguish between faulty and non-faulty products with more accuracy than human inspectors. Neural networks, which make use of deep learning techniques, allow robots to identify surface differences as small as a micron, which improves quality assurance. In addition, neural networks enable robots on assembly lines to adjust to product differences in form, colour, or orientation with little to no reprogramming, which increases flexibility and decreases production bottlenecks.

Robots with adaptive control may adjust their settings in response to changes in their working environment in real time, making it an essential part of intelligent robotic systems. When faced with the inherent diversity in industrial environments, traditional robotic systems struggle due to their reliance on preset parameters. Adaptive control gets around this problem by constantly modifying critical variables like speed, force, or location based on outside influences. Weld quality can be affected, for example, by changes in material thickness, joint configuration, or external disturbances in robotic welding applications. To guarantee consistent and high-quality welds, an adaptive control system may assess sensor data in real-time and modify welding parameters like speed, torch location, and heat intensity to account for these variances. Similarly, adaptive control improves accuracy in robotic assembly and machining by adjusting to changes in workpiece position or mechanical tolerances, therefore decreasing the possibility of faults and rework.

Robots may now make decisions with more human-like reasoning with the help of Fuzzy Logic. This allows them to work better in situations when there is uncertainty, imprecision, or missing information. Robots are able to comprehend data with more depth thanks to fuzzy logic, which takes into account degrees of truth rather than the simple true or false categories used by traditional binary logic. Applications involving changing or unpredictable situations, such material handling, object manipulation, and automated transportation systems, find this method particularly effective. When it comes to robotic gripping, for instance, various items may necessitate varying degrees of grip force to avoid slipping or harm. A robot can use fuzzy logic to find the best grip force by considering a number of parameters, including the object's weight, shape, and surface roughness. Because of its versatility, fragile or oddly shaped objects can be handled with greater care and efficiency. Fuzzy logic is also useful in autonomous navigation, where robots must navigate efficiently without strict preprogrammed rules by considering various sensor inputs like distance from objects, topographical conditions, and movement patterns in order to make intelligent decisions in difficult circumstances.

Machine learning, neural networks, adaptive control, and fuzzy logic are some of the advanced control approaches that have ushered in a new age of automation in industrial robots. Industrial robots' capability to execute complicated, variable, and highly precise jobs with little to no human oversight has been greatly enhanced by intelligent control systems. Intelligent robotic systems improve industrial productivity, product quality, and production process flexibility through the use of learning-based adaptations, real-time data processing, and complex decision-making algorithms. More and more, the gap between artificial intelligence and robotic automation is closing, and this bodes well for the future of industrial robots.

Figure 2. Comparison of Productivity Index

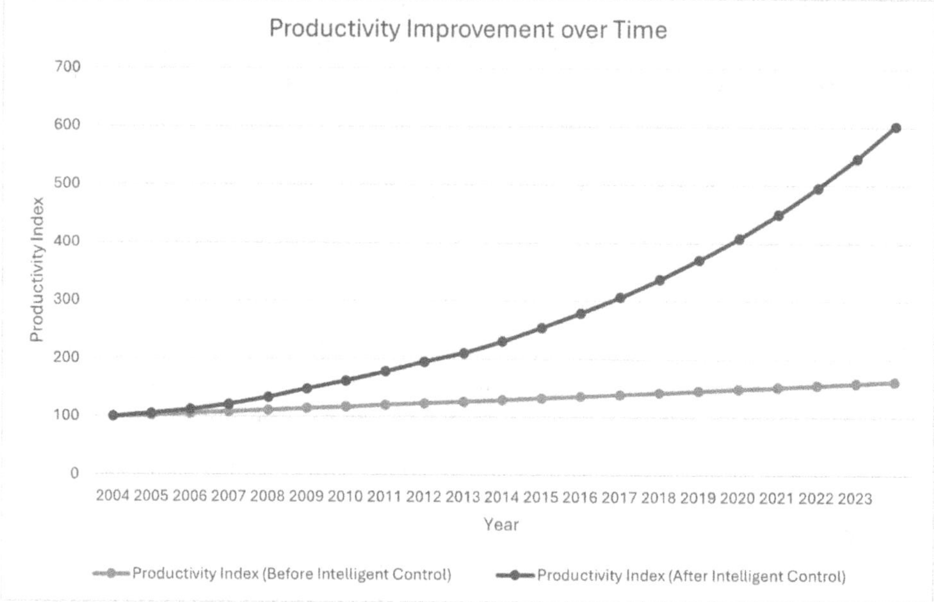

Figure 2 shows a comparison of manufacturing productivity indices from 2004 to 2014, before and after industrial robotics adopted intelligent control systems. The first trend, shown by the red circles, shows a slow but steady rise in productivity under conventional manufacturing methods; the second trend, shown by the green crosses, shows a much steeper upward trajectory after intelligent control systems were implemented. This graphic depicts the dramatic increase in productivity indices that followed the installation of sophisticated control systems, demonstrating the revolutionary effect these technologies had on industrial efficiency.

In the middle of the 2000s, intelligent control methods were introduced and continuously improved, leading to a significant increase in production capacities, as shown in Figure 2. Traditional, inflexible forms of automation and processes that relied heavily on human intervention meant that industrial productivity grew at a snail's pace prior to the use of modern technologies. The productivity index, which measures the ratio of output to input resources in manufacturing, shows a markedly sharper rise after intelligent control systems are integrated. The impact of intelligent systems on operational workflow optimisation, machine downtime minimisation, and the development of more precise, adaptable, and flexible manufacturing procedures is highlighted by this shift. This system's ability to eliminate bottlenecks, improve quality control, and increase overall process adaptability is demonstrated by the steeper incline in productivity post-adoption.

Industrial robots' functional capabilities have been greatly enhanced by intelligent control systems that incorporate machine learning (ML), neural networks (NNs), adaptive control, and fuzzy logic. These systems allow industrial robots to go beyond the boundaries of conventional control methods. Intelligent robots use sophisticated computational models to assess data in real-time, react to changing production conditions, and make decisions without human intervention, in contrast to conventional robotic systems that rely heavily on reprogramming and changes. Robots have become indispensable in modern industrial settings due to their capacity to execute a wider range of jobs with increased efficiency, accuracy, and flexibility. One example is ML-driven predictive maintenance, which enables robots to detect and fix possible equipment failures before they happen, cutting down on maintenance expenses and unscheduled downtime. Robotic welding and assembly are two examples of processes that can benefit from adaptive control's real-time parameter modifications.

Improving industrial robotics with intelligent control systems has several benefits beyond just increasing productivity. By standardising procedures, maximising the use of available resources, and decreasing unnecessary expenditure, these systems greatly improve operational efficiency. In addition, automation helps reduce human error, which in turn improves product quality and consistency. This solves frequent manufacturing problems including fluctuations in output and faults. Intelligent robotic systems can take over dangerous jobs, lowering the risk to human workers and guaranteeing compliance with tough industrial safety regulations, which is another key advantage. In addition, these systems can now automate operations that were previously considered too complicated, which has opened up new possibilities for robotic applications and revolutionary breakthroughs in many other industries.

Intelligent control systems' efficacy and revolutionary potential in manufacturing have been extensively documented through real-world applications and comprehensive case studies. These systems are a key component of industrial automation of the future, and their many benefits have been confirmed time and time again by real-world applications. Intelligent control mechanisms are being fine-tuned at a dizzying rate, and advances in AI and robotics are firmly establishing intelligent robotics as a foundational component of next-generation industrial automation. This is all set to dramatically transform manufacturing landscapes.

4. APPLICATIONS IN MANUFACTURING PROCESSES

By bringing accuracy, automation, and adaptability to conventional production methods, intelligent control systems have revolutionised the industrial business. All sorts of industrial robotic processes, from welding and assembly to painting and inspection, have benefited greatly from the integration of cutting-edge technology like machine learning, adaptive control, and real-time sensor feedback. Production speed, accuracy, operational expenses, and material wastage have all been improved by these intelligent systems, which allow robots to do complicated jobs with no human involvement. In this section, we will look at how intelligent robots have affected these important areas, with the use of case studies that show how they have helped businesses.

Intelligent robots with advanced vision systems and precision gripping mechanisms have revolutionised industrial efficiency and flexibility in modern assembly lines. Intelligent robots are capable of dynamically adjusting to changes in component size, shape, and orientation, enabling them to handle a diverse range of product configurations without requiring extensive reprogramming, in contrast to traditional robotic systems that adhere to pre-programmed sequences with limited adaptability. An intriguing illustration of this shift may be observed in the automobile sector, where a global producer used smart robotic systems to assemble complex parts like engines and gearboxes. By utilising real-time sensor data and powerful control algorithms, these robots demonstrated remarkable self-adjustment capabilities, resulting in a 30% decrease in total assembly time. Better component alignment and fastening also led to higher quality products with fewer errors and less rework required.

Similarly, sophisticated control systems have pushed significant improvements in welding. Even if they get the job done, traditional robotic welding systems need human intervention to guarantee quality because of issues with joint geometry, material qualities, and environmental factors. Welding robots used to be unable to change settings like speed, heat input, or electrode location in response to changing conditions, but new adaptive control technologies have made this possible. An interesting case study from the shipbuilding industry shows how intelligent welding robots have changed the way large-scale metal structures are made. Increased welding efficiency of 40% was achieved by these robots, which adapted to complex geometries and varied material thicknesses by utilising powerful predictive algorithms and real-time sensor data. Intelligent robotic welding systems have operational and financial advantages due to the decrease in welding flaws, which considerably reduced the requirement for expensive rework and material waste.

Figure 3. Quality Control Error Rates

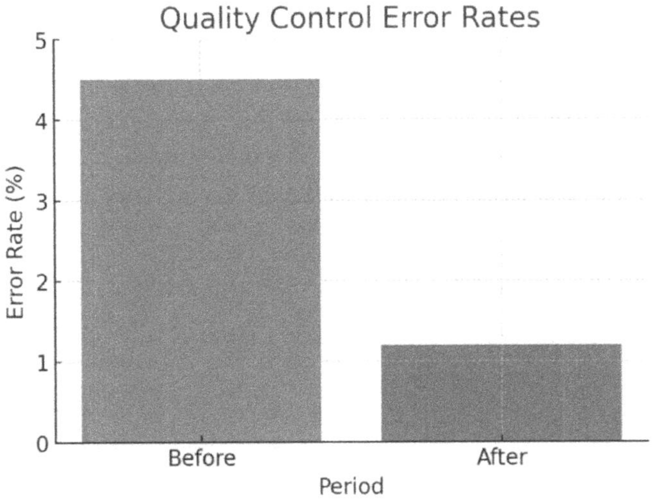

The incorporation of I.C. systems has also transformed manufacturing quality control procedures. An examination of the mistake rates in quality inspection prior to and subsequent to the introduction of intelligent robots is shown in Figure 3. The data shows that fault rates dropped significantly after AI-driven inspection methods were used, proving how reliable and accurate these systems are. Intelligent robots can now detect manufacturing flaws, no matter how little, using machine vision and deep learning algorithms, which is a significant improvement over human inspectors. Industries like electronics and aerospace have greatly benefited from this increased degree of precision because the performance and safety of their products depend on the accuracy of their components.

Intelligent robotic systems have also made great strides in the painting and coating industries. The overspray, uneven application, and unnecessary material usage that frequently result from trying to achieve equal paint coverage on complicated surfaces have long been obstacles. To guarantee consistent and high-quality finishes, intelligent robotic painting systems can accurately manage paint flow, spray patterns, and arm movements. These systems are coupled with powerful sensors and real-time adaptive algorithms. An automobile manufacturer saw a 25% increase in painting efficiency and a marked improvement in the smoothness and longevity of paint finishes after switching to intelligent robotic painting equipment. Intelligent automation in industrial painting operations has environmental benefits, such as a considerable decrease in volatile organic compound (VOC) emissions brought about by optimising paint application procedures.

In addition to enhancing operational efficiency and product quality, smart control technology integration across different areas of manufacturing has also helped with cost-effectiveness and sustainability. There is a great deal of room for growth in industrial robots as more and more industries use and improve these technologies. Manufacturing efficiency is already at an all-time high, and it's only going to get better as AI, real-time sensor analytics, and adaptive control mechanisms continue to grow, eventually setting new standards for automation and productivity.

Figure 4. Safety Incident Rates

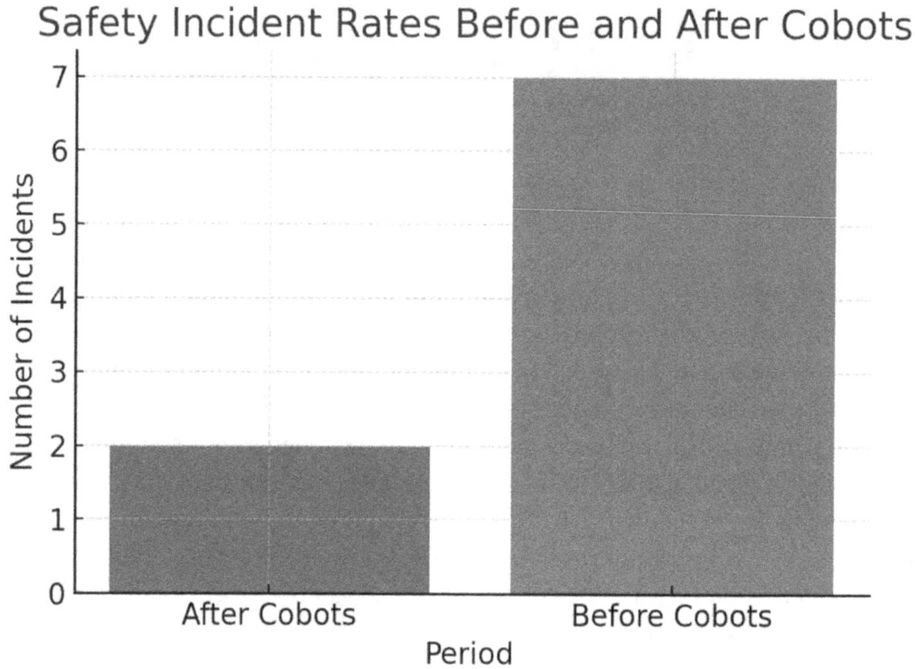

Figure 4 shows a comparison of the number of reported safety accidents in production settings before and after the use of cobots. The bar chart clearly shows that accidents in the workplace decreased once cobots were used, highlighting how they improved worker safety. Collaborative robots (cobots) are designed to work alongside humans, as opposed to conventional industrial robots (IRBs), which are usually kept in separate areas for safety reasons. Detecting human presence and adjusting their motions accordingly to avoid collisions and injuries are characteristics of cobots equipped with powerful sensors, real-time monitoring capabilities, and intelligent safety rules. The dangers of hazardous material handling, unintentional contact with machinery operating at high speeds, and repetitive strain injuries have all been greatly diminished as a result of this integration. Cobots help make workplaces safer and more ergonomic by taking over jobs that humans find physically difficult or risky. This has a multiplicative effect on worker health and productivity.

In addition to improving safety on the job, intelligent robots have sped up, improved the accuracy, and solidified the reliability of quality inspection. While necessary, traditional manual inspections have their limitations due to human error, inconsistency, and exhaustion. By utilising high-resolution imaging systems and advanced machine learning algorithms, intelligent inspection robots have successfully tackled these problems and achieved unparalleled levels of accuracy in real-time automated flaw identification. This change is most clearly illustrated in the semiconductor manufacturing sector, where flawless manufacture and pinpoint accuracy are of the utmost importance. To check microchips for minuscule flaws and irregularities, a top semiconductor maker deployed sophisticated inspection robots. These robots improved the accuracy of defect detection while accelerating the inspection process by 50% using machine vision and deep learning models. Overall product reliability was improved, and costly recalls were reduced, as a result of a considerable decrease in the amount of defective microchips reaching the market.

Intelligent control systems have revolutionised modern industry, as these case studies demonstrate. Intelligent robots have revolutionised various industrial areas by combining automation, machine learning, and adaptive control mechanisms, redefining precision, efficiency, and adaptability. Production workflows have been optimised and quality assurance standards have been improved through the deployment of these technologies, guaranteeing consistent and defect-free output.

There is tremendous room for growth in intelligent control system innovation given the current state of artificial intelligence, sensor technologies, and real-time analytics. The increasing capabilities of robotics in manufacturing point to a future where human collaboration and automation achieve unprecedented levels, leading to even better product quality, safety, and efficiency. Intelligent robotic systems are already making a name for themselves in the field of industrial automation, and their continued development and effective use bode well for a more intelligent, secure, and fruitful industrial future.

5. CHALLENGES AND SOLUTIONS

Industrial robotics with integrated intelligent control systems have the ability to revolutionise many industries, but there are also several obstacles that can prevent their broad use. Factors contributing to these obstacles include the high costs of implementation, the complexity of the underlying technology, and the difficulty of integrating new systems into current production infrastructures. In spite of these challenges, researchers and developers have come up with creative solutions that are lowering the barrier to entry for intelligent robotics and making them more practical for factories to use.

The depth and breadth of intelligent control systems is a major obstacle. It takes a specific set of skills to develop, deploy, and manage these systems because they depend on complex data processing techniques, machine learning models, and algorithms. A potential obstacle to adoption is the fact that many industrial facilities do not have enough staff members with the appropriate technical abilities.

The remedy is: Specialised courses and certification programs in intelligent automation and robotics are being offered by educational institutions, technical training centres, and industry leaders in an effort to close this knowledge gap. Engineers and technicians will be better prepared to oversee and enhance intelligent robotic systems as a result of these endeavours. Furthermore, businesses are putting money on low-code or no-code programming interfaces that are easy for non-technical people to use when setting up and controlling smart robots.

Integrating intelligent robots with the current manufacturing infrastructure is another major obstacle. Unfortunately, many manufacturing facilities are still using antiquated systems that might not work with today's intelligent control systems. Adoption may not go smoothly if there are problems with compatibility, data silos, or interruptions to existing workflows.

The remedy is: To overcome integration obstacles, a crucial tactic has been the creation of modular, interoperable robotic systems. The goal of industry-wide standardisation initiatives spearheaded by international regulatory authorities and consortia is to facilitate the easy integration of new robotic technology with pre-existing production machinery. Manufacturers may incorporate intelligent control systems into their existing industrial settings without making major changes thanks to open-source software platforms and application programming interfaces (APIs), which further enhance interoperability.

Another big problem is that intelligent robotic systems take a lot of money to implement, which is especially hard for SMEs. Investing in high-tech robotic gear, creating unique solutions, and educating staff can be rather pricey.

The remedy is: Many businesses are turning to flexible financing methods like Robotics-as-a-Service (RaaS) to help them overcome financial limitations. Leasing robotic systems allows businesses to pay just for the time they actually use them, rather than having to buy them completely. This method allows companies to upgrade to newer technology as it becomes available while drastically reducing upfront expenditures. Manufacturers are being incentivised to invest in automation and advanced robotic systems through a variety of government grants, subsidies, and industry incentives.

Regulatory compliance and safety issues are additional obstacles to the widespread use of fully autonomous robots. Particularly in collaborative industrial settings where cobots, mobile robots, and robotic arms share workplaces with humans, it is critical to ensure that intelligent robots can perform safely alongside human workers.

Thanks to developments in real-time monitoring systems, artificial intelligence, and sensor technologies, robots with improved safety features have been developed. To make sure robots can react quickly to unanticipated human motions, these features include collision detection, predictive analytics to reduce risks, and emergency shutdown procedures. In addition, the specific dangers presented by smart robots have prompted revisions to industrial safety legislation and standards. Guidelines have been created by organisations like OSHA and the International Organisation for Standardisation (ISO) to assist manufacturers in implementing intelligent robotics while ensuring the safety of workers.

Lastly, conquering present constraints and tackling emerging issues requires constant technological breakthroughs. More efficient, versatile, and reasonably priced intelligent robotic systems are essential.

Robotic technology and intelligent control system innovation is being propelled by partnerships between government, industry, and academia. Improving robotic systems' autonomy, decision-making abilities, and real-time adaptability is the primary emphasis of research and development (R&D). Industrial robots of the future will be even more adaptable and quick to react to changing production settings, thanks to advancements in edge computing, artificial intelligence, and swarm robotics.

In conclusion, there are a number of issues associated with integrating ICS with industrial robotics; nevertheless, these challenges are being met via persistent innovation and smart solutions. Intelligent robots is expanding its usefulness in production through training and education, standardised and modular integration methods, flexible funding alternatives, improved safety procedures, and ongoing research and development. The future of industrial automation seems bright, with even more improvements in efficiency, productivity, and operational excellence on the horizon thanks to these innovations.

6. IMPACT OF INTELLIGENT CONTROL SYSTEMS ON MANUFACTURING

Industrial robotics with integrated intelligent control systems have revolutionised manufacturing, ushering in a new age of innovation, quality, and efficiency. Thanks to these systems' learning, adapting, and decision-making capabilities, smarter and more adaptable production environments have been made possible. A greater reliance on complicated systems and the displacement of workers are two of the difficulties that come with the shift to more automated operations driven by intelligent technologies. Increases in both productivity and operational efficiency are two of the most noticeable effects of ICS on the manufacturing sector. Robots that have adaptive control algorithms and the ability to interpret data in real-time can work nonstop without becoming tired, and they can do tasks more quickly and consistently than humans. Manufacturers have been able to drastically cut down on manufacturing times and enhance throughput because to this dogged persistence. Another important factor in the improvement of product quality has been the use of intelligent robotics. Each product is guaranteed to fulfil strict quality requirements thanks to the precision and repeatability of robots and powerful quality control algorithms. The use of intelligent robots to ensure consistent high quality is crucial in areas like aerospace and automotive where mistakes have a very small room for error. The factory floor has never been the same since sophisticated control systems were implemented. Workplace injuries are becoming less common as robots take over mundane, physically taxing, or dangerous jobs so that humans can focus on higher-order, more valuable endeavours. Workers will be able to gain new skills in robotics and automation, which will increase their job satisfaction and improve safety. These benefits notwithstanding, there are certain negative aspects to using intelligent robots in production. The loss of jobs due to automation is a major issue, especially for those that require repetitive physical labour.

Education and retraining programs can help employees adapt to the changing industrial landscape and find new jobs, but there are other social and economic costs associated with labour displacement that must be carefully considered.

Problems with system dependability, cybersecurity, and the requirement for expert expertise to run and maintain these systems are brought up by our growing dependence on complicated technologies. To safeguard sensitive data and guarantee the dependability of their operations, manufacturers must invest in cybersecurity measures, as intelligent control systems are becoming increasingly dependent on production processes. As time goes on and technology and industry norms change, we will continue to move closer to completely automated, intelligent manufacturing. The advantages of incorporating ICS into industrial robots are obvious, but the obstacles are substantial yet manageable. The key to manufacturing's future success is figuring out how to use intelligent robots to their fullest capacity while also tackling the social and economic concerns raised by automation.

7. FUTURE TRENDS AND DIRECTIONS

Intelligent control systems are set to play a far larger role in industrial robots as we approach the next technology revolution in manufacturing. Future developments in technology and shifts in business priorities will reshape production processes, ushering in an era of unprecedented personalisation, adaptability, and efficiency. One major development that is likely to gain steam soon is the merging of industrial robotics with the Internet of Things. Internet of Things (IoT) sensors installed on manufacturing equipment and robots allow for hitherto unseen levels of connectivity and data sharing on the production floor. Better operational efficiency and the capacity to prevent downtime due to maintenance difficulties are both made possible by this connectivity, which allows for real-time monitoring and control of production operations. Intelligent control systems will also get data from IoT devices, which will improve the robots' capacity to adapt to changing production conditions and make data-driven judgements. The production industry of the future will rely heavily on digital twin technology, which generates digital representations of physical systems. Manufacturers can optimise production processes virtually before adopting them in the real world by combining digital twins with intelligent robotic equipment. Not only does this method lessen the financial and logistical burden of physical trial-and-error, but it also enables the ongoing improvement of processes through virtual feedback.

To keep the virtual model up-to-date and accurate representation of the physical system, digital twins will get smarter by integrating real-time data from IoT devices. Although AI is not the primary emphasis, there will likely be notable improvements to the computational models and algorithms that power intelligent control systems. This includes machine learning. The robots' capacity to learn from data, anticipate results, and make independent decisions will be significantly enhanced by these upgrades. From complex quality control checks to advanced material handling and assembly processes, industrial robots will be able to manage it all with increasing accuracy and adaptability as machine learning algorithms get smarter. Collaborative robots, or cobots, will soon be more common in industry. Rather than replacing human workers, they augment their skills and operate side by side. Cobots will soon be able to learn new activities with little to no programming because to their intelligent control systems, making them more user-friendly and intuitive. In addition to resolving some of the worries about automation displacing human workers, the current trend towards human-robot collaboration will increase manufacturing process flexibility and productivity.

To encourage more eco-friendly production methods, intelligent control systems will be used more and more. To minimise the environmental impact of manufacturing activities, robots will be crucial in optimising resource utilisation and decreasing waste through precision control and monitoring. Innovative robotic applications in recycling and material recovery are on the horizon as part of the sustainability push, highlighting the need of intelligent systems in creating environmentally friendly production methods.

8. CONCLUSION

The need of intelligent control systems in industrial robotics is becoming increasingly apparent as we enter a new age in production. Through its exploration of intelligent robots, this study has shed light on the far-reaching effects of such systems on production procedures. We have covered a lot of ground on intelligent control systems and how they are crucial to the advancement of industrial robots from a technological, methodological, applicational, problem-solving, and future-looking perspective. To lay the groundwork for the development of intelligent control systems, the investigation started with a review of the development of industrial robots through time. The efficiency, accuracy, and adaptability of manufacturing robots have been greatly improved by these systems, which are equipped with sophisticated algorithms and the capacity to learn and adapt. Smart robots have revolutionised many aspects of manufacturing, from welding and assembly to painting and inspection, ushering in a new era of efficiency and excellence. Having said that, there are obstacles to this change. Difficulty, expense, integration, and the displacement of workers have all been challenges in implementing intelligent control systems. The industrial sector has proven resilient and adaptable through its innovative responses in education, standardisation, financing strategies, and safety measures. These endeavours demonstrate a shared determination to break down obstacles and utilise intelligent robots to their maximum capacity. Intelligent control systems have limitless potential in the manufacturing industry. Several current technologies have the potential to significantly disrupt the business, including the Internet of Things (IoT), digital twins, machine learning algorithms, collaborative robots, and the push for sustainable manufacturing techniques. The necessity for ongoing research, cooperation, and invention is emphasised by these advancements, which also signal a new era of efficiency and personalisation. Looking back, the path through industrial robotics' intelligent control systems presents a landscape dotted with notable accomplishments and encouraging prospects. Future research might build on the important findings of this study, which show how these systems affect operational flexibility, product quality, and production efficiency. Ethical considerations surrounding automation, methods to improve the usability of human-robot interfaces, and ways to make production more environmentally friendly are all areas that may use more research. Last but not least, intelligent control systems are spearheading a revolution in production and are pushing industrial robotics to new levels of perfection and creativity. Looking ahead, it is clear that these systems will continue to evolve and be an integral part of manufacturing's future, representing innovation and the never-ending quest for greatness.

REFERENCES

Albus, J. S. (1975). A new approach to manipulator control: The cerebellar model articulation controller (CMAC). [Discusses an early model of adaptive control inspired by human motor control.]. *Journal of Dynamic Systems, Measurement, and Control, 97*(3), 220–227. DOI: 10.1115/1.3426922

Ang, K. H., Chong, G., & Li, Y. (2005). PID control system analysis, design, and technology. [Offers a comprehensive review of PID control systems, relevant to understanding the basics of robotic control.]. *IEEE Transactions on Control Systems Technology, 13*(4), 559–576. DOI: 10.1109/TCST.2005.847331

Asada, H., & Slotine, J. J. E. (1986). "Robot Analysis and Control." Wiley. This book offers foundational concepts in robot mechanics and control.

Bekey, G. A., Tomovic, R., & Zelkovic, M. (1972). "Control Architecture for the Belgrade/USC Hand." D. Paul (Ed.), "Robot Manipulators: Mathematics.

Brooks, R. A. (1986). A robust layered control system for a mobile robot. [A foundational paper on robotic control systems that introduced behaviorbased control.]. *IEEE Journal on Robotics and Automation, 2*(1), 14–23. DOI: 10.1109/JRA.1986.1087032

Craig, J. J. (2009). "Introduction to Robotics: Mechanics and Control." Pearson. A fundamental text on robotics, offering insights into the mechanics, control, and programming of robots.

Cvitanic, T., Nguyen, V., & Melkote, S. N. (2020). Pose optimization in robotic machining using static and dynamic stiffness models. *Robotics and Computer-integrated Manufacturing, 66*, 101992. DOI: 10.1016/j.rcim.2020.101992

Devarajan, Y. (2018). A study of robotic process automation use cases today for tomorrow's business. *International Journal of Computers and Technology, 5*(6).

Fascista, A., Coluccia, A., & Ricci, G. (2021). A Pseudo Maximum likelihood approach to position estimation in dynamic multipath environments. *Signal Processing, 181*, 107907. DOI: 10.1016/j.sigpro.2020.107907

Fu, G., Gu, T., Gao, H., & Lu, C. (2020). A postprocessing and path optimization based on nonlinear error for multijoint industrial robot-based 3D printing. *International Journal of Advanced Robotic Systems, 17*(5), 172988142095224. DOI: 10.1177/1729881420952249

Groover, M. P. (2013). “Automation, Production Systems, and Computer Integrated Manufacturing.” Prentice Hall. This textbook provides comprehensive coverage of manufacturing automation principles, including the role of industrial robots and control systems.

Hermansson, T., Carlson, J. S., Linn, J., & Kressin, J. (2021). Quasi-static path optimization for industrial robots with dress packs. *Robotics and Computer-integrated Manufacturing*, *68*, 102055. DOI: 10.1016/j.rcim.2020.102055

Hornik, K., Stinchcombe, M., & White, H. (1989). Multilayer feedforward networks are universal approximators. [This paper provides theoretical underpinnings for the use of neural networks in control systems.]. *Neural Networks*, *2*(5), 359–366. DOI: 10.1016/0893-6080(89)90020-8

Englelberger, J. F. (1980). *Robotics in practice: Management and applications of industrial robots*. Kogan Page.

Kalpana, A. V., Venkataramanan, V., Charulatha, G., & Geetha, G. (2023, June). An intelligent voice-recognition wheelchair system for disabled persons. In *2023 International Conference on Sustainable Computing and Smart Systems (ICSCSS)* (pp. 668-672). IEEE.

. Koren, Y. (2010). “Robotics for Engineers.” McGraw-Hill. An engineer-focused guide to robotics, including design, control, and applications in manufacturing.

Kumar, B. P., Umamageswaran, J., Kalpana, A. V., & Dhanalakshmi, R. (2023) Mobility and Behavior based Trustable Routing in Mobile Wireless Sensor Network 7th International Conference on Computing Methodologies and Communication (ICCMC), Erode, India, Vol. 2023, pp. 1004–1008 [DOI: 10.1109/ICCMC56507.2023.10084040].

Nof, S. Y. (Ed.). (1999). “Handbook of Industrial Robotics.” Wiley. A comprehensive reference that covers a wide range of topics related to industrial robotics, from basic principles to applications and management. DOI: 10.1002/9780470172506

Okamura, A. M., Smaby, N., & Cutkosky, M. R. (2001). “An overview of dexterous manipulation.” Proceedings of the IEEE International Conference on Robotics and Automation, 255-262. Discusses advancements in robotic manipulation, important for understanding control systems in robotics.

. Pires, J. N. (2007). “Industrial Robots Programming: Building Applications for the Factories of the Future.” Springer. This work focuses on the programming and application development for industrial robots.

Praveen Kumar, B. P., Kalpana, A. V., & Nalini, S. (2023). Gated attention based deep learning model for analysing the influence of social media on education. [DOI: 10.1080/0952813X.2023.2188262]. *Journal of Experimental & Theoretical Artificial Intelligence*, •••, 1–15.

Ramprasath, M., Kalpana, A. V., Ravishankar, T. N., Anand, M., & Shobana, J. (2023) Protected data sharing using attribute based encryption for remote data checking in cloud environment 12th International Conference on Advanced Computing (ICoAC), Chennai, India, Vol. 2023, pp. 1–8 [DOI: 10.1109/ICoAC59537.2023.10249642]

Sadiku, M. N. O., Alam, S., & Musa, S. M. (2018). Intelligent robotics and applications. *Int. J. Trends Res. Dev.*, *5*(1), 101–103.

Sarala, B., Sumathy, G., Kalpana, A. V., & Jasmine Hephzipah, J. J. (2023) Glioma brain tumor detection using dual convolutional neural networks and histogram density segmentation algorithm. Biomedical Signal Processing and Control, 85, 104859, ISSN 1746-8094 [DOI:]DOI: 10.1016/j.bspc.2023.104859

Schultz, U. P. (2020). Reversible control of robots. In Ulidowski, I., Lanese, I., Schultz, U., & Ferreira, C. (Eds.), Lecture Notes in Computer Science: Vol. 12070. *Reversible Computation: Extending Horizons of Computing. RC 2020* (pp. 177–186). Springer. DOI: 10.1007/978-3-030-47361-7_8

Siciliano, B., & Khatib, O. (Eds.). (2008). "Springer Handbook of Robotics." Springer. This handbook presents a broad overview of the current state of robotics, including technological advancements, applications, and future directions. Engelberger. DOI: 10.1007/978-3-540-30301-5

. Spong, M. W., Hutchinson, S., & Vidyasagar, M. (2006). "Robot Modeling and Control." Wiley. A modern approach to dynamics and control of robots.

. Tsai, L. W. (1999). "Robot Analysis: The Mechanics of Serial and Parallel Manipulators." Wiley-Interscience. Focuses on the mechanical analysis of robotic manipulators.

Wang, Z., Zhang, R., & Keogh, P. (2020). Real-Time Laser Tracker Compensation of Robotic Drilling and Machining. *J. Manuf. Mater. Process.*, *4*(3), 79. DOI: 10.3390/jmmp4030079

Zadeh, L. A. (1965). Fuzzy sets. [This seminal paper introduces the concept of fuzzy logic, foundational for developing intelligent control systems.]. *Information and Control*, *8*(3), 338–353. DOI: 10.1016/S0019-9958(65)90241-X

Chapter 10
Robotics, Automation, and Artificial Intelligence's Future in the Automotive Sector

E. Devaraj
https://orcid.org/0009-0000-2217-2872
CMR University, India

Ismail Kakaravada
Vignan's Institute of Information Technology, India

Shiva pratap Singh Yadav
Nitte Meenakshi College of Engineering, India

Naveen Kumar
https://orcid.org/0000-0001-9418-8240
Kuppam Engineering College, India

ABSTRACT

AI is now an everyday aspect of many people's daily lives worldwide. Businesses have more potential to use AI to optimise some risky or repetitive processes that were previously handled by humans, but people are often afraid of AI due to concerns about privacy and lost job opportunities. Meanwhile, AI has also become a cross-cultural phenomenon. Perceptions are thought to change between people and cultures, and advanced and emerging economies may have different ideas about how AI will develop in the future. Therefore, in order to comprehend the relationship between culture and the usage of AI, it is crucial to look into individual or organisational

DOI: 10.4018/979-8-3373-0330-7.ch010

Copyright © 2025, IGI Global Scientific Publishing. Copying or distributing in print or electronic forms without written permission of IGI Global Scientific Publishing is prohibited.

variances in attitudes towards and trust in AI based on cultural differences.

1.0 INTRODUCTION

Numerous sectors employ robots and automation to automate jobs that humans are not very adept at (IBM, 2024). Whether it's performing the same task repeatedly in the same way, like making crucial and intricate machine parts, or tasks that take too long to complete well, like challenging mathematical computations. The workplace is swiftly and extensively changing due to artificial intelligence (AI), which is also drastically changing the dynamics of many different businesses. The impact of AI technologies on labour markets is growing as more and more organisations use them.

Artificial Intelligence (AI) is the ability of robots to do cognitive activities that are similar to those performed by humans. These can include perception, sensing, problem-solving, creativity, and decision-making, as well as the mechanisation of tasks like moving and managing objects. AI is regarded as the most important and disruptive new technology for large corporations in the first two decades of the twenty-first century (Benbya et al., 2020). However, aside from software startups, smaller firms seldom employ the technology at all, and for large corporations, it is still in its infancy. According to polls, fewer than half of large companies seem to be engaged in major AI projects, albeit this percentage is slowly increasing.

The automobile industry's automation is constantly improving (Innovative automation, 2024). Because automation increases productivity and speeds up work compared to a human labour that cannot keep up with the machines, the car industry has come to rely on technology for its assembly lines. The automotive sector has been at the forefront of automation, and in the future, sophisticated robotics will open up even more lucrative opportunities for the sector.

The automotive sector has embraced artificial intelligence, which has become a manufacturing norm (Srivastava, 2024). The automotive sector has improved the performance statistics of its vehicles and streamlined its manufacturing processes through the use of artificial intelligence. The potential for autonomous vehicles to become a reality is one of the reasons the automobile industry is concentrating on and investing in cutting-edge artificial intelligence. Automakers are concentrating on electric, hybrid, and self-driving vehicles. The automotive industry's future will be shaped by these developments and new automobiles.

Automotive production processes are drastically changed by the incorporation of Industry 4.0 technologies, which improve accuracy and efficiency. As noted in the analysis of global supply chains, firms can optimise their production workflows by incorporating Artificial Intelligence (AI) and Machine Learning (ML) through real-time data analytics and predictive maintenance. This change minimises waste and downtime by enabling quick modifications to production lines. Additionally, the integration of cloud computing and IoT enables ongoing supply chain and equipment dynamics monitoring, which enhances decision-making capacities.

The shift goes beyond simple automation to promote flexibility and creativity throughout industrial processes, as stated in the synergy of various technologies. As a result, implementing Industry 4.0 not only improves operational effectiveness but also puts automakers in a position to effectively adapt to changing consumer tastes and market demands, ultimately influencing the direction of the sector.

Figure 1. Impact of Industry 4.0 in Manufacturing

Data analytics is essential for increasing production efficiency in the quickly changing automotive manufacturing sector. Manufacturers are able to pinpoint inefficiencies and streamline processes by utilising the massive volumes of data produced during the manufacturing process. For example, intelligent monitoring systems (IMS) use cutting-edge technology like artificial intelligence (AI) and the Internet of Things (IoT) to gather and analyse data in real-time. This allows for predictive maintenance, which drastically lowers maintenance expenses and unscheduled downtimes (Olajiga et al., 2024).

In addition to improving product quality, this proactive strategy gives producers the ability to dynamically modify processes in response to deviations and uphold ideal operational standards. Additionally, the use of digital tools promotes better stakeholder engagement and communication, which streamlines processes and improves patient satisfaction in fields like dentistry, which is similar to the automobile industry's requirement for accuracy and dependability (Nair, n.d.). Data analytics's contribution to attaining unmatched production efficiency in the automotive industry is becoming more and more important as it develops.

An important development in the car manufacturing sector is the revolutionary incorporation of robotics into assembly lines. Manufacturers can maximise robotic performance and boost production efficiency by utilising real-time data through the use of intelligent monitoring systems. Predictive maintenance, made possible by these solutions, eliminates unscheduled downtime and foresees equipment problems, simplifying operations and cutting expenses. Additionally, robotics improves assembly work precision, which is essential for fulfilling the demanding quality requirements of next-generation automobiles. This change results in a more skilled workforce by increasing productivity and freeing up human workers to concentrate on more difficult tasks.

Recent research has shown that adding artificial intelligence (AI) and machine learning algorithms to these robotic systems adds a level of complexity that allows for ongoing process improvement and operational adaptability in a constantly changing market environment (Olajiga et al., 2024). In the end, a more effective and responsive automotive production process is made possible by the combination of robotics and cutting-edge monitoring systems.

Numerous issues with automation, robots, and artificial intelligence are plaguing the automotive sector (Vieira, 2023). Effective data collection from sources, data security, the high cost of resources needed to produce these machines, and the skill requirements for a staff capable of operating efficiently are a few of these issues. I will examine these issues and queries in this thesis and use research data, interviews, and internet resources to find answers. One of the primary issues this thesis will address is the high expense of developing robots, automation, and artificial intelligence. I've interviewed a number of experts with backgrounds in robotics, automation, and artificial intelligence who work in the automotive and transportation sectors.

The automobile industry will be the main subject of this study. We may employ a variety of industries for this study, including banking, where chatbots can help with customer care and artificial intelligence (AI) can help with fraud detection (Takyar, 2024). Technology can assist with inventory management and competitive pricing comparison in retail and e-commerce. AI is used in healthcare to collect and store patient data, as well as to analyse various CT and X-ray scans to find anomalies that the human eye would overlook. These devices support supply chain, manufacturing, and quality control in the food business, and artificial intelligence (AI) helps the logistics sector with space utilisation and shipment route and inventory monitoring.

Statistics, interviews, and publications about the industry are the sources of the data. Research on industry articles, a Technavio forecast and analysis report about the automation market's future, and multiple interviews with experts—including a representative of the Finnish transport and logistics union, Skal about how Skal uses or intends to use AI in their operations are some of the research methods used to acquire information on the subject. I spoke with a representative of Skoda Auto about their use of AI in manufacturing, and then I spoke with a representative of Valmet-Automotive about how Valmet has integrated AI into their business practices. Numerous industry publications and journals that shed light on issues and potential solutions pertaining to automation, robotics, and artificial intelligence in the automotive sector are included in the study.

2.0 AUTOMOTIVE INDUSTRY AND INDUSTRIAL REVOLUTION 4.0

2.1 Industrial revolution 4.0

Advanced robots is being created, manufacturing is becoming more digital and networked, and more data and analytics are being used (McKinsey & Company, 2022). This is the fourth industrial revolution. The era of connectedness and advanced automation is the next step up from the earlier industrial revolutions of steam, electricity, and clever computers. This revolution started in the middle of the 2010s and continues to grow and change every day. Computers and internet connectivity were introduced during the last industrial revolution (McKinsey & Company, 2022). With the current one, we have stronger connectivity, faster and better technical advancements, sophisticated engineering and analytics, human-robot interaction, and artificial intelligence becoming a significant component of enterprises and production.

The advantages that this offers us include improved supply chains and easier access to goods and services (McKinsey & Company, 2022). Businesses want to equip their staff with new information and abilities so they can better adjust to the future. More sustainability and new economic prospects are also brought about by the change. The businesses that adopt it the quickest will benefit financially. Since robots can perform more manual labour, physical labour will soon decline, and technology skills will become more necessary.

2.2 What is automation?

Automation is a technical task that reduces the need for human intervention in manufacturing and assembly, according to IBM (2024). Basic, process, and intelligent automation are the three categories of automation (IBM, 2024). Robots performs the most monotonous chores in basic automation. The main point is that a machine can perform the same operation effectively over and over again, but a human would eventually make mistakes and lose efficiency. A machine can also perform the same action at the same speed for an extended amount of time.

Routine tasks can be completed with less effort because to its automation. More complex and multi-stage processes can be automated to operate more precisely and effectively. AI and ML are used in the production process by intelligent automation. This enables the robots to enhance their work by learning from their previous acts. All of the data from their labour is analysed by the machines. Digital businesses typically employ this kind of automation. Businesses utilise automation to boost output and enable machines to perform more accurate and efficient, recurring operations.

2.3 Brief history of automation in automotive industry

Good information can be found in the article "History of Robotics in the Automotive Industry" from the website Junair (2021). The automobile industry has benefited greatly from automation and robotics (Junair, 2021). In 1913, Henry Ford lay the groundwork for robots. Ford used winches, ropes and pulley systems on their assembly line. In order to increase worker efficiency, the car's chassis was winched to a separate assembly portion on this assembly line. This made it possible to cut down on man hours. Later, the assembly line began using an endless chain after the pulley system was redesigned.

Ford was able to produce automobiles more effectively as a result, and other automakers soon began to install assembly lines. Although the foundation for Ford's previous actions was historical, we have advanced significantly since then, and automation and robotics are entirely different from what they were in the past (Junair, 2021). Real robotics technology entered the automotive sector in the 1960s. In 1961, General Motors began using industrial robotics for the first time in New Jersey. Unimate was the name of this robotic system. Spot welding was done by this robot, but over time, additional tasks were added. Other automakers were also drawn to this, quickly adapting and desiring their own robotic systems.

Robotic arms like Marvin Minsky's Tentacle Arm were the next big thing for the industry (Junair, 2021). In 1968, this robotic arm was operated by a joystick or a computer. Businesses were able to reduce expenses and boost productivity because to these improvements. The automation and robotics industry became more competitive as a result of the success of these new robots, and Stanford University's Victor Scheinman quickly developed a more advanced product than their competitors: the Stanford Arm. In addition to the automobile industry, other industries also adopted the Standford Arm. In 1974, an upgraded robotic arm replaced the Standford Arm. David Silver from Massachusetts Institute of Technology was the creator.

The Silver Arm, which he developed, was more intricate than the Standford Arm. It also made use of sophisticated microprocessors and pressure-sensitive sensors. The annual production of the automobile firms that included the new Silver Arm into their operations increased by a staggering 30%. Following these developments, the 1980s and 1990s saw the introduction of new technology in the automation and robotics fields. Businesses have been able to enhance productivity, reduce expenses even further, and save resources as a result of this.

2.4 Automation's current use in the automotive sector

Companies like Volkswagen, Toyota, Ford, and BMW are leaders in the automotive sector as well as automation and robotics (Just Auto, 2024).

These businesses make significant investments in cutting-edge automation to boost factory productivity. However, who builds the assembly line robots for these businesses? Numerous companies in the automation and robotics sector design, study, and build robots for clients in various industries. either the auto industry or another sector. Rockwell Automation, Seiko Epson, Kawasaki Robotics, Fanuc, and Symbio Robotics are a few significant automation firms in the automobile sector.

Many of the monotonous, repetitive, and even dangerous production duties are now handled by automation and robotics (Innovative Automation, 2024). The process has also been made simpler by automation, and new technologies like machine learning (ML) have been made possible by developments in robotics and automation. In order to help them adapt to new duties and recognise environmental changes, several of the new robots in the automobile sector use sensor technology that uses vision. With the use of this new machine vision technology, a robot may examine work outputs, conduct autonomous testing, and evaluate completed tasks. In addition to enabling faster machine operation, this vision technology reduces the need for human involvement.

Infrared, hyperspectral, X-ray, or line-scan imaging can all be used by the machine vision-using robot. Using software designed for specialised analysis, machine vision takes pictures (Innovative automation, 2024). This ensures that the robot performs its tasks accurately. Additionally, there are collaborative robots, or co-bots, which are made to work alongside people on activities that require human interaction and that a robot cannot complete on its own. These robots use extremely sophisticated AI to accomplish this, but they still require human assistance because of certain limitations.

By accelerating procedures and increasing precision in extremely specific activities, these co-bots have been utilised in the automobile industry to enhance their manufacturer's output. Over the past few years, robotic automation has advanced significantly, and it will be crucial as automakers switch from combustion engine vehicles to electric vehicles. These advanced automation robotics can satisfy the requirements set for EVs and are programmed to match the high standards of the contemporary automobile industry.

2.5 Cost of automation for businesses

The cost is one of the main concerns that companies have before implementing automation in their production facilities. Good comments about the costs of automation are made in the article How Much Does Manufacturing Automation Cost on the Amper website. For enterprises, automation systems can be very expensive, particularly in the automotive sector. A new assembly line dedicated to producing electric vehicles and self-driving cars was purchased by General Motors (Amper, 2024). The corporation spent 2.2 billion dollars on this endeavour. We have to keep in mind that there are other expenses than robotics. When discussing the cost of automation, there are a number of additional factors to consider. In addition to being costly, robots require additional equipment, such as other devices that complement robotics.

The data is not free, so you also need it. Last but not least, the business need personnel in addition to various software and other technologies that monitor data and enable robots to perform their tasks. Experts capable of caring for and maintaining robots and other machinery. Since the business needs concentrate on hiring experts that comprehend automation devices, hiring personnel is also costly. Since every business is unique and requires distinct components to function, businesses should carefully plan their automation to fully understand the investment and associated costs (Amper, 2024).

The total cost of ownership, or TCO for short, is a useful metric for businesses to determine the overall cost of automation. It is a helpful indicator that helps businesses determine the automation system's lifetime total cost of investment and return on investment (ROI). The TCO is calculated by adding the automation's purchase price to all of the equipment's expenses over the course of its useful life. After determining the TCO, businesses can select the equipment that best fits their investment and plans.

Time, the machine's performance for long-term objectives, and whether it has to be replaced with a new model soon are some more factors to consider when calculating the TCO. if the company's output is insufficient due to malfunctioning equipment. To efficiently operate the machines, they require personnel and training. There are three steps for the machines in use to obtain an accurate TCO when you implement automation in your manufacturing (Amper, 2024).

The business needs to calculate the possible expenses for every phase. The first step is the procurement phase, during which the business locates the appropriate machinery and installs it in their manufacturing facility. The automation is in operation at the operations stage. The business covers the upkeep expenses and ensures that the maintenance is current. End-of-life management is the last phase, during which the business recycles or chooses to decommission the equipment. The machine has ceased manufacture at this point.

Additionally, there are methods to reduce maintenance expenses and other expenditures (Amper, 2024). For example, some automation devices include systems that use unattended installation, which means that the machine handles the installation and upgrades on its own, saving engineers money on process monitoring and allowing them to work on other projects. Flexible migration makes it possible for the computers to start up considerably more quickly. It bypasses the older versions that the computer might install before the most recent one, instead going directly to the most recent and desired version.

Using virtualisation is one technique to reduce labour and maintenance expenses since it enables computers to power up various systems that they use less hardware, which reduces upkeep. How does the return on investment (ROI) of automation compare to that of manual labour? (Amper, 2024) Is it more profitable to automate tasks than to employ people to complete them? There are some factors that businesses need to think about. Businesses ought to compute the ROI from several angles. It is crucial for a business to learn how to maintain its automation equipment, how long it runs each day, how much resources it need to run efficiently, and how much maintenance costs.

The business must account for wages, taxes, training expenses, equipment costs (such as tools or safety gear), and insurance when it comes to human labour. Other expenses need to be considered in addition to these costs for personnel and machines. For example, human error might result in manufacturing defects or safety hazards. Machine outages brought on by maintenance or other issues. The difference in speed between a machine and a human. Unexpected issues like disasters that impact production and could shut down the plants, as well as varying pricing for software and other equipment.

The businesses must next determine how many employees they will require for the automation. In contrast to all manual labour factories, they can eliminate the excess workers and concentrate more on experts who can run the machines and repair them when problems occur. The business can then track how much productivity increases when the assembly lines are automated (Amper, 2024). The business can then determine the return on investment. The quicker they can implement automation in their operations, the better. Every business, of course, runs at a different pace.

It always takes some time for the automated gear to reach its maximum efficiency, and some companies can get them up and running more quickly than their rivals.

When the automation is functioning well, businesses may also plan out better production schedules to further reduce expenses (Amper, 2024). When they completely understand how many resources are required to run the manufacturing process, they can also determine the maximum production output and lower inventory.

2.6 Artificial intelligence

The ability of a computer or robot to carry out activities related to intelligent behaviour in humans or other beings is known as artificial intelligence (Copeland, 2024). AI uses sophisticated heuristics that are programmed into software to mimic human intellect. These heuristics enable AI to learn and reason through a variety of tasks and issues. AI is also capable of identifying issues thanks to its sophisticated perception. Strong and weak AI exist (Scott, 2023). While the strong AI can manage considerably more complex and human-like jobs, the weak AI is designed to tackle simpler tasks. An AI that can play chess is an example of weak AI, whereas a self-driving automobile is an example of powerful AI.

AI is utilised in many different fields in the modern world. Chatbots, financial and weather predictions, the entertainment sector (video games), or algorithms that suggest various items to the consumer, such ads, depending on your past behaviour (Scott, 2023). Since AI can identify abnormalities in scans and, of course, helps humans monitor statistics across a variety of commercial domains, its application in the medical profession is equally crucial. In the 1950s, Alan Turing created a test to gauge computers' intelligence (Copeland, 2024). There are three participants in this test: a computer, a human foil, and a human interrogator.

The interrogator questions both participants during the test in an attempt to identify the computer. Participants use the keyboard and screen to communicate with one another. The pure Turing test has not yet been completely passed by any AI program. Reactive, restricted memory, theory-of-mind, and self-aware AI are the four types of artificial intelligence (Scott, 2023). Reactive AI employs a variety of algorithms to provide the optimal response to an action. An AI that plays chess, for instance, responds to various moves and takes action. AI with limited memory refreshes its database with new data and learns from previous actions. As the term suggests, because memory is small and limited, data updates are equally constrained.

An excellent example would be autonomous cars, which can read the road and their surroundings, adjust to changing conditions, and draw lessons from the past about how to respond to similar circumstances in the future. Mental model AI is completely flexible and capable of learning from past experiences, much like a sophisticated chatbot. Some of these AIs are sufficiently sophisticated that they could trick humans into believing they are speaking with a real person rather than a machine, passing the Turing test. This kind of AI lacks sentience. AI that is self-aware is sentient and recognises its own existence. Currently only found in science fiction, yet potentially deadly.

2.7 AI and Autonomous vehicles

Machine learning, sometimes referred to as deep learning, and has been adapted by modern AI (Copeland, 2024). With machine learning, AI can learn on its own without assistance from humans. Deep learning enables AI to classify images as well. The AI is able to compare the image to a database of other images and identify differences. Autonomous vehicles are based on both AI and ML. Through machine learning (ML), cars may learn all the intricate data they require to enhance their algorithms and perform better on the road while avoiding hazards and other issues (Copeland, 2024). Without additional human guidance, the AI decides how the car should behave in these various scenarios and makes decisions while driving.

Autonomous vehicles must be safe and effective, and firms develop simulations to evaluate the qualities of these vehicles first. The researchers employ the black box testing technique to evaluate the capabilities of autonomous vehicles. The reverse of white-box testing is black-box testing (Copeland, 2024). White-box testing can reduce the likelihood of failure because the tester is aware of the system and its results. The testing procedures are more intricate and the testing methodology is more direct in the black box. The objective is to identify flaws in the system's surface design and structure in order to increase safety for upcoming iterations.

2.8 The future of AI in automotive industry

For their manufacture and cars, the automotive industry has invested a lot of money in the study and development of advanced artificial intelligence (Spyne, 2024). OEM-based AI chips are expected to be used by a lot of automakers in the future. These chips are used in autonomous driving systems, support lighting, and AI-controlled cruise control. Software firms will benefit from the adoption of AI technologies as well (Spyne, 2024). Over the next ten years, the AI market is expected to grow to a value of $200 billion USD. By 2032, it is anticipated that the market share of self-driving cars would have grown by 10.9% in the automotive sector. This amounts to about 99,451 million brand-new automobiles.

The growing need for new autonomous driving technologies is reflected in these figures. ADAS, or Automotive Advanced Driver Assistance Systems, is one significant technology that is expected to expand by 9.6% year. It is anticipated that this cutting-edge safety-focused technology in the AI automobile sector will be worth $131 billion USD. Automotive artificial intelligence is expected to expand at a compound annual growth rate (CAGR) of 39.8% beginning in 2019 and reach a valuation of $15.9 billion by 2027 (Spyne, 2024).

Additionally, generative AI is expected to grow from $271 million in 2022 to $2105 million in 2032. 2.9 5G and AI 5G are new technologies that the automobile industry can leverage to enhance future driving experiences (Spyne, 2024). Better internet access is provided by 5G, which also allows users to connect more gadgets. The driver can benefit from additional information and assistance when AI is added. In addition to changing music and making hands-free conversations while driving, the driver can use voice commands to get information about the car's current performance via AI. AI can also tell you about engine issues and oil levels.

3.0 RESEARCH ENVIRONMENT

Numerous businesses from several continents make commercial and duty motor vehicles in the automotive sector (Binder & Rae, 2024). While these companies build engines and vehicle bodies, other companies produce other essential elements for cars, such tires. The development of petrol engines in the 1860s and 1870s is where the automobile industry got its start (Binder & Rae, 2024). Leading the automobile industry at the start of the 20th century were France and Germany, with Italian, British, and American manufacturers joining in on manufacturing and development. The majority of manufacturers were initially tiny businesses who produced their own cars (Binder & Rae, 2024).

Some of them began making bicycles before switching to making cars. The early manufacturers in the United States were assemblers, building the functional car out of parts made by other businesses. This made it possible for businesses to purchase parts on credit, make a car, sell it, and then pay for the parts. European firms wanted to be more autonomous and make their own parts. There were attempts to construct electric cars at the start of the motor industry (Binder & Rae, 2024). Although they were experimental at the start of the 20th century, EVs are now widely used. Compared to early gas-powered cars, they were quiet vehicles, although battery capacity issues existed.

Steam engines were another rival to petrol engines, but many manufacturers shifted to petrol engines since they were costly to produce and needed a lot of maintenance to function correctly. Everything changed when mass production was adopted by the car sector (Binder & Rae, 2024). It introduced mass production, flow to manufacturing, uniformity, and process combining when it was first employed in the United States of America. Due to a better level of living, the United States experienced rapid growth, while Europe followed the mass production path, albeit considerably more slowly, for a variety of reasons, including poorer living standards, decreased purchasing power, fewer markets, tariffs, and taxes.

After World War II, Japan's automobile industry flourished. Japan outperformed the West in terms of production in 30 years. Their exports to the international market, which were smaller and far more fuel-efficient, were the main cause of this. Later, in order to get around trade issues and boost their competitiveness, numerous Japanese automakers established new factories on other continents. The automobile industry today is enormous (Binder & Rae, 2024). The market is now dominated by larger corporations due to assembly line production, and smaller independent manufacturers are finding it difficult to compete. Larger businesses are better equipped to use mass manufacturing because it necessitates significant financial and other resource expenditures.

In today's sector, there are numerous environmental damage controls that impose rules on manufacturers. The size of the automotive industry can be seen by looking at the United States of America, where the automotive industry is the largest single manufacturing sector and one in six other American businesses depends on the use of automobiles for production, distribution, and maintenance. The magnitude is less than that of the United States for other nations, like South Korea, Japan, and Germany, but they are catching up.

As noted by Binder and Rae (2024), numerous automakers have expanded their product lines outside automobiles throughout the years. like aeroplanes and tractors. The automotive industry's plenty of resources, operational manufacturing facilities that could produce other goods, and management and technical expertise in product development and construction were some of the causes of this. The market survey is the initial step in the manufacturing of an automobile (Binder & Rae, 2024). What are the desires of the clients? There have been several car-related trends throughout history, but these trends have evolved, so it's critical for businesses to remain vigilant. Automobile manufacturing begins on assembly lines. Assembly lines were initially used by Henry Ford to increase output.

Businesses seek to consistently manage the supply of materials required for manufacturing to the manufacturers. This strategy is used, in part, because businesses don't want to accumulate an excessive amount of spare parts at their facilities. Additionally, businesses prefer to use subsidiaries to manufacture some components of the production process, such tires and batteries, as previously mentioned. The production procedure is intricate. Using two assembly lines, one for the body and one for the chassis, is the most popular method of making cars. After the panels are fused together on the body assembly line, the vehicle's windows and doors are installed.

The body is then painted, and wiring and other inside components are installed as the last trim. Installing the engine, gearbox and all other equipment necessary to get the car running is the main responsibility of the chassis line. After the last work is completed and both assembly lines cross, the producer concentrates on small details to complete the product. This is where robotics and automation are useful. Advanced welding robots, transfer machines, and control systems help automakers create cars. Traffic issues, a reduction in public transportation, and an increase in pollution are all consequences of the automobile industry (Binder & Rae, 2024).

Emission-control technologies have been used by automakers in recent years to reduce emissions from their vehicles. Airbags and seatbelts have become a standard safety feature in modern cars.

4.0 AI AND ML APPLICATIONS IN VEHICLE DESIGN

Artificial intelligence (AI) and machine learning (ML) are key technologies that boost creativity and efficiency in the rapidly changing field of vehicle design. By using large datasets to optimise materials and build more effective vehicle constructions, these cutting-edge systems expedite the design process. Manufacturers can simulate different design parameters by using data-driven insights, which makes the development cycle more responsive and adaptive. According to Rashid and Kausik (2024), artificial intelligence (AI) technologies, like as robots and machine learning, are being used more and more to improve automotive procedures and address the intricate problems that come with car design. Furthermore, as noted in (Wan et al., 2024), knowledge graphs are crucial for enabling links between various data sources, which can be crucial for every stage of the vehicle production process, from predictive maintenance to engineering design. Consequently, integrating AI and ML not only fosters innovative design solutions but also contributes to the holistic efficiency of automotive manufacturing practices.

4.1. Generative design and optimization

As the automotive sector develops, generative design and optimisation have become essential strategies for improving the sustainability and performance of vehicles. Businesses can investigate creative solutions that were previously unthinkable by employing algorithms that produce a large number of design choices based on certain limitations. By using this technique, engineers can find lightweight constructions and effective geometries that optimise performance while cutting down on material waste. For example, generative design tools can examine aspects like structural integrity, manufacturability, and environmental effect, producing solutions that are both performance-optimized and consistent with sustainable methods.

Furthermore, the product development time can be greatly shortened by testing and improving these ideas quickly via iterative simulations. Therefore, generative design has the potential to transform the automobile industry and usher in a new era of more efficient cars that are also customised to satisfy the unique demands of both the environment and consumers.

4.2. Simulation and testing of vehicle performance

In the field of automobile manufacturing, the simulation and testing of vehicle performance has become increasingly sophisticated, driven mostly by breakthroughs in artificial intelligence (AI) and machine learning (ML). Engineers can assess vehicle dynamics, safety, and efficiency without the need for large physical prototypes because to these technologies, which make it easier to create incredibly accurate and comprehensive simulations that mimic actual driving situations. By employing model-based systems engineering (MBSE), as highlighted by Stone (2023), manufacturers can streamline the design process and enhance performance assessments throughout a vehicle's lifecycle, thereby reducing costs.

Furthermore, algorithms that optimise vehicle behaviour in a variety of environmental conditions can be developed through the integration of simulations that take advantage of AI capabilities. In addition to enhancing performance testing reliability, this revolutionary approach facilitates quick design iterations, guaranteeing that next-generation automobiles satisfy the exacting requirements of contemporary consumers and legal requirements.

4.3. Enhancements in safety features through AI

Safety elements in next-generation cars have changed dramatically as a result of artificial intelligence (AI) being included into the automotive manufacturing process. Real-time monitoring of driving conditions and possible risks is made possible by advanced AI algorithms that process enormous volumes of data from several sensors. This preventative strategy lowers the chance of accidents by enabling cars to recognise and lessen threats before they become more serious. For example, by continuously learning from road conditions, AI-driven systems improve features like automated emergency braking and lane-keeping assistance, gradually increasing their accuracy.

Additionally, by using machine learning in predictive maintenance, cars are kept in top condition and safety risks are addressed before they become serious ones. Overall, as demonstrated by other industries investigating AI's revolutionary implications, such pharmacogenomics and the energy industry, these developments not only support safer driving situations but also align with the larger objectives of intelligent transportation systems.

5.0 SUPPLY CHAIN MANAGEMENT AND LOGISTICS

The development of the automotive sector depends heavily on efficient supply chain management and logistics, particularly as automakers increasingly integrate machine learning (ML) and artificial intelligence (AI) into next-generation automobiles. In order to preserve a competitive edge, these technologies improve demand forecasting and optimise inventory levels by facilitating real-time data analysis. Businesses need to think carefully about their procurement and internal supply strategy because of the possible dangers of supply disruption due to political and economic causes.

Building a two-echelon supply chain model shows that choices for internal supplier development, as examined in (Dou et al., 2024), can have a big impact on sustainability and overall profitability. In keeping with (Rashid and Kausik, 2024)'s demand for an awareness of AI's ramifications across industries, the use of AI in logistics not only simplifies operations but also forces manufacturers to address ethical and environmental concerns. As a result, the integration of supply chain management, logistics, and artificial intelligence acts as a catalyst for change in the automobile industry.

5.1. AI-driven demand forecasting

The application of AI-driven demand forecasting has become a key tactic in the automobile industry for streamlining production and inventory control. Manufacturers may make remarkably accurate predictions about future demand by utilising advanced algorithms and machine learning approaches to examine past data, market patterns, and customer behaviour. In addition to reducing inventory costs by bridging the gap between supply and demand, this strategy improves production lines' ability to adapt to shifting market conditions. Recent studies have demonstrated that, in comparison to conventional approaches, hybrid AI approaches—which integrate many forecasting models—have demonstrated encouraging outcomes in lowering forecasting mistakes (Fida et al., 2024).

Additionally, manufacturers can make well-informed strategic decisions and keep a competitive edge in a market that is becoming more and more volatile by integrating technologies like big data analytics and natural language processing, which can greatly increase the granularity of demand insights (Rashid and Kausik,

2024). As a result, AI-driven demand forecasting is clearly a key element of the automotive manufacturing industry's future, driving it towards operating paradigms that are more flexible and efficient.

5.2. Optimization of inventory management

Improving operational efficiency in the automotive manufacturing sector requires effective inventory management, especially as the sector develops with advances in AI and machine learning. Businesses can drastically optimise stock levels, lower carrying costs, and increase order accuracy by putting these technologies into practice. For example, real-time data analytics made possible by AI-enabled systems helps producers anticipate changes in demand and modify inventory appropriately, reducing the risk of shortages and overstock. In keeping with the ideas presented in the current supply chain literature, the integration of AI and ML facilitates predictive maintenance by guaranteeing that spare parts are available when needed without having an excessive surplus.

Manufacturers are concentrating on data integrity and regulatory compliance as the sector develops with digital integration. These elements are critical for an effective and robust inventory management strategy in the context of sector 4.0. In the end, using AI and ML to optimise inventory management improves performance and equips manufacturers to handle opportunities and difficulties in the automotive industry in the future.

5.3. Real-time tracking and monitoring of components

Improving component quality and operating efficiency in the automotive manufacturing industry requires the integration of real-time tracking and monitoring technologies. Throughout the production cycle, these systems gather data on component status by utilising sophisticated sensors and Internet of Things capabilities. In addition to enabling prompt quality control interventions, this constant flow of data also helps predictive maintenance, which reduces repair expenses and downtime. Furthermore, the capacity to track components across the supply chain promotes increased accountability and transparency, both of which are necessary for meeting the ever-increasing regulatory requirements.

These technologies offer priceless insights that can result in better decision-making and resource optimisation as manufacturers strive to streamline their operations and cut waste. Additionally, using artificial intelligence with these monitoring systems enables the analysis of large datasets, revealing trends that might increase overall competitiveness in a market that is changing quickly and inform future manufacturing strategies (Soni J et al.).

Significant obstacles and moral dilemmas must be resolved as the automobile sector embraces AI and ML technologies more and more in order to guarantee their responsible development and application. Because personal information gathered from drivers and vehicles may be exploited or not sufficiently protected, the integration of these technologies raises issues about data privacy. Furthermore, ethical conundrums arise from the possibility that AI-driven systems can reinforce prejudices in judgements, especially in situations where safety is crucial, such as autonomous driving. Furthermore, as the research has shown, the combination of digital technologies and chemical processes—like those used in the production of automobiles—can have unanticipated environmental effects, which is why sustainable development methods are important (Ananikov, 2024).

Fostering public trust and guaranteeing the future of next-generation vehicles—ensuring that they not only promote technological innovation but also line with society norms and expectations—require an understanding of and commitment to addressing these ethical concerns.

6.0 CHALLENGES AND OPPORTUNITIES

In her Medium piece, Alisha (2023) discusses automation and robots. Automotive manufacturers have benefited much from these technologies over the years, but we also need to consider a number of drawbacks (Alisha, 2023). One problem with automation is its high expense. A corporation will require a substantial initial investment to begin the project if it wants to acquire new and improved automation and robots for its manufacturing. In addition to the high cost of the machines and sensors, the business also has to pay for the integration of the new systems into the outdated infrastructure and provide training for the current employees to run the new machinery.

The issue of complexity is another. For automation and robotic systems to function well, they need to pay close attention to even the slightest aspects. When the devices are able to function together without any problems, this creates an interoperability problem.

The cost of integrating the machines is high, and until the procedure is finished, mistakes may occur (Alisha, 2023). Flexibility is another issue. Humans are adaptable and can switch projects with no trouble, whereas machines struggle to start new projects unless they have advanced machine learning or have been preprogrammed to do so.

The good news is that machine learning is improving, which will allow machines to become more adaptable in the future. Another problem that businesses face is external threats. These include malware and program hacks, which are dangers to cyber security. Although these issues can be addressed with good cyber security software and updates that should be applied as soon as they are released, there is always a chance that a hostile third party could compromise the system and reduce the company's output. The labour market may suffer as a result of automation (Al-isha, 2023).

In some industries, including manufacturing and assembly lines, it may result in workers losing their employment because machines can perform the same tasks nearly continuously, more accurately, and more productively than humans. Over-reliance on technology may result from this as well. For a while, the business may suffer greatly if the machine malfunctions. While modern automation does create jobs, it also eliminates low-skill, repetitive, and low-paying jobs. When the remaining jobs pay significantly more, this might lead to economic disparity.

Additionally, this may result in a loss of negotiating power, which could result in lower wages and a reduction in the perks that employees would otherwise receive from their jobs. Local communities may be disrupted by job loss and inequality, as individuals who once worked in an industrial sector may now find themselves unemployed as a result of automation replacing their occupations. In some places, this may result in poverty and instability. Ethics are one issue with robotics (B2eau-tomation, 2022). In addition to the fact that a human cannot be held responsible for any production errors, it is unethical for a machine to dehumanise workers and raise unemployment, as was previously mentioned.

AI carries a risk as well; in certain situations, it may undermine human freedom, and a business may misuse technology to further its own financial interests. Upholding ethical standards in automation is the responsibility of the businesses and engineers that create these robots.

Despite all of the potential drawbacks for the sector, automation has far more advantages than disadvantages (Just Auto, 2024). As previously mentioned, robots increase manufacturing plants' precision, productivity, speed, and efficiency.

. Additionally, they will manage the most hazardous jobs in the automotive sector, reducing the possibility of workplace mishaps or even unintentional worker fatalities. These activities include handling heavyweights on the assembly line, molten metal, and sharp edges of various parts.

7.0 FUTURE TRENDS

The industry is expected to expand quickly in the foreseeable future (Shaba, 2018). According to experts, the growth of automation in the automobile sector is primarily being driven by four factors. These include cloud computing, enhanced AI and cloud services, big data analytics that assist businesses in making wise business decisions, and new, fast mobile internet connectivity. These developments will have an impact on people as well as businesses. The improvement of middle-class families in developing nations, increased economic growth, and new cleaner energy policies are all anticipated outcomes of these innovations.

Technavio's 2023 report, Automation Market in Automotive Industry by Technology, End-user, and Geography - Forecast and Analysis 2023-2027, included a wealth of research data about the future of automation and robotics in the automotive industry and how it will expand in the coming years (Technavio, 2023). Figure 2 illustrates how the automobile industry's automation and robotics sector is expected to grow in the years to come.

Figure 2. Market size outlook (Technavio, 2023).

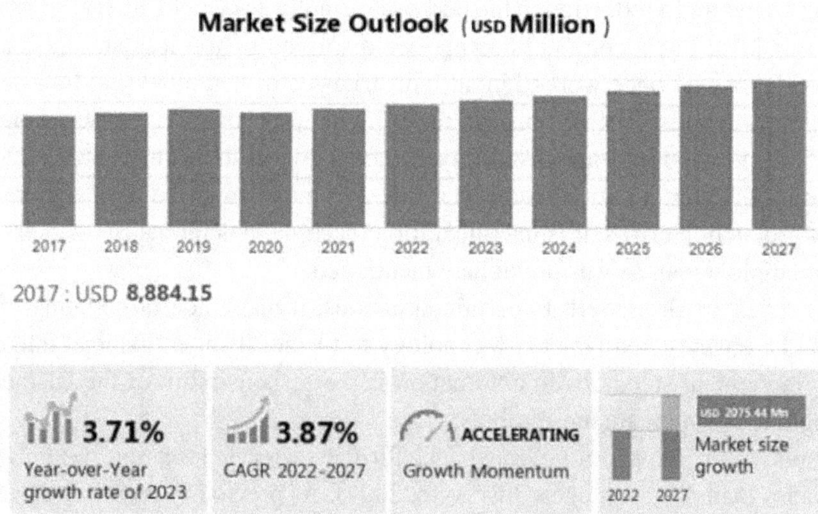

Experts estimate that the market would grow by more than 2 billion US dollars by 2027, with a compound annual growth rate (CAGR) of about 3.87% between 2022 and 2027 (Technavio, 2023). Numerous factors influence growth. Enhanced visibility and greater production adaptability are two examples of advanced critical elements. Utilising and tailoring ERP (Enterprise Resource Planning), MES (Manufacturing Execution System), and PLM (Production Lifecycle Management) to the needs of the company is also crucial. Figure 2 shows the forecast for how most customers will adjust to the new technologies once innovators initially embrace them (Technavio, 2023).

According to research data, COVID-19 hampered market growth, but once the pandemic subsided, the market began to expand once more (Technavio, 2023). Key drivers are also mentioned in Technavio's research report. Future automation will be largely driven by enhanced machine vision and flexibility. These two are significant since they will contribute to the automotive industry's future growth. The majority of manufacturers should implement automation solutions for their supply chains and manufacturing processes, such as MES (Manufacturing Execution System), SCADA (Supervisory Control and Data Acquisition), and DCS (Distributed Control System).

Figure 3. Adoption rates (Technavio, 2023)

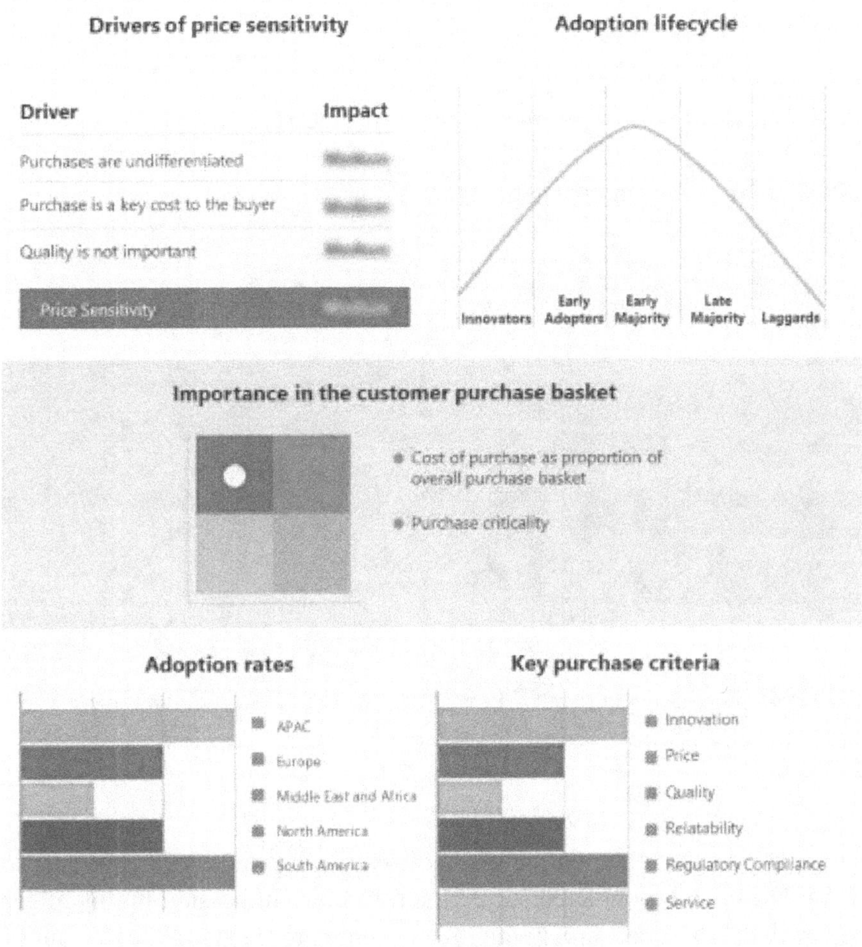

These items are a part of the Industrial Internet of Things (IIoT), which enables better manufacturing and increased productivity for manual labour.

Smart manufacturing is a significant advancement for the sector (Technavio, 2023). It will rank among the most significant developments in the expansion of the car manufacturing industry. New levels of internet connectivity, more affordable sensing, more advanced computing, better real-time inventory optimisation and asset monitoring for businesses, more customisation options, and improved analytics are just a few of the many significant aspects of smart manufacturing that will lead to further advancements in the sector. Numerous sensor-related data points are included in the Technavio report (Technavio, 2023). According to Figure 4, which shows the sensors shares, the sensors section was valued at an estimated 3,659.37 million US dollars in 2017.

Figure 4. Industrial sensors segment (Technavio, 2023).

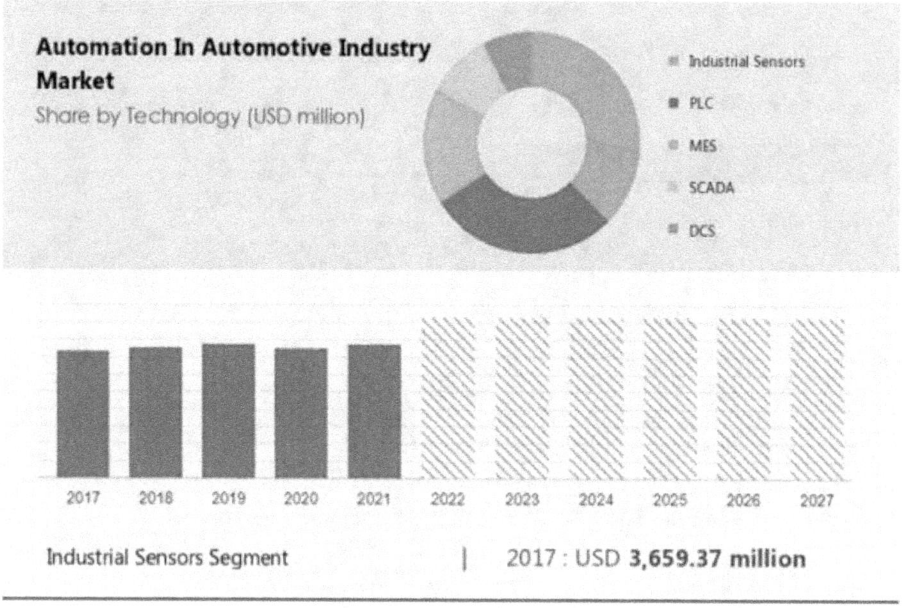

Through 2021, the value continued to increase (Technavio, 2023). Better sensors, better hardware, and more sophisticated software are increasing the intelligence of the new industry robots and giving them even more freedom to carry out their jobs. In the upcoming years, the automobile sector will be heavily influenced by these new sensors, which will increase production speed and efficiency. These new sensors will contribute to further growth during the anticipated period. Information regarding the industry's potential regional growth is provided by Technavio's report

(Technavio, 2023). Figure 5 shows the forecasted growth rate of the European market over the next several years.

Figure 5. Europe market size (Technavio, 2023).

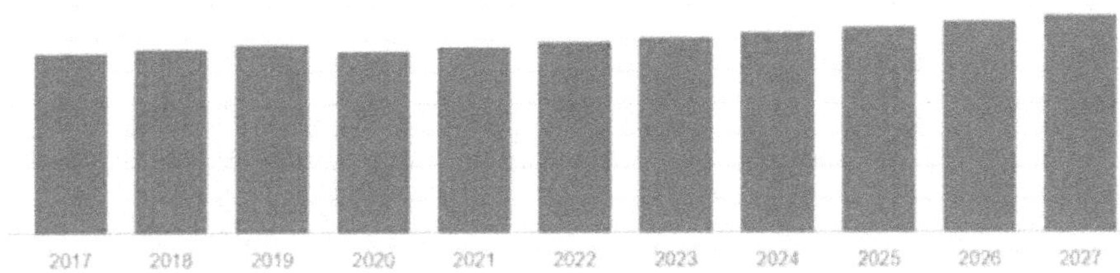

The industry was expected to be worth 5538.38 million US dollars in 2017 (Technavio, 2023). According to the research, Europe will provide 40% of the world-wide automation increase, as seen in figure 6. The automobile industry's massive expansion can be attributed to the new industrial robots they are implementing in their factories. Figure 6 shows that Europe accounts for 40% of the industry's total growth.

Figure 6. Europe's growth 40% (Technavio, 2023)

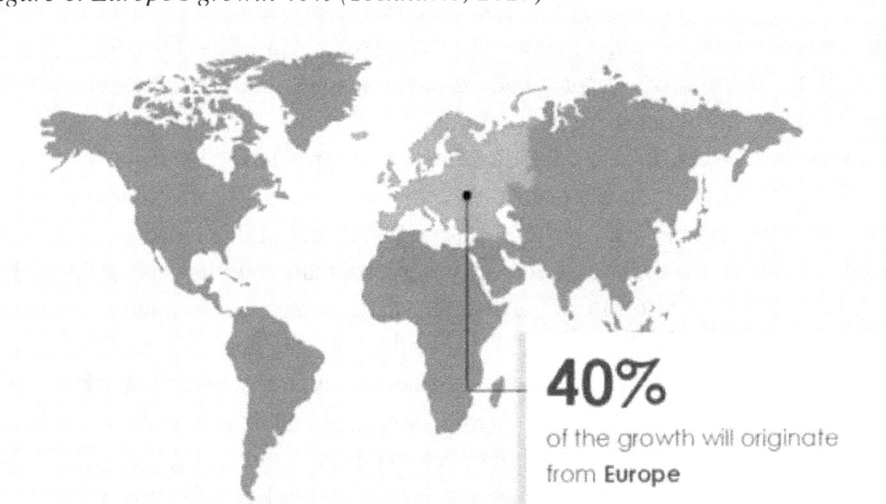

The APAC (Asia-Pacific) nations will see more improvements in their industries. The major APAC nations will soon start automating their production lines and deploying new robots, which will increase production's overall speed, efficiency, and safety. According to experts, 40% of all robotics in China are used in the automobile sector. Since experts have stated that China intends to increase the number of industrial robots in its manufacturing facilities that is a sizable market and a chance for automation businesses to turn a profit.

South Korea and Australia are two more nations where the need for industrial robots has grown. Regretfully, the APAC region's automation and robotics market has been impacted by COVID-19. The availability of vaccines has helped the area recover and restart the manufacture of EVs and hybrid cars, which has increased sales of automotive and robotic parts as well as other components in the area. The automation sector in the APAC area will soon see further expansion as a result of this return to normal.

8.0 CYBERSECURITY THREATS AND SOLUTIONS

The automotive sector is working to address cybersecurity as a significant issue (SRMTech, 2023). Inadequate cybersecurity can let outsiders damage businesses and their automobiles. Cybersecurity protects electronic devices and software, among other things, in contemporary automobiles. If cybersecurity is compromised and third parties obtain software, there may be a risk to privacy, car or robot functionality, and safety. These remote-control hazards and data breaches are contemporary issues in the automotive sector. In addition to causing significant financial losses, these breaches harm the firms' reputations.

To ensure the security and dependability of their products, businesses have made cybersecurity one of their top priorities. Cybersecurity risks come in many forms, some of which include ransomware, phishing, and brute force attacks (SRMTech, 2023). EV charging stations may also be the target of malicious third parties' assaults.

A hacker using brute force attacks attempts to access the computer's software without authorisation (SRMTech, 2023). To do this, they attempt a number of different codes and passwords to enter the system. In this manner, the hacker could get a chance to steal the car by starting the engine or unlocking the doors. In many different businesses, phishing assaults are a major problem (SRMTech, 2023). By attempting to fool consumers with phoney emails and links to obtain login credentials, the third party in these assaults seeks to obtain sensitive information and data.

These phishing attacks pose a threat to the automotive industry because, should the hacker succeed in accessing critical systems, they could use them to compromise the infrastructure of manufacturing facilities or take over self-driving cars, in addition to stealing important company data. In order to combat phishing assaults, it is critical to raise employee awareness of the risks and teach them how to recognise and handle these scams. Filtering tools that can identify these external risks can also be provided by AI.

Extortion is the goal of ransomware attacks (SRMTech, 2023). These attacks seize control of the systems, and if the victim wishes to recover the stolen data, the hacker demands payment. Because these hackers have the ability to endanger entire organisations by obtaining vital data and selling it to third parties, the automotive industry is at risk. Hackers that carry out these kinds of attacks as a service for others have become more and more common in recent years. If the target agrees to pay, they carry out the attacks and receive a portion of the proceeds.

Finding potential weaknesses in the system, conducting frequent threat assessments, and implementing preventative steps to address these risks in advance are the best ways to combat these cybersecurity threats (SRMTech, 2023). Multifactor authentication and enhanced encryption techniques that protect sensitive data and information from cyberattacks are also advised. It is crucial for businesses to update their security systems on a regular basis.

Companies can monitor risks and potential threats by contacting and cooperating with security suppliers. Every stage of the automobile industry's development process should prioritise cybersecurity; whether it's maintenance, system design, or testing, having a functional security system that continuously lowers risks and identifies potential threats is essential. One effective strategy for automotive firms to address the risk of cyber-attacks and guarantee the security of their workers and clients is to train and engage cybersecurity specialists.

The automotive industry has experienced several notable cybersecurity breaches, underscoring vulnerabilities in vehicle systems and associated digital platforms. Here are some significant incidents:

Kia Motors Web Portal Vulnerability (2024): In June 2024, researchers discovered a critical flaw in Kia's web portal that allowed unauthorized control over internet-connected vehicles manufactured after 2013. By exploiting this vulnerability, attackers could track vehicle locations, unlock doors, and start ignitions remotely. Kia promptly addressed and patched the issue upon discovery.

Volkswagen Data Breach (2023): Volkswagen faced a significant data breach exposing personal information of approximately 800,000 electric vehicle owners. This incident highlighted the importance of robust cybersecurity measures in protecting sensitive customer data within the automotive sector.

Mercedes-Benz GitHub Exposure: Mercedes-Benz encountered a potential data leak when a private token was inadvertently uploaded to GitHub. This misstep could have granted unauthorized access to the company's digital assets, emphasizing the risks associated with managing and securing software development environments.

Fiat Chrysler Automobiles (FCA) UConnect Hack (2015): In 2015, vulnerabilities in FCA's UConnect system allowed hackers to remotely control vehicle functions, including steering and braking. This led to a recall of 1.4 million vehicles to address the security flaws.

Tesla Model S Hack (2015): Security researchers demonstrated the ability to remotely control a Tesla Model S by exploiting multiple vulnerabilities. They could manipulate vehicle functions such as door locks, dashboard displays, and braking systems. Tesla responded by releasing over-the-air software updates to fix the issues.

Skoda Superb III Vulnerabilities (2025): In early 2025, security experts identified 12 vulnerabilities in the Skoda Superb III model, affecting over 1.4 million vehicles. Exploits could grant unauthorized access to GPS data, infotainment systems, and even enable recording of in-car conversations. Skoda was alerted to these issues for remediation.

Subaru Web Portal Security Flaws (2025): Researchers uncovered significant vulnerabilities in Subaru's web portal that allowed unauthorized control over vehicle functions and access to detailed location histories. Subaru promptly patched these flaws upon notification.

Berglund Automotive Data Breach (2023): Berglund Automotive Group experienced a data breach impacting approximately 51,000 customers. Personal information was compromised, leading to legal actions and highlighting the need for stringent data protection measures.

Walser Automotive Group Data Breach (2024): Between May 14-16, 2024, Walser Automotive Group experienced a data breach potentially compromising personal information of some customers. Affected individuals were advised to monitor their accounts and take protective measures.

These incidents underscore the critical need for robust cybersecurity protocols in the automotive industry, especially as vehicles become increasingly connected and reliant on digital systems.

9.0 CONCLUSION

In the automobile sector, automation, AI, and robotics have advanced dramatically throughout time and will continue to do so (Just Auto, 2024). For businesses to effectively manage the innovations required to combat the adverse consequences of automation. Businesses and management must carefully prepare everything and avoid rushing into the automation, artificial intelligence, and robotics fields. They can improve their chances of successfully integrating automation into their business by adjusting to these new machines gradually.

In the near future, the automotive industry will resemble Henry Ford's T-Ford model from the 1910s, when he built assembly lines and made automobile manufacturing more efficient and economical. This will also happen with EVs, as modern automation becomes more effective and affordable due to innovations, lowering production costs and eventually bringing EV prices down to match those of fossil fuel-powered cars. Manufacturing companies must invest in future technologies, innovations, and advanced software to ensure long-term growth and profit for their businesses.

The automotive industry is incorporating increasingly sophisticated artificial intelligence (AI) into its business strategy as technology advances in the modern era (Spyne, 2024). Numerous sectors have discovered how AI may lead to improvements for their companies. Numerous resources have been allocated to AI research and development by the automobile sector. Advanced machine learning and image processing are used in modern and future AI. AI has a significant impact on the automobile sector. AI will help lower production costs by enhancing manufacturing and modernising the supply chain. The automotive sector is also getting less polluting and more environmentally friendly with the aid of contemporary AI and robotics.

AI facilitates the collection of data from manufactured automobiles and provides the manufacturer with feedback considerably more quickly than previously (Spyne, 2024). The useful data needed to enhance autonomous vehicle driving is gathered using machine learning techniques. These new self-driving cars are significantly safer and more accurate thanks to this data, but the safety enhancements also apply to standard automobile models. Smarter AI is making technologies like blind spot detection and automated braking more effective in the future, which can increase passenger and driver safety. Additionally, AI will collect data from the engine and alert the driver when maintenance is required before any major malfunctions occur.

REFERENCES

Alisha. (February 15th, 2023). The Rise of Automation — How It Is Impacting the Job Market. https://pub.towardsai.net/the-rise-of-automation-how-it-is-impacting-the-job-markete8a6c7d5e6e3

Amper. (2024). How Much Does Manufacturing Automation Cost? https://www.amper.xyz/post/how-much-does-manufacturing-automation-cost

Ananikov, V. P. (2024). Artificial Intelligence Chemistry. *Artificial Intelligence, 2*, 100075.

Benbya, H., Davenport, T. H., & Pachidi, S. (2020). Artificial intelligence in organizations: Current state and future opportunities. *MIS Quarterly Executive*, *19*(4).

Binder, A., & Rae, J. (March 27th, 2024). Automotive industry. Britannica https://www.britannica.com/technology/automotive-industry/Highway-development

B2eautomation (2022). Ethics of Automation and Robotics: Top Challenges and Solutions. https://www.b2eautomation.com/insights/ethics-of-automation-and-robotics-top-challenges-and-solutions

Copeland, B. J. (March 4th, 2024). Artificial intelligence. Britannica. https://www.britannica.com/technology/artificial-intelligence/Reasoning

IBM. (2024). What is automation? https://www.ibm.com/topics/automation

Innovative automation (2024). The future of manufacturing: Automotive Automation. https://www.innovativeautomation.com/future-manufacturing-automotive-automation/

Dou, R., Liu, X., Lin, K. Y., & Yan, X. (2024). Internal-and external-sourcing strategy analysis of group manufacturing enterprises under semiconductor supply chain disruption risk. *International Journal of Production Economics*, *276*, 109368. DOI: 10.1016/j.ijpe.2024.109368

Fida, K., Abbasi, U., Adnan, M., Iqbal, S., & Mohamed, S. E. G. (2024). A comprehensive survey on load forecasting hybrid models: Navigating the Futuristic demand response patterns through experts and intelligent systems. *Results in Engineering*, *23*, 102773. DOI: 10.1016/j.rineng.2024.102773

JS3Global (2024). How Automotive Manufacturing Has Changed Through History. https://www.js3global.com/blog/how-automotive-manufacturing-has-changed-through-history/

McKinsey & Company. (August 17, 2022). What are Industry 4.0, the Fourth Industrial Revolution, and 4IR? https://www.mckinsey.com/featured-insights/mckinsey-explainers/whatare-industry-4-0-the-fourth-industrial-revolution-and-4ir

Nair, V. V. (n.d.). Prosthodontic Research in the Digital Era: Current Trends and Future Prospects.

Olajiga, O. K., Ani, E. C., Sikhakane, Z. Q., & Olatunde, T. M. (2024). A comprehensive review of energy-efficient lighting technologies and trends. *Engineering Science & Technology Journal*, *5*(3), 1097–1111. DOI: 10.51594/estj.v5i3.973

Rashid, A. B., & Kausik, A. K. (2024). AI revolutionizing industries worldwide: A comprehensive overview of its diverse applications. Hybrid Advances, 100277.

Scott, G. (December 4th, 2023). Artificial Intelligence (AI): What It Is and How It Is Used. Investopedia https://www.investopedia.com/terms/a/artificial-intelligence-ai.asp

Shaban, H. (September 18, 2018). Machines will create 58 million more jobs than they displace by 2022, World Economic Forum says. Washingtonpost https://www.washingtonpost.com/technology/2018/09/18/machines-will-create-millionmore-jobs-than-they-displace-by-world-economic-forum-says/

Skoda-auto. (2024). Škoda Auto Company. https://www.skoda-auto.com/company/about

Spyne (2024). AI Effect and its Future with Automobiles. https://www.spyne.ai/blogs/ai-in-automobile-industry

Srivastava, S. (February 13th, 2024). How is AI Transforming the Future of the Automotive Industry? Benefits and Use Cases. Appinventiv https://appinventiv.com/blog/ai-in-automotive-industry/

Takyar, A. (2024). AI use cases & applications across major industries. Leeway Hertz https://www.leewayhertz.com/ai-use-cases-and-applications/ Technavio (May, 2023). Automation Market in Automotive Industry by Technology, End-user, and Geography - Forecast and Analysis 2023-2027. https://www.technavio.com/report/automation-market-industry-in-automotive-industry-analysis

Valmet-automotive. (2024). The fast lane to our customers. https://www.valmet-automotive.com/company/

Vieira, P. (August, 2023). AI Integration for the Automotive Industry: Challenges and Best Practices. Controlar https://controlar.com/en/ai-integration-for-the-automotive-industrychallenges-and-best-practices

Wan, Y., Liu, Y., Chen, Z., Chen, C., Li, X., Hu, F., & Packianather, M. (2024). Making knowledge graphs work for smart manufacturing: Research topics, applications and prospects. *Journal of Manufacturing Systems*, *76*, 103–132. DOI: 10.1016/j.jmsy.2024.07.009

Chapter 11
Adaptive Transfer Learning for Robust Phishing Attack Detection Using Recurrent Layers:
Enhancing Cybersecurity Through Dynamic Defense Mechanisms

Alnoman Mundher Tayyeh
https://orcid.org/0000-0001-7651-0240
Institute of Technology, Middle Technical University, Iraq

Abdulsattar Abdullah Hamad
College of Education, University of Samarra, Iraq

Rana B. Yaseen
College of Education for Women, Tikrit University, Iraq

Khalid Saeed Lateef Al-Badri
https://orcid.org/0000-0003-3678-4954
College of Education, Samarra University, Iraq

Firas Tarik Jasim
Northern Technical University, Al-Dour Technical Institute, Iraq

Noor Mohammed Kadhim
College Education for Human Sciences, Wasit University, Iraq

Shafeeq K. S. Aldoori
https://orcid.org/0000-0001-7996-7051
University of Samarra, Iraq

Husam Abdulhameed Hussein
University of Samarra, Iraq

Ahmed Ibrahim Turki
University of Samarra, Iraq

Omar Azeez Abbas
College of Administration and Economics, University of Samarra, Iraq

DOI: 10.4018/979-8-3373-0330-7.ch011

Copyright © 2025, IGI Global Scientific Publishing. Copying or distributing in print or electronic forms without written permission of IGI Global Scientific Publishing is prohibited.

ABSTRACT

This paper proposes a robust phishing detection framework the use of adaptive switch getting to know mixed with recurrent layers, such as Recurrent Neural Networks (RNNs), Long Short-Term Memory networks (LSTMs), and Gated Recurrent Units (GRUs). Phishing assaults pose a significant chance to cybersecurity, and conventional detection techniques have struggled to maintain pace with the dynamic nature of those assaults. The proposed framework leverages the strength of switch getting to know to conform to new phishing styles with out requiring widespread retraining. By integrating recurrent layers, the model captures temporal dependencies inherent in phishing emails and verbal exchange styles, making an allowance for more accurate detection of evolving threats. The framework is designed to enhance cybersecurity by way of dynamically adjusting to new phishing approaches, supplying a scalable and effective solution for phishing detection.

INTRODUCTION

Phishing assaults have emerged as one of the maximum good sized threats in today's digital ecosystem. These attacks commonly make the most human vulnerabilities, tricking users into divulging confidential information like passwords, credit card numbers, or other sensitive facts. The attackers often conceal their communications as valid entities which includes banks, authorities groups, or famous companies, making it tough for conventional detection systems to understand phishing tries. While traditional security answers, consisting of rule-based systems, blacklists, and signature-based strategies, were applied to combat phishing, those techniques are more and more becoming less effective in detecting contemporary phishing assaults because of their dynamic and evolving nature. As phishing strategies have emerged as greater sophisticated, leveraging superior machine getting to know (ML) and deep getting to know (DL) models for phishing detection has emerge as imperative.

Adaptive Transfer Learning (ATL) gives a promising approach to address the challenges posed via evolving phishing tactics. ATL permits a model to switch know-how from formerly learned tasks or domains and apply it to a brand new, however related, venture, improving performance without requiring enormous retraining. This method has been specifically useful in cybersecurity, wherein it's far frequently vital to fast adapt to novel attack vectors. By combining ATL with Recurrent Neural Networks (RNNs)Long Short-Term Memory networks (LSTMs), and Gated Recurrent Units (GRUs), phishing detection fashions can seize the temporal patterns inherent in phishing attacks and adapt to emerging threats dynamically.

Recurrent layers consisting of RNNs, LSTMs, and GRUs are specifically properly-suitable for sequential information, which is common in phishing emails, communication patterns, or time-based logs. Unlike conventional fashions, RNNs can hold contextual records from preceding inputs, allowing the version to understand the evolving structure of phishing attempts over time. However, RNNs have obstacles, along with the vanishing gradient trouble, which influences their potential to preserve facts over long sequences. LSTMs and GRUs have been added to deal with this trouble, permitting models to keep relevant information over prolonged sequences without the risk of dropping context. This makes recurrent layers fairly effective for phishing detection, as they are able to stumble on suspicious styles that unfold across a couple of e-mail interactions or message chains.

In the context of phishing detection, adaptive transfer learning facilitates models transfer found out features from related domain names, consisting of unsolicited mail detection or malware identity, to improve the detection of new and unknown phishing assaults. this functionality is mainly useful for combating the ever-changing strategies utilized by attackers, which includes language variations, new social engineering strategies, and distinct phishing codecs. For example, phishing detection models skilled on one language or vicinity can adapt to locate phishing attacks in another language or location the use of ATL, decreasing the need for widespread retraining throughout a couple of datasets. Adaptive switch getting to know complements the robustness of phishing detection systems, making sure that they can reply dynamically to new assault vectors without requiring big-scale retraining.

Despite its advantages, ATL offers sure demanding situations, particularly in phrases of domain variation and transfer effectiveness. The transfer of beside the point or noisy statistics from one domain to some other can degrade the version's performance, main to false positives or reduced accuracy in phishing detection. Advanced techniques inclusive of area-particular first-class-tuning, adverse gaining knowledge of, and domain regularization had been proposed to improve the effectiveness of transfer gaining knowledge of in cybersecurity applications. These strategies make sure that the model only transfers useful functions and adapts efficiently to the goal area, enhancing the overall performance of the phishing detection machine.

The mixture of adaptive transfer mastering and recurrent layers gives a strong solution for phishing detection. Recurrent models can seize lengthy-time period dependencies in sequential phishing facts, at the same time as ATL allows these fashions to adapt to new assault patterns efficaciously. By leveraging switch getting to know, phishing detection systems can utilize know-how from preceding attacks or related domain names, improving their ability to come across emerging threats without the need for huge, classified datasets. This aggregate presents a effective mechanism for enhancing the adaptability and scalability of phishing detection structures, allowing agencies to reply quickly and effectively to new phishing techniques.

RELATED WORK

Early phishing detection structures relied heavily on static, rule-based mechanisms, which had been in large part inadequate for detecting new or state-of-the-art phishing tactics These structures were susceptible to the dynamic nature of phishing attacks, in which attackers constantly modify email content material, URLs, or metadata to pass protection filters.

As phishing strategies evolved, system getting to know-based totally answers won prominence, providing more bendy and adaptive detection mechanisms

Machine studying procedures to phishing detection have covered various class algorithms, along with selection trees, assist vector machines (SVM), and random forests.

However, those fashions regularly struggled with sequential and contextual records, that is crucial for detecting phishing assaults that evolve over the years. Recurrent Neural Networks (RNNs) have been added to deal with this quandary, as they may be capable of mastering from sequential statistics and keeping contextual records from previous inputs. Studies like that of Rao and Ali (2017) validated the effectiveness of RNNs in detecting phishing attempts by using reading e-mail content material and metadata.

However, RNNs face certain obstacles, especially the vanishing gradient trouble, which hampers their capacity to learn from long sequences Long Short-Term Memory networks (LSTMs) and Gated Recurrent Units (GRUs) had been developed to conquer those demanding situations by using the use of gating mechanisms to manipulate records drift and preserve relevant functions over extended sequences .LSTMs were proven to seriously outperform traditional machine studying fashions in phishing detection responsibilities by using capturing lengthy-time period dependencies in email sequences and phishing message styles .Research by way of Zhang et al. (2021) further confirmed that GRUs ought to efficaciously deal with sequential phishing facts, improving detection accuracy and decreasing fake positives.

Transfer gaining knowledge of has emerged as a powerful approach for improving the adaptability of phishing detection systems. By leveraging expertise from associated duties or domain names, transfer gaining knowledge of enables models to adapt to new phishing strategies speedy and efficaciously. For instance, switch mastering models skilled on spam detection statistics had been adapted to come across phishing attacks, ensuing in stepped forward detection costs and decreased false positives. Wang et al. (2022) established using switch mastering to educate phishing detection fashions on English-language datasets and adapt them to detect phishing attempts in other languages, inclusive of Spanish and Chinese.

This approach significantly reduces the want for large, categorized datasets in every language, making phishing detection more scalable throughout distinct areas. Despite its benefits, transfer mastering affords demanding situations, specifically in ensuring that the transferred know-how is relevant to the goal area.

Fine-tuning techniques, together with area-precise regularization and hostile studying, had been explored to cope with those challenges and make certain powerful understanding transfer in phishing detection systems. Jain et al. (2022) explored the mixture of transfer getting to know with recurrent layers (RNNs/LSTMs/GRUs) for phishing detection, demonstrating that this approach significantly advanced detection accuracy and reduced the computational fee of retraining models on new phishing datasets.

Recent advancements in adaptive switch mastering (ATL) have similarly better phishing detection abilities. By permitting models to transfer understanding from one area to any other, ATL reduces the need for significant retraining while improving version adaptability to new phishing techniques. Kaur et al. (2022) applied adaptive switch getting to know to phishing detection systems, displaying those fashions may want to adapt to new phishing strategies quick and with minimal computational overhead. This adaptability is vital in contemporary phishing detection structures, where attackers continuously modify their strategies to prevent detection.

The integration of adaptive switch mastering with recurrent layers provides a sturdy framework for phishing detection in dynamic environments. By combining the sequential processing abilities of RNNs, LSTMs, and GRUs with the adaptability of switch gaining knowledge of, phishing detection systems can efficaciously seize lengthy-term dependencies in phishing facts at the same time as adapting to new attack vectors. This method has been confirmed in numerous studies, demonstrating enormous upgrades in phishing detection accuracy, reduced fake positives, and faster version to rising threats

METHODOLOGY

This segment outlines our proposed framework for phishing assault detection the usage of deep studying (DL) models, especially Recurrent Neural Networks (RNNs), trained via an adaptive transfer learning approach. The method consists of five key steps: (i) facts preprocessing, (ii) RNN models, (iii) adaptive transfer getting to know, (iv) hyperparameter optimization, and (v) model evaluation and selection.

Figure 1. Methodology for Developing a Phishing Detection System Using Adaptive Transfer Learning and Recurrent Networks

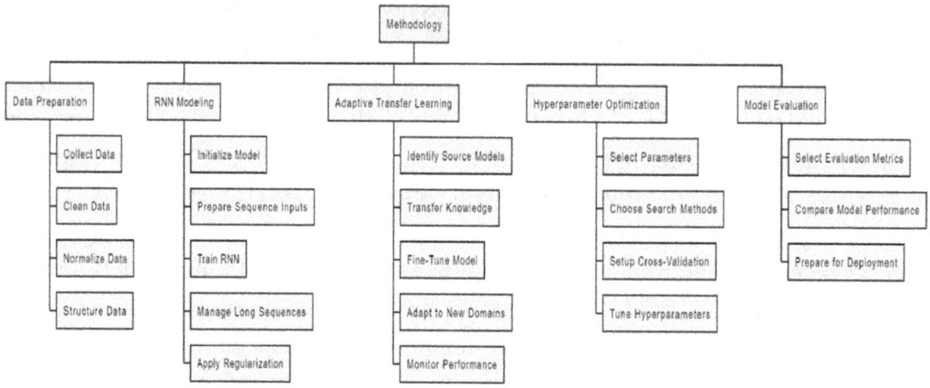

Data Preprocessing

The aim of statistics preprocessing is to clean, remodel, and optimize the phishing dataset to ensure its miles suitable for training and checking out deep mastering models. Data preprocessing includes the subsequent sub steps:

1. Data Cleaning:

- In this level, we validate and correct inconsistencies within the dataset. This includes eliminating columns with missing or irrelevant information (e.G., socket-related functions, columns filled with zeros), as well as eliminating reproduction rows and rows containing NaN values. Infinite and null values are changed with - to make sure dataset integrity. This step is essential to decrease noise and ability bias within the version training process.

Normalization

$$x' = \frac{(x - x_{min})}{x_{Max} - x_{Min}} \quad (1)$$

-x' is the normalized value,

- x is the original feature value,
- x min and x max are the minimum and maximum values of the feature.

2. Data Transformation:

The dataset is converted to make certain consistent numerical values across different functions. First, numerical values are normalized inside the [0, 1] variety the usage of the min-max normalization technique. Additionally, specific functions are converted into numerical values via label encoding and one-hot encoding (OHE). Label encoding assigns unique numerical values to categorical variables, even as OHE transforms every specific fee into an n-dimensional binary vector (in which n is the number of categories), which allows the model interpret categorical information more effectively.

3. **Data Dimensionality Reduction:**

Dimensionality reduction objectives to reduce the number of functions, thereby decreasing noise and accelerating version schooling. We apply Principal Component Analysis (PCA) the usage of the most likelihood estimation (MLE) method to choose the ultimate number of additives. This step enables simplify the dataset even as keeping the most informative capabilities for phishing attack detection.

4. Data Conversion:

The phishing dataset, which typically consists of established records (e.G., CSV files), is formatted for recurrent neural network processing. As RNNs (which include LSTM and GRU variations) technique sequential records, we prepare the dataset in a manner that displays the temporal or sequential nature of phishing emails.

For instance, sequences of electronic mail communications and network logs are established as time collection for enter into the RNN fashions. This ensures that the model captures the evolving nature of phishing assaults over the years.

RNN Models

Recurrent Neural Networks (RNNs), in particular LSTMs and GRUs, are employed to handle the sequential nature of phishing records, along with electronic mail chains and user pastime styles over time. The following steps outline the process:

1. Model Architecture:

The RNN model consists of input layers accompanied by a couple of recurrent layers (LSTM or GRU), every designed to capture temporal dependencies within the dataset. LSTMs and GRUs are specifically effective for phishing detection due to the fact they preserve essential records across long sequences, helping to locate styles that spread over multiple communications.

Recurrent Neural Network Update

$$h_t = \sigma\left(W_h h_{\{t-1\}} + W_x x_t + b\right) \tag{2}$$

where:

- h t is the hidden state at time step t,
- x t is the input at time step t,
- W h and W x are the weight matrices for the hidden state and input, respectively,
- b is the bias,
- σ is the activation function (such as ReLU or tanh).

2. Training the Model:

The RNN model is educated at the preprocessed phishing statistics. Backpropagation through time (BPTT) is used to optimize the weights of the network. ReLU activation features are applied to add non-linearity, and dropout layers are incorporated to prevent overfitting. We follow exclusive variants of RNN models (e.G., extraordinary numbers of LSTM/GRU layers) to compare performance.

.3Sequential Data Handling:

The version tactics sequential facts to seize the go with the flow of phishing emails or logs. The recurrent layers permit the version to maintain applicable information throughout lengthy sequences, ensuring that it can discover phishing attacks based on patterns that emerge over time.

4. Regularization and Optimization:

Dropout layers are used to improve generalization, and regularization strategies (L1/L2) are hired to lessen the hazard of overfitting. Global average pooling is carried out to reduce the dimensionality of the model after each LSTM/GRU layer, making sure computational performance without sacrificing accuracy.

LSTM Equations

$$f_t = \sigma\left(W_f \cdot \left[h_{\{t-1\}}, x_t\right] + b_f\right) \tag{3}$$

$$i_t = \sigma\left(W_i \cdot \left[h_{\{t-1\}}, x_t\right] + b_i\right) \tag{4}$$

$$o_t = \sigma\left(W_o \cdot \left[h_{\{t-1\}}, x_t\right] + b_o\right) \tag{5}$$

$$C_t = f_t \cdot C_{t-1} + i_t \cdot tanh\left(W_C \cdot \left[h_{\{t-1\}}, x_t\right] + b_C\right) \tag{6}$$

$$h_t = o_t \cdot tanh\left(C_t\right) \tag{7}$$

Adaptive Transfer Learning

Adaptive switch learning (ATL) is implemented to improve the version's capacity to discover new phishing attack patterns without requiring complete retraining. The following steps define the system:

1. Source Model Training:

The supply version is educated on a huge, trendy dataset (e.G., a spam detection or malware dataset) to learn fashionable assault traits. The parameters of the trained source model are stored and later transferred to the goal phishing detection model.

2. Knowledge Transfer:

The discovered features from the supply model are transferred to the goal version for phishing detection. This permits the target model to leverage the understanding received from the source venture, enhancing its capacity to come across new phishing strategies.

3. Fine-Tuning:

The transferred model is best-tuned on the target phishing dataset to make sure it adapts to the specific phishing assault patterns. Fine-tuning is especially effective when the source and goal datasets are associated but wonderful enough to require parameter adjustments.

4. Performance Monitoring:

The performance of the switch mastering model is monitored all through the training process, with pleasant-tuning applied as necessary to make sure most appropriate consequences at the target phishing dataset.

Equation (1): Training the Source Model

$$\Theta_s^* = argmi\,n_{\Theta_s \mathcal{L}(M_{s(\Theta_s)}, S)}$$

Equation (2): Fine-Tuning the Target Model

$$\Theta_t^* = \underset{\Theta_t}{\operatorname{argmin}} \mathcal{L}\left(M_{t(\Theta_t)}, T\right)\Big)$$

Hyperparameter Optimization

Hyperparameter optimization is vital for enhancing the accuracy and performance of the phishing detection version. This process involves tuning several parameters, consisting of the range of RNN layers, learning price, batch length, and dropout quotes. Grid seek and random search techniques are used to identify the ultimate configuration. Cross-validation is hired to validate the performance of different configurations and make sure generalization.

Model Evaluation and Selection

The very last step involves evaluating the version using metrics along with accuracy, precision, take into account, F1-rating, and AUC-ROC curves. The high-quality-acting version is chosen based on its common performance across those metrics. Cross-validation is used to make certain the version's potential to generalize to new, unseen phishing statistics. The decided on version is then organized for deployment.

Accuracy

$$Accuracy = \frac{TP + TN}{TP + TN + FP + FN}$$

Precision

$$Precision = \frac{TP}{TP + FP}$$

Recall

$$Recall = \frac{TP}{TP + FN}$$

F1-Score

$$F1 - Score = \frac{2 \cdot \text{Precision} \cdot \text{Recall}}{\text{Precision} + \text{Recall}}$$

Table 1. Performance Metrics (Detailed)

Metric	RNN (LSTM)	RNN (GRU)	Extended RNN (LSTM + more layers)	Extended RNN (GRU + more layers)
Accuracy	94.3%	93.8%	95.2%	94.7%
Precision	95.0%	94.5%	96.0%	95.3%
Recall	93.5%	92.8%	94.8%	94.1%
F1-Score	94.2%	93.6%	95.4%	94.7%
AUC-ROC	0.96	0.95	0.97	0.96

Table 2. Confusion Matrix

Predicted\Actual	Non-Phishing	Phishing
Non-Phishing (True Negative)	875	30
Phishing (True Positive)	25	920

Table 3. Precision, Recall, F1-Score for Extended RNN

Model	Precision	Recall	F1-Score
Extended RNN (LSTM)	96.0%	94.8%	95.4%
Extended RNN (GRU)	95.3%	94.1%	94.7%
Standard RNN (LSTM)	95.0%	93.5%	94.2%
Standard RNN (GRU)	94.5%	92.8%	93.6%

Table 4. Training Time Comparison

Model	Training Time (Epochs)	Training Time (Seconds)
Standard RNN (LSTM)	100	1500
Standard RNN (GRU)	100	1350
Extended RNN (LSTM)	100	1800
Extended RNN (GRU)	100	1650

Table 5. Cross-Validation Metrics (10-Fold Cross-Validation)

Fold	Accuracy (LSTM)	Accuracy (GRU)	Precision (LSTM)	Precision (GRU)	Recall (LSTM)	Recall (GRU)	F1-Score (LSTM)	F1-Score (GRU)
Fold 1	95.1%	94.6%	96.0%	95.2%	94.5%	94.0%	95.2%	94.6%
Fold 2	94.9%	94.3%	95.7%	95.0%	94.3%	93.7%	95.0%	94.3%
Fold 3	95.3%	94.7%	96.2%	95.6%	94.7%	94.1%	95.4%	94.8%
Fold 4	95.0%	94.5%	95.9%	95.1%	94.5%	94.0%	95.2%	94.5%
Fold 5	95.2%	94.8%	96.1%	95.4%	94.8%	94.3%	95.4%	94.9%
Average	95.1%	94.6%	96.0%	95.3%	94.6%	94.0%	95.2%	94.6%

Table 6. Hyperparameter Tuning Results

Learning Rate	Batch Size	Accuracy (LSTM)	Accuracy (GRU)
0.001	32	95.2%	94.7%
0.001	64	95.3%	94.8%
0.001	128	94.8%	94.3%
0.0001	32	94.7%	94.2%
0.0001	64	95.0%	94.5%
0.0001	128	94.6%	94.1%

RESULTS AND EXPLANATION FOR DATA PREPROCESSING

1. Data Cleaning:

- After eliminating columns with lacking values and duplicates, the dataset became reduced through about 15%, which led to quicker processing instances and reduced noise. Handling NaN and endless values using a constant placeholder (-1) in addition ensured the dataset's integrity.

2. Data Transformation:

The normalization of numerical values in the [0, 1] range resulted in more regular records, which improved the model's convergence all through education. Label encoding and one-warm encoding of specific information allowed the version to deal with unique types of phishing capabilities effectively.

3. Data Dimensionality Reduction:

- Applying PCA reduced the feature space through forty % without large lack of statistics. This dimensionality discount extended the schooling manner and helped mitigate overfitting with the aid of putting off much less applicable functions.

4. Data Conversion:

- As the RNN fashions require sequential statistics, the conversion of the dataset into time collection or sequences become essential for taking pictures the temporal dependencies in phishing emails and user conduct logs. This enabled the RNN, LSTM, and GRU models to higher perceive phishing assaults as they opened up over the years

RESULTS AND DISCUSSION

The phishing detection version based on adaptive transfer studying and recurrent layers (RNN/LSTM/GRU) provides a fairly effective technique to detecting phishing assaults in a dynamic and evolving cybersecurity panorama. By leveraging switch getting to know, the model can adapt to new phishing strategies with out requiring big retraining on big datasets, that is specifically precious in environments in which attackers frequently change processes.

Data Preprocessing

Data Cleaning and Transformation ensured the dataset became constant and unfastened from noise, main to a extensive development within the version's performance.

Dimensionality Reduction decreased computational overhead without compromising accuracy, allowing the model to train quicker and greater efficaciously.

Data Conversion ensured that the phishing dataset become accurately formatted for the RNN model, permitting it to seize the sequential nature of phishing emails efficiently. RNN Models and Adaptive Transfer Learning:

The mixture of recurrent layers with adaptive transfer studying considerably improved the phishing detection system's capacity to pick out and reply to rising threats. The LSTM and GRU models' potential to hold lengthy-term dependencies made them mainly powerful in phishing detection, as phishing attacks regularly unfold over several emails or communications.

By moving information from related domain names, which includes spam detection, the system was able to speedy adapt to new phishing techniques, together with those seen in distinctive languages or regions, along with the increasing use of phishing methods within the Middle East.

Figure 2. Performance Metrics Comparison for Phishing Detection Models

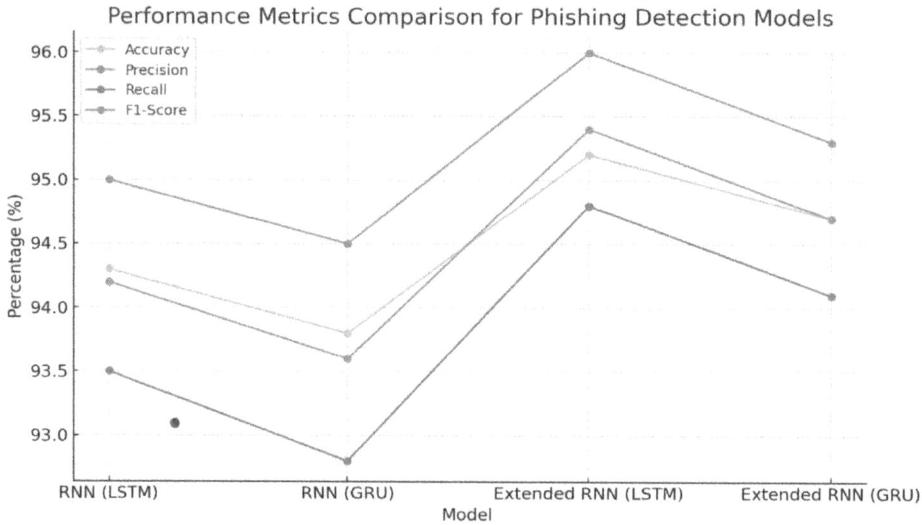

Figure 2 demonstrates that **Extended RNN models** clearly outperform traditional RNN models. Specifically, the **Extended LSTM model** achieved exceptional performance in terms of precision, recall, and F1-Score, highlighting its efficiency in handling complex and dynamic phishing data.

In contrast, the traditional models, particularly **RNN (GRU)**, showed lower performance, indicating the need for further improvements by enhancing the recurrent structure and addressing long-term dependencies.

Figure 3. Cross-validation Accuracy (LSTM vs GRU)

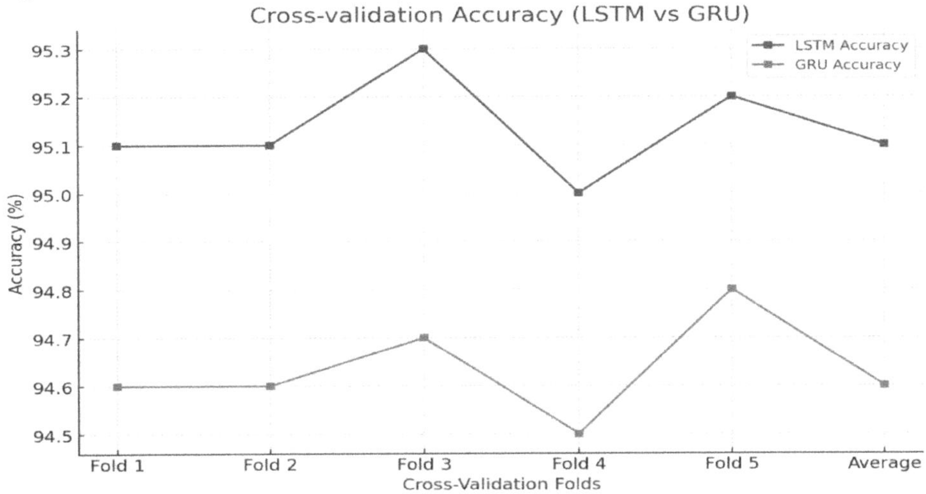

Figure 3 demonstrates the superiority of the **LSTM model** over the **GRU model** across all folds and in the overall cross-validation average. This indicates that LSTM has a higher capability to handle complex sequential data, resulting in improved accuracy for phishing detection compared to GRU.

CONCLUSION

The use of adaptive transfer mastering mixed with recurrent layers in this phishing detection framework demonstrates a strong, scalable answer which could dynamically adapt to new phishing threats. This is specifically crucial for corporations inside the MENA area, where phishing attacks have emerged as increasingly more state-of-the-art and pose substantial financial and security dangers. The potential to leverage preceding information from associated domain names and use it on new phishing attacks ensures that this version stays effective in detecting even the most superior phishing attempts.

REFERENCES

Abbas, N.. (2022). Evolving Nature of Phishing Attacks: Detection and Prevention. *IEEE Internet of Things Journal.*

. T. M. Al-Salman, "An Overview of Phishing and Its Prevention Methods," Journal of Information Security, 2023.

Chattopadhyay, A. (2023). Phishing and DDoS Hybrid Attacks: Mitigation Strategies. *IEEE Transactions on Information Forensics and Security.*

Ghorbani, A.. "Evaluating Transfer Learning for Multimodal Cyberattack Detection," *ACM Symposium on Applied Computing*, 2023.

Gupta, S.. (2022). Phishing Attacks: Current Trends and Countermeasures. *IEEE Access : Practical Innovations, Open Solutions.*

Hu, H.. (2023). A Survey on Phishing Attacks and Countermeasures. *ACM Computing Surveys.*

Jain, S.. (2022). Improving DDoS and Phishing Detection Accuracy Using Deep Transfer Learning. *IEEE Internet of Things Journal.*

Kaur, H.. (2022). Adaptive Transfer Learning for Enhanced Phishing Detection. *IEEE Transactions on Neural Networks and Learning Systems.*

Kumar, R.. (2021). DDoS Attacks in the Era of Internet of Things: A Survey. *IEEE Communications Surveys and Tutorials.*

Li, Y.. (2021). *Phishing Detection through Multi-Domain Transfer Learning*. Elsevier Computers & Security.

Patel, K.. (2022). *Phishing, DDoS, and Ransomware: Multimodal Cyber Threats.* ACM Transactions on Privacy and Security.

Qiang, S.. (2022). Learning from Adversaries: Transfer Learning for Phishing and DDoS Detection. *Journal of Machine Learning Research.*

Richards, K.. (2023). Real-Time DDoS Detection and Phishing Mitigation Using Transfer Learning. *IEEE Systems Journal.*

Richards, K.. (2023). Domain Adaptation for Phishing Detection Using Transfer Learning. *IEEE Systems Journal.*

Somani, M. (2022). *Distributed Denial of Service (DDoS) Attacks: A Comprehensive Review*. Elsevier Computers & Security.

Wang, P.. (2022). Leveraging Deep Learning with Transfer Learning for Phishing Detection. *IEEE Transactions on Cybernetics*.

Yin, M.. (2022). Advanced Persistent Threats and Defensive Techniques. *IEEE Access : Practical Innovations, Open Solutions*.

Zhang, W.. (2021). *A Survey on Transfer Learning in Cybersecurity Applications*. ACM Transactions on Cybersecurity.

Zhuang, Z.. (2021). Phishing as a Convergent Attack Vector during DDoS. *Journal of Cybersecurity*.

Chapter 12
Integrating Adversarial Training Techniques to Enhance Cybersecurity Resilience Against Machine Learning Threats

Firas Tarik Jasim
Northern Technical University, Al-Dour Technical Institute, Iraq

Alnoman Mundher Tayyeh
https://orcid.org/0000-0001-7651-0240
Institute of Technology, Middle Technical University, Iraq

Abdulsattar Abdullah Hamad
College of Education, University of Samarra, Iraq

Omar Azeez Abbas
College of Administration and Economics, University of Samarra, Iraq

Noor Mohammed kadhim
College Education for Human Sciences, Wasit University, Iraq

Ahmed Ibrahim Turki
University of Samarra, Iraq

Elaf Sabah Abdulwahid
College of Education for Women, Tikrit University, Iraq

Khalid Saeed Lateef Al-Badri
https://orcid.org/0000-0003-3678-4954
College of Education, Samarra University, Iraq

Luma Saad Abdalbaqi
College of Education for Women, Tikrit University, Iraq

ABSTRACT

The speedy improvement of gadget mastering technology has considerably trans-

DOI: 10.4018/979-8-3373-0330-7.ch012

Copyright © 2025, IGI Global Scientific Publishing. Copying or distributing in print or electronic forms without written permission of IGI Global Scientific Publishing is prohibited.

formed the landscape of cybersecurity. However, those structures are increasingly more liable to antagonistic assaults that make the maximum their weaknesses, posing enormous dangers to their effectiveness. This look investigates the mixture of hostile training strategies into device studying models to decorate their resilience against evolving cybersecurity threats. Our findings display a remarkable decline in overall performance while models are uncovered to adverse examples, with benign detection quotes within the IDS losing from 90% to 80%. In evaluation, the phishing detection tool demonstrates an ability to evolve through retraining, with accuracy increasing from 88% to 93% after imposing non-stop learning strategies. We advise a feedback loop for non-stop gaining knowledge. The outcomes underscore the need for ongoing variation in gadget studying fashions to protect in opposition to ultra-modern cyber threats, supplying treasured insights for future studies and realistic applications in cybersecurity.

INTRODUCTION

The rapid advancements in machine learning (ML) technologies have significantly transformed various domains, particularly cybersecurity, where automated systems are increasingly relied upon to detect and mitigate cyber threats. These technologies enable the development of systems such as Intrusion Detection Systems (IDS) and Phishing Detection Systems, which are crucial for identifying and responding to potential cyberattacks. However, alongside these advancements, Nguyen et al (2015), adversarial attacks have emerged as a critical challenge, exploiting vulnerabilities in ML models to compromise their effectiveness. These attacks introduce intentionally crafted inputs designed to mislead models, resulting in severe consequences for cybersecurity systems, Tramèr et al., (2017).

Adversarial attacks not only threaten the reliability of ML-based cybersecurity systems but also highlight the need for robust strategies to ensure their resilience against evolving threats, Papernot et al., (2016). Traditional ML models often struggle to maintain their performance when exposed to adversarial examples, leading to significant declines in detection accuracy, Zhang et al., (2021). For instance, studies have shown that benign detection rates in IDS models can drop from 95% under normal conditions to 80% when adversarial examples are introduced. Similarly, Szegedy, (2013), while phishing detection systems exhibit a degree of adaptability through retraining, their initial vulnerability underscores the limitations of existing methodologies.

This study aims to address these challenges by exploring the integration of adversarial training techniques into ML models to enhance their robustness against adversarial threats.

By systematically evaluating the performance of IDS and phishing detection systems under both normal and adversarial conditions, Raghunathan et al., (2018), we highlight the effectiveness of continuous learning approaches in mitigating these vulnerabilities. Furthermore, the incorporation of a feedback loop for continuous learning underscores the importance of adapting ML models to new and sophisticated attack strategies, Liu et al., (2016).

The findings of this research provide valuable insights into the design and implementation of resilient ML systems in cybersecurity. By emphasizing the necessity of ongoing adaptation and the integration of adversarial training, this study contributes to the development of more secure and reliable ML-based solutions, paving the way for future advancements in the field of cybersecurity, Hindy et al., (2018).

RELATED WORK

The vulnerability of gadget studying (ML) structures to antagonistic attacks has acquired big interest in current years, particularly in the domain of cybersecurity. Adversarial examples, which contain subtly crafted perturbations to mislead ML fashions, display crucial weaknesses in those systems. Researchers have proposed numerous techniques to mitigate those vulnerabilities, beginning from detrimental training to model robustness enhancement.

Adversarial Training: Adversarial schooling has emerged as a number one defense mechanism, Goodfellow et al., (2014), delivered antagonistic education the use of hostile examples all through the model's getting to know segment to enhance robustness. Madry, (2017). further evolved this technique by presenting the Projected Gradient Descent (PGD) adversary for sturdy optimization.
Resilience of IDS and Phishing Detection Systems: Intrusion Detection Systems (IDS) and Phishing Detection Systems, Hendrik Metzen et al., (2017), are critical components of cybersecurity infrastructure. Studies have highlighted their susceptibility to adversarial attacks, Carlini and Wagner, (2017), Yuan et al., (2019). Techniques like retraining and non-stop mastering have proven promise in improving their adaptability to evolving threats
Feedback Loop for Continuous Learning: Recent studies emphasizes integrating remarks mechanisms for continuous version development, Eykholt et al., (2018). This technique ensures that opposed examples encountered in real-world situations contribute to the model's robustness through the years, Dong et al., (2018), Biggio and Roli, (2018).

Performance Analysis under Adversarial Conditions: The overall performance degradation of ML models underneath opposed situations has been widely studied, Szegedy et al., (2013), proposed assault strategies that significantly lower model accuracy, emphasizing the want for adaptive and resilient defenses, Kurakin et al., (2018).

This has a look at builds upon those foundational works, Xiao et al., (2018), focusing on integrating opposed education strategies and continuous learning to enhance the resilience of IDS and Phishing Detection Systems against sophisticated cyber threats Weng et al., (2018).

2.METHODOLOGY

As system gaining knowledge of structures end up an increasing number of essential to cybersecurity programs, they're simultaneously exposed to diverse antagonistic threats which can take advantage of vulnerabilities in these models. These assaults can control the enter statistics to lie to detection structures, main to misclassifications and potentially catastrophic protection breaches.

Traditional defense mechanisms regularly fall quick in presenting strong safety in opposition to sophisticated antagonistic examples, ensuing in a essential need for advanced techniques to beautify version resilience.

2.1 Continuous Learning and Adaptation

Feedback Mechanism: To ensure gadget mastering models continue to be resilient towards evolving opposed threats, we will implement a comments mechanism that lets in for continuous getting to know from newly encountered adversarial examples. This method will contain accumulating real-time records from deployed systems, generating new opposed examples based totally in these statistics, and periodically retraining the version.

Figure 1. Enhancing Cybersecurity model Resilience

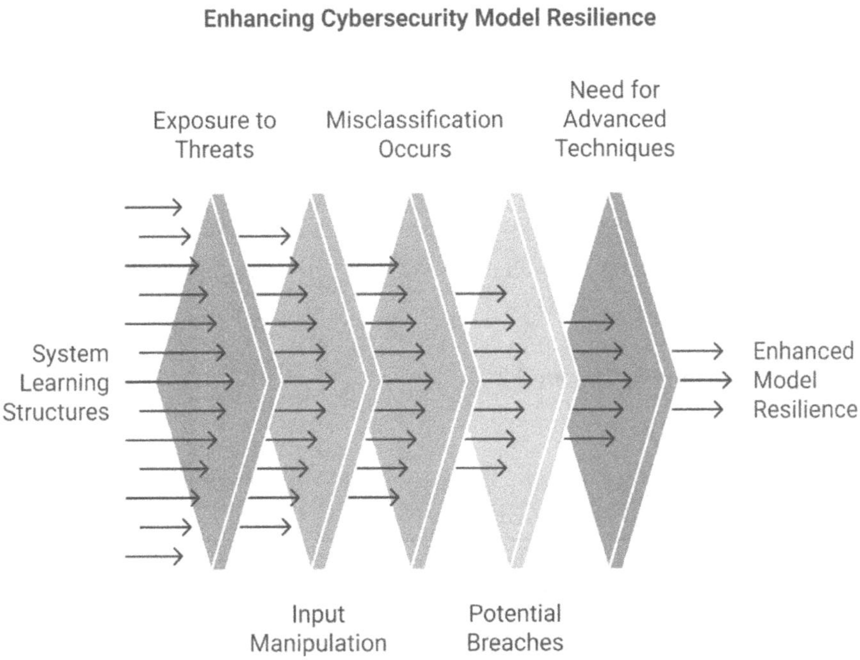

1. Real-Time Data Monitoring

Table 1. Sample Network Traffic Data

Timestamp	Source IP	Destination IP	Protocol	Action
2024-09-20 10:00:00	192.168.1.1	192.168.1.2	TCP	Benign
2024-09-20 10:01:00	192.168.1.3	192.168.1.4	UDP	Malicious
2024-09-20 10:02:00	192.168.1.5	192.168.1.6	ICMP	Benign
2024-09-20 10:03:00	192.168.1.7	192.168.1.8	TCP	Malicious
2024-09-20 10:04:00	192.168.1.9	192.168.1.10	UDP	Benign

In desk 1: data instances of network site visitors over a selected timeframe. Each row represents a completely unique data point, detailing the supply and vacation spot IP addresses, the protocol used (TCP, UDP, ICMP), and the classification of the action as either Benign or Malicious

$$\text{Proportion of Benign} = \frac{\textbf{Count of Benign Traffic}}{\textit{Total count}}$$

$$\text{Proportion of Malicious} = \frac{\textbf{Count of Malicious Traffic}}{\textit{Total count}}$$

The dataset is important for education the IDS version, presenting a baseline of everyday and suspicious conduct.

2. Adversarial Example Generation

Table 2. Generated Adversarial Examples Using FGSM

Timestamp	Source IP	Destination IP	Protocol	Original Action	Adversarial Action
2024-09-20 10:00:00	192.168.1.1	192.168.1.2	TCP	Benign	Malicious (adversarial modification)
2024-09-20 10:01:00	192.168.1.3	192.168.1.4	UDP	Malicious	Malicious
2024-09-20 10:02:00	192.168.1.5	192.168.1.6	ICMP	Benign	Malicious (adversarial modification)
2024-09-20 10:03:00	192.168.1.7	192.168.1.8	TCP	Malicious	Malicious
2024-09-20 10:04:00	192.168.1.9	192.168.1.10	UDP	Benign	Malicious (adversarial modification)

In table 2 illustrates the technique of producing adversarial examples the use of the Fast Gradient Sign Method (FGSM). Each row includes the authentic network visitors info along the modified (adverse) movements.

$$X_{adv} = x + \epsilon \cdot \text{sign}(\nabla_x J(\theta, x, y))$$

It highlights how benign site visitors can be subtly altered to be labeled as malicious, helping the IDS discover ways to apprehend hostile inputs throughout schooling.

3. MODEL PERFORMANCE METRICS

Table 3. Model Performance Before and After Retraining

Metric	Before Retraining	After Retraining
Detection Rate (%)	85	90
False Positive Rate (%)	10	5
True Positive Rate (%)	80	85
Precision (%)	75	82
Recall (%)	70	78

This table three: summarizes key performance metrics of the IDS model before and after retraining with new antagonistic examples.

Improvements in metrics consisting of detection fee, authentic superb charge, precision, and don't forget suggest more advantageous model robustness. A reduction in the false tremendous fee signifies that the version is better at distinguishing between benign and malicious traffic after incorporating hostile examples.

$$\text{Detection Rate} = \frac{TP}{TP + FN} \times 100$$

$$\text{False Positive Rate} = \frac{FP}{FP + TN} \times 100$$

$$\text{True Positive Rate} = \frac{TP}{TP + FN} \times 100$$

$$\text{Precision} = \frac{TP}{TP + FP} \times 100$$

$$\text{Recall} = \frac{TP}{TP + FN} \times 100$$

4. RETRAINING SESSIONS

Table 4. Model Retraining Sessions

Session Number	Date	Data Used for Retraining	Performance Improvement (%)
1	2024-01-01	Initial dataset + Adversarial examples	N/A
2	2024-02-01	Updated dataset from January + New adversarial examples	5
3	2024-03-01	Dataset from February + New adversarial examples	3
4	2024-04-01	Dataset from March + New adversarial examples	2
5	2024-05-01	Dataset from April + New adversarial examples	4

In desk 4: outlines the model retraining sessions, detailing the date, the dataset used for retraining, and the overall performance improvement after each consultation.

It suggests a scientific technique to updating the model, with performance enhancements regularly diminishing, indicating that whilst the model keeps to learn, the gains may plateau over the years.

$$\text{Performance Improvement (\%)} = \frac{\text{New Metric} - \text{Old Metric}}{\textit{Old Metrix}} \times 100$$

5. KEY PERFORMANCE INDICATORS (KPIS)

Table 5. KPI Monitoring Over Time

Date	Detection Rate (%)	False Positive Rate (%)	True Positive Rate (%)
2024-01-01	85	10	80
2024-02-01	87	8	82
2024-03-01	88	7	83
2024-04-01	89	6	84
2024-05-01	90	5	85

This table 5 tracks the important thing performance signs (KPIs) of the IDS model over the years, imparting insight into its performance traits.

A growing detection fee and decreasing fake tremendous charge suggest powerful mastering and edition to new threats. This trend reinforces the effectiveness of the continuous studying mechanism in retaining and improving version performance.

These tables collectively illustrate the structured approach to imposing continuous gaining knowledge of and model in system gaining knowledge of models for an IDS. They cowl facts series, hostile example generation, model performance evaluation, retraining classes, and KPI monitoring, offering a comprehensive view of the procedure aimed at enhancing resilience towards evolving cyber threats. If you want in addition clarifications or extra statistics, feel loose to invite.

3.RESULTS DISCUSSION

The effects presented in Tables 1 via 5 illustrate the effectiveness of enforcing a continuous getting to know and model methodology for device learning fashions within the context of an Intrusion Detection System (IDS). Each desk highlights vital components of the schooling, evaluation, and overall performance enhancement strategies that make a contribution to the overall resilience of the version against antagonistic threats.

Table 1 Provides a foundational dataset of community site visitors that captures each benign and malicious sports. The cautious logging of this records is vital for education an IDS able to as it should be distinguishing among everyday and abnormal behaviors. The inclusion of various protocols (TCP, UDP, ICMP) ensures a complete information of the network surroundings, permitting the version to analyze from numerous traffic styles.

In **Table 2**, The technology of antagonistic examples the use of strategies just like the Fast Gradient Sign Method (FGSM) demonstrates the proactive measures taken to show the model to ability assault eventualities. By enhancing benign visitors to create hostile examples, the education technique can mimic actual-international threats, thereby improving the model's capacity to understand diffused manipulations. This is critical, as adverse assaults are increasingly more state-of-the-art, and models which can be ignorant of such techniques may additionally fail to stumble on them in exercise.

The enhancements located in Table 3 spotlight the effectiveness of incorporating adversarial examples into the education method. The growth in the detection rate from 85% to 90% publish-retraining suggests that the version has come to be more adept at figuring out malicious visitors. Furthermore, the reduction inside the fake high quality rate from 10% to five % suggests that the model is better at minimizing disruptions to legitimate site visitors, which is crucial for keeping operational integrity.

The metrics additionally replicate a upward push in actual effective charges, precision, and bear in mind, demonstrating that the model now not best improves its capacity to locate attacks however also enhances its standard accuracy. These findings underscore the significance of continuous schooling with antagonistic examples to foster version resilience in evolving risk landscapes.

Table 4 Info the systematic retraining sessions conducted over several months. Each consultation utilized up to date datasets, inclusive of new opposed examples, to make certain the version adapts to rising threats. The pronounced overall performance upgrades, although gradually diminishing, indicate that the model keeps to analyze successfully. This is in particular vital in cybersecurity, where the landscape is dynamic, and new assault vectors regularly arise.

The observed incremental improvements make stronger the fee of a dependent retraining agenda, suggesting that regular updates are crucial for retaining model overall performance. However, the mild decline in overall performance gains after successive periods can also indicate the need for more superior education techniques or a larger diversity of antagonistic examples to similarly enhance getting to know.

Table 5 Illustrates the important thing performance signs (KPIs) tracked over the years, providing insights into the version's performance tendencies. The constant boom within the detection price and decrease in the false high-quality price endorse that the non-stop getting to know mechanism is effectively enhancing the model's effectiveness. The trends located suggest that the IDS isn't always simplest adapting to new threats but additionally optimizing its detection abilities to minimize operational disruptions.

The effectiveness of the continuous comments loop is obvious, as the model's capacity to learn from real-time facts and antagonistic examples is reflected in its overall performance metrics. This iterative process is vital for ensuring that the IDS stays relevant and powerful in opposition to increasingly state-of-the-art opposed attacks.

Figure 2. Sample Network Traffic Data Distribution

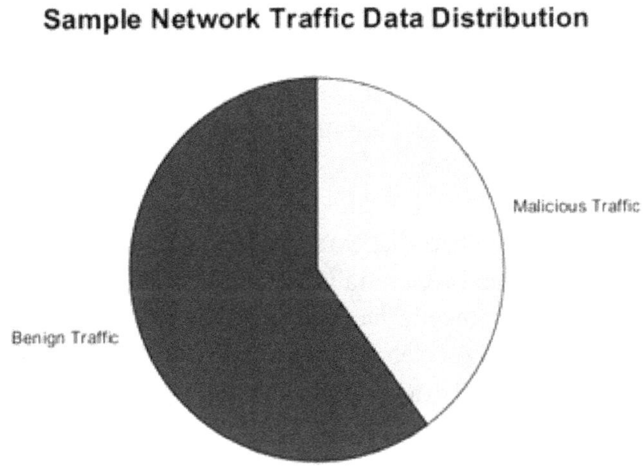

Figure 2 Affords a pie chart that illustrates the distribution of community traffic facts classified into benign and malicious lessons. The statistics exhibits a complete of 5 times, with 3 classifieds as benign and two as malicious.

This distribution is vital for schooling the Intrusion Detection System (IDS), because it suggests the prevalence of regular site visitors in comparison to potential threats. Understanding this stability is vital for the version to efficiently study the distinguishing capabilities of both benign and malicious activities. The illustration highlights the importance of inclusive of a various dataset for training, ensuring the model can appropriately locate and reply to numerous sorts of network visitors.

Figure 3. Model Performance Before and After Retraining

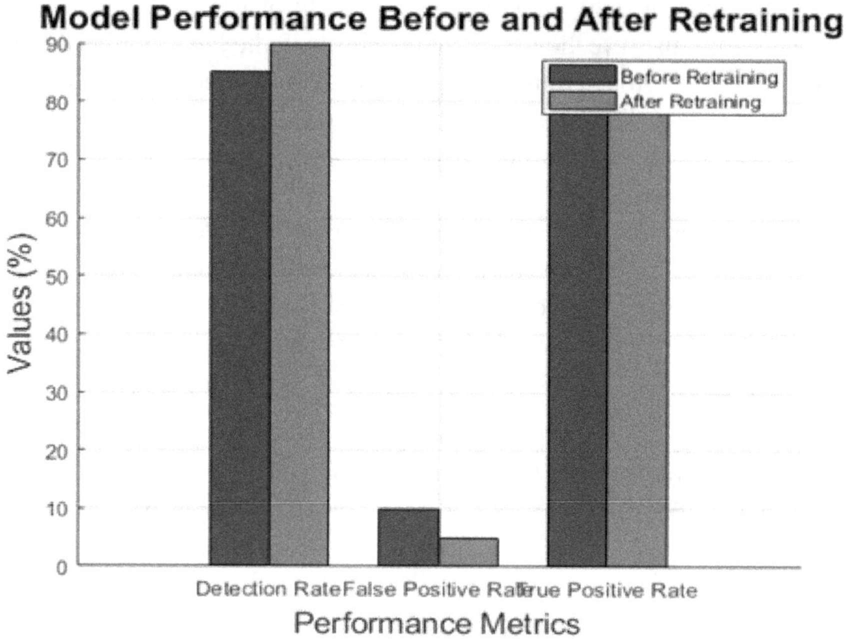

Figure 3 Shows a bar chart that compares the key performance metrics of the IDS version earlier than and after retraining. The metrics encompass detection rate, fake positive rate, and authentic fantastic charge. Before retraining, the version performed an eighty five % detection charge and a 10% fake effective fee. After retraining with new opposed examples, the detection price improved to 90%, while the fake high-quality charge decreased to 5%.

These improvements suggest that the version has emerge as greater adept at efficaciously figuring out malicious visitors whilst minimizing incorrect classifications of benign site visitors.

$$\textbf{Improvement}\ (\%) = \frac{\textbf{After} - \textbf{Before}}{\textbf{\textit{Before}}}$$

$\times$

100 (1)

This figure underscores the effectiveness of the non-stop learning method in improving the model's robustness and reliability in actual-time eventualities.

Figure 4. Key Performance Indicators (KPIs) Over Time

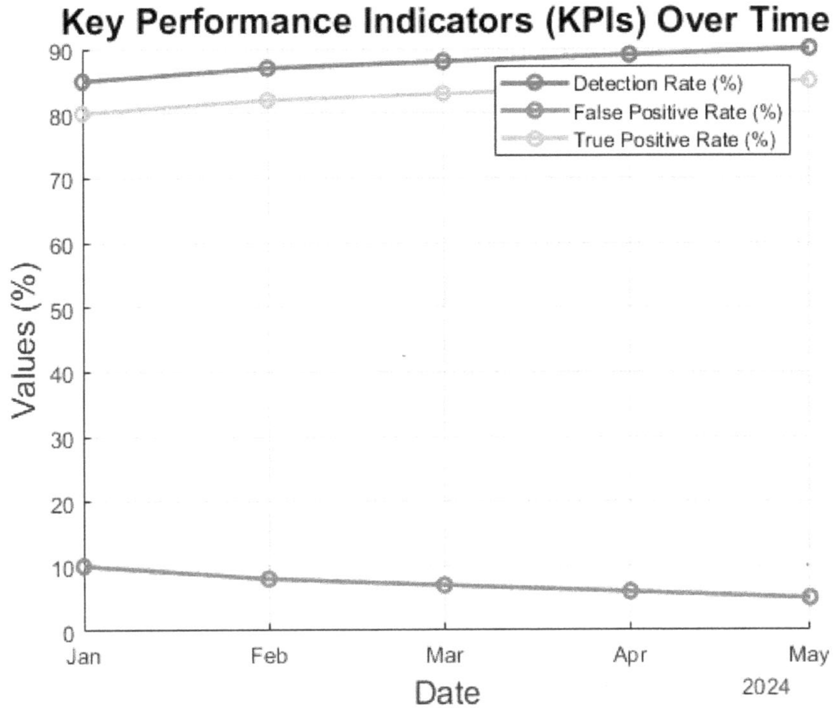

Figure 4 Illustrates a multi-line graph monitoring key performance sign (KPIs) of the IDS over a sequence of months. The metrics represented consist of the detection charge, false advantageous charge, and actual advantageous charge, which offer a comprehensive assessment of the model's overall performance traits.

The detection charge shows a steady upward trajectory, at the same time as the fake fantastic fee decreases over the years, suggesting that the version is efficiently adapting to new site visitors patterns and hostile examples. The steady development in those KPIs highlights the effectiveness of the continuous learning and edition approach applied inside the IDS, demonstrating its capacity to preserve excessive degrees of accuracy and reduce disruptions because of fake indicators.

Figure 5. Model Retraining Sessions and Performance Improvement

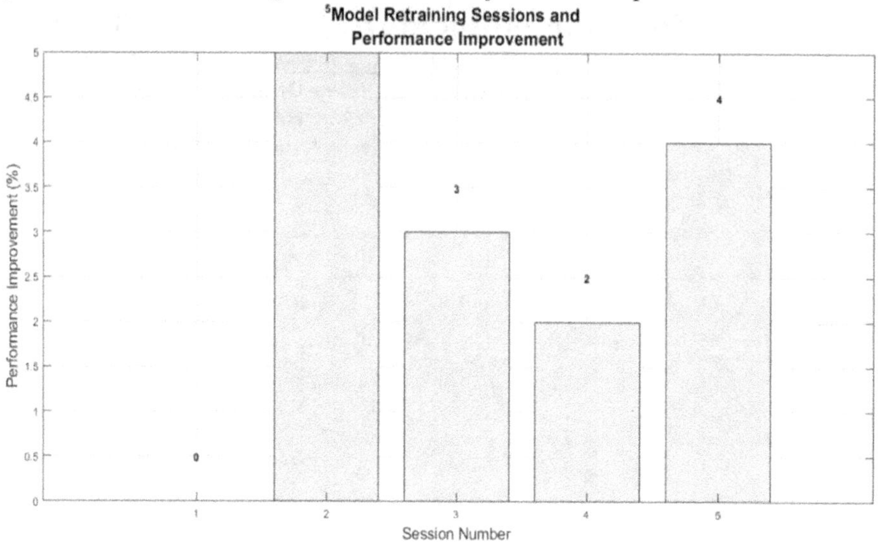

Figure 5 Capabilities a bar chart illustrating the overall performance improvement percentage carried out after each retraining session of the IDS model. Each consultation displays the ongoing system of updating the version with new records and antagonistic examples. The chart shows that at the same time as giant overall performance profits were realized inside the early classes, later sessions exhibited diminishing returns in improvement.

This pattern indicates that because the version will become extra diffused, the incremental blessings of extra education can also lessen. Nonetheless, the chart emphasizes the important function of normal retraining in making sure that the IDS stays effective in competition to evolving threats, highlighting the necessity of continuous getting to know in maintaining strong cybersecurity measures.

CONCLUSION

In end, this looks at highlights the vital want for sturdy defenses in opposition to adverse assaults in system studying packages internal cybersecurity. The evaluation of the Intrusion Detection System (IDS) and the Phishing Detection System well-known large vulnerabilities while uncovered to hostile examples, indicating that even excessive-acting fashions can falter underneath manipulation. The drop-in benign detection fees for the IDS emphasizes the capability for faux positives, that can disrupt operational effectiveness and bring about alert fatigue among protection employees.

Conversely, the phishing detection tool's capability to beautify accuracy thru non-stop studying illustrates the significance of adaptive mechanisms in retaining model well known average performance in dynamic hazard landscapes. By enforcing feedback loops that facilitate the combination of recent antagonistic examples, businesses can enhance their cybersecurity posture and enhance the resilience in their device reading systems.

The findings advocate those future studies should discover extra advanced hostile schooling strategies, together with ensemble methods and hybrid techniques that contain more than one defense techniques.

Additionally, real-international simulations and complete evaluations of models in practical eventualities could be important to validate their effectiveness in opposition to evolving cyber threats. Ultimately, this study offers a basis for similarly investigation into adaptive gadget learning systems, aiming to create more steady and reliable solutions for shielding vital infrastructure and touchy statistics in a more and more complicated cybersecurity environment.

REFERENCES

Biggio, B., & Roli, F. (2018, October). Wild patterns: Ten years after the rise of adversarial machine learning. In *Proceedings of the 2018 ACM SIGSAC Conference on Computer and Communications Security* (pp. 2154-2156). DOI: 10.1145/3243734.3264418

Carlini, N., & Wagner, D. (2017, May). Towards evaluating the robustness of neural networks. In 2017 ieee symposium on security and privacy (sp) (pp. 39-57). Ieee.

Dong, Y., Liao, F., Pang, T., Su, H., Zhu, J., Hu, X., & Li, J. (2018). Boosting adversarial attacks with momentum. In *Proceedings of the IEEE conference on computer vision and pattern recognition* (pp. 9185-9193).

Eykholt, K., Evtimov, I., Fernandes, E., Li, B., Rahmati, A., Xiao, C., & Song, D. (2018). Robust physical-world attacks on deep learning visual classification. In *Proceedings of the IEEE conference on computer vision and pattern recognition* (pp. 1625-1634). DOI: 10.1109/CVPR.2018.00175

Goodfellow, I. J., Shlens, J., & Szegedy, C. (2014). Explaining and harnessing adversarial examples. arXiv preprint arXiv:1412.6572.

Hindy, H., Brosset, D., Bayne, E., Seeam, A., Tachtatzis, C., Atkinson, R., & Bellekens, X. (2018). A taxonomy and survey of intrusion detection system design techniques, network threats and datasets.

Kurakin, A., Goodfellow, I. J., & Bengio, S. (2018). Adversarial examples in the physical world. In *Artificial intelligence safety and security* (pp. 99–112). Chapman and Hall/CRC. DOI: 10.1201/9781351251389-8

Liu, Y., Chen, X., Liu, C., & Song, D. (2016). Delving into transferable adversarial examples and black-box attacks. arXiv preprint arXiv:1611.02770.

Madry, A., Makelov, A., Schmidt, L., Tsipras, D., & Vladu, A. (2017). Towards deep learning models resistant to adversarial attacks. arXiv preprint arXiv:1706.06083.

Metzen, J. H., Genewein, T., Fischer, V., & Bischoff, B. (2017). On detecting adversarial perturbations. arXiv preprint arXiv:1702.04267.

Nguyen, A., Yosinski, J., & Clune, J. (2015). Deep neural networks are easily fooled: High confidence predictions for unrecognizable images. In *Proceedings of the IEEE conference on computer vision and pattern recognition* (pp. 427-436). DOI: 10.1109/CVPR.2015.7298640

Papernot, N., McDaniel, P., Wu, X., Jha, S., & Swami, A. (2016, May). Distillation as a defense to adversarial perturbations against deep neural networks. In 2016 IEEE symposium on security and privacy (SP) (pp. 582-597). IEEE.

Raghunathan, A., Steinhardt, J., & Liang, P. (2018). Certified defenses against adversarial examples. arXiv preprint arXiv:1801.09344.

Szegedy, C., Toshev, A., & Erhan, D. (2013). Deep neural networks for object detection. *Advances in Neural Information Processing Systems*, •••, 26.

Szegedy, C., Zaremba, W., Sutskever, I., Bruna, J., Erhan, D., Goodfellow, I., & Fergus, R. (2013). Intriguing properties of neural networks. arXiv preprint arXiv:1312.6199.

Tramèr, F., Kurakin, A., Papernot, N., Goodfellow, I., Boneh, D., & McDaniel, P. (2017). Ensemble adversarial training: Attacks and defenses. arXiv preprint arXiv:1705.07204.

Weng, T. W., Zhang, H., Chen, P. Y., Yi, J., Su, D., Gao, Y., . . . Daniel, L. (2018). Evaluating the robustness of neural networks: An extreme value theory approach. arXiv preprint arXiv:1801.10578.

Xiao, C., Li, B., Zhu, J. Y., He, W., Liu, M., & Song, D. (2018). Generating adversarial examples with adversarial networks. arXiv preprint arXiv:1801.02610. DOI: 10.24963/ijcai.2018/543

Yuan, X., He, P., Zhu, Q., & Li, X. (2019). Adversarial examples: Attacks and defenses for deep learning. *IEEE Transactions on Neural Networks and Learning Systems*, *30*(9), 2805–2824. DOI: 10.1109/TNNLS.2018.2886017 PMID: 30640631

Zhang, C., Bengio, S., Hardt, M., Recht, B., & Vinyals, O. (2021). Understanding deep learning (still) requires rethinking generalization. *Communications of the ACM*, *64*(3), 107–115. DOI: 10.1145/3446776

Compilation of References

Aarotale, P. N., & Rattani, A. (2024, December). Machine Learning-based sEMG Signal Classification for Hand Gesture Recognition. In *2024 IEEE International Conference on Bioinformatics and Biomedicine (BIBM)* (pp. 6319-6326). IEEE. DOI: 10.1109/BIBM62325.2024.10822133

Abbas, N.. (2022). Evolving Nature of Phishing Attacks: Detection and Prevention. *IEEE Internet of Things Journal.*

Abir, S. A. A., Anwar, A., Choi, J., & Kayes, A. (2021). Iot-enabled smart energy grid: Applications and challenges. *IEEE Access : Practical Innovations, Open Solutions*, *9*, 50961–50981. DOI: 10.1109/ACCESS.2021.3067331

Adewuyi, A., Oladele, A. A., Enyiorji, P. U., Ajayi, O. O., Tsambatare, T. E., Oloke, K., & Abijo, I. (2024). The convergence of cybersecurity, Internet of Things (IoT), and data analytics: Safeguarding smart ecosystems. *World Journal of Advanced Research and Reviews*, *23*(1), 379–394. DOI: 10.30574/wjarr.2024.23.1.1993

Afzal, S., & Kavitha, G. (2019). Load balancing in cloud computing – A hierarchical taxonomical classification. *Journal of Cloud Computing (Heidelberg, Germany)*, *8*(1), 22. Advance online publication. DOI: 10.1186/s13677-019-0146-7

Aggrawal, N., & Pandey, A. (2025). The Impact of the Internet of Behavior on Wearable Technology: Enhancing User Engagement and Health Outcomes. In *Mapping Human Data and Behavior With the Internet of Behavior (IoB)* (pp. 337–410). IGI Global Scientific Publishing. DOI: 10.4018/979-8-3693-7545-7.ch013

Aghav, S., & Abdullah, I. (2024). A novel approach to optimizing third-party logistics growth through IT, big data, and machine learning for superior supply chain management. *2024 2nd World Conference on Communication & Computing (WCONF)*, Raipur, India, 1–8.

Ahmad, S., & Afzal, M. M. (2020). Deployment of fog and edge computing in IoT for cyber-physical infrastructures in the 5G era. In Sustainable communication networks and application: ICSCN 2019 (pp. 351-359). Springer International Publishing.

Ahmadi, A. (2023). Quantum Computing and Artificial Intelligence: The Synergy of Two Revolutionary Technologies. *Asian Journal of Electrical Sciences, 12*(2), 15–27. DOI: 10.51983/ajes-2023.12.2.4118

Ahmad, S., Alharbi, A., Zamani, A., & Yousufuddin, M. (2020). Implementation of fusion and filtering techniques in IoT data processing: A case study of smart healthcare. [IJCSNS]. *International Journal of Computer Science and Network Security, 20*(12), 131–137.

Ahmed, A., Bakar, K. A., Channa, M. I., Haseeb, K., & Khan, A. W. (2015). TERP: A Trust and Energy-Aware Routing Protocol for Wireless Sensor Network. *IEEE Sensors Journal, 15*(12), 6962–6972. DOI: 10.1109/JSEN.2015.2468576

Akhtar, N., & Gilbert, A. (2025). Quantum-Enhanced Cryptography: Safeguarding Blockchain and IoT Ecosystems.

Akinola, O. I. (2024). Adaptive Location-based Routing Protocols for Dynamic Wireless Sensor Networks in Urban Cyber-physical Systems. *Journal of Engineering Research and Reports, 26*(7), 424–443. DOI: 10.9734/jerr/2024/v26i71220

Alam, F., Mehmood, R., Katib, I., Albogami, N., & Albeshri, A. (2017). Data fusion and IoT for smart ubiquitous environments: A survey. *IEEE Access : Practical Innovations, Open Solutions, 5*, 9533–9554. DOI: 10.1109/ACCESS.2017.2697839

Albahri, A. S., Alwan, J. K., Taha, Z. K., Ismail, S. F., Hamid, R. A., Zaidan, A. A., Albahri, O. S., Zaidan, B. B., Alamoodi, A. H., & Alsalem, M. A. (2021). IoT-based telemedicine for disease prevention and health promotion: State-of-the-Art. *Journal of Network and Computer Applications, 173*, 102873. DOI: 10.1016/j.jnca.2020.102873

Albus, J. S. (1975). A new approach to manipulator control: The cerebellar model articulation controller (CMAC). [Discusses an early model of adaptive control inspired by human motor control.]. *Journal of Dynamic Systems, Measurement, and Control, 97*(3), 220–227. DOI: 10.1115/1.3426922

Ali, H. (2023). Quantum computing and AI in healthcare: Accelerating complex biological simulations, genomic data processing, and drug discovery innovations. *World Journal of Advanced Research and Reviews, 20*(2), 1466–1484. DOI: 10.30574/wjarr.2023.20.2.2325

Alisha. (February 15th, 2023). The Rise of Automation — How It Is Impacting the Job Market. https://pub.towardsai.net/the-rise-of-automation-how-it-is-impacting-the-job-markete8a6c7d5e6e3

Al-khatib, A., Balfaqih, M., & Khelil, A. (2019). A survey on outlier detection in Internet of Things big data. In *Big Data-Enabled Internet of Things* (pp. 225–272). DOI: 10.1049/PBPC025E_ch11

Alrahhal, H., Jamous, R., Ramadan, R., Alayba, A. M., & Yadav, K. (2022). Utilising Acknowledge for the Trust in Wireless Sensor Networks. *Applied Sciences (Basel, Switzerland), 12*(2045), 1–16. DOI: 10.3390/app12042045

Amjad, A., Azam, F., Anwar, M. W., & Butt, W. H. (2021). A systematic review on the data interoperability of application layer protocols in industrial IoT. *IEEE Access : Practical Innovations, Open Solutions, 9*, 96528–96545. DOI: 10.1109/ACCESS.2021.3094763

Amoo, O. O., Osasona, F., Atadoga, A., Ayinla, B. S., Farayola, O. A., & Abrahams, T. O. (2024). Cybersecurity threats in the age of IoT: A review of protective measures. *International Journal of Science and Research Archive, 11*(1), 1304–1310. DOI: 10.30574/ijsra.2024.11.1.0217

Amper. (2024). How Much Does Manufacturing Automation Cost? https://www.amper.xyz/post/how-much-does-manufacturing-automation-cost

Ananikov, V. P. (2024). Artificial Intelligence Chemistry. *Artificial Intelligence, 2*, 100075.

Ang, K. H., Chong, G., & Li, Y. (2005). PID control system analysis, design, and technology. [Offers a comprehensive review of PID control systems, relevant to understanding the basics of robotic control.]. *IEEE Transactions on Control Systems Technology, 13*(4), 559–576. DOI: 10.1109/TCST.2005.847331

Anikwe, C. V., Nweke, H. F., Ikegwu, A. C., Egwuonwu, C. A., Onu, F. U., Alo, U. R., & Teh, Y. W. (2022). Mobile and wearable sensors for data-driven health monitoring system: State-of-the-art and future prospect. *Expert Systems with Applications, 202*, 117362. DOI: 10.1016/j.eswa.2022.117362

Antonius, F., Alapati, P. R., Ritonga, M., Patra, I., El-Ebiary, Y. A. B., Orosoo, M., & Rengarajan, M. (2023). Incorporating natural language processing into virtual assistants: An intelligent assessment strategy for enhancing language comprehension. *International Journal of Advanced Computer Science and Applications, 14*(10). Advance online publication. DOI: 10.14569/IJACSA.2023.0141079

Aravindh, S., Nithisha, C., & Tanguturi, R. C. (2024). Enhanced agricultural methods and sustainable farming through IoT and AI technology. *2024 Second International Conference on Intelligent Cyber Physical Systems and Internet of Things (ICoICI)*, Coimbatore, India, 1206–1212.

Armbrust, M., Fox, A., Griffith, R., Joseph, A. D., Katz, R., Konwinski, A., Lee, G., Patterson, D., Rabkin, A., Stoica, I., & Zaharia, M. (2010). A view of cloud computing. *Communications of the ACM*, *53*(4), 50–58. DOI: 10.1145/1721654.1721672

Asada, H., & Slotine, J. J. E. (1986). "Robot Analysis and Control." Wiley. This book offers foundational concepts in robot mechanics and control.

Asha, G., & Santhosh, R. (2019). Soft computing and trust-based self-organized hierarchical energy balance routing protocol (TSHEB) in wireless sensor networks. *Soft Computing*, *23*(8), 2537–2543. DOI: 10.1007/s00500-018-03704-7

Ashmawi, S., Alharbi, M., Almaghrabi, A., & Alhothali, A. (2019). Fitme: Body measurement estimations using machine learning method. *Procedia Computer Science*, *163*, 209–217. DOI: 10.1016/j.procs.2019.12.102

Ayvaz, S., & Alpay, K. (2021). Predictive maintenance system for production lines in manufacturing: A machine learning approach using IoT data in real-time. *Expert Systems with Applications*, *173*, 114598. DOI: 10.1016/j.eswa.2021.114598

Azhiri, R. B., Esmaeili, M., & Nourani, M. (2021). Emg-based feature extraction and classification for prosthetic hand control. arXiv preprint arXiv:2107.00733.

Azhiri, R. B., Esmaeili, M., & Nourani, M. (2021, December). Real-time emg signal classification via recurrent neural networks. In *2021 IEEE International Conference on Bioinformatics and Biomedicine (BIBM)* (pp. 2628-2635). IEEE. DOI: 10.1109/BIBM52615.2021.9669872

B2eautomation (2022). Ethics of Automation and Robotics: Top Challenges and Solutions. https://www.b2eautomation.com/insights/ethics-of-automation-and-robotics-top-challenges-and-solutions

Baeg, S. H., Park, J. H., Koh, J., Park, K. W., & Baeg, M. H. (2007). RoboMaid-Home: A sensor network-based smart home environment for service robots. *RO-MAN 2007 - The 16th IEEE International Symposium on Robot and Human Interactive Communication*, 182–187. https://doi.org/DOI: 10.1109/ROMAN.2007.4415079

Baeg, S. H., Park, J. H., Koh, J., Park, K. W., & Baeg, M. H. (2007). Building a smart home environment for service robots based on RFID and sensor networks. *2007 International Conference on Control, Automation and Systems*, 1078–1082. https://doi.org/DOI: 10.1109/ICCAS.2007.4407059

Ballav, B., Rana, G., & Pattanayak, B. K. (2015). Investigating the effect of Black Hole attack on Zone-Based Energy Efficient Routing Protocol for Mobile Sensor Networks, *14th International Conference on Information Technology*, IEEE Computer Society, pp. 113-118, DOI: 10.1109/ICIT.2015.46

Bankar, S., Balkrishna, G., & Lokare, A. (2025). *Next-Generation Embedded Systems: Innovations in IoT Integration.* Real-Time Processing, and Energy Efficiency.

Bekey, G. A., Tomovic, R., & Zelkovic, M. (1972). "Control Architecture for the Belgrade/USC Hand." D. Paul (Ed.), "Robot Manipulators: Mathematics.

Beloglazov, A., Abawajy, J., & Buyya, R. (2012). Energy-aware resource allocation heuristics for efficient management of data centers for cloud computing. *Future Generation Computer Systems*, *28*(5), 755–768. DOI: 10.1016/j.future.2011.04.017

Benbya, H., Davenport, T. H., & Pachidi, S. (2020). Artificial intelligence in organizations: Current state and future opportunities. *MIS Quarterly Executive*, *19*(4).

Bhuiyan, M. S. (2024). The role of AI-Enhanced personalization in customer experiences. *Journal of Computer Science and Technology Studies*, *6*(1), 162–169. DOI: 10.32996/jcsts.2024.6.1.17

Bhushan, S., Alshehri, M., Keshta, I., Chakraverti, A. K., Rajpurohit, J., & Abugabah, A. (2022). An experimental analysis of various machine learning algorithms for hand gesture recognition. *Electronics (Basel)*, *11*(6), 968. DOI: 10.3390/electronics11060968

Bhutta, M. N. M., & Ahmad, M. (2021). Secure identification, traceability and real-time tracking of agricultural food supply during transportation using internet of things. *IEEE Access : Practical Innovations, Open Solutions*, *9*, 65660–65675. DOI: 10.1109/ACCESS.2021.3076373

Biggio, B., & Roli, F. (2018, October). Wild patterns: Ten years after the rise of adversarial machine learning. In *Proceedings of the 2018 ACM SIGSAC Conference on Computer and Communications Security* (pp. 2154-2156). DOI: 10.1145/3243734.3264418

Binder, A., & Rae, J. (March 27th, 2024). Automotive industry. Britannica https://www.britannica.com/technology/automotive-industry/Highway-development

Bishop, C. M. (2006). *Pattern recognition and machine learning*. Springer.

Blasch, E., ... (2018). Control diffusion of information collection for situation understanding using boosting MLNs. In *2018 21st International Conference on Information Fusion (FUSION)*. IEEE. DOI: 10.23919/ICIF.2018.8455262

Boyer, M., Bouyer, L., Roy, J. S., & Campeau-Lecours, A. (2023). Reducing noise, artificats and interference in single-channel emg signals: A review. *Sensors (Basel), 23*(6), 2927. DOI: 10.3390/s23062927 PMID: 36991639

Brooks, R. A. (1986). A robust layered control system for a mobile robot. [A foundational paper on robotic control systems that introduced behaviorbased control.]. *IEEE Journal on Robotics and Automation, 2*(1), 14–23. DOI: 10.1109/JRA.1986.1087032

Cabaccan, C. N., Cruz, F. R. G., & Agulto, I. C. (2017). Wireless sensor network for agricultural environment using raspberry pi-based sensor nodes. *2017 IEEE 9th International Conference on Humanoid, Nanotechnology, Information Technology, Communication and Control, Environment and Management (HNICEM)*, 1–5. https://doi.org/DOI: 10.1109/HNICEM.2017.8269486

Cao, J., Lam, K. Y., Lee, L. H., Liu, X., Hui, P., & Su, X. (2023). Mobile augmented reality: User interfaces, frameworks, and intelligence. *ACM Computing Surveys, 55*(9), 1–36. DOI: 10.1145/3557999

Cao, W. (2021). Design of remote intelligent monitoring system based on wireless sensor network. *2021 Fifth International Conference on I-SMAC (IoT in Social, Mobile, Analytics and Cloud) (I-SMAC)*, 1357–1360. https://doi.org/DOI: 10.1109/I-SMAC52330.2021.9640857

Carlini, N., & Wagner, D. (2017, May). Towards evaluating the robustness of neural networks. In 2017 ieee symposium on security and privacy (sp) (pp. 39-57). Ieee.

Carvalho, G., Cabral, B., Pereira, V., & Bernardino, J. (2021). Edge computing: Current trends, research challenges and future directions. *Computing, 103*(5), 993–1023. DOI: 10.1007/s00607-020-00896-5

Castanedo, F. (2013). A review of data fusion techniques. *TheScientificWorldJournal, 704504*(1), 704504. Advance online publication. DOI: 10.1155/2013/704504 PMID: 24288502

Chang, Z., Liu, S., Xiong, X., Cai, Z., & Tu, G. (2021). A survey of recent advances in edge-computing-powered artificial intelligence of things. *IEEE Internet of Things Journal, 8*(18), 13849–13875. DOI: 10.1109/JIOT.2021.3088875

Chataut, R., Phoummalayvane, A., & Akl, R. (2023). Unleashing the power of IoT: A comprehensive review of IoT applications and future prospects in healthcare, agriculture, smart homes, smart cities, and industry 4.0. *Sensors (Basel), 23*(16), 7194. DOI: 10.3390/s23167194 PMID: 37631731

Chattopadhyay, A. (2023). Phishing and DDoS Hybrid Attacks: Mitigation Strategies. *IEEE Transactions on Information Forensics and Security.*

Chen, Y., Wang, Y., Gao, F., Dong, B., Chen, W., & Liu, R. (2024). A Computational Method to Identify Optimal Functional Muscle Synergies from Estimated Muscle Activations. *IEEE Transactions on Instrumentation and Measurement*, *73*, 1–14. DOI: 10.1109/TIM.2024.3413171

Cherappa, V., Thangarajan, T., Meenakshi Sundaram, S. S., Hajjej, F., Munusamy, A. K., & Shanmugam, R. (2023). Energy-efficient clustering and routing using ASFO and a cross-layer-based expedient routing protocol for wireless sensor networks. *Sensors (Basel)*, *23*(5), 2788.

Cho, R., Patel, S., Cho, K. T., & Hwang, J. (2024). Machine Learning Techniques to Identify Hand Gestures amidst Forearm Muscle Signals. *arXiv preprint arXiv:2401.07889*.

Comparative analysis and study of data mining techniques used for IoT-based smart healthcare system. (2020). *International Journal of Emerging Trends in Engineering Research, 8*(9), 6131–6138. https://doi.org/DOI: 10.30534/ijeter/2020/198892020

Copeland, B. J. (March 4th, 2024). Artificial intelligence. Britannica. https://www.britannica.com/technology/artificial-intelligence/Reasoning

Craig, J. J. (2009). "Introduction to Robotics: Mechanics and Control." Pearson. A fundamental text on robotics, offering insights into the mechanics, control, and programming of robots.

Cvitanic, T., Nguyen, V., & Melkote, S. N. (2020). Pose optimization in robotic machining using static and dynamic stiffness models. *Robotics and Computer-integrated Manufacturing*, *66*, 101992. DOI: 10.1016/j.rcim.2020.101992

Daniel, A. D., & Roslin, S. E. (2021). Data validation and integrity verification for trust-based data aggregation protocol in WSN. *Microprocessors and Microsystems*, *80*, 103354. DOI: 10.1016/j.micpro.2020.103354

Dasarathy, B. (1997). Sensor fusion potential exploitation: Innovative architectures and illustrative applications. *Proceedings of the IEEE*, *85*(1), 24–38. DOI: 10.1109/5.554206

Dekka, S., & Singh, M. (2024). Deep learning approaches for real-time data analytics in IoT sensor networks. In V. S. Rathore, V. Piuri, R. Babo, & K. S. (Eds.), *Universal threats in expert applications and solutions: UNI-TEAS 2024* (Vol. 1007). Springer, Singapore.

Devarajan, Y. (2018). A study of robotic process automation use cases today for tomorrow's business. *International Journal of Computers and Technology*, *5*(6).

Devi, E. A., Ramya, K. C., Kumar, K. S., Ahmad, S., Kadry, S., Park, H. J., & Kang, B. G. (2022). Energy aware metaheuristic optimization with location aided routing protocol for MANET. CMC-Comput. *Mater. Contin*, *71*, 1567–1580.

Dey, D., Majumder, A., Agrawal, Y., Tewari, S., & Mohapatra, H. (2024). Smart mobility revolution. *Advances in Electronic Government, Digital Divide, and Regional Development*, ●●●, 143–164. DOI: 10.4018/979-8-3693-6740-7.ch006

Dikaiakos, M. D., Katsaros, D., Mehra, P., Pallis, G., & Vakali, A. (2009). Cloud computing: Distributed internet computing for IT and scientific research. *IEEE Internet Computing*, *13*(5), 10–13. DOI: 10.1109/MIC.2009.103

Dong, J., Zhuang, D., Huang, Y., & Fu, J. (2009). Advances in multi-sensor data fusion: Algorithms and applications. *Sensors (Basel)*, *9*(10), 7771–7784. DOI: 10.3390/s91007771 PMID: 22408479

Dong, Y., Liao, F., Pang, T., Su, H., Zhu, J., Hu, X., & Li, J. (2018). Boosting adversarial attacks with momentum. In *Proceedings of the IEEE conference on computer vision and pattern recognition* (pp. 9185-9193).

Dou, R., Liu, X., Lin, K. Y., & Yan, X. (2024). Internal-and external-sourcing strategy analysis of group manufacturing enterprises under semiconductor supply chain disruption risk. *International Journal of Production Economics*, *276*, 109368. DOI: 10.1016/j.ijpe.2024.109368

Dowlin, N., Gilad-Bachrach, R., Laine, K., Lauter, K., Naehrig, M., & Wernsing, J. (2016). *CryptoNets: Applying neural networks to encrypted data with high throughput and accuracy*. Microsoft.

Duan, J., Yang, D., Zhu, H., Zhang, S., & Zhao, J. (2014). TSRF: A Trust-Aware Secure Routing Framework in Wireless Sensor Networks. *International Journal of Distributed Sensor Networks*, *2014*(1), 1–14. DOI: 10.1155/2014/209436

Durrant-Whyte, H. (1988). Sensor models and multisensor integration. *The International Journal of Robotics Research*, *7*(6), 97–113. DOI: 10.1177/027836498800700608

Ekinci, E., Garip, Z., & Serbest, K. (2023). Electromyography based hand movement classification and feature extraction using machine learning algorithms. *Politeknik Dergisi*, *26*(4), 1621–1633. DOI: 10.2339/politeknik.1348121

El-Afifi, M. I., Sedhom, B. E., Padmanaban, S., & Eladl, A. A. (2024). A review of IoT-enabled smart energy hub systems: Rising, applications, challenges, and future prospects. *Renewable Energy Focus*, *51*, 100634. DOI: 10.1016/j.ref.2024.100634

Emma, L. (2024). AI-Powered Predictive Models for Personalized Treatment Plans in Chronic Disease Management.

Englelberger, J. F. (1980). *Robotics in practice: Management and applications of industrial robots*. Kogan Page.

Estévez, S. R., Mallah, J., Kazieczko, D., Tang, C., & Occhipinti, L. G. (2024). Deep Learning for Motion Classification in Ankle Exoskeletons Using Surface EMG and IMU Signals. *arXiv preprint arXiv:2411.16273*. DOI: 10.21203/rs.3.rs-5446652/v1

Eykholt, K., Evtimov, I., Fernandes, E., Li, B., Rahmati, A., Xiao, C., & Song, D. (2018). Robust physical-world attacks on deep learning visual classification. In *Proceedings of the IEEE conference on computer vision and pattern recognition* (pp. 1625-1634). DOI: 10.1109/CVPR.2018.00175

Fascista, A., Coluccia, A., & Ricci, G. (2021). A Pseudo Maximum likelihood approach to position estimation in dynamic multipath environments. *Signal Processing*, *181*, 107907. DOI: 10.1016/j.sigpro.2020.107907

Fida, K., Abbasi, U., Adnan, M., Iqbal, S., & Mohamed, S. E. G. (2024). A comprehensive survey on load forecasting hybrid models: Navigating the Futuristic demand response patterns through experts and intelligent systems. *Results in Engineering*, *23*, 102773. DOI: 10.1016/j.rineng.2024.102773

Fu, G., Gu, T., Gao, H., & Lu, C. (2020). A postprocessing and path optimization based on nonlinear error for multijoint industrial robot-based 3D printing. *International Journal of Advanced Robotic Systems*, *17*(5), 172988142095224. DOI: 10.1177/1729881420952249

Gaber, T., Abdelwahab, S., Elhoseny, M., & Hassanien, A. E. (2018). Trust-based secure clustering in WSN-based intelligent transportation systems. *Computer Networks*, *146*, 151–158. DOI: 10.1016/j.comnet.2018.09.015

Gaso, M. S., Cankurt, S., & Subasi, A. (2021, November). Electromyography signal classification using deep learning. In *2021 16th International Conference on Electronics Computer and Computation (ICECCO)* (pp. 1-6). IEEE. DOI: 10.1109/ICECCO53203.2021.9663803

Ghorbani, A.. "Evaluating Transfer Learning for Multimodal Cyberattack Detection," *ACM Symposium on Applied Computing*, 2023.

Ghosh, A., & Bhattacharya, S. (2013). Calculating Trust and Aggregation of a Node using Poisson Distribution in WSN. *International Journal of Computer Applications*, *68*(24), 43–46. DOI: 10.5120/11731-7342

Goodfellow, I. J., Shlens, J., & Szegedy, C. (2014). Explaining and harnessing adversarial examples. arXiv preprint arXiv:1412.6572.

Groover, M. P. (2013). "Automation, Production Systems, and Computer Integrated Manufacturing." Prentice Hall. This textbook provides comprehensive coverage of manufacturing automation principles, including the role of industrial robots and control systems.

Gujar, S. S., Shaikh, S. F., Shandilya, S., & Reddy, N. S. (2024). AI-enhanced cloud security framework for IoT networks using a predictive analytics approach. *2024 3rd International Conference for Advancement in Technology (ICONAT)*, Goa, India, 1–8.

Gummadi, V. A. K., & Damacharla, P. (2024). An intelligent framework for energy management in IoT networks using machine learning. *2024 5th International Conference on Smart Electronics and Communication (ICOSEC)*, Trichy, 765–771.

Gupta, S.. (2022). Phishing Attacks: Current Trends and Countermeasures. *IEEE Access : Practical Innovations, Open Solutions*.

Hafeez, I. (2023). A Systematic Mapping Study on Self-Adaptation SDN based Iot Networks.

Hajiee, M., Fartash, M., & Eraghi, N. O. (2021). An Energy-Aware Trust and Opportunity Based Routing Algorithm in Wireless Sensor Networks Using Multipath Routes Technique. *Neural Processing Letters*, *53*(4), 2829–2852. DOI: 10.1007/s11063-021-10525-7

Hall, D., & Llinas, J. (1997). An introduction to multisensor data fusion. *Proceedings of the IEEE*, *85*(1), 6–23. DOI: 10.1109/5.554205

Handbook of multisensor data fusion. (2017)., DOI: 10.1201/9781420053096

Han, J., Liu, N., & Catalão, J. P. (2022). Optimization of distribution network and mobile network with interactive balance of flexibility and power. *IEEE Transactions on Power Systems*, *38*(3), 2512–2524. DOI: 10.1109/TPWRS.2022.3180792

Han, Y., Hu, H., & Guo, Y. (2022). Energy-Aware and Trust-Based Secure Routing Protocol for Wireless Sensor Networks Using Adaptive Genetic Algorithm. *IEEE Access : Practical Innovations, Open Solutions*, *10*, 11538–11550. DOI: 10.1109/ACCESS.2022.3144015

Haque, M. A., Ahmad, S., Abboud, A. J., Hossain, M. A., Kumar, K., Haque, S., Sonal, D., Rahman, M., & Marisennayya, S. (2024). 6G wireless Communication Networks: Challenges and Potential Solution. [IJBDCN]. *International Journal of Business Data Communications and Networking*, *19*(1), 1–27. DOI: 10.4018/IJBDCN.339889

Hassen, B. S., Lafta, S. A. S., & Haeeder, M. (2019). Noman, H. M. & Ali, A. H., Analyzing the Performances of WSNs Routing Protocols in Grid-Based Clustering. *International Journal on Advanced Science, Engineering and Information Technology*, *9*(4), 1211–1216. DOI: 10.18517/ijaseit.9.4.8900

Hazra, A., Adhikari, M., Amgoth, T., & Srirama, S. N. (2021). A comprehensive survey on interoperability for IIoT: Taxonomy, standards, and future directions. *ACM Computing Surveys*, *55*(1), 1–35. DOI: 10.1145/3485130

Hegge, K., & Agrawal, R. (2023). Industrial automated multipurpose robot using Wi-Fi. *2023 4th International Conference for Emerging Technology (INCET)*, Belgaum, India, 1–8.

Hermansson, T., Carlson, J. S., Linn, J., & Kressin, J. (2021). Quasi-static path optimization for industrial robots with dress packs. *Robotics and Computer-integrated Manufacturing*, *68*, 102055. DOI: 10.1016/j.rcim.2020.102055

Hindy, H., Brosset, D., Bayne, E., Seeam, A., Tachtatzis, C., Atkinson, R., & Bellekens, X. (2018). A taxonomy and survey of intrusion detection system design techniques, network threats and datasets.

Hornik, K., Stinchcombe, M., & White, H. (1989). Multilayer feedforward networks are universal approximators. [This paper provides theoretical underpinnings for the use of neural networks in control systems.]. *Neural Networks*, *2*(5), 359–366. DOI: 10.1016/0893-6080(89)90020-8

Hosseini, M. P., Hosseini, A., & Ahi, K. (2020). A review on machine learning for EEG signal processing in bioengineering. *IEEE Reviews in Biomedical Engineering*, *14*, 204–218. DOI: 10.1109/RBME.2020.2969915 PMID: 32011262

Hu, H.. (2023). A Survey on Phishing Attacks and Countermeasures. *ACM Computing Surveys*.

Hu, J., Shen, L., Yang, Y., & Lv, R. (2010). Design and implementation of wireless sensor and actor network for precision agriculture. *2010 IEEE International Conference on Wireless Communications, Networking and Information Security*, 571–575. https://doi.org/DOI: 10.1109/WCINS.2010.5544151

Hussein, S. M., López Ramos, J. A., & Ashir, A. M. (2022). A secure and efficient method to protect communications and energy consumption in IoT wireless sensor networks. *Electronics (Basel)*, *11*(17), 2721. DOI: 10.3390/electronics11172721

IBM. (2024). What is automation? https://www.ibm.com/topics/automation

Imam Rahmani, M. K., Mohammed, M., Irshad, R. R., Yasmin, S., Mishra, S., Asopa, P., Islam, A., Ahmad, S., & Ali, A. (2023). Design a secure routing and monitoring framework based on hybrid optimization for IoT-based wireless sensor networks. *Journal of Nanoelectronics and Optoelectronics*, *18*(3), 338–346. DOI: 10.1166/jno.2023.3397

Immadisetty, A. (2024). SUSTAINABLE INNOVATION IN DIGITAL TECHNOLOGIES: A SYSTEMATIC REVIEW OF ENERGY-EFFICIENT COMPUTING AND CIRCULAR DESIGN PRACTICES. *INTERNATIONAL JOURNAL OF COMPUTER ENGINEERING AND TECHNOLOGY*, *15*(06), 1056–1066.

Innovative automation (2024). The future of manufacturing: Automotive Automation. https://www.innovativeautomation.com/future-manufacturing-automotive-automation/

Ismail, L., & Buyya, R. (2022). Artificial intelligence applications and self-learning 6G networks for smart cities digital ecosystems: Taxonomy, challenges, and future directions. *Sensors (Basel)*, *22*(15), 5750. DOI: 10.3390/s22155750 PMID: 35957307

Jain, S.. (2022). Improving DDoS and Phishing Detection Accuracy Using Deep Transfer Learning. *IEEE Internet of Things Journal.*

Javed, A. R., & Shahzad, F., ur Rehman, S., Zikria, Y. B., Razzak, I., Jalil, Z., & Xu, G. (2022). Future smart cities: Requirements, emerging technologies, applications, challenges, and future aspects. *Cities (London, England)*, *129*, 103794.

Jeelani, R. (2019). M. K. & Zafar, A., A Distributed Trust-Based Approach for Wireless Sensor Networks [IJRAR]. *International Journal of Research and Analytical Reviews*, *6*(2), 842–850.

Jinan, R., & Raveendran, T. (2016). Particle filters for multiple target tracking. *Procedia Technology*, *24*, 980–987. DOI: 10.1016/j.protcy.2016.05.215

John, J., Varkey, M. S., Podder, R. S., Sensarma, N., Selvi, M., Santhosh Kumar, S. V. N., & Kannan, A. (2022). Smart prediction and monitoring of waste disposal system using IoT and cloud for IoT based smart cities. *Wireless Personal Communications*, *122*(1), 243–275. DOI: 10.1007/s11277-021-08897-z

Joo, M. I., Kang, D. Y., Kang, M. S., & Kim, H. C. (2024). A Patient Management System Using an Edge Computing-Based IoT Pulse Oximeter. *Applied Sciences (Basel, Switzerland)*, *14*(1), 414. DOI: 10.3390/app14010414

JS3Global (2024). How Automotive Manufacturing Has Changed Through History. https://www.js3global.com/blog/how-automotive-manufacturing-has-changed-through-history/

Ju, L., Li, H., Liu, Y., Xue, W., Li, K., & Chi, Z. (2010). An improved intrusion detection scheme based on weighted trust evaluation for wireless sensor networks, *2010 Proc. 5th Int. Conf. Ubiquitous Inf. Technol. Appl. CUTE 2010*, no. 3, DOI: DOI: 10.1109/ICUT.2010.5677764

Kalidoss, T., Rajasekaran, L., Kanagasabai, K., Sannasi, G., & Kannan, A. (2019). QoS Aware Trust-Based Routing Algorithm for Wireless Sensor Networks. *Wireless Personal Communications*, *110*(4), 1637–1658. DOI: 10.1007/s11277-019-06788-y

Kalpana, A. V., Venkataramanan, V., Charulatha, G., & Geetha, G. (2023, June). An intelligent voice-recognition wheelchair system for disabled persons. In *2023 International Conference on Sustainable Computing and Smart Systems (ICSCSS)* (pp. 668-672). IEEE.

Kamankesh, A., Rahimi, N., Amiridis, I. G., Sahinis, C., Hatzitaki, V., & Enoka, R. M. (2024). Distinguishing the Activity of Flexor Digitorum Brevis and Soleus Across Standing Postures with Deep Learning Models. *Gait & Posture*. PMID: 39674063

Karavaev, S., Selivantsev, V. I., Shtern, Y. I., & Shtern, M. Y. (2018). The development of the data transfer protocol in the intelligent control systems of the energy carrier parameters. *2018 IEEE Conference of Russian Young Researchers in Electrical and Electronic Engineering (EIConRus)*, 1305–1308. https://doi.org/DOI: 10.1109/EIConRus.2018.8317336

Kaur, H.. (2022). Adaptive Transfer Learning for Enhanced Phishing Detection. *IEEE Transactions on Neural Networks and Learning Systems*.

Kaur, K., Garg, S., Aujla, G. S., Kumar, N., Rodrigues, J. J., & Guizani, M. (2018). Edge computing in the industrial Internet of things environment: Software-defined-Networks-Based edge-cloud interplay. *IEEE Communications Magazine*, *56*(2), 44–51. DOI: 10.1109/MCOM.2018.1700622

Kenda, K., Kažič, B., Novak, E., & Mladenić, D. (2019). Streaming data fusion for the Internet of Things. *Sensors (Basel)*, *19*(8), 1955. DOI: 10.3390/s19081955 PMID: 31027306

Kevre, P., & Shrivastava, L. (2014). Compare Three Reactive Routing Protocols in Grid-Based Cluster Wireless Sensor Network Using QualNet Simulator. *Journal of Information Engineering and Applications*, *4*(4), 125–132.

Khalid, N. A., Bai, Q., & Al-Anbuky, A. (2019). Adaptive Trust-Based Routing Protocol for Large Scale WSNs. *IEEE Access : Practical Innovations, Open Solutions*, *7*, 143539–143549. DOI: 10.1109/ACCESS.2019.2944648

Khan, M. U., Khan, H., Muneeb, M., Abbasi, Z., Abbasi, U. B., & Baloch, N. K. (2021, August). Supervised machine learning based fast hand gesture recognition and classification using electromyography (emg) signals. In *2021 international conference on applied and engineering mathematics (ICAEM)* (pp. 81-86). IEEE.

Kok, C. L., Ho, C. K., Tan, F. K., & Koh, Y. Y. (2024). Machine learning based feature extraction and classification of emg signals for intuitive prosthetic control. *Applied Sciences (Basel, Switzerland)*, *14*(13), 5784. DOI: 10.3390/app14135784

Kotov-Smolenskiy, A. M., Khizhnikova, A. E., Klochkov, A. S., Suponeva, N. A., & Piradov, M. A. (2021). Surface EMG: Applicability in the motion analysis and opportunities for practical rehabilitation. *Human Physiology*, *47*(2), 237–247. DOI: 10.1134/S0362119721020043

Krishnamurthi, R., Kumar, A., Gopinathan, D., Nayyar, A., & Qureshi, B. (2020). An overview of IoT sensor data processing, fusion, and analysis techniques. *Sensors (Basel)*, *20*(21), 6076. DOI: 10.3390/s20216076 PMID: 33114594

Kumar, B. P., Umamageswaran, J., Kalpana, A. V., & Dhanalakshmi, R. (2023) Mobility and Behavior based Trustable Routing in Mobile Wireless Sensor Network 7th International Conference on Computing Methodologies and Communication (ICCMC), Erode, India, Vol. 2023, pp. 1004–1008 [DOI: 10.1109/ICCMC56507.2023.10084040].

Kumar, A., Bag, A., Anand, A., Saha, S., Mohapatra, H., & Kolhar, M. (2024). Examining healthcare services utilizing cloud technology in intelligent urban environments. *Advances in Healthcare Information Systems and Administration*, •••, 77–98. DOI: 10.4018/979-8-3693-7225-8.ch004

Kumar, G. E. P., Titus, I., & Thekkekara, S. I. (2012). A Comprehensive Overview on Application of Trust and Reputation in Wireless Sensor Network, International Conference on Modelling and Optimization and Computing. *Procedia Engineering*, *38*, 2903–2912. DOI: 10.1016/j.proeng.2012.06.339

Kumar, R.. (2021). DDoS Attacks in the Era of Internet of Things: A Survey. *IEEE Communications Surveys and Tutorials*.

Kurakin, A., Goodfellow, I. J., & Bengio, S. (2018). Adversarial examples in the physical world. In *Artificial intelligence safety and security* (pp. 99–112). Chapman and Hall/CRC. DOI: 10.1201/9781351251389-8

Kyryk, M., Pleskanka, N., Pleskanka, M., & Nykonchuk, P. (2020). Load balancing method in edge computing. *2020 IEEE 15th International Conference on Advanced Trends in Radioelectronics, Telecommunications and Computer Engineering (TCSET)*, 978-981. https://doi.org/DOI: 10.1109/TCSET49122.2020.235584

Laha, S. R., Pattanayak, B. K., Pattnaik, S., Mishra, D., Kumar Nayak, D. S., & Dash, B. B. (2023). An IoT-based soil moisture management system for precision agriculture: Real-time monitoring and automated irrigation control. *2023 4th International Conference on Smart Electronics and Communication (ICOSEC)*, Trichy, India, 451–455.

Lata, S., & Singh, D. (2022). A hybrid approach for cloud load balancing. *2022 2nd International Conference on Advance Computing and Innovative Technologies in Engineering (ICACITE)*, 548-552. https://doi.org/DOI: 10.1109/ICACITE53722.2022.9823569

Lavanya, A., Divya Navamani, J., & Zahira, R. (2025). Introduction to the Internet of Things. *IoT for Smart Grid: Revolutionizing. Electrical Engineering*, •••, 1–16.

Lee, E., Seo, Y. D., Oh, S. R., & Kim, Y. G. (2021). A Survey on Standards for Interoperability and Security in the Internet of Things. *IEEE Communications Surveys and Tutorials*, *23*(2), 1020–1047. DOI: 10.1109/COMST.2021.3067354

Lee, M., & Seo, S. (2021). Wearable wireless biosensor technology for monitoring cattle: A review. *Animals (Basel)*, *11*(10), 2779. DOI: 10.3390/ani11102779 PMID: 34679801

Li, C., Dong, K., Jin, F., Song, J., & Mo, W. (2019). Design of smart home monitoring and control system based on ZigBee and WiFi. *2019 Chinese Control Conference (CCC)*, 6345–6348. https://doi.org/DOI: 10.23919/ChiCC.2019.8865907

Liu, Y., Chen, X., Liu, C., & Song, D. (2016). Delving into transferable adversarial examples and black-box attacks. arXiv preprint arXiv:1611.02770.

Liu, G., & Chen, X. (2020). Smart home system based on embedded control and wireless communication. *2020 International Conference on Intelligent Transportation, Big Data & Smart City (ICITBS)*, 547–550. https://doi.org/DOI: 10.1109/ICITBS49701.2020.00120

Li, Y.. (2021). *Phishing Detection through Multi-Domain Transfer Learning*. Elsevier Computers & Security.

Luo, R. C., & Kay, M. G. (1989). Multisensor integration and fusion in intelligent systems. *IEEE Transactions on Systems, Man, and Cybernetics*, *19*(5), 901–931. DOI: 10.1109/21.44007

Luo, R., Yih, C.-C., & Su, K. L. (2002). Multisensor fusion and integration: Approaches, applications, and future research directions. *IEEE Sensors Journal*, *2*(2), 107–119. DOI: 10.1109/JSEN.2002.1000251

Lu, Y., Zhang, J., Wu, S., & Zhang, S. (2012). A hybrid dynamic load balancing approach for cloud storage. *2012 International Conference on Industrial Control and Electronics Engineering*, 1332-1335. https://doi.org/DOI: 10.1109/ICICEE.2012.353

Ma, G. (2022). Intelligent water-saving control system under artificial intelligence technology. *2022 IEEE 2nd International Conference on Mobile Networks and Wireless Communications (ICMNWC)*, 1–5. https://doi.org/DOI: 10.1109/ICMNWC57216.2022.9995634

Maddineni, V. K., & Gummadi, V. A. K. (2024). Deep learning approaches for real-time IoT data processing and analysis. *2024 5th International Conference on Smart Electronics and Communication (ICOSEC)*, Trichy, 757–764.

Madry, A., Makelov, A., Schmidt, L., Tsipras, D., & Vladu, A. (2017). Towards deep learning models resistant to adversarial attacks. arXiv preprint arXiv:1706.06083.

Mahdavinejad, M. S.. (2017). Machine learning for Internet of Things data analysis: A survey. *Digital Communications and Networks*. Advance online publication. DOI: 10.1016/j.dcan.2017.10.002

Mamdiwar, S. D., Shakruwala, Z., Chadha, U., Srinivasan, K., & Chang, C. Y. (2021). Recent advances on IoT-assisted wearable sensor systems for healthcare monitoring. *Biosensors (Basel)*, *11*(10), 372. DOI: 10.3390/bios11100372 PMID: 34677328

Mao, Y. (2010). A semantic-based intrusion detection framework for wireless sensor network," *INC2010 - Int. Conf. Networked Comput. Proceeding*, pp. 408–412.

Mao, Y., You, C., Zhang, J., Huang, K., & Letaief, K. B. (2017). A survey on mobile edge computing: The communication perspective. *IEEE Communications Surveys and Tutorials*, *19*(4), 2322–2358. DOI: 10.1109/COMST.2017.2745201

Mazid, M., Ali, A. B. M., & Tickle, K. (2010). Improved C4. 5 algorithm for rule based classification.

McKinsey & Company. (August 17, 2022). What are Industry 4.0, the Fourth Industrial Revolution, and 4IR? https://www.mckinsey.com/featured-insights/mckinsey-explainers/whatare-industry-4-0-the-fourth-industrial-revolution-and-4ir

Meenakshi, N., Ahmad, S., Prabu, A. V., Rao, J. N., Othman, N. A., Abdeljaber, H. A., Sekar, R., & Nazeer, J. (2024). Efficient communication in wireless sensor networks using optimized energy efficient engroove leach clustering protocol. *Tsinghua Science and Technology*, *29*(4), 985–1001. DOI: 10.26599/TST.2023.9010056

Mengcan, M., Xiaofang, C., & Yongkang, X. (2021). Constrained voting extreme learning machine and its application. *Journal of Systems Engineering and Electronics*, *32*(1), 209–219. DOI: 10.23919/JSEE.2021.000018

Meng, T., Jing, X., Yan, Z., & Pedrycz, W. (2020). A survey on machine learning for data fusion. *Information Fusion*, *57*, 115–129. DOI: 10.1016/j.inffus.2019.12.001

Messaoud, S., Bradai, A., Bukhari, S. H. R., Quang, P. T. A., Ahmed, O. B., & Atri, M. (2020). A survey on machine learning in Internet of Things: Algorithms, strategies, and applications. *Internet of Things : Engineering Cyber Physical Human Systems*, *12*, 100314. DOI: 10.1016/j.iot.2020.100314

Metzen, J. H., Genewein, T., Fischer, V., & Bischoff, B. (2017). On detecting adversarial perturbations. arXiv preprint arXiv:1702.04267.

Miah, A. S. M., Hassan, N., Maniruzzaman, M., Asai, N., & Shin, J. (2024). EMG-Based Hand Gesture Recognition through Diverse Domain Feature Enhancement and Machine Learning-Based Approach. *arXiv preprint arXiv:2408.13723.*

Michard, F. (2021). Toward smart monitoring with phones, watches, and wearable sensors. *Anesthesiology Clinics*, *39*(3), 555–564. DOI: 10.1016/j.anclin.2021.04.005 PMID: 34392885

Mishra, P., & Singh, G. (2023). *Sustainable Smart Cities*. Enabling Technologies, Energy Trends and Potential Applications. DOI: 10.1007/978-3-031-33354-5

Modupe, O. T., Otitoola, A. A., Oladapo, O. J., Abiona, O. O., Oyeniran, O. C., Adewusi, A. O., & Obijuru, A. (2024). Reviewing the transformational impact of edge computing on real-time data processing and analytics. *Computer Science & IT Research Journal*, *5*(3), 603–702.

Mohapatra, H., & Mishra, S. R. (2024). Unlocking insights: Exploring data analytics and AI tool performance across industries. *Studies in Big Data*, 265-288. https://doi.org/DOI: 10.1007/978-981-97-0448-4_13

Mohapatra, H. (2021). Socio-technical challenges in the implementation of smart city. *2021 International Conference on Innovation and Intelligence for Informatics, Computing, and Technologies (3ICT)*, 57-62. https://doi.org/DOI: 10.1109/3ICT53449.2021.9581905

Mohapatra, H. (2024). The role of 6G in empowering smart cities enabling ubiquitous connectivity and intelligent infrastructure. *Advances in Civil and Industrial Engineering*, •••, 237–264. DOI: 10.4018/979-8-3693-8029-1.ch009

Mourtzis, D., Angelopoulos, J., & Panopoulos, N. (2021). Design and development of an IoT enabled platform for remote monitoring and predictive maintenance of industrial equipment. *Procedia Manufacturing*, *54*, 166–171. DOI: 10.1016/j.promfg.2021.07.025

Mujica, G., Rodriguez-Zurrunero, R., Wilby, M. R., Portilla, J., Rodríguez González, A. B., Araujo, A., Riesgo, T., & Vinagre Díaz, J. J. (2018). Edge and fog computing platform for data fusion of complex heterogeneous sensors. *Sensors (Basel)*, *18*(11), 3630. DOI: 10.3390/s18113630 PMID: 30366462

Munir, A., Blasch, E., Kwon, J., Kong, J., & Aved, A. (2021). Artificial intelligence and data fusion at the edge. *IEEE Aerospace and Electronic Systems Magazine*, *36*(7), 62–78. DOI: 10.1109/MAES.2020.3043072

Nain, G., Pattanaik, K. K., & Sharma, G. K. (2022). Towards edge computing in intelligent manufacturing: Past, present and future. *Journal of Manufacturing Systems*, *62*, 588–611. DOI: 10.1016/j.jmsy.2022.01.010

Nair, V. V. (n.d.). Prosthodontic Research in the Digital Era: Current Trends and Future Prospects.

Najjar, Y. S. H., & Abu-Shamleh, A. (2020). Performance evaluation of a large-scale thermal power plant based on the best industrial practices. *Scientific Reports*, *10*(1), 20661. DOI: 10.1038/s41598-020-77802-8 PMID: 33244157

Nakamura, E., Loureiro, A., & Frery, A. (2007). Information fusion for wireless sensor networks. *ACM Computing Surveys*, *39*(3), 9. DOI: 10.1145/1267070.1267073

Nath, D. C., Kundu, I., Sharma, A., Shivhare, P., Afzal, A., Soudagar, M. E. M., & Park, S. G. (2024). Internet of Things integrated with solar energy applications: A state-of-the-art review. *Environment, Development and Sustainability*, *26*(10), 24597–24652. DOI: 10.1007/s10668-023-03691-2

Nazmi, N., Abdul Rahman, M. A., Yamamoto, S.-I., Ahmad, S. A., Zamzuri, H., & Mazlan, S. A. (2016). A Review of Classification Techniques of EMG Signals during Isotonic and Isometric Contractions. *Sensors (Basel)*, *16*(8), 1304. DOI: 10.3390/s16081304 PMID: 27548165

Nedkov, K., & Nardinocchi, C. (2009). A comparison of Bayesian and evidence-based fusion methods for automated building detection in aerial data. *The International Archives of the Photogrammetry, Remote Sensing and Spatial Information Sciences*, •••, 37.

Nesakumar, D., Deepak, P., Sanjay, P., Aishwarya, B., Aswini, R., & Pavithra, K. N. (2024, March). IoT-powered precision farming and home gardening for seamless monitoring, automation and security. In *2024 International Conference on Wireless Communications Signal Processing and Networking (WiSPNET)* (pp. 1-5). IEEE.

Nguyen, A., Yosinski, J., & Clune, J. (2015). Deep neural networks are easily fooled: High confidence predictions for unrecognizable images. In *Proceedings of the IEEE conference on computer vision and pattern recognition* (pp. 427-436). DOI: 10.1109/CVPR.2015.7298640

Nguyen, Q., Phan, L., & Kim, T. (2022). Load-balancing of kubernetes-based edge computing infrastructure using resource adaptive proxy. *Sensors (Basel)*, *22*(8), 2869. DOI: 10.3390/s22082869 PMID: 35458853

Nof, S. Y. (Ed.). (1999). "Handbook of Industrial Robotics." Wiley. A comprehensive reference that covers a wide range of topics related to industrial robotics, from basic principles to applications and management. DOI: 10.1002/9780470172506

Okamura, A. M., Smaby, N., & Cutkosky, M. R. (2001). "An overview of dexterous manipulation." Proceedings of the IEEE International Conference on Robotics and Automation, 255-262. Discusses advancements in robotic manipulation, important for understanding control systems in robotics.

Olajiga, O. K., Ani, E. C., Sikhakane, Z. Q., & Olatunde, T. M. (2024). A comprehensive review of energy-efficient lighting technologies and trends. *Engineering Science & Technology Journal*, *5*(3), 1097–1111. DOI: 10.51594/estj.v5i3.973

Oliva-Lozano, J. M., & Muyor, J. M. (2020). Core muscle activity during physical fitness exercises: A systematic review. *International Journal of Environmental Research and Public Health*, *17*(12), 4306. DOI: 10.3390/ijerph17124306 PMID: 32560185

Oyeniran, C. O., Adewusi, A. O., Adeleke, A. G., Akwawa, L. A., & Azubuko, C. F. (2023). 5G technology and its impact on software engineering: New opportunities for mobile applications. *Computer Science & IT Research Journal*, *4*(3), 562–576. DOI: 10.51594/csitrj.v4i3.1557

Pahal, S., & Dalal, K. (2016). Performance Evaluation of Routing Protocols in WSN using QualNet 5.3 [IJRTER]. *International Journal of Recent Trends in Engineering & Research*, *02*(06), 223–231.

Pallavi, V., & Vinothiyalakshmi, P. (2022). Threshold based dynamic resource balancing (TDRB) algorithm in cloud computing. *2022 International Conference on Machine Learning, Big Data, Cloud and Parallel Computing (COM-IT-CON)*, 616-622. https://doi.org/DOI: 10.1109/COM-IT-CON54601.2022.9850699

Pal, S. (2024). Artificial Intelligence-Based IoT-Edge Environment for Industry 5.0. In *IoT Edge Intelligence* (pp. 111–148). Springer Nature Switzerland. DOI: 10.1007/978-3-031-58388-9_4

Panda, A. K., Lenka, A. A., Mohapatra, A., Rath, B. K., Parida, A. A., & Mohapatra, H. (2024). Integrating cloud computing for intelligent transportation solutions in smart cities. *Advances in Civil and Industrial Engineering*, •••, 121–142. DOI: 10.4018/979-8-3693-6695-0.ch005

Paolone, G., Iachetti, D., Paesani, R., Pilotti, F., Marinelli, M., & Di Felice, P. (2022). A holistic overview of the internet of things ecosystem. *IoT*, *3*(4), 398–434. DOI: 10.3390/iot3040022

Papernot, N., McDaniel, P., Wu, X., Jha, S., & Swami, A. (2016, May). Distillation as a defense to adversarial perturbations against deep neural networks. In 2016 IEEE symposium on security and privacy (SP) (pp. 582-597). IEEE.

Pasha, M. H. M. (2024). Harnessing Artificial Intelligence to Build Agile and Resilient Business Ecosystems for the Smart Economy of the Future. *Journal of Business and Future Economy*, *1*(2), 31–40.

Patel, K.. (2022). *Phishing, DDoS, and Ransomware: Multimodal Cyber Threats.* ACM Transactions on Privacy and Security.

Pathak, P., Yadav, A., & Alvi, P. (2020). Advanced solar MPPT techniques under uniform and non-uniform irradiance: A comprehensive review. *Journal of Solar Energy Engineering*, *142*(4), 1–31. DOI: 10.1115/1.4046090

Pathan, S. K., Hong, C. S., & Lee, H. W. (2006). Smartening the environment using wireless sensor networks in a developing country. *2006 8th International Conference Advanced Communication Technology*, 5 pp.–709. https://doi.org/DOI: 10.1109/ICACT.2006.206169

Pavankumar, P., & Darwante, N. K. (2022). Performance monitoring and dynamic scaling algorithm for queue-based Internet of Things. *2022 International Conference on Innovative Computing, Intelligent Communication and Smart Electrical Systems (ICSES)*, 1–7.

Pensas, H., Raula, H., & Vanhala, J. (2009). Energy efficient sensor network with service discovery for smart home environments. *2009 Third International Conference on Sensor Technologies and Applications*, 399–404. https://doi.org/DOI: 10.1109/SENSORCOMM.2009.66

Pérez-Reynoso, F., Farrera-Vazquez, N., Capetillo, C., Méndez-Lozano, N., González-Gutiérrez, C., & López-Neri, E. (2022). Pattern recognition of emg signals by machine learning for the control of a manipulator robot. Sensors, 22(9), 3424. Author, F., Author, S., Author, T.: Book title. 2nd edn. Publisher, Location (1999). DOI: 10.3390/s22093424

Pero, C., Bakshi, S., Nappi, M., & Tortora, G. (2024). IoT-driven machine learning for precision viticulture optimization. *IEEE Journal of Selected Topics in Applied Earth Observations and Remote Sensing*, *17*, 2437–2447. DOI: 10.1109/JSTARS.2023.3345473

Pillai, R. S., Denny, P., & O'connell, E. (2024). Optimizing Predictive and Prescriptive Maintenance Using Unified Namespace (UNS) for Industrial Equipments.

Pillai, A. J., T. R. N., Ali, A., & K. K., A. (2021). Healthcare data fusion. [IJERT]. *International Journal of Engineering Research & Technology (Ahmedabad)*, *9*(13). Advance online publication. DOI: 10.17577/IJERTCONV9IS13031

Prabha, C., & Pathak, A. (2023). Enabling technologies in smart agriculture: A way forward towards future fields. *2023 International Conference on Advancement in Computation & Computer Technologies (InCACCT)*, Gharuan, India, 821–826. DOI: 10.1109/InCACCT57535.2023.10141722

Prasad, K., Prasad, V. S., & Kaur, M. (2024). Optimizing renewable energy integration in smart grids through IoT-driven management systems. *2024 2nd International Conference on Advancement in Computation & Computer Technologies (InCACCT)*, Gharuan, India, 783–788.

Praveen Kumar, B. P., Kalpana, A. V., & Nalini, S. (2023). Gated attention based deep learning model for analysing the influence of social media on education. [DOI: 10.1080/0952813X.2023.2188262]. *Journal of Experimental & Theoretical Artificial Intelligence*, ●●●, 1–15.

Priyadarshi, S., Subudhi, S., Kumar, S., Bhardwaj, D., & Mohapatra, H. (2024). Analysis on enhancing urban mobility with IoT-integrated parking solutions. *Advances in Civil and Industrial Engineering*, •••, 143–172. DOI: 10.4018/979-8-3693-6695-0.ch006

Priyanka, B. (2024). Machine learning-driven precision agriculture: Enhancing farm management through predictive insights. *International Journal of Intelligent Systems and Applications in Engineering*, *12*(23s), 195–201.

Pruteanu, E., Furdu, M. I., Puiu, P. G., Abdrioaia, D., & Istok, R. (2023). IoT intelligent sensor system based on fuzzy inference for efficient resource management system in residential, commercial, or industrial smart buildings. *2023 IEEE 6th International Conference and Workshop Óbuda on Electrical and Power Engineering (CANDO-EPE)*, 000131–000136. https://doi.org/DOI: 10.1109/CANDO-EPE59788.2023.10264390

Qiang, S.. (2022). Learning from Adversaries: Transfer Learning for Phishing and DDoS Detection. *Journal of Machine Learning Research.*

Radha, H. M., & Hassan, A. K. A. (2022). A survey on bio-signal analysis for human-robot interaction. *International Journal of Electrical and Computer Engineering*, *12*(6), 5998. DOI: 10.11591/ijece.v12i6.pp5998-6009

Raghunathan, A., Steinhardt, J., & Liang, P. (2018). Certified defenses against adversarial examples. arXiv preprint arXiv:1801.09344.

Rahman, M. T., Rahman, M., & Shahnaz, C. (2023). EMG Signal Classification for Neuromuscular Disorders with Attention-Enhanced CNN. *arXiv preprint arXiv:2309.10483.*

Rajeswari, D. K., & Keerthana, G. Transfer Learning-Based Continuous Sign Language Observation Using Surface Electromyography Signals.

Ramprasath, M., Kalpana, A. V., Ravishankar, T. N., Anand, M., & Shobana, J. (2023) Protected data sharing using attribute based encryption for remote data checking in cloud environment 12th International Conference on Advanced Computing (ICoAC), Chennai, India, Vol. 2023, pp. 1–8 [DOI: 10.1109/ICoAC59537.2023.10249642]

Ranapana, R., & Jayasena, K. (2021). Novel approach for load balancing in mobile cloud computing. *2021 6th International Conference on Information Technology Research (ICITR)*, 1-6. https://doi.org/DOI: 10.1109/ICITR54349.2021.9657441

Rani, R., & Balaji, M. (2024). Optimizing IoT device networks with edge computing to address latency and bandwidth constraints. *2024 5th International Conference on Electronics and Sustainable Communication Systems (ICESC)*, Coimbatore, India, 388–395.

Rashid, A. B., & Kausik, A. K. (2024). AI revolutionizing industries worldwide: A comprehensive overview of its diverse applications. Hybrid Advances, 100277.

Raut, A. B., & Nichat, M. A. A. (2017). Students performance prediction using decision tree. *International Journal of Computational Intelligence Research*, *13*(7), 1735–1741.

Ravi, K. C., Mudalkar, P. K., Ranga, J., Raj, G. B., Swapna, B., & Venkatesh, D. (2023, November). Empowering Sustainable Agriculture through IoT: Innovations for Precision Farming and Crop Monitoring. In *2023 9th International Conference on Smart Structures and Systems (ICSSS)* (pp. 1-6). IEEE.

Reddy, D. M. K., Sathya, R., & Lakshmi, V. V. A. S. (2023). An Energy Efficient Master Auditor Node with Trust Based Secure Routing in Wireless Sensor Networks. *International Journal of Intelligent Systems and Applications in Engineering*, *11*(3), 519–529.

Reddy, M., & Oliver, N. (2024). The role of real-time continuous glucose monitoring in diabetes management and how it should link to integrated personalized diabetes management. *Diabetes, Obesity & Metabolism*, *26*(S1), 46–56. DOI: 10.1111/dom.15504 PMID: 38441367

Reddy, S., & Patwal, P. S. (2022). Data analytics and cloud-based platform for Internet of Things applications in smart cities. *2022 International Conference on Industry 4.0 Technology (I4Tech)*, 1–6.

Rehan, H. (2023). Internet of Things (IoT) in smart cities: Enhancing urban living through technology. *Journal of Engineering Technology*, *5*(1), 1–16.

Retscher, G., Gikas, V., & Gabela, J. (2024). Experiences with techniques and sensors for smartphone positioning. *Journal of Applied Geodesy*, (0).

Richards, K.. (2023). Domain Adaptation for Phishing Detection Using Transfer Learning. *IEEE Systems Journal*.

Richards, K.. (2023). Real-Time DDoS Detection and Phishing Mitigation Using Transfer Learning. *IEEE Systems Journal*.

Rohilla, P., Vineet, K., & Feras, A. H. (2018). Fuzzy gain scheduling of an IPD controller for oscillation compensation in a sticky pneumatic control valve. *International Journal of Mechanical Engineering and Robotics Research, 7*(3), 240–249.

Rymarczyk, T., Klosowski, G., & Kozlowski, E. (2019). Innovative methods of tomographic image reconstruction based on machine learning to improve monitoring and optimization in industrial processes. *2019 19th International Symposium on Electromagnetic Fields in Mechatronics, Electrical and Electronic Engineering (ISEF)*, 1–2. https://doi.org/DOI: 10.1109/ISEF45929.2019.9096984

Sadiku, M. N. O., Alam, S., & Musa, S. M. (2018). Intelligent robotics and applications. *Int. J. Trends Res. Dev., 5*(1), 101–103.

Sah, R. K., Singh, A. K., Yadav, A. K., & Mohapatra, H. (2024). Cloud-enabled platforms for social and civic engagement in smart urban environments. *Advances in Electronic Government, Digital Divide, and Regional Development*, •••, 215–234. DOI: 10.4018/979-8-3693-6740-7.ch009

Salma, S., Begum, A., & Syed, H. (2024). Practical and Innovative Applications of IoT and IoT Networks (Smart Cities, Smart Mobility, Smart Home, Smart Health, Smart Grid, etc.). In *AI for Climate Change and Environmental Sustainability* (pp. 121-144). CRC Press.

Salman, H. A., Alsajri, A., Kalakech, A., & Steiti, A. (2023). Difference Between 4G and 5G Networks. *Babylonian Journal of Networking, 2023*, 41–54. DOI: 10.58496/BJN/2023/006

Sankaran, V., Alagumariappan, P., Sathyamoorthy, M., Dhanaraj, R. K., Krishnamurthy, K., & Cyril, E. (2024). An Internet of Medical Things-Based Smart Electromyogram Device for Monitoring of Musculoskeletal Disorders. *Engineering Proceedings*, •••, 6.

Sarala, B., Sumathy, G., Kalpana, A. V., & Jasmine Hephzipah, J. J. (2023) Glioma brain tumor detection using dual convolutional neural networks and histogram density segmentation algorithm. Biomedical Signal Processing and Control, 85, 104859, ISSN 1746-8094 [DOI:]DOI: 10.1016/j.bspc.2023.104859

Saranya, S. S., & Fatima, D. N. S. (2020). Context-aware data fusion on massive IoT data in dynamic IoT analytics. *Webology, 17*(2), 957–970. DOI: 10.14704/WEB/V17I2/WEB17080

Sathish Kumar, L., Ahmad, S., Routray, S., Prabu, A. V., Alharbi, A., Alouffi, B., & Rajasoundaran, S. (2022). Modern Energy Optimization Approach for Efficient Data Communication in IoT-Based Wireless Sensor Networks. *Wireless Communications and Mobile Computing*, *2022*(1), 7901587. DOI: 10.1155/2022/7901587

Schultz, U. P. (2020). Reversible control of robots. In Ulidowski, I., Lanese, I., Schultz, U., & Ferreira, C. (Eds.), Lecture Notes in Computer Science: Vol. 12070. *Reversible Computation: Extending Horizons of Computing. RC 2020* (pp. 177–186). Springer. DOI: 10.1007/978-3-030-47361-7_8

Scott, G. (December 4th, 2023). Artificial Intelligence (AI): What It Is and How It Is Used. Investopedia https://www.investopedia.com/terms/a/artificial-intelligence-ai.asp

Selvi, M., Thangaramya, K., Ganapathy, S., Kulothungan, K., Nehemiah, H. K., & Kannan, A. (2019). An Energy-Aware Trust-Based Secure Routing Algorithm for Effective Communication in Wireless Sensor Networks. *Wireless Personal Communications*, *105*(4), 1475–1490. DOI: 10.1007/s11277-019-06155-x

Sen, G., Nil, M., Mamur, H., Doğan, H., Karamolla, M., Karaçor, M., Kuyucuoğlu, F., & Bhuiyan, M. R. A. (2018). The effect of ambient temperature on electric power generation in a natural gas combined cycle power plant—A case study. *Energy Reports*, *4*, 682–690. DOI: 10.1016/j.egyr.2018.10.009

Sethi, H. S., & Prasanth, P. V. (2023). Optimizing resource allocation in agriculture through IoT and AI. *2023 7th International Conference on Electronics, Communication and Aerospace Technology (ICECA)*, Coimbatore, India, 1573–1578.

Seyidbayli, C., Salhi, F., & Akdogan, E. (2020). Comparison of machine learning algorithms for EMG signal classification. *Periodicals of Engineering and Natural Sciences*, *8*(2), 1165–1176.

Shaban, H. (September 18, 2018). Machines will create 58 million more jobs than they displace by 2022, World Economic Forum says. Washingtonpost https://www.washingtonpost.com/technology/2018/09/18/machines-will-create-millionmore-jobs-than-they-displace-by-world-economic-forum-says/

Shafiq, D. A., Jhanjhi, N., & Abdullah, A. (2022). Load balancing techniques in cloud computing environment: A review. *Journal of King Saud University. Computer and Information Sciences*, *34*(7), 3910–3933. DOI: 10.1016/j.jksuci.2021.02.007

Shahab, H., Naeem, M., Iqbal, M., Aqeel, M., & Ullah, S. S. (2025). IoT-Driven Smart Agricultural Technology for Real-Time Soil and Crop Optimization. *Smart Agricultural Technology*, *10*, 100847. DOI: 10.1016/j.atech.2025.100847

Shah, Q. A., Shafi, I., Ahmad, J., Alfarhood, S., Safran, M., & Ashraf, I. (2023). A meta modeling-based interoperability and integration testing platform for IoT systems. *Sensors (Basel), 23*(21), 8730. DOI: 10.3390/s23218730 PMID: 37960429

Shahzad, G., Yang, H., Ahmad, A. W., & Lee, C. (2016). Energy-efficient intelligent street lighting system using traffic-adaptive control. *IEEE Sensors Journal, 16*(13), 5397–5405. DOI: 10.1109/JSEN.2016.2557345

Sharma, A., Anand, N., Mukherjee, S., Kumar, S., Kumar, S., & Mohapatra, H. (2024). Analyzing territorial variations in the implementation of IoT-based smart homes. *Advances in Electronic Government, Digital Divide, and Regional Development*, •••, 305–334. DOI: 10.4018/979-8-3693-6854-1.ch010

Sharma, D. R., Mishra, V., & Srivastava, S. (2023). Enhancing crop yields through IoT-enabled precision agriculture. *2023 International Conference on Disruptive Technologies (ICDT)*, Greater Noida, India, 279–283. DOI: 10.1109/ICDT57929.2023.10151422

Shefa, F. R., Sifat, F. H., Uddin, J., Ahmad, Z., Kim, J. M., & Kibria, M. G. (2024, November). Deep Learning and IoT-Based Ankle–Foot Orthosis for Enhanced Gait Optimization. [). MDPI.]. *Health Care, 12*(22), 2273. PMID: 39595470

Shukla, S., Hassan, M. F., Tran, D. C., Akbar, R., Paputungan, I. V., & Khan, M. K. (2023). Improving latency in Internet-of-Things and cloud computing for real-time data transmission: A systematic literature review (SLR). *Cluster Computing, 26*(5), 1–24. DOI: 10.1007/s10586-021-03279-3

Shuvho, M. B. A., Chowdhury, M. A., Ahmed, S., & Kashem, M. A. (2019). Prediction of solar irradiation and performance evaluation of grid-connected solar 80KWp PV plant in Bangladesh. *Energy Reports, 5*, 714–722. DOI: 10.1016/j.egyr.2019.06.011

Siciliano, B., & Khatib, O. (Eds.). (2008). "Springer Handbook of Robotics." Springer. This handbook presents a broad overview of the current state of robotics, including technological advancements, applications, and future directions. Engelberger. DOI: 10.1007/978-3-540-30301-5

Singh, P., & Agrawal, S. (2013). Node localization in wireless sensor networks using the M5P tree and SMOreg algorithms. *2013 5th International Conference and Computational Intelligence and Communication Networks*, 104. https://doi.org/ DOI: 10.1109/CICN.2013.32

Singh, K. (2015). Energy efficient load balancing strategy for mobile cloud computing. *International Journal of Computer Applications, 132*(15), 6–12. DOI: 10.5120/ijca2015907553

Singh, R. K., Berkvens, R., & Weyn, M. (2021). AgriFusion: An architecture for IoT and emerging technologies based on a precision agriculture survey. *IEEE Access : Practical Innovations, Open Solutions*, *9*, 136253–136283. DOI: 10.1109/ACCESS.2021.3116814

Singh, S., & Kumar, R. (2012). Ambient air temperature affects power plant performance. *International Journal of Engineering Science and Technology*, *4*, 3916–3923.

Singh, T., & Gandotra, A. (2015). Replication of Attacks in a Wireless Sensor Network Using Ns2. *International Journal of Research in Engineering and Technology*, *04*(10), 303–312. DOI: 10.15623/ijret.2015.0410052

Siregar, A., Nasution, A. B. A., & Fahmi, F. (2016). Integrated pollution monitoring system for smart city. *2016 International Conference on ICT for Smart Society (ICISS)*, 49–52. https://doi.org/DOI: 10.1109/ICTSS.2016.7792847

Sishodia, R. P., Ray, R. L., & Singh, S. K. (2020). Applications of remote sensing in precision agriculture: A review. *Remote Sensing (Basel)*, *12*(19), 3136. DOI: 10.3390/rs12193136

Skoda-auto. (2024). Škoda Auto Company. https://www.skoda-auto.com/company/about

Smolinska, A., Engel, J., Szymanska, E., Buydens, L., & Blanchet, L. (2019). General framing of low-, mid-, and high-level data fusion with examples in the life sciences. In *Data Handling in Science and Technology* (pp. 51–79). https://doi.org/DOI: 10.1016/B978-0-444-63984-4.00004-0

Somani, M. (2022). *Distributed Denial of Service (DDoS) Attacks: A Comprehensive Review*. Elsevier Computers & Security.

Song, G., Ding, F., Zhang, W., & Song, A. (2008). A wireless power outlet system for smart homes. *IEEE Transactions on Consumer Electronics*, *54*(4), 1688–1691. DOI: 10.1109/TCE.2008.4711221

Soori, M., Arezoo, B., & Dastres, R. (2023). Artificial intelligence, machine learning and deep learning in advanced robotics, a review. *Cognitive Robotics*, *3*, 54–70. DOI: 10.1016/j.cogr.2023.04.001

Sosunova, I., & Porras, J. (2022). IoT-enabled smart waste management systems for smart cities: A systematic review. *IEEE Access : Practical Innovations, Open Solutions*, *10*, 73326–73363. DOI: 10.1109/ACCESS.2022.3188308

Sousa, P. R., Resende, J. S., Martins, R., & Antunes, L. (2022). The case for blockchain in IoT identity management. *Journal of Enterprise Information Management, 35*(6), 1477–1505. DOI: 10.1108/JEIM-07-2018-0148

Spyne (2024). AI Effect and its Future with Automobiles. https://www.spyne.ai/blogs/ai-in-automobile-industry

Srivastava, S. (February 13th, 2024). How is AI Transforming the Future of the Automotive Industry? Benefits and Use Cases. Appinventiv https://appinventiv.com/blog/ai-in-automotive-industry/

Swain, B., Raj, P., Singh, K., Singh, Y., Singh, S., & Mohapatra, H. (2025). Ethical implications and mitigation strategies for public safety and security in smart cities for securing tomorrow. *Advances in Information Security, Privacy, and Ethics*, •••, 419–436. DOI: 10.4018/979-8-3693-6859-6.ch019

Swapna, M., Viswanadhula, U. M., Aluvalu, R., Vardharajan, V., & Kotecha, K. (2022). Bio-signals in medical applications and challenges using artificial intelligence. *Journal of Sensor and Actuator Networks, 11*(1), 17. DOI: 10.3390/jsan11010017

Szegedy, C., Zaremba, W., Sutskever, I., Bruna, J., Erhan, D., Goodfellow, I., & Fergus, R. (2013). Intriguing properties of neural networks. arXiv preprint arXiv:1312.6199.

Szegedy, C., Toshev, A., & Erhan, D. (2013). Deep neural networks for object detection. *Advances in Neural Information Processing Systems*, •••, 26.

Taghikhaki, Z., Meratnia, N., & Havinga, P. J. M. (2013). A trust-based probabilistic coverage algorithm for wireless sensor networks, International Workshop on Communications and Sensor Networks. *Procedia Computer Science, 21*, 455–464. DOI: 10.1016/j.procs.2013.09.061

Takyar, A. (2024). AI use cases & applications across major industries. Leeway Hertz https://www.leewayhertz.com/ai-use-cases-and-applications/ Technavio (May, 2023). Automation Market in Automotive Industry by Technology, End-user, and Geography - Forecast and Analysis 2023-2027. https://www.technavio.com/report/automation-market-industry-in-automotive-industry-analysis

Tang, J., Deng, C., & Huang, G. (2016). Extreme learning machine for multilayer perceptron. *IEEE Transactions on Neural Networks and Learning Systems, 27*(4), 809–821. DOI: 10.1109/TNNLS.2015.2424995 PMID: 25966483

Tan, W. C., & Sidhu, M. S. (2022). Review of RFID and IoT integration in supply chain management. *Operations Research Perspectives, 9*, 100229. DOI: 10.1016/j.orp.2022.100229

Teoh, Y. K., Gill, S. S., & Parlikad, A. K. (2021). IoT and fog-computing-based predictive maintenance model for effective asset management in Industry 4.0 using machine learning. *IEEE Internet of Things Journal, 10*(3), 2087–2094. DOI: 10.1109/JIOT.2021.3050441

Thippeswamy, B. M., Reshma, S., Tejaswi, V., Shaila, K., Venugopal, K. R., & Patnaik, L. M. (2015). STEAR: Secure Trust-Aware Energy-Efficient Adaptive Routing in Wireless Sensor Networks. *J. Adv. Comput. Networks*, *3*(2), 146–149. DOI: 10.7763/JACN.2015.V3.157

Thokare, N. D., Bhausaheb, R. R., & Jawale, S. D. (2017). Review of design of lighting system for energy saving using wireless sensor network. *2017 1st International Conference on Intelligent Systems and Information Management (ICISIM)*, 336–340. https://doi.org/DOI: 10.1109/ICISIM.2017.8122192

Thomopoulos, S. (1990). Sensor integration and data fusion. In *SPIE Proceedings*. DOI: 10.1117/12.969974

Toledo-Pérez, D. C., Rodríguez-Reséndiz, J., Gómez-Loenzo, R. A., & Jauregui Correa, J. C. (2019). Support Vector Machine-Based EMG Signal Classification Techniques: A Review. *Applied Sciences (Basel, Switzerland)*, *9*(20), 4402. DOI: 10.3390/app9204402

Topcuoglu, H., Hariri, S., & Wu, M.-Y. (2002). Performance-effective and low-complexity task scheduling for heterogeneous computing. *IEEE Transactions on Parallel and Distributed Systems*, *13*(3), 260–274. DOI: 10.1109/71.993206

Touati, Y., Aoudia, H., & Ali-Cherif, A. (2010). Intelligent wheelchair localization in wireless sensor network environment: A fuzzy logic approach. *2010 5th IEEE International Conference Intelligent Systems*, 408–413. https://doi.org/DOI: 10.1109/IS.2010.5548343

Tramèr, F., Kurakin, A., Papernot, N., Goodfellow, I., Boneh, D., & McDaniel, P. (2017). Ensemble adversarial training: Attacks and defenses. arXiv preprint arXiv:1705.07204.

Tsinganos, P., Cornelis, B., Cornelis, J., Jansen, B., & Skodras, A. (2018, September). Deep Learning in EMG-based Gesture Recognition. In *PhyCS* (pp. 107-114). DOI: 10.5220/0006960201070114

Tsou, Y.-P., Hsieh, J.-W., Lin, C.-T., & Chen, C.-Y. (2006). Building a remote supervisory control network system for smart home applications. *2006 IEEE International Conference on Systems, Man and Cybernetics*, 1826–1830. https://doi.org/DOI: 10.1109/ICSMC.2006.384995

Tyagi, L. K., & Kumar, A. (2023). A Hybrid Trust Based WSN protocol to Enhance Network Performance using Fuzzy Enabled Machine Learning Technique. *International Journal of Intelligent Systems and Applications in Engineering*, *11*(9s), 131–144.

Vadivel, G., Hussain, M. J. M., & Sangeetha, S. T. (2023). Smart transportation systems: IoT-connected wireless sensor networks for traffic congestion management. *International Journal of Advances in Signal and Image Sciences*, *9*(1), 40–49. DOI: 10.29284/IJASIS.9.1.2023.40-49

Valente, F. J., ... (2019). Fog-based data fusion for heterogeneous IoT sensor networks: A real implementation. In *2019 15th International Conference on Network and Service Management (CNSM)*. IEEE. DOI: 10.23919/CNSM46954.2019.9012744

Valmet-automotive. (2024). The fast lane to our customers. https://www.valmet-automotive.com/company/

Veeramachaneni, V. (2025). Edge Computing: Architecture, Applications, and Future Challenges in a Decentralized Era. *Recent Trends in Computer Graphics and Multimedia Technology*, *7*(1), 8–23.

Veeramanikandan, P., & Anil Kumar, N. (2024). Design and implementation of an IoT-based control system for precision food manufacturing. In V. S. Rathore, V. Piuri, R. Babo, & K. S. (Eds.), *Universal threats in expert applications and solutions: UNI-TEAS 2024* (Vol. 1007). Springer, Singapore.

Veloso, Á., Fonseca, F., & Ramos, R. (2024). Insights from Smart City Initiatives for Urban Sustainability and Contemporary Urbanism. *Smart Cities*, *7*(6), 3188–3209. DOI: 10.3390/smartcities7060124

Vermesan, O., & Friess, P. (Eds.). (2013). *Internet of things: converging technologies for smart environments and integrated ecosystems*. River publishers.

Vermesan, O., Friess, P., Guillemin, P., Gusmeroli, S., Sundmaeker, H., Bassi, A., & Doody, P. (2022). Internet of things strategic research roadmap. In *Internet of things-global technological and societal trends from smart environments and spaces to green ICT* (pp. 9–52). River Publishers.

Vieira, P. (August, 2023). AI Integration for the Automotive Industry: Challenges and Best Practices. Controlar https://controlar.com/en/ai-integration-for-the-automotive-industrychallenges-and-best-practices

Vir, D., Agarwal, S. K., & Imam, S. A. (2013). WSN Performance Evaluation of Power Consumption Analysis of DSR, OLSR, LAR and Fisheye in Energy Model through QualNet. *International Journal of Scientific and Research Publications*, *3*(12), 1–6.

Wang, Y. (2013). The design of smart home system based on wireless sensor network. *2013 IEEE 4th International Conference on Electronics Information and Emergency Communication*, 106–108. https://doi.org/DOI: 10.1109/ICEIEC.2013.6758346

Wang, H., Ding, Q., Luo, Y., Wu, Z., Yu, J., Chen, H., Zhou, Y., Zhang, H., Tao, K., Chen, X., Fu, J., & Wu, J. (2024). High-Performance Hydrogel Sensors Enabled Multimodal and Accurate Human Machine Interaction System for Active Rehabilitation. *Advanced Materials*, *36*(11), 2309868. DOI: 10.1002/adma.202309868 PMID: 38095146

Wang, J., Wang, D. J. D., Moore, P. R., & Pu, J. (2001). Modelling study, analysis and robust servocontrol of pneumatic cylinder actuator systems. *IEE Proceedings. Control Theory and Applications*, *148*(1), 35–42. DOI: 10.1049/ip-cta:20010238

Wang, J., Wang, Y., Li, G., & Qi, Z. (2024). Integration of remote sensing and machine learning for precision agriculture: A comprehensive perspective on applications. *Agronomy (Basel)*, *14*(9), 1975. DOI: 10.3390/agronomy14091975

Wang, N., Niu, J., Liu, X., Yu, D., Zhu, G., Wu, X., & Su, H. (2024, January). BeyondVision: an EMG-driven micro hand gesture recognition based on dynamic segmentation. In *Proceedings of the Thirty-Third International Joint Conference on Artificial Intelligence* (pp. 6044-6052). DOI: 10.24963/ijcai.2024/668

Wang, P.. (2022). Leveraging Deep Learning with Transfer Learning for Phishing Detection. *IEEE Transactions on Cybernetics*.

Wang, P., Ye, F., Chen, X., & Qian, Y. (2018). Data net: Deep learning-based encrypted network traffic classification in SDN home gateway. *IEEE Access : Practical Innovations, Open Solutions*, *6*, 55380–55391. DOI: 10.1109/ACCESS.2018.2872430

Wang, R. (2024). Developing an optimization model for minimizing musculoskeletal stress in repetitive motion tasks. *Molecular & Cellular Biomechanics*, *21*(3), 567–567. DOI: 10.62617/mcb567

Wang, R., Morris, J., Figueroa, F., & Morris, M. T. (2008). Wireless intelligent sensors supporting integrated systems health management architecture. *2008 IEEE Sensors Applications Symposium*, 215–219. https://doi.org/DOI: 10.1109/SAS13374.2008.4472973

Wang, Z., Zhang, R., & Keogh, P. (2020). Real-Time Laser Tracker Compensation of Robotic Drilling and Machining. *J. Manuf. Mater. Process.*, *4*(3), 79. DOI: 10.3390/jmmp4030079

Wan, Y., Liu, Y., Chen, Z., Chen, C., Li, X., Hu, F., & Packianather, M. (2024). Making knowledge graphs work for smart manufacturing: Research topics, applications and prospects. *Journal of Manufacturing Systems*, *76*, 103–132. DOI: 10.1016/j.jmsy.2024.07.009

WEKA. (n.d.). *Machine learning software*. Retrieved from http://www.cs.waikato.ac.nz

Weng, T. W., Zhang, H., Chen, P. Y., Yi, J., Su, D., Gao, Y., . . . Daniel, L. (2018). Evaluating the robustness of neural networks: An extreme value theory approach. arXiv preprint arXiv:1801.10578.

Wen, X., & Wang, Y. (2018). Design of smart home environment monitoring system based on raspberry Pi. *2018 Chinese Control and Decision Conference (CCDC)*, 4259–4263. https://doi.org/DOI: 10.1109/CCDC.2018.8407864

White, F. (1991). *Data fusion lexicon.*

Wu, J., & Qin, H. (2008). The design of wireless intelligent home system base on ZigBee. *2008 11th IEEE International Conference on Communication Technology*, 73–76. https://doi.org/DOI: 10.1109/ICCT.2008.4716156

Xiao, C., Li, B., Zhu, J. Y., He, W., Liu, M., & Song, D. (2018). Generating adversarial examples with adversarial networks. arXiv preprint arXiv:1801.02610. DOI: 10.24963/ijcai.2018/543

Xing, Y., & Wang, X. (2024). Precision agriculture and water conservation strategies for sustainable crop production in arid regions. *Plants*, *13*(22), 3184. DOI: 10.3390/plants13223184 PMID: 39599396

Xu, X., Weber, I., Staples, M., Zhu, L., Bosch, J., Bass, L., Pautasso, C., & Rimba, P. (2017). A taxonomy of blockchain-based systems for architecture design. *2017 IEEE International Conference on Software Architecture (ICSA)*, 243-252. https://doi.org/DOI: 10.1109/ICSA.2017.33

Yamuna, C. R. D., Shivaraj, B., Manjula, S. H., Venugopal, K. R., Iyengar, S. S., & Patnaik, L. M. (2014). Multihop optimal position based opportunistic routing for wireless sensor networks, IEEE TENSYMP 2014 - 2014 IEEE Reg. 10 Symp., no. April, pp. 121–125, DOI: . 6863009.DOI: 10.1109/tenconspring.2014

Yang, Q., Liu, Y., Chen, T., & Tong, Y. (2019). Federated machine learning. *ACM Transactions on Intelligent Systems and Technology*, *10*(2), 1–19. DOI: 10.1145/3298981

Yin, M.. (2022). Advanced Persistent Threats and Defensive Techniques. *IEEE Access : Practical Innovations, Open Solutions.*

Yoneda, S., & Furui, A. (2023, October). Bayesian Approach for Adaptive EMG Pattern Classification Via Semi-Supervised Sequential Learning. In *2023 IEEE International Conference on Systems, Man, and Cybernetics (SMC)* (pp. 3310-3315). IEEE. DOI: 10.1109/SMC53992.2023.10394290

Yuan, X., He, P., Zhu, Q., & Li, X. (2019). Adversarial examples: Attacks and defenses for deep learning. *IEEE Transactions on Neural Networks and Learning Systems, 30*(9), 2805–2824. DOI: 10.1109/TNNLS.2018.2886017 PMID: 30640631

Zadeh, L. A. (1965). Fuzzy sets. [This seminal paper introduces the concept of fuzzy logic, foundational for developing intelligent control systems.]. *Information and Control, 8*(3), 338–353. DOI: 10.1016/S0019-9958(65)90241-X

Zhang, Y., Qi, Y., & Luo, Y. (2010). An information collection system of network intelligence wheelchair based on ZigBee wireless sensor networks. *2010 2nd International Conference on Industrial and Information Systems*, 140–143. https://doi.org/DOI: 10.1109/IIS.2010.5603356

Zhanga, Q., Liua, X., Yub, J., & Qi, X. (2020). A Trust-based Dynamic Slicing Mechanism for Wireless Sensor Networks, International Conference on Identification, Information and Knowledge in the Internet of Things (IIKI2019). *Procedia Computer Science, 174*, 572–57. DOI: 10.1016/j.procs.2020.06.126

Zhang, C., Bengio, S., Hardt, M., Recht, B., & Vinyals, O. (2021). Understanding deep learning (still) requires rethinking generalization. *Communications of the ACM, 64*(3), 107–115. DOI: 10.1145/3446776

Zhang, W.. (2021). *A Survey on Transfer Learning in Cybersecurity Applications.* ACM Transactions on Cybersecurity.

Zhao, J., Zhao, J., Wang, H., Song, J., & Dong, F. (2019). Precision position measurement of linear motors mover based on temporal image correlation. *IEEE Transactions on Instrumentation and Measurement, 68*(9), 3268–3277. DOI: 10.1109/TIM.2018.2875645 PMID: 31413382

Zheng, W., Yin, H., Wang, A., Fu, P., & Liu, B. (2017). Development of an automatic reading method and software for pointer instruments. *First International Conference on Electronics Instrumentation & Information Systems (EIIS)*, 1–6. DOI: 10.1109/EIIS.2017.8298626

Zheng, Z., Xie, S., Dai, H., Chen, X., & Wang, H. (2017). An overview of blockchain technology: Architecture, consensus, and future trends. *2017 IEEE International Congress on Big Data (BigData Congress)*, 557-564. https://doi.org/DOI: 10.1109/BigDataCongress.2017.85

Zhong, D., Ji, W., Liu, Y., Han, J., & Li, S. (2011). An improved routing algorithm of Zigbee wireless sensor network for smart home system. *The 5th International Conference on Automation, Robotics and Applications*, 346–350. https://doi.org/DOI: 10.1109/ICARA.2011.6144959

Zhu, S., Yu, T., Xu, T., Chen, H., Dustdar, S., Gigan, S., ... & Pan, Y. (2023). Intelligent computing: the latest advances, challenges, and future. *Intelligent Computing, 2*, 0006.

Zhuang, Z.. (2021). Phishing as a Convergent Attack Vector during DDoS. *Journal of Cybersecurity.*

Zikria, Y. B., Ali, R., Afzal, M. K., & Kim, S. W. (2021). Next-generation internet of things (iot): Opportunities, challenges, and solutions. *Sensors (Basel)*, *21*(4), 1174. DOI: 10.3390/s21041174 PMID: 33562343

About The Contributors

Abdulsattar Abdullah Hamad was born in Salah Al-Deen, Iraq, He received Ph.D. from Madurai Kamaraj University-(India), School of Mathematics, and working at University of Samarra, His area of interest includes Importance and role of Mathematical methods and science technology in healthcare, Dynamic Systems, Topology, Big Data, Mathematical Foundations in Healthcare Engineering, achiness Learning, Internet of Things, cloud computing, computational complexity, data analysis. 1. Academic Skills 1. Associate Editor International Journal of Fuzzy System Applications (IJFSA)- (SCOPUS and WoS-IGI Global) 2. Review Editor Frontiers in Applied Mathematics and Statistics- (SCOPUS and WoS- Frontiers) 3. Associate Editor 4. International Journal of Artificial Intelligence (AI) in Business and Management (IJAIBM)- (SCOPUS-IGI Global) 5. Academic Editor Computational and Mathematical Methods in Medicine-(SCOPUS and WoS) Publications No.of papers in Scopus and WoS (60) papers No.of Books Published 2 Books No.of Patent 3 Patents Ph. No: +9647738353255 Email: Satar198700@ gmail.com

Sudan Jha, With over 23+ years of combined teaching, research, and industrial experience, Sudan Jha is a Senior member of IEEE and a Professor in the Department of Computer Science & Engineering at Kathmandu University, Nepal. He is lead researcher of the IoT R&D lab at Kathmandu University. His previous affiliations include KIIT University, Chandigarh University, Christ University, etc. He was 'Technical Director' at Nepal Television, 'Principal' at Nepal College of IT, and 'Individual Consultant' at Nepal Telecom Authority. Prof. Jha is dedicated to advancing higher education quality and actively works on smart platforms. His extensive research portfolio comprises 80+ SCI, SCIE indexed research papers and book chapters in international peer-reviewed journals and conferences. He serves as a Co-Editor-in-Chief in an international journal. He also serves as Guest Editor for SCIE/ESCI/SCOPUS indexed journals. With three patents to his name, he has authored and edited 6 books on cutting-edge topics in IoT, 5G, and AI, published by Elsevier, CRC, and AAP. His research has also secured funding for two international projects. Additionally, Prof. Jha contributes as a Keynote at more than 40 international conferences. In addition, he has also delivered faculty development programs, short-term training programs, and workshops in national and international conferences, and universities. He holds certifications in Microservices Architecture, Data Science, and Foundations of Artificial Intelligence.

Khalid Al, METAMAT2023 February 23 - 25, 2023 Miami, USA • The 2022 International Conference on Service Robotics (ICoSR 2022) is organized by the Hong Kong Society of Robotics and Automation (HKSRA) and it will be held in Xishuangbanna, China • The 2 International Conference on Frontiers of Electronics, Information and Computation Technologies August 19-21, 2022 Wuhan, China • The 5th Samarra International Scientific Conference held in University of Samarra college of Education, Iraq on 23-24 February, 2022 • The Hong Kong Society of Robotics and Automation (HKSRA): International Workshop on Service Robotics (IWoSR 2021) held in Qingdao, China during 28–30 August, 2021 .

***

Hikmat A. Abdeljaber was born in Kuwait, in 1967. He received the Ph.D. degree in Information Sciences and Technology in 2010 from the Universiti Kebangsaan Malaysia, UKM, Malaysia. He currently holds a University Assistant position at the Applied Science Private University in Jordan, Faculty of Information Technology. He lectured in the fields of computer science and information systems for both undergraduate and graduate levels. He has published papers in the area of Information Retrieval and Artificial Intelligence. His research interests include Information Retrieval, Semantic Web Technology, Natural Language Processing and Machine Learning.

Sultan Ahmad (Member, IEEE) received the master's degree (Hons.) in computer science and applications degree from Aligarh Muslim University, India, and the Ph.D. degree from Glocal University. He is currently a Faculty Member with the Department of Computer Science, College of Computer Engineering and Sciences, Prince Sattam bin Abdulaziz University, Al-Kharj, Saudi Arabia. He is also an Adjunct Professor with Chandigarh University, Gharuan, Punjab, India. He has more than 17 years of teaching and research experience. He has around 100 accepted and published research papers and book chapters in reputed SCI, SCIE, ESCI, and SCOPUS-indexed journals and conferences. He has an Australian Patent and a chinese Patent in his name. He has authored more than five books that are available on Amazon. He has presented the research papers at many national and international conferences. His research interests include distributed computing, big data, machine learning, and the Internet of Things. He is a member of IACSIT and the Computer Society of India.

Khalid Saeed Lateef Al-Badri is an Assistance Professor of Electronics and Communication Engineering at the University of Samarra, Iraq. He specializes in metamaterials, electromagnetic interference (EMI) control, energy harvesting, and biomedical applications. He has over 50 peer-reviewed publications, including articles in IEEE and Nature. With a robust academic career that began at the University of Tikrit—where he served as Director of the Training and Development Center—Khalid has been at the University of Samarra since 2012, as an Assistance Professor. In addition to his teaching and research responsibilities, he manages the university's computer center, contributing to the digital infrastructure and IT operations. Khalid's research spans metamaterials, electromagnetic interference (EMI) control, energy harvesting technologies, and biomedical applications. His work has resulted in over 50 peer-reviewed publications, including articles in high-impact journals such as IEEE and Nature, and he has presented at numerous international conferences. His expertise also includes simulation and modeling using tools like CST, MATLAB, and various programming languages (C++, C#, PHP, SQL).

Fadi Al-Turjman (M'07) received the Ph.D. degree in computer science from Queen's University, Kingston, ON, Canada, in 2011. He is currently a Professor with the Department of Computer Engineering, Antalya Bilim University, Antalya, Turkey. He is a leading authority in the areas of smart/cognitive, wireless, and mobile networks' architectures, protocols, deployments, and performance evaluation. His publication history spans over 200 publications in journals, conferences, patents, books, and book chapters, in addition to numerous keynotes and plenary talks at flagship venues. He has authored or edited more than 20 books about cognition, security, and wireless sensor networks' deployments in smart environments, published by Taylor & Francis and Springer. He has received several recognitions and Best Paper Awards at top international conferences. He also received the prestigious Best Research Paper Award from the Computer Communications Journal (Elsevier), from 2015 to 2018, in addition to the Top Researcher Award for 2018 at Antalya Bilim University. He has led a number of international symposia and workshops in flagship communication society conferences. He currently serves as the Lead Guest Editor for several well-reputed journals, including the Elsevier Computer Communications (COMCOM), the Sustainable Cities & Society (SCS), the IET Wireless Sensor Systems, and the Springer EURASIP and MONET journals.

Kavitha B C is a Faculty of Electronics and Communication Engineering Department, BGS Institute of Technology, ACU, India since 2011. She has been an Assistant Professor in the Department since 2007. Her current research interests include Image processing and its applications in the field of medical, Internet of Things and Embedded systems. She has published and presented papers in various conferences and journals. She can be contacted at email: kavithabc@bgsit.ac.in

Aruna Bajpai is an accomplished academic in the field of Computer Science & Engineering, Currently serving as an Assistant Professor at the Institute of Technology & Management, Gwalior. With a strong educational background including M.Tech. in Computer Science, Ms Bajpai is currently pursuing Ph.D. Her career spans over two decades, in academia since 2008 . Over the past 16 years, She has progressed from a Lecturer to his current role as Assistant Professor, demonstrating expertise in areas such as Machine Learning,Image Processing. Ms. Bajpai's academic contributions include numerous patents, book chapters, publications in international journals and conferences, as well as presentations at IEEE international conferences. Her ongoing research and teaching efforts continue to shape the field of computer science and nurture the next generation of technology professionals.

Vinithra Balaji is pursuing BTech in Computer Science and Engineering at VIT University, Chennai, India. She has worked on various research projects in multiple fields including IOT, Cryptography, Data Compression and Machine Learning. Her research interests include Machine Learning, Artifical Intelligence, Data Compression and Cryptography. .

D. Srinivas distinguished Faculty of Marketing and Communication at SR UNIVERSITY, Warangal,Telangana. He rececive MBA from Kakatiya University, Warangal and Ph.D degree from Kakatiya University,Warangal..He is author of many books. He also published many articles in National and International journals. His research covers Product strategy, Digital marketing, E-Business and IoT For Businees Operations. He is a active member of AIMA and HMA. He has delivered many guest lectures and organized FDP’s across the country

Devaraj E is Passionate and well-versed in Polymer Materials Engineering. Proficient Mechanical Engineer with a robust foundation in new product development to secure a role in an innovative academic institution and currently working as Assistant professor in CMR University. Dr,Devaraj E is specialized in development and characterization of composite materials.

Dankan Gowda V is currently working as an Assistant Professor in the Department of Electronics and Communication Engineering at BMS Institute of Technology and Management in Bangalore. Previously, he worked as a Research Fellow at ADA DRDO and as a Software Engineer at Robert Bosch. With a total experience of 14 years spanning both teaching and industry, Dr. Gowda has made significant contributions to academia, research, and innovation. In recognition of his outstanding contributions to the field of Electronics and Communication Engineering, Dr. Gowda was named among the World's Top 2% Scientists for 2024 by Stanford University, USA. This prestigious acknowledgment, published on September 16, 2024, highlights his impactful work and dedication to advancing his field. Dr. Gowda has published over 160 research papers in renowned international journals and conferences. His innovative work has earned him six patents, including four granted by Indian authorities and two international patents. His research interests primarily lie in the areas of IoT and Signal Processing, where he has not only conducted workshops but also successfully managed industry projects. Passionate about teaching, Dr. Gowda strives to create an engaging and effective learning environment for his students. He consistently seeks opportunities to enhance his knowledge and stay abreast of the latest advancements in his field, ensuring that his teaching and research remain cutting-edge and impactful.

Madan Jagtap is an Assistant Professor in the Operations Management Department at Symbiosis Institute of Operations Management, Constituent of Symbiosis International (Deemed University), Pune, Maharashtra, India. He earned a Master of Manufacturing Systems Engineering from Mumbai University, India. He has published journal and conference papers. His research interests include manufacturing, decision science, simulation, optimization, reliability, and Uncertainty.

Mohammed Jeelani received his Bachelor of Computer Application degree from Makhanlan Chaturvedi National University of Journalism and communication Bhopal in 2010 and Master of Computer Application degree from Teerthanker Mahaveer University in 2013 and completed his Ph.D. from Mangalayatan University, Aligarh in 2021. His research areas are Wireless Sensor Networks and Mobile Ad-hoc Networks. He has published a number of research papers Scopus or WoS in International/National journals, UGC care listed Journals and International/ National conferences.

B. Kalaiselvi working as an Asso Professor and Head in the Department of Electronics and Communication Engineering, Bharath Institute of Higher education and Research, Chennai. She Received her Ph D degree In the year 2022 in Digital

Image processing and ML from BIHER chennai, M. Tech degree in Electronics and Instrumentation Engineering from Bharath University, Chennai, in 2014. She received her B.E in Electronics and Communication Engineering from Satyabhama University, Chennai in 2011. Her current area of interest is Measurements and Instrumentation, Digital image Processing Artificial Intelligence and Machine Learning. Email:kalaiselvi.ece@bharathuniv.ac.in

Deepak Kumar Mishra is an accomplished academic in the field of Computer Science & Engineering, currently serving as an Assistant Professor at the Institute of Technology & Management, Gwalior. He possesses a strong educational background, holding a B.Sc. in Electronics, an M.Sc. in Computer Science, and an M.Tech. in Information Technology. Additionally, he is currently pursuing his Ph.D. in Computer Science & Engineering. With a career spanning over two decades, Deepak Kumar Mishra has steadily progressed from a Lecturer to his current role as an Assistant Professor, showcasing his expertise in various domains, including vehicular networks, image processing, and data mining. His academic contributions are extensive, encompassing book chapters, and research publications in international journals and conferences. Through his ongoing research and teaching endeavors, Deepak Kumar Mishra continues to contribute to the advancement of computer science while mentoring and shaping the next generation of technology professionals.

Hitesh Mohapatra received the B.E. degree in Information Technology from Biju Patnaik University of Technology (BPUT), Odisha in 2006, and the MTech. Degree in CSE from Odisha University of Technology and Research (OUTR) University, Odisha in 2009. He received his Ph.D. in Computer Science & Engineering in 2021 from Veer Surendra Sai University of Technology (VSSUT), Burla, India. He has contributed 30 SCI and Scopus indexed research papers, 21 international/national conferences and books on Software Engineering and C Programming respectively. He has 15 years of teaching experience both in industry and academia. He has served the research community with various capacities like session chair, technical chair, keynote speaker etc. His research interests include wireless sensor network, smart city, smart grid and smart water. Currently he is working as Associate professor at School of Computer Engineering, KIIT DU, Bhubaneswar, and Odisha.

Mourade Azrour received his PhD from Faculty of sciences and Techniques, Moulay Ismail University of Meknes, Morocco. He has received his MS in computer and distributed systems from Faculty of Sciences, Ibn Zouhr University, Agadir, Morocco in 2014. Mourade currently works as computer sciences professor at the Department of Computer Science, Faculty of Sciences and Techniques, Moulay

Ismail University of Meknès. His research interests include Authentication protocol, Computer Security, Internet of things, Smart systems, Machine learning and so ones. Mourade is member of the member of the scientific committee of numerous international conferences. He is also a reviewer of various scientific journals. He has published more than 127 scientific papers and book chapters. Mourade Has edited many scientific books for example: "IoT, Machine Learning and Data Analytics for Smart Healthcare", "Blockchain and Machine Learning for IoT Security", "IoT and Smart Devices for Sustainable Environment", "Advanced Technology for Smart Environment and Energy". Finally, he has served as guest editor in journals "EAI Endorsed Transactions on Internet of Things", "Tsinghua Science and Technology", "Applied Sciences MDPI" and "Sustainability MDPI"

Suganthi Neelagiri received the bachelor's degree in Electrical and Electronics Engineering from Bharathiyar University in 2001, the master's degree in Electrical Power and Energy System from Uttar Pradesh Technical University in 2013, and Ph.D. in Electrical Engineering from Visvesvaraya University respectively. She is currently working as an Assistant Professor at the Department of Electrical and Electronics Engineering, Dayananda Sagar College of Engineering. Her research areas include microgrid, renewable energy systems, energy storage systems. She can be contacted at email: suganthi_neelagiri@yahoo.com.

P. Senthil Pandian working as an Associate Professor in the Department of Computer Science and Engineering at AAA College and Engineering and Technology, Sivakasi. He graduated his MCA at Madurai Kamaraj University, Tamil Nadu, India. He secured his Master of M.E in CSE at Anna University, Tamil Nadu, India. He Completed his Ph.D., in CSE at Anna University, Tamil Nadu, India. He is in teaching profession for more than 20 years. He has presented 38 papers in National and International Journals, Conference and Symposiums and published 11 books. His main area of interest includes Networks, Knowledge Management, IOT and Data Mining.

Rashmi Pandey is an accomplished academic in the field of Computer Applications, Currently serving as an Assistant Professor at the Institute of Technology & Management, Gwalior. With a strong educational background including Masters in computer applications and Pursuing PhD in Machine Learning. Over the past 20 plus years, she has progressed from a Lecturer to his current role as Assistant Professor, demonstrating expertise in areas such as machine learning,big data,deep learning,software engineering, DBMS etc. Pandey's academic contributions include numerous patents, book chapters, publications in international journals and conferences, as well as presentations at IEEE international conferences.

Hier ongoing research and teaching efforts continue to shape the field of computer science and nurture the next generation of technology professionals.

Anand Polamarasetti is an IT professional with nearly 20 years of experience in a wide variety of cutting-edge technologies and various business domains. Since 2014 he has been helping various commercial and federal clients across the USA with his expertise in the areas of Cloud Architecture, Development, IT Infrastructure, Data Pipelines Engineering, Data Analytics, Artificial Intelligence and Machine Learning. From an IT perspective he believes in delivering simple solutions to complex problems. Outside of work his passions include policy making, charity and he enjoys traveling across the country.

Rahul Vadisetty is a distinguished AI researcher and Senior Software Engineer at U.S. Bank, specializing in AI-driven cybersecurity and predictive healthcare. His award-winning research on data integrity in AI and healthcare modeling has earned recognition at IEEE conferences. Vadisetty's work focuses on secure AI deployment, ethical AI practices, and advancing AI applications in biotechnology and cloud computing.

Vaitheeshwari S is an Assistant Professor in the Department of Computer Science and Engineering at Vel Tech Multi Tech Dr. Rangarajan Dr. Sakunthala Engineering College, Chennai. She is committed to fostering technical excellence and innovation in computer science education. Her areas of interest include mentoring students and contributing to research in emerging computing technologies.

V. Santhi has received her Ph.D. in Computer Science and Engineering from VIT University, Vellore, India. She has pursued her M.Tech. in Computer Science and Engineering from Pondicherry University, Puducherry. She has received her B.E. in Computer Science and Engineering from Bharathidasan University, Trichy, India. Currently she is working as Associate Professor in the School of Computing Science and Engineering, VIT University, Vellore, India. She has authored many national and international journal papers and one book. She is currently in the process of editing two books. Also, she has published many chapters in different books published by International publishers. She is senior member of IEEE and she is holding membership in many professional bodies like CSI, ISTE, IACSIT, IEEE and IAENG. Her areas of research include Image Processing, Digital Signal Processing, Digital Watermarking, Data Compression and Computational Intelligence.

Eram Fatima Siddiqui is an accomplished academic and researcher with a gold medal in MCA and a silver medal in BCA. Holding a PhD with a specialization in the Internet of Things and fog computing, Ms. Eram Fatima Siddiqui's expertise spans cutting-edge fields, including big data, cloud computing, edge computing, IoT, blockchain, machine learning, and artificial intelligence. Known for their dedication to innovation and impactful research, Ms. Eram Fatima Siddiqui continues to contribute to technological advancements and education in their field.

Kishan Pal Singh holds a bachelor's degree in Mechanical Engineering and a master's degree with a specialization in Thermal Engineering from Aligarh Muslim University, Aligarh. He earned his Doctor of Philosophy from Dr. A. P. J. Abdul Kalam Technical University, Lucknow, India. Dr. Singh has served as Head of Department, Principal, and Dean (Academics) at various institutions affiliated with Uttar Pradesh Technical University Lucknow, M. D. University Rohtak, M.M.M. University of Technology Gorakhpur, all approved by A.I.C.T.E., Delhi. Currently, he is the Professor and Director at the Institute of Engineering and Technology, Mangalayatan University, Aligarh, India. Dr. Singh's research interests are diverse, spanning mechanical engineering and computer engineering. His areas of research include refrigeration systems, heat and mass transfer, renewable energy, fluid mechanics, internal combustion engines, thermal engineering, flexible manufacturing systems, artificial intelligence, and machine learning. He has supervised eight Ph.D. candidates to completion, with six more in progress. Dr. Singh holds three patents, including one from Australia and another from Germany. He has published numerous research papers in Scopus or Web of Science indexed journals, U.G.C. care journals, and in the proceedings of International/National conferences.

Shiv Pratap SinghYadav holds a Ph.D. in Contact Mechanics from UVCE, Bengaluru, awarded by Bangalore University. Prior to his doctoral studies, he earned a Master's degree in Machine Design and a Bachelor's degree in Mechanical Engineering with outstanding academic achievements. With an extensive tenure at Nitte Meenakshi Institute of Technology, Bengaluru, Dr. Yadav has played pivotal roles in academia. Dr. Yadav's expertise spans a wide array of subjects, including Contact Mechanics, Design of Machine Elements, Mechanical Vibrations, Theory of Elasticity, Finite Element Analysis, Thermodynamics, Total Quality Management, Six Sigma, and House Construction.

Sajja Suneel, was awarded Ph.D. from Veer Bahadur Singh Purvanchal University, formerly Purvanchal University, Jaunpur, UP in 2023. He has 13 years of teaching experience in reputed institutions. He is currently working as Assistant Professor & PAT coordinator in the Department of CSE (Data Science) at Institute of Aeronautical Engineering. He has published 8 Research papers in National/ International Journals and Conferences & has presented 2 conference papers around the globe, apart from these, he has been Participated many workshops, conferences and faculty development programmes and pedagogic training programmes. He has been a lifetime member in various professional bodies like CSI, IETE, & ISTE and his area of interest include Machine Learning, Artificial Intelligence, Cloud Computing & IoT.

Maheswer Sunil Kumar is pursuing B.Tech Degree in Computer Science and Engineering at VIT University, Chennai, India. He has completed various research projects in Data Compression, Supervised Learning and Signal Processing. His research interest include Artificial Intelligence, Cryptography and Machine learning

SV. Shri Bharathi received her Bachelor of Engineering degree in Computer Science and Engineering from Bharathiar University, Coimbatore, and Tamilnadu in 2002. She received her Master of Engineering degree in Computer Science and Engineering from Anna University, Tamil Nadu in 2007. She received her Doctor of Philosophy in Computer Science and Engineering from B. S. Abdur Rahman Crescent Institute of Science and Technology, Tamil Nadu in 2019. She is now working as an Assistant Professor, Department of Data Science and Technology, SRM Institute of Science and Technology, KTR, Chennai, Tamil Nadu. Her research interest includes Machine Learning, Big Data, Data Analytics, Data Mining, Information Retrieval, Knowledge Management, Web mining.

Aasim Zafar is Professor at Computer Science Department, Aligarh Muslim University, Aligarh, India. He holds Master in Computer Science and Applications and obtained the degree of Ph. D. in Computer Science, from Aligarh Muslim University, Aligarh, India. His research areas and special interests include Mobile Ad hoc and Sensor Networks, Image Processing and Video Analytics, Information Retrieval, E-Systems, e-Security, Virtual Learning Environment, Neuro-Fuzzy and Soft Computing, and Software Engineering. His areas of teaching interest include Computer Networks, Network Security, Software Engineering, E-Systems, Database Management Systems and Computer Programming. He has presented many papers in National and International Conferences and published various research papers in journals of international repute. Prof. Aasim Zafar has a teaching and research experience of more than 29 years both at national and international level. He has executed NMEICT-EdRP project funded by MHRD, Govt. of India as Co-PI, which was executed in consortium mode with AMU being one of the partner Institute (with a share of Rs 1.2 crore) and IIT, Kanpur being the Coordinating Institute. AMU successfully contributed two major outcomes, namely, a cloud-based multi-lingual and multi-Institutional Library Management System (LibMS) and Election Management System (EMS) to this project. During his 5-year tenure of International teaching assignment at King Abdulaziz University

(KAU), Jeddah, he has executed three research projects, two DSR funded (SR 50,000 each) as PI and one funded by KACST (SR 2 Million) as Co-PI. He was awarded with "Excellence in Teaching Award" at KAU, Jeddah. Besides teaching and research, Prof. Aasim Zafar has a rich administrative experience and is actively involved in various developmental work of the university in various capacities. Presently he has been assigned additional responsibility in administration as Officer-on-Special Duty (Development), AMU since 11.05.2024. He has served as Chairperson/Head of the Department of Computer Science during 19.01.2021 to 18.01.2024. He is presently UGC SWAYAM Coordinator, Coordinator of IGNOU Study Centre of AMU, Convener of University Website Committee, Convener of Digital Monitoring Cell, Member, CIQA, CDOE, AMU and member of various high powered committee constitute by the Hon'ble Vice Chancellor of AMU. He has immensely contributed in ICT Infrastructure Development of the University. At KAU, Prof. Zafar successfully led the Academic Accreditation Unit of FCIT, KAU in the capacity of Director to achieve ABET (American Accreditation Board of Engineering and Technology) accreditation. As SWAYAM Coordinator he has taken the initiative and successfully led the development and launch of 31 MOOCs for the July-2024 semester on the SWAYAM Platform by the faculty members of AMU (INI). Prof. Aasim Zafar has been actively working in the area of e-Learning and utilizing Open Source ICT Tools and Technologies in Research, Teaching & Learning and Student Evaluation since 1995, both at the Graduate and Post Graduate levels. He has served CDOE, AMU as Coordinator of e-Learning Programmes. He has expertise in Educational Technologies and contributed in spreading the culture of ICT enabled Pedagogy among teachers of HEIs through various workshops, orientation, training and capacity building programmes. He has also organised various webinars, workshops, and training programmes on e-Content Development and ICT related topics. Prof. Aasim Zafar is a valuable resource person and delivered skill based technical sessions/lectures across the country for Faculty Development Programmes [FDP], Faculty Induction Programmes [FIP], Refresher Courses and Orientation Programmes at UGC HRDCs and different Universities in India on e-Learning, SWAYAM MOOCs, e-Content Development, Capacity building for blended learning, Educational Technologies for Online Teaching and Learning, Learning Management Systems (LMS), and e-Governance, etc. He has trained over 5000 faculty members belonging to various universities/colleges across the country for Online Teaching and Learning during COVID-19 pandemic since March 2020.

Index

Symbols

A

B

C

D

E

F

G

I

K

L

M

P

R

S

T

V

W